T0330207

Investing in the United States

STUDIES IN INTERNATIONAL INVESTMENT

Series Editor: Karl P. Sauvant, *Executive Director, Vale Columbia Center on Sustainable International Investment (a joint center of Columbia Law School and the Earth Institute), Columbia University, USA*

Columbia Law School
Columbia Law School, founded in 1858, stands at the forefront of legal education and of the law in a global society. Columbia Law School graduates have provided leadership worldwide in a remarkably broad range of fields: government, diplomacy, the judiciary, business, nonprofit, advocacy, entertainment, academia, science and the arts. Led by Dean David M. Schizer, Columbia Law School joins its traditional strengths in international and comparative law, constitutional law, administrative law and human rights law with pioneering work in intellectual property, digital technology, sexuality and gender and criminal law. For further information, visit http://www.law.columbia.edu.

The Earth Institute at Columbia University
The Earth Institute at Columbia University is the world's leading academic center for the integrated study of Earth, its environment and society. Led by Professor Jeffrey D. Sachs, the Earth Institute builds upon excellence in the core disciplines – earth sciences, biological sciences, engineering sciences, social sciences, and health sciences – and stresses cross-disciplinary approaches to complex problems. Through research, training and global partnerships, it mobilizes science and technology to advance sustainable development, while placing special emphasis on the needs of the world's poor. For more information, visit: http://www.earth.columbia.edu.

The Vale Columbia Center on Sustainable International Investment
The Vale Columbia Center on Sustainable International Investment (VCC) is a joint center of Columbia Law School and the Earth Institute at Columbia University. It seeks to be a leader on issues related to foreign direct investment (FDI) in the global economy, paying special attention to the sustainability dimension of this investment. The Vale Columbia Center focuses on the analysis and teaching of the implications of FDI for public policy and international investment law. Its objectives are to analyze important topical policy-oriented issues related to FDI, develop and disseminate practical approaches and solutions, and provide students with a challenging learning environment. To learn more about the VCC, please visit our website at www.vcc.columbia.edu.

Titles in the series include:

The Rise of Transnational Corporations from Emerging Markets
Threat or Opportunity?
Edited by Karl P. Sauvant

Investing in the United States
Is the US Ready for FDI from China?
Edited by Karl P. Sauvant

Investing in the United States

Is the US Ready for FDI from China?

Edited by

Karl P. Sauvant

Executive Director, Vale Columbia Center on Sustainable International Investment (a joint center of Columbia Law School and the Earth Institute) at Columbia University, USA

STUDIES IN INTERNATIONAL INVESTMENT

Edward Elgar
Cheltenham, UK • Northampton, MA, USA

Published by
Edward Elgar Publishing Limited
The Lypiatts
15 Lansdown Road
Cheltenham
Glos GL50 2JA
UK

Edward Elgar Publishing, Inc.
William Pratt House
9 Dewey Court
Northampton
Massachusetts 01060
USA

A catalogue record for this book
is available from the British Library

Library of Congress Control Number: 2009937891

Mixed Sources
Product group from well-managed
forests and other controlled sources
www.fsc.org Cert no. SA-COC-1565
© 1996 Forest Stewardship Council
FSC

ISBN 978 1 84844 859 9

Printed and bound by MPG Books Group, UK

Contents

Contributors

Lorraine Eden is a Professor of Management at Texas A&M University. She is best known for her work on transfer pricing (the pricing of goods, services and intangibles traded within multinational enterprises). Her more than 100 scholarly publications appear in journals such as *Academy of Management Journal, Academy of Management Review, Accounting, Organizations and Society*, and *Journal of International Business Studies*. She is Editor-in-Chief of the *Journal of International Business Studies* and a Fellow of the Academy of International Business.

David N. Fagan's practice covers national security law, international trade and investment, and global privacy and data security. He has represented clients before federal and state government agencies and Congress in connection with a range of issues, including regulatory approvals of international investments, national security-related criminal investigations, high-profile congressional investigations, and federal and state regulatory and enforcement actions in the data security area. On investment issues, he has represented foreign and domestic clients in various industries (including defense, software, information technology, communications, energy, aviation, maritime transportation, ports, and biotechnology/pharmaceuticals) in securing the approval of the Committee on Foreign Investment in the United States (CFIUS), as well as in connection with ongoing compliance matters related to mitigation agreements with CFIUS. He also frequently handles matters related to the mitigation of foreign ownership, control or influence (FOCI) under applicable national industrial security regulations. He is an Adjunct Professor of Law at Georgetown University Law Center, teaching a seminar on "National Security Law and the Private Sector."

Timothy Frye is the Marshall D. Shulman Professor of Post-Soviet Foreign Policy in the Department of Political Science at Columbia University and is the Director of the Harriman Institute for Eurasian and East European Studies. He has published broadly on the politics and economics of postcommunist transformation. He is currently (2009) working on a book manuscript, *Property Rights and Property Wrongs: What Russia Teaches Us About the Rule of Law*. He has worked as a consultant for the World Bank, the European Bank for Reconstruction and Development, the Bloomberg Foundation, and the US Agency for International Development.

Steven Globerman is the Kaiser Professor of International Business and the Director of the Center for International Business at Western Washington University's College of Business and Economics. He writes and consults widely on a range of issues related to international trade and foreign direct investment, and he is a member of the editorial review board for the *Journal of International Business*. He received his PhD from New York University.

Carla A. Hills is Chairperson and Chief Executive Officer of Hills & Company, International Consultants, which provides advice to international firms on investment, trade, and risk assessment issues abroad. She served in the Cabinets of President George H.W. Bush as United States Trade Representative and President Gerald R. Ford as Secretary of the Department of Housing and Urban Development. She serves on several non-profit organizations focused on international policy, including as Co-Chair of the Council on Foreign Relations and of the International Advisory Board of the Center for Strategic and International Studies; Chair of the National Committee on US–China Relations and of the Inter-American Dialogue; and is a member of the Executive Committee of the Peterson Institute for International Economics and the board of the International Crisis Group. She received her Bachelor's degree from Stanford University and her law degree from Yale University.

Mark Kantor was a partner in the Corporate and Project Finance Groups of Milbank, Tweed, Hadley & McCloy until he retired. He currently serves as an arbitrator and mediator, and teaches courses in International Business Transactions and in International Arbitration as an Adjunct Professor at the Georgetown University Law Center. He is also a Senior Research Fellow at the Vale Columbia Center on Sustainable International Investment. He is the Editor-in-Chief of *Transnational Dispute Management*, an online global portal focusing on transnational disputes. He is also a member of numerous other legal advisory and editorial boards. He is Vice-Chair of the DC Bar International Dispute Resolution Committee and Chair of the Washington, DC chapter of The Chartered Institute of Arbitrators. Among other publications, he is the author of *Valuation for Arbitration: Compensation Standards, Valuation Methods and Expert Evidence* (Kluwer Law International, 2008), named Best Book of 2008 in the OGEMID Awards.

Curtis J. Milhaupt is the Fuyo Professor of Japanese Law, Professor of Comparative Corporate Law, and Director of the Center for Japanese Legal Studies at Columbia Law School. In addition to numerous scholarly articles, he has co-authored or edited seven books, including *Law and Capitalism: What Corporate Crises Reveal about Legal Systems and Economic Development Around the World* (with Katharina Pistor, University of Chicago Press, 2008) and *Transforming Corporate Governance in East Asia* (Routledge Press, 2008). He served from 1997 to 2000 as a member of an international project team charged with creating an "institutional blueprint" for a unified Korean peninsula, drawing on lessons from German unification. Prior to entering academia, he practiced corporate law in New York and Tokyo with a major law firm. He holds a JD from Columbia Law School, where he was an editor of the Columbia Law Review, and a BA with high honors in Government and International Studies from the University of Notre Dame.

Stewart R. Miller is Associate Professor of Management at the University of Texas San Antonio. His research focuses on multinational enterprises, in particular liability of foreignness (foreign subsidiary performance) and internationalization. It appears in the *Journal of International Business Studies*, *Academy of Management Journal*, *Strategic Management Journal*, *Organization Science*, *Long-Range Planning* and *Management International Review*, among others. He is a member of the editorial review board of the *Journal of International Business Studies*. He received his PhD from Indiana University.

Pablo M. Pinto is an Assistant Professor in the Political Science Department at Columbia University. He is a resident member of the Saltzman Institute of War and Peace Studies, a research fellow of the Institute for Social and Economic Research and Policy, and member of the advisory committee of the Institute of Latin American Studies at Columbia. His areas of expertise are international and comparative political economy. His research analyzes the causes and consequences of foreign direct investment and has appeared in journals such as *Comparative Political Studies*, *Economics & Politics*, and the *Review of International Political Economy*, among others. He received his PhD from the University of California San Diego, an MA in international politics from Aoyama Gakuin University, Japan, and a degree in law from the National University of La Plata, Argentina.

Karl P. Sauvant is the founding Executive Director of the Vale Columbia Center on Sustainable International Investment, Research Scholar and Lecturer in Law at Columbia Law School, Co-Director of the Millennium Cities Initiative, and Guest Professor at Nankai University, China. Before that, he was Director of UNCTAD's Investment Division. He is the author of, or responsible for, a substantial number of publications. In 2006, he was elected an Honorary Fellow of the European International Business Academy. He received his PhD from the University of Pennsylvania in 1975.

Daniel Shapiro is the Dean and Lohn Foundation Professor at the Faculty of Business Administration, Simon Fraser University. He is the author or co-author of five books and monographs and over 50 journal articles, mainly in the areas of international investment, comparative corporate governance and industrial structure. He has been a visiting professor or lecturer at universities on five continents, has consulted for a wide variety of institutions, and has twice won the TD Canada Trust Award for teaching excellence. He received his PhD in 1974 from Cornell University.

Foreword

Since the 1940s, under both Democratic and Republican administrations, the United States has led the world in opening global markets for goods, services and investment. This has facilitated the spread of technology and encouraged the development of faster and cheaper communications and transport. As a result, the world's economies have become increasingly entwined since the early 1980s.

The results have been spectacular. The explosion of world trade and investment has caused standards of living to soar at home and abroad. Economist Gary Hufbauer, in a comprehensive study published in 2005,[1] calculates that the opening of global markets since World War II has increased our nation's gross domestic product (GDP) by roughly $1 trillion per year, thus raising the average American household yearly income by $9500. Cross-border investment has contributed significantly to that gain. According to the International Monetary Fund such direct investment rose from 6.5 percent of world GDP in 1980 to 32 percent in 2006. Supply chains encircle the globe.

Poor countries have also gained from the opening of global markets. According to studies by the World Bank, those economies that opened their markets grew more than three times faster than those that kept their markets closed. A recent paper by the staff of the International Monetary Fund pointed out that: "over the past 20 years, as a number of countries have become more open to global economic forces, the percentage of the developing world living in extreme poverty – defined as living on less than $1 per day – has been cut in half."[2]

Notwithstanding the proven benefits that result from cross-border transactions, in recent years we have seen an erosion of the bipartisan consensus favoring the free flow of goods, services, and investment. Our nation is struggling with an economic crisis of historic proportions, one that is accompanied by steady increases in unemployment. Last year we completed a lengthy election process in which a number of candidates for President, the Senate and the House of Representatives placed the blame for our economic ills at the doorstep of globalization, open trade and, too often, China. China is criticized for manipulating its currency to maximize its exports which, in turn, is blamed for the loss of millions of American jobs and the build-up of our massive trade deficit and China's huge foreign exchange reserves. Nightly television newscasters amplify these complaints.

The combination of bad economic news and election rhetoric has intensified Americans' fears about job security and fueled their concerns that their future economic opportunities may be eroded, as a country of 1.3 billion people and the world's fastest-growing large economy becomes ever more active in the global market place.

There is increasing concern expressed by members of Congress about cross-border investments by both sovereign wealth funds and state-owned companies. China, with one of the largest funds and numerous state-owned enterprises, is an object of particular concern.

Sovereign wealth funds are not new; the first sovereign wealth fund was the Kuwait Investment Authority, established in 1953 to invest excess oil revenue. But since 2000 the number of such funds has multiplied, spurred by the sharp rise in oil and commodity prices and by growing fiscal surpluses, which has resulted in a huge increase in the number of governments owning and managing assets. This fact has forced a rethinking of global finance by policy-makers in the United States and in other industrialized countries which, until the beginning of the economic crisis in 2008, have expressed a strong preference for governments to limit their role in the world's economic and financial systems.

The authors of the present volume provide concrete reasons why they give an affirmative response to the question addressed in this volume: is the United States ready for foreign direct investment from China? They also discuss a number of complex legal, regulatory and political issues that foreign investors in general need to address to be successful. This highly readable analysis will be helpful not only to foreign investors but also to their potential domestic partners and to state and local governments seeking to attract job-creating investments. The authors are to be congratulated for the careful manner in which they have dissected the various issues connected to cross-border investment into the United States.

Carla A. Hills
Washington, DC, April 2009

NOTES

1. Gary Hufbauer, "The payoff to America from globalization," in *United States and the World Economy* (Washington, DC: Institute for International Economics, 2005).
2. Julian Di Giovanni, Glenn Gottselig, Florence Jaumotte, Luca Antonio Ricci and Stephen Tokarick, "Globalization: a brief overview", *IMF Staff papers*, 08/02, May 2008, p. 1, http://imf.org/external/np/exr/ib/2008/pdf/053008.pdf.

Preface

One of the world's most important bilateral relationships is that between China and the United States. An increasingly visible component of that relationship concerns foreign direct investment (FDI).

United States firms have invested in China for years – some US$96 billion since China opened to the world in 1978. They have been welcomed and play an important role in many sectors of that country's economy. Chinese firms are only now beginning to establish themselves in the United States, pushed in many ways by the same factors that drive their competitors from other countries to enter the world market.

And like their competitors, Chinese firms enter foreign markets not only through greenfield investments but increasingly through mergers and acquisitions (M&As) as well. Naturally, like all firms, they need to observe the regulatory framework of the United States, both when establishing themselves in that country and when operating in it. They also need to become accepted insiders that contribute to their host country's economy and society.

All indications are that a growing number of Chinese firms are interested in investing in the United States, and are prepared to allocate considerable resources for that purpose. This raises an important question: is the United States ready to receive foreign direct investment from China, including in the form of cross-border mergers and acquisitions?

The United States certainly has an open and welcoming investment climate, and its market is one of the most dynamic ones in the world. Not surprisingly, therefore, the United States is the most important host country, having attracted $233billion in 2007 alone, about 16 percent of global flows that year. It is also a highly sophisticated and competitive market with a well-developed regulatory framework. Investors, especially from emerging markets, are therefore well advised to familiarize themselves thoroughly with the entry and operating conditions in the United States. This is particularly important for Chinese firms, not only because many of them are relatively inexperienced newcomers in the global FDI market and especially the United States, but also because recent events suggest that they are receiving more scrutiny than their competitors when they enter via cross-border M&As.

This volume contains the results of a joint project between the US Chinese Services Group of Deloitte LLP and the Vale Columbia Center on Sustainable International Investment. It looks at the principal issues with which Chinese firms – and, for that matter, any foreign firms – need to deal with when investing in the United States. Anyone interested in direct investment in the United States will hopefully find this volume useful, be it from a business, policy or academic perspective.

Karl P. Sauvant
New York, March 2009

Acknowledgments

I would like to acknowledge with gratitude the US Chinese Services Group of Deloitte LLP, under the leadership of National Managing Partner Clarence Kwan, for its contribution to the original idea for, and the subsequent development of, a project on "Is the United States ready for foreign direct investment in China?" and the series of papers that resulted from it.

I am also grateful to the contributors to this volume for preparing the individual chapters on the various aspects of the *problematique* covered here. Special thanks as well to Michael O'Sullivan, succeeded by Lisa Sachs, for managing the project and providing numerous substantive comments that improved the manuscript. Lisa Sachs was also central to bringing this manuscript to fruition.

To all of them: thank you very much!

Karl P. Sauvant
New York, March 2009

To John H. Dunning, friend, mentor, inspiration.

1. Is the United States ready for FDI from China? Overview*

Karl P. Sauvant

INTRODUCTION

Important new players are entering the world market for foreign direct investment (FDI): firms from emerging markets.[1] While there have always been multinational enterprises (MNEs) based in these economies, it is only recently that their outward FDI has become significant. Thus, in 2007 alone, emerging-market MNEs invested some $300 billion abroad,[2] more than ten times total world FDI outflows 25 earlier. This investment is being undertaken by more than 20,000 emerging market multinationals, in all economic sectors, in all parts of the world.

Among emerging-market MNEs, none have received more attention than those head-quartered in China. Within the span of fewer than ten years (2000–2007), they invested an estimated $68 billion abroad, for a total stock of $96 billion at the end of 2007 (Figures 1.1 and 1.2), catapulting China into the ranks of the leading outward investors among emerging markets. This investment takes place in all sectors (and especially services – Table 1.1) and regions of the world (Table 1.2), "through more than 5000 Chinese investment entities hav[ing] established nearly 10,000 overseas enterprises through direct investment across 172 countries and/or economies."[3]

While there are many firms that undertake outward foreign direct investment (OFDI), the great majority of the largest Chinese MNEs consists of state-owned enterprises administered by the central government. They accounted for 83 percent of OFDI flows in 2005; by the end of 2005, their share of OFDI stock was 84 percent.[4] Eighteen among the largest had, in 2006, $79 billion of foreign assets, employed over 120,000 persons abroad and had $79 billion in sales by their foreign affiliates (Table 1.3). Like their competitors from developed countries (and, for that matter, also increasingly from other emerging markets), Chinese firms rely more and more on mergers and acquisitions (M&As) when entering foreign markets, as opposed to greenfield investment (Tables 1.4 and 1.5).

While China's outward FDI position may not look that impressive when compared with that of other, especially developed, countries it needs to be taken into account that it is only recently that Chinese firms have begun their outward expansion and that it is only since the beginning of this decade that the government supports this trend through its "Go Global" policy. Moreover, outflows may well grow considerably in the coming years. During the first half of 2008 alone, non-financial Chinese MNEs invested more abroad ($26 billion) than during all of 2007 ($22 billion), raising the possibility that total outflows in 2008 might be $50–60 billion. If China's sovereign wealth fund, the China Investment Corporation, should become more active in the FDI market, this figure could

Investing in the United States

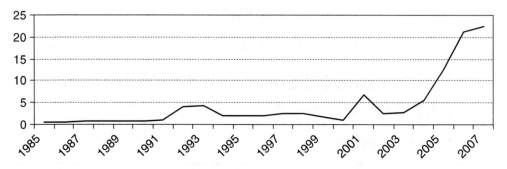

Source: UNCTAD, http://stats.unctad.org/FDI/.

Figure 1.1   China's outward FDI flows, 1985–2007 (US$ billions)

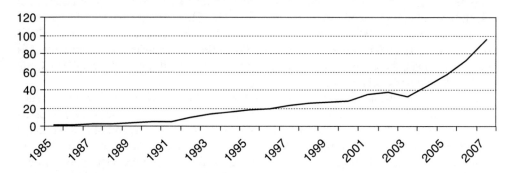

Source: UNCTAD, http://stats.unctad.org/FDI/.

Figure 1.2   China's outward FDI stock, 1985–2007 (US$ billions)

rapidly become higher, although the financial crisis and recession may well temporarily slow down outward FDI flows.

These developments raise an important question, namely: is the world ready for FDI – and especially M&As – from emerging markets? To put it differently: can emerging-market MNEs be integrated smoothly into the world FDI market, as part of a broader integration of these economies into the world economy? It is a question that needs to be asked because there are some indications that some countries have difficulties accepting "the new kids on the block."[5] And it is a question to be asked especially for MNEs based in China, as their outward expansion – from Africa to the US – is getting considerable attention in the media and from policy-makers.

This volume focuses on one subset of this question, namely: is the US ready for FDI – and especially M&As – from China? The question is all the more important, as Chinese FDI in the US while still small (Table 1.6 and Figure 1.3), is bound to rise. After all, the US is the single biggest and most attractive market in the world, and most firms think they need to establish themselves there, to include it in their portfolios of locational assets. This applies also to Chinese firms.

Table 1.1   Sectoral distribution of China's OFDI stock, 2006 (US$ millions)

OFDI stock	US$ m	Percentage of total
Primary sector	18718	(25)
Agriculture, forestry, husbandry and fishery	807	(1)
Mining, quarrying and petroleum	17902	(24)
Secondary sector (Manufacturing)	7530	(10)
Tertiary sector	48778	(65)
Lease and business services	19464	(26)
Wholesale and retail	12955	(17)
Transport and storage	7568	(10)
Others	8791	(12)
Total	75026	(100)

Source: OECD (2008), p. 136.

Table 1.2   Regional distribution of OFDI stock from China, 2006 (US$ millions)

OFDI stock	US$ m	Percentage of total
Asia	47978	(64)
Hong Kong, China (as a share of Asia)	42270	(88)
Latin America (LA)	19694	(26)
3 Offshore Financial Centres (as a share of LA)	18977	(96)
Europe	2270	(3)
Western Europe (as a share of Europe)	1050	(46)
Central and Eastern Europe (as a share of Europe)	1220	(54)
Africa	2557	(3)
North America	1584	(2)
Oceania	939	(1)
Total	75026	(100)

Source: OECD (2008), p. 135.

The short answer to that question is "yes." Indeed, the US has one of the most open investment frameworks in the world and its states and many municipalities actively seek to attract FDI. The long answer is still "yes," but with a number of qualifications attached to it, as there are all sorts of tricky and difficult issues that need to be taken into account by emerging-market MNEs in general, and Chinese MNEs wishing to enter the US market in particular. The focus of this volume is precisely on these tricky and difficult issues and how foreign firms can deal with them, in terms of entering the US market, operating in it, and prospering in it.

Table 1.3 FUDAN-VCC ranking of 18 large Chinese multinational enterprises in terms of foreign assets, 2006 (US$ millions)

Rank	Name	Industry	Foreign assets	Foreign sales	Foreign employment
1	CITIC Group	Diversified	17623	2482	18305
2	China Ocean Shipping (Group) Company	Transport and storage	10397	8777	4432
3	China State Construction Engineering Corp	Construction, real estate	6831	4376	5820
4	China National Petroleum Corp	Petroleum expl./ref./ distr.	6374	3036	22000
5	Sinochem Corp.	Petroleum and fertilizer	5326	19374	220
6	China Poly Group Corporation	Trade, real estate	5113	1750	n.a.
7	China National Offshore Oil Corp.	Petroleum and natural gas	4984	3719	984
8	Shougang Group	Diversified	4875	2250	n.a.
9	China Shipping (Group) Company	Diversified	4600	4324	2433
10	TCL Corporation	Electrical and electronic equipment	3875	3366	32078
11	Lenovo Group	Computer and related activities	3147	9002	6200
12	China Minmetals Corp	Metals and metal products	1266	2527	630
13	China Communications Construction Corp	Construction	1162	2855	1078
14	Shum Yip Holdings Company Limited	Real estate	972	123	28
15	Baosteel Group Corporation	Diversified	968	4231	170
16	Shanghai Automotive Industry Corporation(Group)	Automotives	442	4133	7175
17	China Metallurgical Group Corporation	Diversified	439	314	745
18	Haier Group	Manufacturing, telecommunications, IT	394	1870	6800
TOTAL			78788	78509	123670

Source: FUDAN-VCC survey of Chinese multinational enterprises, at www.vcc.columbia.edu.

Table 1.4   M&As versus China's OFDI, 1988–2006

	1988–89 (average)	1990–91 (average)	2000–02 (average)	2003	2004	2005	2006
China's deals (US $ millions)	109	430	3 561	1 647	1 125	5 279	14 904
As a ratio in total OFDI flow (%)	13.9	16.7	43.6	57.7	20.5	43.1	84.5

Source: OECD (2008), p. 75.

1.1   ENTERING THE US MARKET

1.1.1   Mergers and Acquisitions versus Greenfield FDI

For many firms, the typical way to establish themselves in a foreign country is through mergers and acquisitions (M&As), as opposed to greenfield investments (that is, the establishment of new production facilities). In fact, in developed countries, the bulk of FDI takes place through this mode of entry. In 2007, there were 10,145 cross-border M&As globally, valued at $1.6 trillion; of these, 78 percent of the M&As and 89 percent of the total value involved developed countries.[6] This compares with FDI inflows to developed countries of $1.2 trillion in the same year.[7] The US is no exception to this pattern. In 2007, there were 2040 M&As undertaken in this country by foreign firms, at a value of $380 billion; in the same year, FDI inflows amounted to $230 billion.[8] M&As and greenfield investments both have a number of advantages and disadvantages for firms and host countries, an issue examined by Steven Globerman and Daniel Shapiro in Chapter 2.

For firms, M&As have the advantage of allowing them to enter a market rapidly – and in today's globalizing world economy, in which competition is everywhere, speed is often of the essence. Moreover, if the acquired firm controls an extensive distribution network, state-of-the-art research and development (R&D) facilities and valuable brand names, the acquiring firm obtains a portfolio of locational and proprietary assets that are key to international competitiveness. Deep market penetration can be achieved quickly in this manner, which is also useful if the acquiring firm already exports to the foreign market. If experienced staff can be retained in the acquired firm, the acquiring firm minimizes learning costs associated with operating in a new market; in fact, it obtains local knowledge and skills, as well as a network of relationships that can be important for prospering in a new environment.

However, cross-border M&As also involve a number of difficulties and risks. To begin with, the proper target needs to be identified and a deal needs to be negotiated. If the corporate cultures of the acquiring and acquired firms differ substantially – and this is likely to be the case if the acquiring firm is from China (or, for that matter, any other emerging market) and the acquired firm is in the US – there is the additional challenge of meshing different cultures. At the same time, the new unit needs to be incorporated into the international production network of the parent firm. This, in turn, may involve

Table 1.5 *Major OFDI deals by Chinese enterprises, 2004–07*

Chinese enterprises	Invested project/ acquired asset	Host country	Estimated investment amount (US$ billion)	Date	Comment	Major motivation
Wuhan Iron and Steel and other three steel mill companies	Wheelara joint-venture with BHP billion for mining iron ore	Australia	9.3	2004	Agreement signed	(1) Iron core
CNPC	Petrokazakhstan	Canada/ Kazakhstan	4.18	2005	Acquired	(1) Oil
China Minmetals	CODELCO	Chile	0.55	2005	Agreement signed	(1) Copper
Sinopec	99.49% stake in Udmurtneft OAO	Russia	3.65	2006	Acquired	(1) Oil
CITIC	Kazakh oil assets of Nations Energy Company	Canada/ Kazakhstan	1.91	2006	Acquired	(1) Oil and (4)
China Metallurgical Group	Aynak copper field and related infrastructure project	Afghanistan	2.8	2007	Agreement signed	(1) Copper
Shanghai Baosteel	Joint-venture with Companhia Vale do Rio Doce for a steel slab plant	Brazil	3–4	2007	Letter of intent signed	(1) Steel
Sinopec	Development of Yadavaran onshore oil field	Iran	2	2007	Agreement signed	(1) Oil
Industrial and Commercial Bank of China	20% stake in Standard Bank	South Africa	5.49	2007	Completed	(2) and (4)
Bank of China	669 branches including a recent opening at London	28 countries	40% of its net profits from overseas	By 2007		(2) and (4)

Lenova	IBM (PC hardware division)	USA	1.75	2004	Completed	(3) Computer
Nanjing Auto	MG Rover	UK	N/A	2005	Completed	(3) Automobile
China Mobile	China Resource Peoples Telephone	Hong Kong, China	0.43	2005	Completed	(4)
Bank of China	Singapore Aircraft Leasing Enterprise	Singapore	3.43	2006	Completed	(4)
State Grid Corporation	Consortium led by the Philippines' Monte Ore Grid for grid operation privatization	Philippines	3.95	2007	Bid awarded	(4)
Failed deals						
China Minmetals	Noranda	Canada	5	2004	Aborted	(1) Copper and zinc
CNOOC	Unocal	USA	19.5	2005	Aborted	(1) Oil
Haier	Maytag	USA	1.28	2005	Aborted	(3) Washing Machine
China Mobile	Millicom International Cellular	Luxembourg	5.3	2007	Aborted	(3)

Note: Major motivations include: (1) resource-seeking, (2) market-seeking, (3) strategic-asset-seeking, (4) diversification-seeking and (5) efficiency-seeking.

Source: OECD (2008), p. 95.

7

Table 1.6   China's foreign direct investment into the US, 2002–07

Year	US$ millions
2002	385
2003	284
2004	435
2005	574
2006	973
2007	1091

Source: US Bureau of Economic Analysis, www. bea.gov.

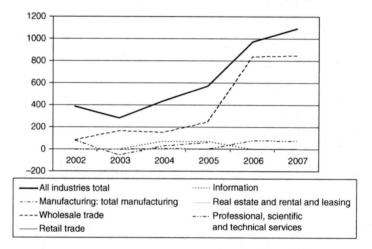

Note: ªForeign direct investment position in the United States on a historical-cost basis.

Source: US Bureau of Economic Analysis data, www.bea.gov.

Figure 1.3   China's FDI in the US by industry, 2002–07ª (US$ millions)

a restructuring of the acquired assets, including the closing down of existing production lines, the relocation of R&D facilities and lay-offs – all actions that may encounter the resistance of labor unions; local, regional or national authorities; and other stakeholders. In fact, resistance may start earlier, especially if stakeholders – rightly or wrongly – anticipate some of the actions just mentioned (and others, such as increase in concentration and therefore a possible decrease in competition) once an M&A is consummated. Resistance in the host country can be particularly high if the target is in a sector that is considered of great economic or strategic importance or involves a national champion, or if the acquirer is a state-owned enterprise, especially from an emerging market (which would typically be the case for Chinese MNEs, as most of the important ones have some percentage of state ownership).

Given all these difficulties and risks, it is not surprising that many M&As have not lived up to their expectations and that a number have even been unwound. Even long-established MNEs may not succeed – witness the acquisition of Chrysler by Daimler Benz, a move that, after a few years, was undone. On the other hand, many M&As do succeed. The secret is careful planning, experience and having the skills and patience to navigate the difficulties and risks that are inherent in a cross-border M&A.

Greenfield investments, on the other hand, allow a firm to start from scratch, beginning with the choice of the location; they are unencumbered by various legacy costs and practices that are established in an acquisition target.[9] However, it takes time to establish a greenfield investment and to develop a network of relationships, and it requires more learning in terms of operating in a new environment.

Moreover, greenfield investments are uniformly welcomed by host countries (and typically even benefit from various incentives) as they create new production capacity, while M&As represent only a change in ownership and, moreover, the shifting of control of a domestic entity to a parent firm headquartered abroad. Greenfield investments also mean new jobs, and they may bring new technologies, skills, competition and exports. Exceptional circumstances apart (like a rescue operation of a firm in danger of failing), governments prefer greenfield investments to M&As. This preference holds even though – as Globerman and Shapiro argue – the positive economic effects of greenfield investments and M&As converge over time and, hence, do not support a discrimination between these two forms of market entry.

1.1.2 The Regulatory Environment

These different perceptions of host countries as regards M&As and greenfield investments find their expression in the regulatory framework that governs FDI in the US, with the former investments potentially facing scrutiny, while the latter are uniformly welcome. In fact, the US has one of the most open investment frameworks in the world, reaffirmed in May 2007 in a statement on "Open Economies" by President George W. Bush[10] and the establishment of "Invest in America" within the Department of Commerce.[11] Moreover, virtually all states of the Union fiercely compete for FDI. Many of them have established investment promotion offices abroad. Hence the short answer of "yes" to the question: "is the US ready for FDI from China?"

But, the "rise of the rest"[12] – meaning especially FDI from emerging markets – is creating adjustment problems that are also visible in US–China relations. As US Secretary of the Treasury, Henry M. Paulson, remarked:

> Economic nationalism . . . has been a growing concern in the United States in recent years . . . Foreign investment into the United States, especially by sovereign wealth funds and state-owned enterprises, is also increasingly viewed with suspicion by some US companies, various members of the national security community, and the American public at large, despite regulations by the Committee on Foreign Investment in the United States that provide sufficient protections in sensitive sectors.[13]

In the aftermath of September 11, 2001, in particular, national security concerns have entered the realm of the FDI field, mixed with apprehension about the rise of emerging-market MNEs, especially from countries that are considered to be potentially unfriendly or strategic competitors. The importance of state-owned enterprises in the outward FDI of a number of emerging markets and the growing role of government-controlled sovereign wealth funds add to this apprehension. Among emerging markets, China receives particular attention, precisely because it is seen as an important strategic competitor and because the bilateral balance-of-payments deficit of the US with China, combined with what is regarded an undervalued Chinese currency, are held responsible for some of the difficulties that the US economy is experiencing.

The result has been the strengthening of the established screening mechanism for FDI, namely the Committee on Foreign Investment in the United States (CFIUS). Originally provided with formal authority to review foreign investments with a nexus on US national security interests in the late 1980s, the committee's role in screening certain FDI was further enhanced through the Foreign Investment and National Security Act of 2007 (FINSA) and the subsequent President's Executive Order of January 2008 and the final regulations issued by the Treasury Department (which entered into force on November 21, 2008). The contribution by David N. Fagan, in Chapter 3, describes and analyzes in detail the regulatory and institutional development for FDI in the US and the implications it has for foreign investors in general and Chinese investors in particular.

In brief, the precise legal and institutional framework for any given investment depends largely on the facts and circumstances relating to it, including the nature of the transaction, the location of an investment (which may determine what local laws or institutions can impact prospects for success), the sector of an investment, the size of the investment, and specific facts of a particular transaction such as the legal compliance reputation of the acquirer and US target and the potential broader legal liabilities of the US target. In the case of M&As, furthermore, US anti-trust legislation may well come into play. All this makes the US FDI framework less predictable than it was in the past.

Foreign investors undertaking M&As in the US must pay special attention to the security review conducted by CFIUS. (Greenfield investments are exempted by statute and regulation from review by CFIUS.) In particular, there is a presumption that M&As by state-controlled entities are subject to additional scrutiny in the form of an "investigation," which follows an initial 30-day review, unless certain statutory triggers (related to senior-level sign-off within the CFIUS process and the absence of any remaining national security issues) for terminating the review at 30 days are met. Figure 1.4 presents, succinctly, the principal aspects of this process. As Fagan points out, the critical threshold questions for a CFIUS review are whether there is foreign control over a US business; if there is control, whether a transaction presents any significant national security concerns; and if there are such concerns, whether they can be mitigated through contractual commitments from the parties involved ("mitigation agreements"). Importantly, "national security" is not defined.

The CFIUS process can be crucial for Chinese MNEs, as most of the biggest ones are state-controlled entities. This creates special challenges for Chinese MNEs (as well as for state-controlled entities of other countries) to obtain regulatory approval and manage the potential for a particular transaction becoming an object of political debate as occurred, for example, in the aborted takeover attempt of Unocal by the China National Offshore Oil Corporation (CNOOC) and the acquisition by Dubai Ports World of the Peninsular and Oriental Steam Navigation Company (which operated terminals at six major US ports).

It reflects the changed investment climate in the US that notifications to CFIUS were up considerably in 2007 and 2008 (Figure 1.5). While no deals were blocked, six were

US Regulatory Due Diligence and Strategy Framework for FDI

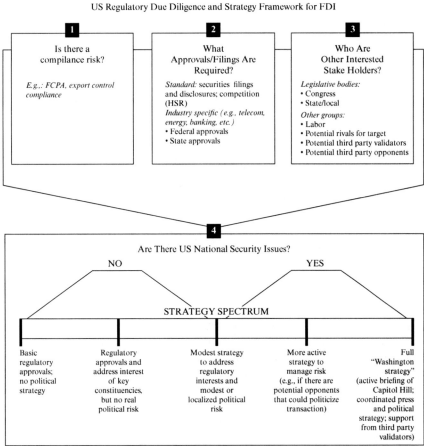

Source: David N. Fagan, Chapter 3 in this volume; copyright Covington & Burling LLP.

Figure 1.4 *The US regulatory and strategic due diligence flow chart for cross-border M&As*

subject to investigation in 2007, and 22 in 2008. In February 2008, a filing involving a minority Chinese investment in a US telecoms firm was withdrawn in the face of national security concerns. While the data certainly shows a substantial increase in scrutiny, the numbers involved pale, however, in comparison to the total number of cross-border M&As in the US. Still, the growing number of CFIUS notifications and investigations signal that the regulatory framework for FDI in the US is changing.

Developing an appropriate regulatory and political strategy is particularly important for MNEs entering the US through M&As and prospering in that country, as it is not only the various agencies comprising CFIUS that decide on a specific deal but Congress itself, and the entire political establishment can get involved. This is especially true when high-profile transactions are contemplated – and any large M&A by a Chinese firm potentially falls into this category. Navigating the US political landscape for FDI is, indeed, a real

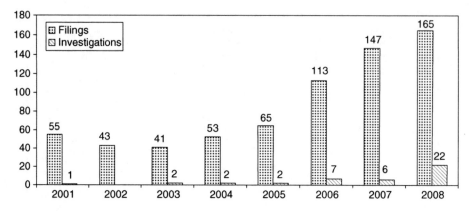

Source: US Treasury Department.

Figure 1.5   CFIUS filings and investigations, 2001–08

challenge for foreign investors (and not only investors from China), as Timothy Frye and Pablo M. Pinto elaborate in Chapter 4.

The dynamics in this landscape are complex. Presidents, responsible for the country as a whole, have generally been supportive of a liberal investment framework, although they also need to take national security concerns into account (see the statement of the President mentioned earlier). Within the Executive branch, the cross-pressures between openness and national security are balanced in CFIUS in the context of specific M&As, as its members represent a wide range of approaches and interests. But for individual members of Congress, the situation is different, because they represent individual districts. As a result, members of Congress need to deliver benefits to their own districts if they want to be re-elected by their constituents, especially if representatives hold marginal seats. Depending on how members of Congress see themselves affected by China in general and the country's FDI in particular, they will seek to shape policies accordingly.

As Frye and Pinto point out, members of Congress interested in China have organized themselves in political groups, most important among them the Congressional China Caucus and the US–China Working Group. The former focuses on the strategic and political concerns associated with China (and is typically critical of China), while the latter focuses on the economic opportunities that result from engaging China (and therefore is typically pro-China) (see Table 1.7). The saliency of these groups can be illustrated in reference to the vote in the House of Representatives in June 2005 on a resolution that called upon the President to "initiate immediately a thorough review of the proposed acquisition, merger or takeover" if Unocal accepted CNOOC's bid. The resolution was passed by a vote of 398 to 15. Tellingly, 8 of the 15 representatives who voted against the resolution were from the US–China Working Group, while not one member of the Congressional China Caucus opposed it. In addition, 6 of the 15 "no" votes came from representatives of districts in the state of Washington, a state that has substantial exports to China.

Moreover, beyond the Executive and Congress, there are many other stakeholders

Table 1.7   US stakeholders' position on economic liberalization toward China

Motivation	General attitude	
	Relatively pro-China	Relatively anti-China
Economic	Financial firms (private equity, M&A players)	Labor leaders and unions
	Business associations (Business Roundtable, Financial Services Forum)	Conservative think-tanks (American Enterprise Inst.; Heritage Foundation)
	Liberal think tanks (IIE; OFFI)	Labor-affiliated think-tanks
	Congress: US–China Working Group	Congress: Congressional China Caucus
	US states actively seeking foreign investment	House membership
	The public: richer, more educated people who value cosmopolitanism	The public: anti-globalization and concerned about trade with China and "US jobs"; human rights advocates
Nationalistic/ strategic	"Panda huggers" in defense community	US military; security community
		Congress: Congressional China Caucus
		The public: slight tendency to be wary of China for people concerned about US military superiority

Source: Timothy Frye and Pablo M. Pinto, Chapter 4 in this volume.

that have an interest in the China–US relationship in general and FDI from China in particular. Table 1.7 lists a number of them and their overall orientation and attitude.

What this underlines is that M&As by Chinese firms in the US are not only an economic issue – they are, especially when it comes to larger acquisitions in sensitive sectors – but as much or more a political issue, even if they make economic sense. Hence, to smooth the entry process, it is important to understand Washington's political landscape, know what the interests of key players are, learn to navigate the committee network in Congress, and build alliances from the local level upward.

1.2   OPERATING

Once the mode of entry (M&A versus greenfield investment) has been chosen and regulatory barriers have been navigated, the challenge for foreign investors – and Chinese ones in particular – is to operate successfully in the highly competitive, sophisticated and litigious US market and prosper in it. To do that, foreign investors need to overcome the "liability of foreignness," discussed by Lorraine Eden and Stewart R. Miller in Chapter 5. As one of the leading academics in the FDI field observed many years ago: "Alien status always imposes some penalty on managerial effectiveness."[14] "Liability of foreignness", therefore, is the liability of being a stranger in a strange land. It revolves around a number of costs that foreign firms – but not domestic ones – incur by operating abroad. These involve, most notably, unfamiliarity costs arising from a lack of knowledge about the host country; the potential (and sometimes subtle) differential treatment of foreign affiliates by host country organizations and institutions; and costs arising out of the need to manage relations between the parent firm and its foreign affiliate, as well as the relations of foreign affiliates and local partners and stakeholders from a distance. These costs can be particularly high if the gap between the regulatory, normative and cognitive situations in the home country (for example, China) and the host country (for example, the US) is high. As Eden and Miller point out, furthermore, the challenge to handle such costs is accentuated in cases in which firms from a country with weaker institutions need to operate in countries with stronger institutions.

Chinese MNEs certainly face the entire range of liability-of-foreignness costs when establishing themselves in the US. On the regulatory side, they need to operate in a country with a highly developed legal system and a strong legal culture. Naturally, the entire set of laws and regulations governing enterprises applies to Chinese foreign affiliates. Some regulatory instruments that are particularly relevant relate to corrupt practices, corporate governance, financial practices, foreign trade, transfer pricing, occupational health, labor safety, civil rights, age discrimination, and employees with disabilities. In addition, a number of industries are subject to sector-specific federal and state regulatory regimes (for example, banking, telecommunications). All this adds up to a complex regulatory framework that is typically enforced at the federal and/or state levels. Foreign affiliates are well advised to observe these laws and regulations scrupulously, lest their operations risk legal difficulties. This is a particular challenge for Chinese firms as they typically have little experience with operating foreign affiliates, including in the US.

At the same time, Chinese firms established in the US (like those of other countries) benefit from various protections against unwarranted action by the authorities, contained in US national and international investment laws. Mark Kantor, in Chapter 6, examines to what extent international investment law provides protection for Chinese investments in the US, even though there is no investment treaty between the US and China. (However, the beginning of negotiations of a bilateral investment treaty was announced in June 2008.) Most important here are the World Trade Organization (WTO) General Agreement on Trade in Services (the GATS, which, in "Mode 3," provides a number of protections to service businesses conducted through a "commercial presence", akin to FDI, in the US) and the WTO Agreement on Trade-Related Investment Measures (the TRIMs agreement) (prohibiting certain performance requirements). The enforcement of both these agreements occurs via the state-to-state dispute settlement mechanism in the WTO Dispute Settlement Understanding. The normal remedy for breach of the GATS or TRIMs agreements is withdrawal of trade benefits, a remedy that is not necessarily valuable to injured investors.

But Chinese investors can obtain the protection of a bilateral investment treaty – and, for that matter, also a double taxation treaty – between the US and a third country by means of "treaty-shopping," that is, by investing in the US via a company they have established in that third country, provided that company has "substantial business activities" in that country. Once they do that, all the protections of that third country's bilateral investment treaty with the US apply. As of 2008, the US had bilateral investment treaties with 47 economies[15] and various types of tax treaties with 65.[16] A similar approach may be taken with respect to establishing an investment vehicle in a third country that has a free trade agreement with the US (including the North American Free Trade Agreement NAFTA), as long as it has applicable investment provisions.

Such protection involves, among other things, payment of fair market value compensation in the case of expropriation, including indirect expropriation. Applicable international investment agreements (IIAs) also provide protection against US legislative, regulatory or judicial treatment contrary to the international investment law principle of "fair and equitable treatment." Subject to specific exceptions, they guarantee non-discrimination on the basis of nationality ("most-favored-nation treatment" and "national treatment"). They guarantee the free repatriation of dividends, the free distribution of the proceeds of the sale of an investment and the free transfer of other payments. They prohibit restrictions on the nationality of senior managers. Finally, they prohibit certain performance requirement (often beyond those already prohibited by the TRIMs agreement). In contrast to the GATS and TRIMs Agreements, however, applicable IIAs also allow foreign investors to initiate investor–state arbitration proceedings. The normal remedy in investor–state arbitration for the breach of an IIA is the payment of damages to compensate for injury.[17]

However, US IIAs (like the WTO agreements) contain an "essential security" exception under which the US is entitled, notwithstanding other provisions of such treaties, to take measures to protect its essential security interests. Furthermore, recent US treaties expressly state that the exception is "self-judging," that is, the US government alone decides whether or not a given measure is necessary in a particular situation. Still, in spite of this (and other) limitations, the protections offered to foreign investors in the US are among the strongest in the world.

1.3 PROSPERING

How to deal with the liability of foreignness? What, in particular, can Chinese firms – and, for that matter, firms from other countries – do to prosper in the US? The answer to this question has many facets – and it can draw on the experience of firms from Japan that were in a situation similar to that of Chinese firms today when they entered the US in the 1980s. Curtis J. Milhaupt examines this experience in Chapter 7.

During the 1980s, the macroclimate of US–Japanese relations was characterized by trade frictions, exchange rate controversies, concerns about the nature of the Japanese economy ("Japan Inc."), fears about Japan's economic ascendance, and cultural misperceptions. The media and politicians had a field day in Japan-bashing.

In spite of this climate, Japanese FDI in the US rose from less than $1 billion annually during the 1970s, to a peak of nearly $20 billion in 1988–90.[18] It received special attention and faced resistance, exacerbated at times by the relative inexperience of Japanese firms: they (like their Chinese counterparts today) had just embarked on an accelerated internationalization process through FDI and hence had not yet accumulated the experience that comes with operating abroad for decades. During the second half of the 1980s, in particular, when M&As became the principal mode of entry for Japanese firms, a number of high-profile acquisitions (for example, that of the Rockefeller Center) received considerable publicity. One attempted acquisition – Fujitsu's bid for Fairchild Semiconductor (already foreign owned) – actually contributed to the adoption of the Exon–Florio Amendment, which is the original statute governing the CFIUS national security review process. Moreover, a number of Japanese affiliates in the US faced legal difficulties in the employment area, with one suit reaching the Supreme Court. All in all, Japanese FDI in the US had a rough time.

The parallels in the macroclimate between the US and Japan then and the US and China now are indeed striking.[19] Some of the reactions to Chinese FDI in the US are also strikingly similar, even as far as the reaction by the media and politicians is concerned, and the strengthening of CFIUS through FINSA. Yet, in the case of Japanese FDI in the US, the controversies died down during the 1990s. Today, Japanese firms are firmly implanted in the US; they have become an integral and valuable part of the country's economic and social fabric, and Japan remains an important source of FDI.

What can we learn from the Japanese experience and, broader, how can Chinese foreign affiliates in the US prosper in the US market? Milhaupt, Eden and Miller, but also virtually every other author in this volume, answer this question, each one from his or her perspective and in the context of their specific subjects. The underlying message is clear, though: Chinese firms – like those from other countries before them– need to become insiders, and they need to build up a positive company brand name, to be accepted in the US. Various strategies can be pursued to that effect.

Where Chinese firms have a choice between entering the US market through an M&A or a greenfield investment, the safer route (politically speaking), is the latter. And even in the case of M&As, follow-on greenfield investments can be important to increase the acceptability of a given investment. Greenfield investments, as was pointed out earlier, are universally welcome as they create new production capacities and employment, and they are not subject to a potential CFIUS review. For Chinese firms exporting to the US, perhaps the best way is to establish assembly facilities and eventually move on to full production capacities (reducing the trade deficit in the process). A number of Japanese firms successfully followed this path, especially in the automotive industry.

In the case of M&As, mention has already been made of the need for an appropriate political strategy, if possible avoiding high-profile takeovers, especially hostile ones. Part of such a strategy is to examine carefully who is affected by a planned acquisition and to understand the interests of the principal stakeholders involved. Stakeholder management and learning how to navigate the political process and institutional system in Washington, DC, are very important, either individually or together with other non-US MNEs[20]; discrete lobbying may be an important part of this process. The objective needs to be to reduce, to the greatest extent possible, negative publicity and hence to avoid starting out on the wrong foot. If this cannot be done, an attempted acquisition may not come to fruition or may be vetoed.

Once established, foreign affiliates need to observe local laws and regulations scrupulously – this goes without saying.[21] This requires a thorough understanding of the country's regulatory framework and its functioning. Compliance training and working with local partners who understand US regulations can be important here.

More than that, foreign affiliates need to integrate themselves as tightly as possible in the communities in which they are established. This means, among other things, growing roots by creating backward linkages with local enterprises, giving them a stake in the well-being of the affiliate. It also means recruiting high-level US citizens for management positions, the board of directors and especially positions in an affiliate that involve an interface with public and private US organizations. Finally, integration involves cultivating the local community which, in turn, has its own links to the state and federal governments. All politics (including in Washington, DC) is, in the end, local. Organizations that foster communications among business people have a role to play as well; the US–China Business Council is important in this regard, and eventually its degree of penetration may be as deep as that of the US–Japan Business Council.

Another important means to advance integration is corporate social responsibility (CSR). It is a concept that has great saliency in the US – firms are expected to pay full heed to it, at the local, state and federal levels. Japanese firms became fully cognizant of the importance of CSR as part of their efforts to become accepted and integrated. Donations to local charities have a role to play here, as has the establishment of foundations in support of education and the endowment of chairs at major universities.[22]

Pursuing these strategies allows foreign affiliates to create a dense network of economic, social and cultural interactions and ties that embed them and their reputation in their communities and, eventually, make them insiders with a good corporate brand name.

Naturally, this requires considerable learning on the part of the managers of foreign affiliates and their parent firms. Building that human capacity is one of the key challenges facing Chinese MNEs. This begins with training when it comes to M&As (and seeking advice where this is needed), learning the ropes of the political system, knowing how to become a good corporate citizen, and demonstrating the contribution that foreign affiliates make to the local and national economy. It also requires that the government of the home country of foreign affiliates (in this case, China) encourages foreign affiliates to become insiders in the host country and acquire a good corporate brand name. And it requires that the media, the public and the political establishment of the host country (in this case, the US) recognize the value of Chinese FDI and respect the principle of non-discrimination in the treatment of such investment; a bilateral investment treaty can help in this respect.

1.4   SUMMARY AND CONCLUSIONS[23]

There are indications worldwide that the climate for FDI is becoming less welcoming just as Chinese enterprises are appearing on the global stage. In particular, a number of developed countries, including the United States, Japan and Germany, are taking a more cautious approach to cross-border M&A, by far the most important mode of entry into foreign markets by MNEs and, increasingly, for Chinese enterprises as well. Particularly since CNOOC withdrew its bid for Unocal in mid-2005, cross-border M&As by Chinese firms have attracted special attention, and there is ample indication they will continue to do so for the foreseeable future.

The reasons for this nervous reaction to Chinese outward FDI are mixed, but they are largely political in nature. Questions are raised about the governance of Chinese firms and the fear that Chinese acquirers, especially when they are state-owned, may enjoy financing advantages. This is less an issue for the shareholders of acquisition targets than for rival firms competing for the same assets. There is also some concern, especially in Europe, about the ability of Chinese firms to manage cross-border M&As successfully and the implication that any failures would have for host countries, especially in terms of unemployment and the business of suppliers. Most importantly, there is the suspicion that cross-border acquisitions by state-owned firms are not necessarily driven by commercial motives alone, but are rather the result of political or strategic calculations determined (or at least influenced) by the government that controls them. The formal launch in September 2007 of the China Investment Corporation, China's new sovereign wealth fund with $200 billion in foreign exchange reserves at its disposal, has only fuelled speculation about the link between Chinese outward FDI and the country's wider geopolitical goals.

If this were not enough, Chinese enterprises are seeking to enter the global FDI market at a time when economic tensions between China and its major trade partners are at an all-time high. In the US, currency valuation has emerged as a lightning rod, while fast-growing trade imbalances with the US, Europe and, more recently, Japan, have deepened frictions as well. In fact, some observers trace a direct link between China's trade surplus and the rapid growth of Chinese outward FDI, especially its state-financed portion.[24] Other issues unrelated to Chinese FDI have helped sour public perceptions of Chinese business, especially the 2007 product recalls involving Chinese-made goods. To the average American or European, unfamiliar with even the largest Chinese companies, it becomes quite easy to allow negative associations to fill the void, with very predictable consequences in the political arena.

Given the speed at which Chinese firms are expected to go global, and the fact that state-owned enterprises account for a substantial portion of China's FDI, Chinese firms are encountering a rapidly evolving political environment in the US and other developed markets. In July 2007, the US revised the Exon–Florio Amendment, including a presumption that filings relating to acquisitions by state-controlled foreign entities will require investigation by CFIUS. Notification to, and investigation by, CFIUS have risen substantially. In a number of European countries, as well as Australia and Canada, investment reviews are now being strengthened, including through the introduction of a CFIUS-like screening process in Russia and Germany. With Japan recently strengthening its oversight of cross-border M&As and political pressure building in Canada, the Republic of Korea and elsewhere, the global investment environment seems to be tightening just as Chinese enterprises are poised to enter the world FDI market.

What to do in light of the vulnerability of Chinese outward FDI? It is only natural that, with the re-emergence of China as a major economy, its firms will spread their wings and become major players in the world FDI market.[25] The world needs to accept that Chinese MNEs are here to stay, and that outward FDI is another aspect of the country's integration into the world economy. The issue for all stakeholders is how to handle this process smoothly.

At the most basic level, it is essential that the non-discrimination principle – which is central to the international law governing cross-border investment – is applied by the US to Chinese outward FDI as it is applied to the investments of other countries; if a bilateral investment treaty should, indeed, be negotiated, non-discrimination would presumably feature prominently in it.

Chinese companies, too, need to be mindful of managing their international growth in light of the sensitivities that exist – rightly or wrongly – about the transnationalization of Chinese business. This begins with the training of executives not only in matters related to the management of their firms, but also in those related to the political economy and culture of the US and other major host countries. Stakeholder management is particularly important here vis-à-vis policy-makers, labor, investors, local communities and the public. Furthermore, any acquisition by a state-owned enterprise and/or investments with a potential impact on national security will need particularly careful preparation. The same goes for acquisitions in sectors that are perceived to be off-limits to foreign investors from China. On the public relations side, it needs to be shown that Chinese FDI is fundamentally no different from that of other countries – and hence contributes to the economic growth and development of its host countries. Naturally, this message will be better received if Chinese companies behave as scrupulously good corporate citizens when operating abroad, not only by observing the laws and regulations of their host countries, but by exercising exemplary corporate social responsibility as well.

Whatever the overall impact and perception of Chinese outward FDI, Chinese firms may want to draw on the experience of Japanese firms in the US. When Japanese companies burst onto the world FDI market in the 1980s (partly through high-profile M&As), there was widespread fear that they would come to dominate the world economy; attitudes in the US in particular were defensive. Some of these fears began to dissipate as Japan entered a period of stagnation in the 1990s. Yet, perhaps more importantly, Japanese firms began to change their basic approach to investing in the US. Their understanding of the US market and ability to build key relationships with governments and communities grew. In addition to M&As, Japanese companies began to establish assembly facilities in the US and, later, full production units. As their readiness to address US market entry challenges increased, they found that the receptivity of the US business environment rose as well, in a virtuous cycle. Under the best of circumstances, Chinese firms and other stakeholders in the US–Chinese investment relationship will embark on a similar trajectory in a more compressed time-frame. Chinese firms, together with their counterparts in other emerging markets, can then look forward to a normalization of their investment relationships with the US.

NOTES

* Very helpful comments on this text were received from Lorraine Eden, David N. Fagan, Timothy Frye, Steven Globerman, Mark Kantor, Curtis J. Milhaupt, Stewart R. Miller, Pablo M. Pinto and Daniel Shapiro. They are gratefully acknowledged. Special thanks go to Lisa Sachs for helping finalize this chapter.
1. "Emerging markets," for the purpose of this chapter, are defined as all members of the Organisation for Economic Co-operation and Development (OECD), including, however, the Republic of Korea and Mexico.
2. UNCTAD (2008).
3. OECD (2008), p. 71. At the same time, the concentration ratio is high (as in the case of other countries), as the top five economies accounted for 86 percent of total outflows and 85 percent of total outward stock, especially in Hong Kong (China) and tax havens (ibid).
4. Cheng and Ma (2007), p. 15. (These figures do not include state-owned enterprises administered by regional governments.) According to the same source, the share of state-owned enterprises in the total number of outward investing entities had dropped from 43 percent in 2003 to 29 percent in 2005.
5. Sauvant (2009).
6. UNCTAD (2008).
7. Since M&As can be financed from sources other than FDI, it is not possible to determine the exact share of FDI accounted for by M&As.

8.   UNCTAD (2008).
9.   It is notable that Japanese automotive firms, when entering the US market, deliberately established themselves in areas in which there had not been an automotive industry previously.
10. "President Bush's Statement on Open Economies," May 10, 2007, http://www.whitehouse.gov/news/releases/2007/05/20070510-3.html.
11. Invest in America, http://www.ita.doc.gov/investamerica/index.asp.
12. Zakaria (2008).
13. Paulson (2008), p. 72.
14. Caves (1971), p. 6.
15. As of December 2008, the United States had signed a bilateral investment treaty with Albania, Argentina, Armenia, Azerbaijan, Bahrain, Bangladesh, Belarus, Bolivia, Bulgaria, Cameroon, Democratic Republic of the Congo, Republic of the Congo (Brazzaville), Croatia, Czech Republic, Ecuador, Egypt, El Salvador, Estonia, Georgia, Grenada, Haiti, Honduras, Jamaica, Jordan, Kazakhstan, Kyrgyzstan, Latvia, Lithuania, Moldova, Mongolia, Morocco, Mozambique, Nicaragua, Panama, Poland, Romania, Russia, Rwanda, Senegal, Slovakia, Sri Lanka, Trinidad & Tobago, Tunisia, Turkey, Ukraine, Uruguay and Uzbekistan (US State Department, http://www.state.gov/e/eeb/rls/fs/2008/22422.htm).
16. As of December 2008, the United States had signed a tax treaty with Australia, Austria, Bangladesh, Barbados, Belgium, Bulgaria, Canada, People's Republic of China, Commonwealth of Independent States (Armenia, Azerbaijan, Belarus, Georgia, Kyrgyzstan, Moldova, Tajikistan, Turkmenistan and Uzbekistan), Cyprus, Czech Republic, Denmark, Egypt, Estonia, Finland, France, Germany, Greece, Hungary, Iceland, India, Indonesia, Ireland, Israel, Italy, Jamaica, Japan, Kazakhstan, Republic of Korea, Latvia, Lithuania, Luxembourg, Mexico, Morocco, Netherlands, New Zealand, Norway, Pakistan, Philippines, Poland, Portugal, Romania, Russia, Slovak Republic, Slovenia, South Africa, Spain, Sri Lanka, Sweden, Switzerland, Thailand, Trinidad & Tobago, Tunisia, Turkey, Ukraine, United Kingdom and Venezuela. (US Department of the Treasury, http://www.irs.gov/pub/irs-pdf/p901.pdf and http://www.ustreas.gov/offices/tax-policy/treaties.shtml).
17. Virtually all of these protections, though, are also found in the US Constitution and US statutory enactments – and US domestic protections are often even stronger than those contained in US treaties. (The principal difference is that the protections of a US IIA can be enforced before a neutral international arbitral panel, while US constitutional and statutory rights are enforced before US courts and administrative agencies.)
18. Flows declined thereafter, when Japan entered a decade of economic difficulties. They only surpassed the 1990 peak in 2007.
19. There is however, one major difference, namely that China is seen, in the political and military areas, as a strategic competitor in the US.
20. The Organization for International Investment, grouping a number of foreign affiliates, is an example.
21. As we know from the experience of Japanese affiliates in the US, employment practices are a particularly sensitive matter.
22. For example, Curtis J. Milhaupt, the author of Chapter 7 in this volume, holds the Fuyo Professorship at Columbia Law School, established in 1980 by the Fuyo Group (one of the six major *keiretsu* corporate groups then in existence).
23. This section draws on Kwan and Sauvant (2008), pp. 39–46.
24. It should be noted that, while a substantial revaluation of the RMB would reduce the trade surplus, it would further encourage outward FDI from China as it would make US and other foreign assets cheaper in terms of that currency.
25. See Sachs (2008), pp. 15–22.

REFERENCES

Caves, R. (1971). "International corporations: the industrial economics of foreign investment," *Economica*, 38, pp. 1–27.

Cheng, Leonard and Zihui Ma (2007). "China's outward FDI: past and future," http://www.nber.org/books_in_progress/china07/cwt07/cheng.pdf, July.

Kwan, Clarence and Karl P. Sauvant (2008). "Chinese direct investment in the United States: the challenges ahead," *Location USA*, pp. 39–46.

OECD (2008). *OECD Investment Policy Reviews: China 2008* (Paris: OECD).

Paulson, Henry M., Jr (2008). "A strategic economic engagement: strengthening US–Chinese ties," *Foreign Affairs*, 87 (55) (September–October), pp. 59–77.

Sachs, Jeffrey D. (2008). "The rise of TNCs from emerging markets: the global context," in Karl P. Sauvant, Kristin Mendoza and Irmak Ince, eds, *The Rise of Transnational Corporations from Emerging Markets: Threat or Opportunity?* (Cheltenham, UK and Northampton, MA, USA: Edward Elgar), pp. 15–22.

Sauvant, Karl P. (2009). "Driving and countervailing forces: a rebalancing of national FDI policies," in Karl P. Sauvant, ed., *Yearbook on International Law and Investment Policy 2008/2009* (Oxford: Oxford University Press).

UNCTAD (2008). *World Investment Report 2008: Transnational Corporations and the Infrastructure Challenge* (Geneva: UNCTAD).

Zakaria, Fareed (2008). *The Post-American World* (New York: Norton).

2. Modes of entry by Chinese firms in the United States: economic and political issues

Steven Globerman and Daniel Shapiro*

INTRODUCTION

The purpose of this chapter is to discuss and assess both the strategic and political environments surrounding inward investment in the United States by investors based in China and, tangentially, other emerging markets. In particular we focus on the differences between foreign greenfield entry, and entry by acquisition, and we do so from two different perspectives. First, we consider whether there is any reason for Chinese investors to favor greenfield investments over other modes of expansion in the United States. At the same time we evaluate whether US authorities should be more or less concerned about greenfield investments made by Chinese investors compared to acquisitions of US companies by those investors.

Of course, these two perspectives are linked. In choosing an entry mode, firms must account for the possible political opposition that such entry may create. In essence, such political costs are part of the "liability of foreignness" discussed in Chapter 5 by Eden and Miller. These costs may not only alter the choice between greenfield entry and entry by acquisition, but may also alter the choice between full ownership (control) and partial ownership (control). Thus, we also consider the possibility of hybrid entry modes that do not involve full ownership or control.

In fact it is now clear that the vast majority of global foreign direct investment (FDI) flows now occurs via mergers and acquisitions (Globerman and Shapiro 2005; UNCTAD 2008). However, Chinese outward FDI has historically concentrated on greenfield and joint venture (JV) investment, although acquisitions of foreign-owned companies have increased in recent years. The Asia Pacific Foundation of Canada (2005, 2006) reports that the majority of Chinese outbound investment projects have been undertaken in the form of joint ventures (61 percent), followed by mergers and acquisitions (23 percent), with the remainder being greenfield investments. Nevertheless, acquisitions have grown more prominent in recent years. According to estimates by Hemerling et al. (2006), since 1986, Chinese companies have invested some $30 billion in non-Chinese companies, with nearly a third of these acquisitions having occurred in 2004 and 2005. Deng (2007) suggests that mergers and acquisitions now constitute the major form of Chinese FDI. Thus, the choice of entry mode remains a relevant consideration for both Chinese firms and the host country.

The existing literature on entry modes, surveyed and summarized below, is primarily focused on firms from developed market economies. In evaluating the choice of entry mode by Chinese firms, and the potential response by host countries, two factors must be borne in mind. The first is that Chinese multinational enterprises (MNEs), like those from other emerging markets are "latecomers" (Mathews 2002). Latecomer firms are not only late entrants to an industry, but they are often initially resource-poor so that part of their strategy is to acquire resources that will allow them to catch up. In this regard, latecomer firms have motivations that differ from traditional MNEs that attempt to leverage existing resources in foreign markets (Deng 2007). The second factor is the Chinese MNEs are often state-owned or state-supported enterprises (Deng 2007; He and Lyles 2008; Yeung and Liu 2008). State ownership may affect the motivation of firms, and their entry choices, but may also affect the response of host countries.

Thus, several attempted acquisitions of United States companies by MNEs headquartered in emerging markets, including China, were accompanied by strong political protests in the United States. For example, strong opposition to the takeover of Unocal by the Chinese National Offshore Oil Corporation (CNOOC) on the part of US politicians, along with the prospect of a prolonged approval process, led to CNOOC withdrawing its takeover bid (see Chapter 3 by David Fagan). While the rationale for the opposition was perhaps not clearly articulated, the opposition was symptomatic of the concerns regarding takeovers of domestically owned companies by MNEs headquartered in China and in other emerging markets populated by state-owned enterprises (SOEs) or state-supported companies. The strong opposition to the attempted Unocal takeover may have discouraged some inward FDI to the United States from emerging markets.[1]

Even in the midst of a domestic financial crisis, worries continue to be expressed about Chinese investment in the United States. A case in point is the media focus in the US on the China Investment Corporation which made major investments in several large US financial companies in 2008. Ironically, those investments proved to be extremely unprofitable, thereby giving rise to complaints in China about wasting valuable financial reserves in an effort to bail out Western companies.[2]

Although there has always been political opposition to inward FDI, particularly when it occurs via acquisitions of domestic firms, legal barriers to inward FDI have been substantially weakened in both developed and emerging markets in recent decades (UNCTAD 2008). This phenomenon reflects a broad consensus among policy-makers, supported by research, that the economic benefits of inward FDI to the host economy generally exceed any associated economic costs. The opposition to outward FDI from China and other emerging markets therefore likely reflects the view that the net benefits of such FDI differ substantially from the net benefits of earlier generations of outward FDI, which originated mainly in developed countries.[3] In addition, while acquisitions of domestic companies by Chinese MNEs can be reviewed by the US government, there is currently no procedure for reviewing greenfield investments.[4]

The chapter proceeds as follows. In sections 2.1 and 2.2 we take the perspective of the investing company. We survey and discuss conceptual and empirical issues associated with foreign entry mode choice in general, and by Chinese firms in particular. Specifically, we focus on entry via foreign acquisitions of domestic companies versus greenfield investments, as well as the evidence bearing upon potential differences between the two modes. We also discuss the advantages and disadvantages of partial ownership and control. In sections 2.3 and 2.4, the perspective taken is that of the host country. Section 2.3 considers general factors influencing the net social benefits of inward FDI, with a focus on the issue of spillover efficiency benefits. We also survey the relevant empirical evidence,

particularly as it relates to the anticipated benefits by mode of entry. In section 2.4 we
address host country issues that might be specific to China, most of which arise from
the fact that many Chinese MNEs are state-owned enterprises (SOEs). Section 2.4 also
evaluates the practical relevance of host country concerns raised about FDI undertaken
by SOEs in light of evidence on the motives and performance of SOEs. The final section
contains a summary and conclusion.

2.1   MODE OF ENTRY: THE INVESTOR'S PERSPECTIVE

2.1.1   Conceptual Issues

Firms can enter foreign markets using alternative strategies. Figure 2.1 summarizes these
strategies along two broad dimensions. One is whether the foreign investment involves the
creation of a new organization (greenfield) or whether it takes place through the takeover (in
part or whole) of an existing organization (acquisition). The second dimension encompasses
the extent of the foreign investor's ownership ranging from a controlling interest to a non-
controlling interest. Figure 2.1 therefore follows the recent academic literature (Brouthers
and Hennart 2007; Slangen and Hennart 2007; Meyer et al. 2009) in suggesting that entry
mode decisions require consideration of both entry method and degree of control.

	Greenfield	Acquisition
Controlling ownership	*Fully controlled new operating entity* Examples: Haier production facilities in South Carolina; Galanz R&D centre in Seattle	*Take over existing operating entity* Examples: Lenovo acquisition of IBM PC Division; TCL acquisition of Schneider Electronics; China National Petroleum (CNPC) acquisition of PetroKazahkstan
Non-controlling ownership	*Joint venture with domestically owned company* Example: Huawei JVs in Russia and India	*Partial acquisition/strategic alliance* Examples: CNPC 40% acquisition in Sudan; Chinalco (original) acquisition of 9% stake in Rio Tinto

Source: Adapted from Brouthers and Hennart (2007).

Figure 2.1   Mode of entry options

While the distinction between greenfield and acquisition investments is relatively straightforward as both a conceptual and empirical matter, controlling ownership is not. Specifically, depending upon the circumstances, any given percentage ownership can be associated with effective managerial control or, at best, with a vocal minority position. For the purposes of this chapter, controlling ownership should be thought of as an ownership stake sufficient to give the foreign investor managerial control of the business in question. Non-controlling ownership therefore encompasses situations ranging from the foreign investor being an active, albeit subordinate, participant in management to being a completely passive minority shareholder.

Specific modes of international entry can be associated with the cells identified in Figure 2.1. Traditionally, greenfield investments are thought of as new operating entities that are fully owned, or at least controlled, by the foreign investor, while acquisitions involve full or controlling ownership takeovers of existing business entities. These two broad strategic options are represented in the top row of Figure 2.1. Non-controlling ownership, as a practical matter, encompasses cases in which the foreign investor typically has no more than a 50 percent ownership share. It thus includes greenfield entry via joint ventures.[5] Non-controlling ownership also includes cross-order "acquisition" cases where the foreign investor is simply a minority and passive investor in a domestically owned and controlled business, or when the investor makes a strategic minority investment, perhaps with a view toward establishing a controlling position in future. It also includes cases of strategic alliances where the minority partner agrees to certain activities. These options are identified in the second row of Figure 1.[6]

We first consider the choice between greenfield entry versus entry by acquisition. Perhaps the most obvious advantage of an acquisition is that it allows relatively quick entry into a foreign market. The relative importance of speed of entry will be greater when profit opportunities that are available to early entrants are not available to later entrants because of entry barriers associated with moving first. Acquisitions are also preferred in relatively slow-growing markets. The rationale here is that greenfield entry increases production capacity in the short run, thereby putting downward pressure on prices, all other things remaining constant. Such downward pressure is likely to be more pronounced when market demand is growing slowly. Hence, it is suggested that acquisitions are preferable to greenfield investments in markets that are either growing relatively slowly and/or where there are strong first-mover advantages, other things remaining constant.

As noted above, the choice of entry mode will depend to some degree on the motivation for the investment. The choice therefore depends on a comparison of the costs associated with developing or obtaining some form of knowledge, technology or brand. Specifically, acquisitions may be the preferred mode of entry when the purpose of the FDI is not to exploit firm-specific proprietary advantages (such as technologies or brands), but rather to acquire them. One major motive for investing abroad is to acquire assets that are complementary to those already possessed by the foreign investor in order to enhance the efficiency and competitiveness of the investor. In principle, complementary assets can be acquired piecemeal or embodied in an existing organization. Examples of complementary assets include marketing and distribution networks in the host country, and technological and managerial knowledge resident in the host country. In practice, complementary assets of specific value to the foreign investor are consolidated under the ownership of one or more host country companies, such that acquiring the relevant assets piecemeal for purposes of establishing a greenfield business is not a viable option.

Obviously, if acquisitions are a more advantageous way to enter foreign markets under specific circumstances, one might expect acquirers to pay a financial premium for such acquisitions. That is, the present value cost of an acquisition will exceed the present value cost of a greenfield investment that creates the same production capacity. For example, if acquisitions are particularly preferable in slower-growing markets, then investors should expect to pay more for acquisitions than greenfield investments in those markets, other things remaining constant. If capital markets are relatively efficient, the takeover premiums established in capital markets should offset the specific advantages to the acquisition mode of entry, at least for the "average" investor; however, specific investors might be more willing and able than others to pay a financial premium in order to avail themselves of the advantages offered by acquisitions. One possibility in this regard is that some investors may have relatively low costs of capital that enable them to outbid other investors for acquisition targets. In this regard, SOEs generally, and Chinese SOEs specifically, have been criticized by managers of US and European-based companies for enjoying an "unfair" financing advantage which presumably enables them to outbid competitors for advantageous acquisitions. This criticism will be discussed in more detail in a later section.

The choice of the acquisition route may also depend on the experience of the entrant in evaluating acquisition opportunities, and integrating merged entities into its global operations. In this regard, foreign entrants without significant acquisition experience in a particular country may well face information asymmetries such that they do not have adequate information regarding the economic value of their targets, or the managerial difficulties that specific acquisitions will pose. As a result, entrants may find the acquisition mode relatively expensive with a high probability of failure. In particular cultural distance between the home and host countries may create difficulties for the foreign acquirer. On the other hand, a foreign investor who is relatively familiar with the host country's economic and institutional environment can more readily justify paying an acquisition premium, all other things remaining constant, since the acquisition target is likely to be more easily integrated into the acquiring company's organization.

To this point, the evaluation of greenfield investments versus acquisitions has not explicitly considered the advantages and disadvantages of controlling ownership versus non-controlling ownership. In fact, as we discuss below, the relevant trade-offs along this strategic dimension may be particularly acute for Chinese companies investing abroad.

The benefits of control revolve around the ability to protect valuable strategic assets from appropriation by partners. The cost of control is that it increases the firm's exposure to a variety of risks (in this case entry risks). Some obvious entry risks are related to finance, culture and politics. If ownership can be shared, financial risk is reduced. If cultural differences are profound, shared ownership reduces entry risk. If political opposition increases entry risk, then shared ownership may diffuse that risk.

However, choices regarding control may also depend on the firm's motivation. One motive for investing abroad is to exploit an investing firm's competitive advantages in the host market. While specific advantages can, in theory, be exploited through channels other than FDI, for example by licensing host country partners to produce and sell the foreign investor's proprietary products in the host country, it is often more profitable to exploit those advantages within the company's own value chain rather than through arm's-length sales of the firm's underlying capabilities. An example is the capability to produce specific products more efficiently because of organizational advantages or production knowledge. While knowledge about "lean production techniques," for example, can in principle be sold, in practice it is extremely difficult to sell knowledge or other intangible assets on an arm's-length basis. In particular, establishing a competitive value for knowledge will often require the divulgence of information that undermines the ability of the seller to maintain proprietary control of the information. As a consequence, exploiting intangible assets in foreign markets is typically best accomplished by internalizing the relevant assets within a wholly owned affiliate.

These various considerations suggest that decisions regarding entry mode are neither simple nor formulaic. The correct decision will always be firm-specific and will rely on a variety of factors, as outlined above. Nevertheless, it is relatively clear that acquisition is the favored mode when speed of entry matters, when the industry is relatively mature, and when the motive for entry is to acquire (rather than exploit) complementary or strategic assets. Full control modes are favored when the entrant is capable of bearing financial, cultural and political risks, and when the firm must protect or acquire critical strategic assets.

2.1.2 Empirical Evidence

Given the complexity of the entry mode decision, it is perhaps not surprising that the empirical evidence on the matter is somewhat ambiguous. In their recent survey of the empirical literature, Slangen and Hennart (2007) note that only six of the 22 variables that they identified across the surveyed studies have fully consistent and significant effects. However, among these are the findings that greenfield entry is indeed preferred when the industry is fast-growing and when the parent firm is highly R&D intensive (implying that it is seeking to exploit its firm-specific advantage). Similarly, other evidence suggests that firms seeking to acquire or protect firm-specific strategic assets will prefer high control modes of entry, although the impact of other factors such as cultural distance appears less clear (Brouthers and Hennart 2007).

2.2 MODE OF ENTRY: PERSPECTIVE OF THE CHINESE INVESTOR

In this section we consider the entry mode choice in the more specific context of a Chinese investor. We begin by noting that Chinese firms in fact populate all of the cells in Figure 2.1, where we provide examples of each. Thus Chinese firms do, in fact, face and make entry mode choices along the dimensions we have described.

As suggested above, the choice of international entry mode by Chinese firms is arguably influenced by the latecomer status of China as a source of FDI. In particular, Chinese managers have relatively limited knowledge of how to manage operating businesses in developed countries, including the United States. The knowledge deficiencies are heightened by differences in national cultures such that differences between the United States and China in their political and social institutions exacerbate the difficulties that Chinese managers face in competing against domestically owned firms in the United States. These various differences contribute to the liabilities that Chinese companies face when operating in the US market.

In this context, acquisitions have been seen as a more favorable international business mode than greenfield investments from the perspective of Chinese MNEs.[7] This is because acquisitions result in integrated host country management teams being made available to Chinese investors. Conversely, in the case of greenfield investments, new management teams must be assembled and integrated into a cohesive organizational culture, *de novo*. Indeed, US companies can be targeted by Chinese investors partly on the basis of unique managerial skills of the target companies that are complementary to the firm-specific advantages of the Chinese investor. In short, acquisitions potentially facilitate a remediation of the knowledge gaps facing Chinese investors expanding into the United States.

In fact, however, acquisitions of US companies will not necessarily bridge the cross-cultural gaps between Chinese managers and US employees or otherwise remediate the knowledge gap. For example, He and Lyles (2008) report problems associated with a lack of trust between Lenovo employees and IBM employees, a problem that ran in both directions. More generally, Boston Consulting Group (Hemerling et al. 2006, pp. 6–7) found that many outright acquisitions had actually destroyed value in the acquired entities and that many emerging-market MNEs lacked managerial expertise in executing large-scale acquisitions.

In addition, the Chinese parent will still need to manage the acquired US affiliate in important ways if the acquisition involves taking a controlling interest, unless the Chinese investor wants to organize its foreign investments into a pure holding company. However, the creation of international holding companies is typically not a motive for foreign direct investment on the part of Chinese companies. More typically, Chinese foreign investment is directed at acquiring assets and resources, including technology and managerial know-how (Deng 2007). In this regard, Chinese companies may at this time have limited abilities to absorb technology and managerial know-how effectively through the acquisition mode. Simply put, it may be too difficult in many cases for Chinese investors to integrate new technology and management practices into their global organizations while at the same time trying to "parent" newly acquired US companies. Indeed, the shortcomings associated with cultural difference referenced earlier may lead Chinese investors to make poor acquisition decisions in the first place. In particular, they may choose acquisition targets that are difficult to integrate or that are politically sensitive with relatively high probabilities of either not working out or being rejected by the host governments. The latter risk is becoming increasingly relevant as Western governments place an increasing emphasis on national security as a criterion for evaluating inward foreign direct investments.

While non-controlling ownership options involve the obvious sacrifice of administrative control, they also represent a relatively low-risk mode for Chinese companies to absorb intangible assets such as technology and know-how, as well as to access physical assets and intellectual property. Certainly, differences in corporate culture can interfere with the success of international business options such as contractual joint ventures. Nevertheless, it is ordinarily less of a challenge to work in partnership with a knowledgeable domestically owned partner than to subsume that partner entirely into the Chinese investor's multinational enterprise.

A recent survey of Chinese executives undertaken by McKinsey reports that the majority of respondents plan to make acquisitions the heart of their long-term global strategies (Deitz et al. 2008).[8] However, McKinsey also highlights the propensity of Chinese companies to misjudge the political, labor and environmental risks presented by foreign business environments, and argues that business partners can be valuable resources for Chinese companies in terms of weighing and addressing such risks.

This argument parallels observations by Dong and Glaister (2007) that international strategic alliances offer Chinese firms opportunities to share costs and risks and to learn new skills and technologies. While differences in national and corporate cultures create difficulties for Chinese and foreign partner relationships in strategic alliances, those differences are often mitigated by the experience that foreign alliance partners have accumulated doing business in China. They are also mitigated by Chinese companies taking minority equity positions in the alliances.

Finally, we suggest that financial risk is not as relevant to Chinese investors. It is obviously true that a larger ownership share will oblige the foreign investor to put more financial capital at risk. While financial risk is certainly not irrelevant to Chinese investors, access to low-cost financial capital arguably reduces the importance of such risk as a critical constraint on the foreign investment strategies of Chinese companies, at least in comparison to foreign investors headquartered elsewhere.[9]

In summary, difference between Chinese and US political and ideological systems, as well as culture-based differences in business practices, constitute major "liabilities of foreignness" for Chinese managers operating in the United States (He and Lyles 2008). In addition, Chinese managers often lack the skills to manage in more sophisticated markets overseas. These observations suggest that modes of global entry that facilitate Chinese companies learning from local partners or acquired firms will be strategically important for the foreseeable future. In this regard, absorption of local expertise will arguably be more effectively accomplished through joint ventures or acquisitions than through pure greenfield investments. Furthermore, joint venture or minority acquisitions in which Chinese investors are not controlling owners impose less economic and political risk on Chinese companies. Hence, a presumptive case can be made that a preference for controlling ownership and administrative control on the part of Chinese companies investing in the US may be problematic and that more attention should be given to how transfers of technology, managerial expertise and other intangible resources can be accomplished through modes of international diversification based on minority equity positions or joint venture partnerships.

2.3 MODE OF ENTRY: THE HOST COUNTRY PERSPECTIVE

From the host country perspective, the issue is whether mode of entry affects the net (social) benefits of FDI. A substantial literature exists comparing and contrasting the economic effects on the host country of the two broad modes of FDI: greenfield and acquisition. A particular focus of the literature is the spillover productivity benefits for the host economy, since such spillovers are the primary gain to the host country associated with inward FDI (Blomstrom et al. 2000). Hence, any distinction between the two forms of FDI from the perspective of the host country needs to focus particularly on potential differences in host country spillover benefits. We note that the literature does not focus on control issues, but rather on the simple distinction between greenfield entry and acquisitions. This simple distinction undoubtedly flows from the fact that in general, in developed economies most FDI takes the form of acquisitions.

2.3.1   Spillover Efficiency Gains

Spillover efficiency benefits from inward FDI result from productivity improvements enjoyed by host country firms that are associated with the activities of foreign affiliates in the same country. The various sources of spillover efficiency benefits are potentially operative in the case of both acquisitions and greenfield investments by foreigners. For example, innovations introduced to the host economy by foreign affiliates can be imitated by domestically owned firms whether the innovations are introduced through the operations of a greenfield facility or an already existing acquired facility. Likewise, learning-by-doing on the part of host country workers and managers can take place in already existing businesses acquired by foreign investors, as well as in new facilities.

Entry by foreign firms increases competition, and can therefore create incentives for local firms to become more efficient. It is typically argued that acquisitions of existing firms result in less competition compared to greenfield investments, because acquisitions reduce the number of competitors. However, this view is too simplistic because foreign acquirers may be willing and able to make investments in the acquired companies that make the latter more competitive than they were under domestic ownership.[10] In addition, acquisitions may facilitate more effective entry (more rapid and at greater scale) so that there is in fact more competition.

Host country spillover benefits from inward FDI might also be indirectly affected by the mode of entry. For example, if foreign companies undertaking greenfield investments are, on average, more efficient than those acquiring local firms, host country spillover benefits might be greater when entry is greenfield. This is because the higher relative efficiency of firms undertaking greenfield investments permits a higher level of transfer of technical and managerial expertise to domestic firms.

It is important to recognize that any spillover benefits to domestic firms will depend on what has been termed absorptive capacity. The absorptive capacity of local firms is essentially their ability to adopt and exploit information and technology spillovers made available through the activities of foreign firms. Because absorptive capacity itself depends upon the nature of accumulated inward FDI, the linkage between spillover benefits and the mode of FDI is likely to be complex. Thus, local firms might be better able to absorb knowledge transferred from foreign firms that employ relatively less complex technologies. In the case of Chinese FDI in the US, the issue of absorption will likely depend more on cultural differences at the organizational level than on the capabilities of US companies to adopt and exploit technology spillovers.

2.3.2   Other Costs and Benefits of Inward FDI

While spillover productivity gains to domestically owned producers are the main conceptual benefit of inward FDI, there are other relevant potential consequences for the host economy, including capital investment and employment levels. While not necessarily directly related to spillover efficiency benefits, domestic policy-makers would undoubt-edly prefer higher levels of employment to lower levels of employment in the domestic economy. Higher levels of non-inflationary employment will, in turn, be related to the production capacity of the domestic economy. Increases in an economy's capacity to produce output allow for increases in the demand for labor without generating con-comitant increases in inflationary pressures. In the long run, an economy's capacity to utilize labor more efficiently will be tied to capital investments. In this regard, greenfield investments are sometimes seen as adding new plant and equipment capacity to the host economy, whereas foreign acquisitions do not. Again, this perspective is simplistic. If acquired domestic firms grow more quickly than they would have done under continued domestic ownership, the overall capital stock of the host economy is also likely to grow faster than it would have in the absence of the foreign acquisitions. This will certainly be true in cases in which domestically owned firms are in danger of failing.

Benefits from inward FDI can also be experienced by domestic owners of assets, as well as by host country consumers. If foreign owners can operate acquired assets more efficiently, they can also afford to bid higher prices for those assets than would be the case for local investors. Competition among foreign investors should therefore result in some or all of the anticipated improvements in efficiency being captured by host country owners in the form of an acquisition price premium. In principle, the premium can be paid for the acquisition of an already existing enterprise or for individual assets such as land or skilled management that are assembled into a greenfield operation. In practice, however, the need to pay a control premium for an already existing company likely means that domestic shareholders will be primary beneficiaries of any efficiency advantages that foreign investors enjoy relative to domestic investors in operating host country assets.

Finally, it is likely that at least some portion of any productivity gains associated with ownership changes will be passed on to domestic consumers in the form of lower prices. This outcome is most likely when there is strong competition in the domestic market that forces efficiency gains to be passed on. As discussed above, it is not necessarily true that greenfield investments lead to more effective competition than do acquisitions, and it is therefore likely that both modes of inward FDI will contribute to host country benefits in the form of lower prices for consumers.

2.3.3 Acquisitions versus Greenfield Investment: The Empirical Evidence

In the preceding sections, a number of conceptual arguments in favor of greater eco-nomic benefits from greenfield investments compared to acquisitions were considered. The broad conclusion to be drawn is that there are no overwhelming theoretical reasons to expect that the host country benefits of greenfield investments exceed those of acqui-sitions. In short, the issue is an empirical one. Unfortunately, the available evidence is fragmented and limited. In particular, there is no evidence of which we are aware that identifies host country spillover efficiency benefits from greenfield FDI separately from those associated with acquisitions of host country firms.

Several studies focus on the characteristics of foreign investors who undertake greenfield investments versus those who undertake acquisitions. For example, Nocke and Yeaple (2008) concluded, on the basis of a theoretical model, that firms engaging in greenfield investments will be systematically more efficient than those engaging in cross-border acquisitions; they argued that this inference is consistent with available evidence. In a similar vein, Raff et al. (2005) proposed that, controlling for industry and country-specific characteristics, the most productive firms, that is, those owning the most assets, will enter through greenfield investments, while less productive ones will choose mergers and acquisitions. They confirm this prediction in an econometric analysis of firm-level data.

Notwithstanding any differences in the underlying efficiencies of foreign investors entering through the greenfield versus the acquisition mode, there is no consistent evidence that the host country effects of the two modes of FDI differ. As noted earlier, greenfield investment involves the creation of new production capacity which, other things remaining constant, should increase domestic competition, at least in the short run. Indeed, UNCTAD (2000) found that the most significant distinction between the two modes is that acquisition FDI is associated with a persistent "concentration effect" relative to greenfield FDI. Hence, one would expect greenfield FDI to make greater contributions to increased competition in host country markets than FDI through acquisitions. Claeys and Hainz (2006) found supportive evidence for this inference in a sample of banks from ten transition economies of Eastern Europe for the period 1995–2003. On the other hand, Chung (2001) found that mode of entry for FDI into the United States over the period 1987–91 had no significant impact on industry price–cost margins – that is, there is no identifiable difference in the competitive impacts of FDI depending upon whether the mode of entry is greenfield versus acquisition.

With respect to domestic wages, Heyman et al. (2004) found that foreign-owned firms entering Sweden through greenfield investments had to pay higher wages to attract new workers. In contrast, foreign acquirers tended to target higher-wage firms but increased wages at a slower rate than non-acquired firms after the change in ownership.[11] Conversely, Blonigen and Slaughter (2001) found that Japanese greenfield investments in the United States in the 1980s were associated with lower, not higher, relative demand for skilled labor.

Other evidence on the effects of greenfield FDI versus foreign acquisitions is also ambivalent. For example, while Mata and Portugal (2000) found that greenfield entrants were more likely to be shut down than acquisition entrants, McCloughan and Stone (1998) found that greenfield entrants faced a lower risk of failure than acquisition entrants. In terms of innovation, Bertrand et al. (2007) found that, controlling for parent, affiliate, industry and country characteristics, acquired affiliates of Swedish MNEs were, on average, more likely to undertake research and development (R&D) and have a higher level of R&D intensity than affiliates created by greenfield investments. This result persisted over time and with the age of affiliates, as well as for different firm types and industries. They interpreted their findings as suggesting that policies that discourage cross-border acquisitions and favor greenfield investments may be counterproductive for a host country aiming at increasing R&D investments.

As noted above, this brief literature review highlights the absence of consistent empirical evidence on the host country effects of greenfield investments versus acquisitions. Moreover, there is virtually no evidence bearing upon this issue for FDI undertaken by Chinese or other emerging-market MNEs. This observation is important, since political opposition to Chinese acquisitions of US companies might be mitigated by evidence that other US companies realized spillover productivity benefits from such acquisitions.

Mathieu (2006) evaluated several Chinese acquisitions of large French companies. In one acquisition, Marionnaud was taken over by A.S. Watson Group, part of the Hutchison Whampoa Corporation. The French company was struggling to stay in business prior to the acquisition. After the acquisition, its performance improved and it expanded its operations substantially. In another case, Blue Star acquired Adisseo, a world-scale producer of animal feed supplements. As part of the deal, Blue Star intends to set up an R&D center in France specializing in biotechnology for the production of amino acids used in animal feed. Apparently, the French experience with Chinese acquisitions has been sufficiently favorable that the Invest in France Agency is increasing the number of employees at its office in China to raise awareness of opportunities in the French market. Unfortunately, there is little other published evidence on possible spillover efficiency benefits to host countries from Chinese FDI.

In summary, based on the currently available evidence, we cannot conclude that the host country benefits of greenfield FDI investments systematically differ from those of foreign acquisitions over the longer run. An implication is that policy-makers should not necessarily promote policies that discourage acquisitions in favor of greenfield investments. This suggestion is supported by the Organisation for Economic Co-operation and Development (OECD) in its survey of the impacts of foreign takeovers on host countries. Specifically, the OECD concluded that "it makes little economic sense" for policy-makers to distinguish greenfield investment from cross-border acquisitions (OECD 2007, p. 86). While the OECD conclusion would seem to suggest that potential entrants into national markets need not worry about mode of entry as a source of political backlash, host governments do tend to worry more about acquisitions than greenfield investments. A separate and, perhaps, more complex issue is whether acquisitions by Chinese companies, as well as companies based in other emerging markets, raise unique host country concerns, thereby perhaps meriting "special treatment" by host countries. We turn now to address this issue.

2.4 CONCERNS ABOUT ACQUISITIONS BY COMPANIES BASED IN CHINA

As noted in the preceding section, most of the available evidence on the host country effects of inward FDI involves acquisitions made by MNEs headquartered in developed countries. There is also some evidence focusing on MNEs from emerging markets acquiring companies based in other emerging markets; however, there is virtually no evidence documenting the experience of MNEs from emerging markets acquiring firms in developed countries. Yet, this latter phenomenon is at the heart of the policy conflict surrounding the FDI process in the United States and Europe at the present time.

In the absence of reliable evidence bearing upon the economic impacts of foreign acquisitions by MNEs based in emerging markets (including China), a policy evaluation of the phenomenon must draw largely upon conceptual analysis. The latter should identify why the economic impacts on the host economy from foreign acquisitions might be different in the case of acquirers from China, as well as the appropriate policy response to the differences identified. The identity of the foreign acquirer might be related to the anticipated economic effects because the motives of acquirers may differ, as well as the market and non-market disciplines that different acquirers face. In this section we focus on the unique issues create by state ownership of Chinese (and other) firms.

2.4.1 State Ownership: Potential Effects

It is typically assumed that when making an acquisition the acquiring firm is driven to maximize the wealth of its owners. Therefore, firms will attempt to acquire other firms only if the acquiring firm's management believes that the acquisition will increase the long-run profitability of the firm. Although principal–agent problems in large, widely held public companies can encourage and allow management to pursue acquisitions that are not necessarily consistent with long-run profit maximization, competitive capital markets provide a potentially strong disciplinary force on managers who systematically fail to make efficient decisions. In theory, managers who sacrifice the interests of shareholders in favor of other goals face the prospect of being replaced through takeovers of their companies.

All of this may change with the ownership of the acquiring firm. In contrast to the model above, managers of SOEs often face no acquisition threat from capital markets. The takeover threat is not relevant for SOEs because the state is often the controlling shareholder and sometimes the only shareholder. In China, state ownership is present in most large MNEs, although it may not involve majority ownership. Ownership can be held by national or local government. As a consequence, financial losses can be subsidized from other sources of government finance. The same issues may also arise in the case of family-owned businesses where there is no necessary compulsion for owner-managers to pursue efficiency goals because they are immune from takeover threats. In addition, growth may be a more prominent goal in order to ensure the employment of family members.

There are other distinct principal–agent problems that distinguish SOEs. An SOE cannot have its board of directors changed via a proxy contest. The absence of proxy contests, like the absence of the threat of takeover, reduces the incentives of board members and managers to maximize the value of the company. In addition, most SOEs cannot go bankrupt. The irrelevance of bankruptcy effectively reduces pressures to contain costs and increase efficiency. Furthermore, an SOE generally has a higher body or bodies that oversee it. This can be one or more ministries, a dedicated government entity, parliament or, frequently, a combination of overseers. The complex agency chain through and across various levels of government may present governance difficulties that are unique to SOEs (see the World Bank 2006). And finally, as noted by Goergen (2007), when majority state ownership is present conflicts emerge, not between owners and managers, but between minority and majority shareholders.

Thus, when state ownership is present, and when capital markets are not very competitive, there is less reason to believe that managers (or majority owners) will be disciplined, even in the long run, for decisions that result in an inefficient allocation of the organization's resources. To the extent that goals unrelated to wealth maximization or efficiency dominate in Chinese MNEs, the latter may choose to make unprofitable foreign acquisitions and may also operate acquired foreign companies inefficiently. Although the latter outcome raises no concerns for the host country, since the subsidies required to perpetuate the inefficient performance of Chinese affiliates in the domestic US economy are presumably provided by China and not by US residents, the inefficient Chinese-owned affiliates are also less likely to be a source of spillover benefits to the host economy. For example, inefficient acquisitions are less likely to promote increased competition in domestic industries than are acquisitions that result in the merged firm becoming more efficient than the incumbent domestically owned firm.

Closely related to the issue of state ownership is that of national security, about which concerns have been raised in a number of proposed foreign takeovers of companies operating in the United States. While national security can be an issue in any foreign acquisition, the problem may be more acute in the case of acquisitions by Chinese and other emerging market companies, particularly if they are state-owned. One notable example was the proposed acquisition by Dubai Ports of a UK company with an affiliate operating a number of major US shipping ports. While the Middle Eastern background of the would-be acquirer certainly figured prominently in the security argument, it is highly likely that a similar "national security" concern would have been expressed by US politicians had a Chinese company proposed the same acquisition. More recently, a proposed buyout of network equipment maker 3Com by Bain Capital Partners was scuttled after Bain was notified by the Committee on Foreign Investment in the United States (CFIUS) that it intended to block the deal which would have given China's Huawei Technologies Co. a minority stake in 3Com. The specific concern was that Huawei, which is not state-owned, would gain access to the telecommunications equipment maker's technology which is used by the US Defense Department, among others.

At issue is the concern that Chinese companies, particularly SOEs, may have no political loyalty to the host country. The implication is that domestically owned companies presumably do. Thus, Chinese SOEs may be less willing than domestically owned companies to sacrifice their organizational objectives for the sake of the national interests of the host country, including national security. In the extreme case, SOE affiliates might even be seen as agents of an unfriendly government whose objective is to damage the economic infrastructure of the United States and other Western countries.

The potential relevance of national security concerns arising from Chinese FDI certainly cannot be dismissed. However the issue is whether special measures must be taken to address these concerns. The rationale for doing so is based on the presumption that the importance of political objectives is more important for Chinese MNEs than it is for MNEs based in other countries. On this question, there is simply no evidence that would permit a definitive judgment.

Woo and Zhang (2006, p. 4) assert that, since 1980, the emphasis on political objectives in determining Chinese outward foreign direct invest (OFDI) policy has gradually given way to the primacy of commercial interests, a view shared by He and Lyles (2008). However, this assertion is certainly debatable (Kang and Liu 2007; Deng 2007). At the same time, the approval process for OFDI has been greatly simplified, with decision-making authority delegated first from the central government to local governments, and more recently to the enterprise itself. The devolution of decision-making authority to MNE managers is consistent with an increasing emphasis on commercial objectives.

A related issue raised about Chinese SOEs is their lack of transparency of structure and organizational form. A specific concern is that many Chinese SOEs do not maximize profits and do not comply with codes of corporate governance and transparency to which OECD companies largely adhere. Firms acquired by Chinese companies may therefore experience financial difficulties under a politically appointed and motivated management pursuing non-profit motives. To the extent that financial losses and other adverse consequences of inefficient management are borne solely by the Chinese parent, no broader externality costs are imposed upon the host economy. However, it remains possible that a lack of financial transparency may impose costs on host country citizens if it results in unanticipated financial performance. Of course, as recent events indicate, the lack of financial transparency is not confined to Chinese SOEs.

Clearly, the potential for such third-party costs also exists in the case of domestically owned companies. The current situation in the US financial sector associated with defaults on what appears to be, in retrospect, an excessively lax and, in some cases even fraudulent extension of subprime mortgages and consumer loans, highlights the potential for systemic economic costs to arise from the activities of domestically owned firms operating in even relatively highly regulated industries. The Enron fiasco further underscores the difficulties in preventing corporate financial misbehavior from having widespread economic implications, even when a corporation is subject to public accounting rules and regulations associated with a New York Stock Exchange listing. Thus, it is by no means clear that the potential consequences of inappropriate governance practices and limited corporate transparency are limited to SOEs from developing countries. Nevertheless, transparency is an important issue (see Box 2.1).

In addition to concerns that SOEs do not pursue efficiency goals, there are concerns that SOEs pursue public policy goals that may sacrifice efficient performance as conventionally measured. For example, SOEs in China are seen as maintaining employment in order to reduce social tensions that might arise through massive lay-offs of workers. While some have argued that making SOEs employers of last resort has social benefits that outweigh the associated inefficiencies, others argue that sustaining the existence of large SOEs unduly impedes the movement of resources from contracting and inefficient sectors of the Chinese economy to the expanding and efficient sectors. It is unlikely that the Chinese government would make employment preservation a goal of SOE affiliates in the US and other developed countries – that is, there is no reason to believe that affiliates of Chinese SOEs operating in the US would employ US workers whose wages exceeded their contributions to profit. A more plausible issue is that Chinese SOEs are targeted at acquiring critical natural resources in the host country in order to ensure long-run security of supply for the Chinese economy. The concern is that in the event of an unexpected short-run or long-run disruption of supply for one or more of those natural resources, Chinese owners would refuse to supply local buyers, even if the latter are willing to pay more than competing Chinese buyers.

These concerns emerge from the dependence of China on the global supply of raw materials and energy, particularly oil and various minerals such as copper, bauxite and uranium. Interestingly, however, Hong and Sun (2004) conclude that while access to natural resources is an important motive for outward FDI from China, in the late 1990s increasingly more Chinese firms used FDI to acquire advanced foreign technologies, as well as managerial skills. Furthermore, since the mid-1990s, more and more Chinese firms have listed on overseas stock markets (Hong Kong, New York) to raise equity capital. It therefore appears to be the case that as Chinese outward FDI has evolved, it has been characterized by an increasingly diverse set of motivations.

This conclusion is also evident from survey evidence. For example, in his survey of

---

BOX 2.1 ENHANCING TRANSPARENCY

There are several approaches that can be taken to enhance transparency. One is to require firms engaged in acquisitions of US companies to follow internationally agreed-upon standards of governance and accountability as set out by organizations such as the World Bank or the OECD. In this case, policy coordination among developed countries would be necessary to avoid the diversion of investment funds to countries that have not implemented the policy.

A second approach is to impose financial reporting and corporate governance measures mandated by domestic regulators such as the New York Stock Exchange, even in the case of foreign acquisitions by non-listed entities. This approach would increase the costs of acquiring US companies and would presumably have to be applied to all foreign acquirers and not just China-based acquirers. Such a measure would likely reduce any net benefits attached to foreign acquisitions, and could also deter future investment.

Given that the risks to the US economy arising from corporate misbehavior are not uniquely associated with Chinese affiliates operating in the US it does not seem necessary to apply country-specific measures. In this regard, the situation facing the US also confronts other countries. Therefore it is likely that significant incentives exist for broad agreement on minimum standards of corporate governance. Although major host countries may well disagree on specific details, there seems to be room for agreement on some "common denominator" standard of governance, such as the OECD's Principles of Corporate Governance.

Similar transparency concerns surround the activities of sovereign wealth funds (SWFs). Proposed solutions include voluntary codes of conduct (Davis 2007), inclusion of corporate governance in global trade negotiations, and reliance on institutions such as the IMF and the World Bank to examine issues related to the activities of SWFs, including the transparency of their operations.[a]

On balance, transparency issues are likely best handled as part of a global policy agenda. It is neither theoretically optimal, nor practical, for the US to impose its own specific governance standards as a condition of allowing inward investment from China or other emerging economies.

---

[a] Abu Dhabi and Singapore have recently agreed to basic principles that call for, among other things, strict disclosure and governance standards for sovereign wealth funds. The agreed-upon guidelines are aimed at complementing efforts under way at the International Monetary Fund and the OECD to write voluntary codes of "best practices" for sovereign wealth funds. See Barkley (2008).

Chinese companies Wu (2005) reports three primary motivations for Chinese FDI, including market-seeking (56 percent), obtaining technology and brands (16 percent), and securing resources (20 percent). Although it is difficult to assess the validity of survey results, it would appear that concerns expressed about outward FDI from China leading to dominant ownership of critical natural resources on the part of Chinese SOEs seem unrealistic based upon the apparent relative unimportance of the "securing resources" motive (He and Lyles 2008). Furthermore, given the relatively dispersed sources of supply for natural resources, outward FDI from China to this sector would have to be massive indeed to create any real threat of control over supply in the hands of Chinese companies.

2.4.2   State Ownership: Empirical Evidence on Behavior and Performance

Available evidence leaves little doubt that the performance of SOEs in developed countries is generally inferior to that of comparable private sector competitors (Estrin et al. 2007). However, there is relatively little evidence on SOEs from emerging markets, including China. Such Chinese evidence as exists is inconclusive. For example, Estrin et al. (2007) report mixed evidence regarding the performance of SOEs in China, although their evidence is based on a limited number of studies whose primary focus is productivity.[12] Perhaps their most important result is that mixed enterprises in China seem to do better than private firms, or wholly state-owned firms. Other studies of Chinese companies also provide equivocal evidence. For example, Aivazian et al. (2005) found that corporatization of SOEs results in improved governance and profitability and suggest that corporatization is, therefore, an alternative to mass privatization. Hovey and Naughton (2007) maintain that the evidence suggests that increasing state ownership is negatively correlated with firm performance (measured in different ways). Similar conclusions were drawn by Dollar and Wei (2007) who found that SOEs have lower returns to capital as compared to private firms and foreign-owned firms, and by Shiu (2002) who found that SOEs are less efficient.

On the other hand, Chen et al. (2009) found that SOEs affiliated to the central government performed better than private firms. Similarly, Ma et al. (2006) discovered little evidence that state ownership has a direct impact on firm financial performance, although it does enhance the performance of firms affiliated with business groups in China; however, Carney et al. (2009) found that increasing state ownership had mixed effect on the profitability of business groups. Nee et al. (2007) also reports that state ownership per se has no impact on firm financial performance in China, but government (and party) interventions into management decision-making have a negative effect. Chen et al. (2006) found that privatization in China did not increase either the productivity or the profitability of firms. Finally, Li and Xia (2008) suggest that although private firms tend to be more profitable, they also rely more on short-term strategies whereas SOEs are more likely to adopt strategies that favor longer-term goals such as the introduction of new products.

Several recent studies examine directly the innovative activities of Chinese firms. Jefferson et al. (2006) suggests that while SOEs are not efficient at knowledge production, once they acquire new knowledge they are able to use the innovations at least as effectively as private firms. At the same time, Girma et al. (2006) found that foreign participation in Chinese SOEs (joint ventures) enhanced innovative activity. These studies therefore suggest that some Chinese SOEs are able to capture knowledge spillovers from foreign (and other) partners that will increase their ability to more effectively use new technology. On the other hand, Zhou and Li (2008) found that state participation in international joint ventures increases innovative activity which suggests that state presence may promote the absorptive capacity of the joint venture. In general, therefore, there is little conclusive evidence to suggest that state ownership of China's largest firms is negatively associated with the innovative performances of those firms.

Woo and Zhang (2006) describe the results of a survey carried out in May–June 2005 by the Asia Pacific Foundation of Canada in partnership with the China Council for the Promotion of International Trade (CCPIT). The survey covered 296 member companies of CCPIT. The survey results suggest that respondents' current investments overseas were driven as much by the Chinese government's "Going Global" policy and related incentives, as by pure business considerations. When asked about future investments, however, the importance of government policy direction and incentives is given much less weight by respondents. Rather, "business potential" is seen as the primary motivation. Similary, Ralston et al. (2006) provide survey evidence indicating that the organizational cultures in Chinese SOEs are closer to those of foreign-controlled firms compared to the domestic private firms. Related to this latter point, Li (2007) discusses several cases of Chinese MNEs listing their stocks in Hong Kong (China), not only to raise financial capital, but also to overcome the ambiguous property rights of either state or collective ownership. In short, for at least some Chinese MNEs, outward FDI might be part of the process of becoming more "market-oriented."

2.4.3 Summary

Although there are real concerns surrounding the entry of Chinese MNEs into the US, it can be argued that those concerns are either substantially overstated or not uniquely relevant to acquisitions by Chinese MNEs, or that they can be addressed by policy instruments already in place. Notwithstanding, if the expected benefits from Chinese FDI in the United States are negligible, any significant expected costs might tilt the balance against expecting such FDI to have net economic benefits for US residents. In this latter case, an argument might be made that Chinese FDI should receive particular scrutiny and monitoring.

The primary basis for questioning whether traditional spillover efficiency benefits to the host economy are likely to be realized from Chinese FDI is the significant amount of state ownership or influence of Chinese MNEs. State ownership or influence can be expected to reduce efficiency pressures on managers of Chinese MNEs, and the spillover benefits from inward FDI to the host country should be a positive function of the efficiency of foreign investors. However, the evidence on the performance of Chinese SOEs is not conclusive.

This does not mean that Chinese SOEs are necessarily well governed. It may well be that they are better protected, better subsidized and less transparent, all of which might explain the ambiguous results of using financial performance measures. It is also likely the case that comparable private sector firms in China themselves suffer from serious, albeit different, governance deficiencies so that governance failures are not necessarily confined to SOEs.

2.5 SUMMARY AND CONCLUSIONS

As Chinese MNEs continue to expand their global operations, they have encountered remarkable success, but also face major challenges. Among the challenges facing Chinese investors is the strategic choice of entry mode. The latecomer status of Chinese firms and the growth of the Chinese economy suggests that resource-seeking (both natural resources and firm-specific strategic resources) is an increasing imperative for Chinese outward FDI, and such resources are often better obtained through acquisitions. Combined with the managerial inexperience of Chinese MNEs and the difficulty posed by cultural differences between China and the US, the acquisition mode has further strong advantages compared to the greenfield mode. On the other hand, acquisitions are more likely to raise political opposition in the US. Such opposition might be mitigated by Chinese investors choosing minority ownership alternatives.[13] While minority ownership involves sacrifice of administrative control, it also involves less risk. Furthermore, the transfer of managerial knowledge and skills from the foreign partner might be more consistently realized if the Chinese investor holds a minority rather than majority ownership stake, since the latter imposes the full burdens of administration on Chinese managers who are unfamiliar with the host country environment. Finally, minority ownership expands the range of options facing the Chinese investor, including the possibility of gradually increasing the ownership share as the investor's familiarity with the host economy improves.

From the host country's perspective, the benefits of inward FDI are typically linked to spillover efficiency benefits to the country's factors of production. To the extent that Chinese entrants are resource-seeking SOEs that are relatively inefficient competitors in the global economy, the spillover efficiency benefits to the US and other host countries associated with Chinese FDI might be relatively small. Based upon available evidence, however, Chinese SOEs seem no less efficient than SOEs in many other emerging markets or, for that matter, many privately owned emerging-market MNEs. Hence, one would need to conclude that all FDI from emerging markets has no net economic benefit for the United States in order to make that argument for Chinese FDI. Such a conclusion is not warranted on the basis of any evidence of which we are aware.

In addition, direct and indirect access to China's domestic market for US-based companies might well be conditioned by the ability of Chinese firms to make investments in, and construct alliances with, US-based companies. As a practical political matter, therefore, the benefits of inward Chinese investment for US companies and workers are more likely to be related to the linkages between such investment and the future openness of China's economy to US trade and capital flows. The rapid growth and large size of China's domestic economy makes it a particularly beneficial trade and investment partner for the United States. In this context, it seems feckless to argue that there is no economic justification for allowing inward FDI and portfolio investment from China.

Indeed, minority investments in US companies by Chinese companies might well facilitate reciprocal investments in Chinese companies by those partially Chinese-owned US companies. The experience of the Blackstone Group is a case in point. Following a major minority Chinese investment in the US-based Blackstone Group, Blackstone acquired a 20 percent equity stake in China National Blue Star (Group) Corporation, a state-owned chemical company. It might be inferred that China's ownership stake in Blackstone facilitated the latter's ability to obtain approval from Chinese officials for the equity investment in Blue Star.[14]

Restrictions on inward Chinese FDI might also have implications for the US economy to the extent that Chinese FDI is complementary to Chinese exports. If so, policies that restrict the former will also restrict the latter. In this context, the economic benefits of inward FDI from China might be seen as similar to the economic benefits of imports from China. There is some consensus that imports from China have contributed to higher real incomes for Americans via lower prices for a range of products. Indeed, if Chinese FDI leads to more value-added production within US affiliates of Chinese MNEs, the "dislocation" effects on US workers associated with Chinese exports might well be reduced by increased Chinese FDI in the United States.

In sum, the future prosperity of the United States will arguably be prominently influenced by the degree to which the economies of China and the United States are integrated through trade and investment. In this context, the relevant question might not be: is the US ready for investment from China? The relevant question might be: can the US afford not to be ready for investment from China? In our view, there is not much additional cost associated with such readiness. As discussed in Chapter 3 by David Fagan, as well as Chapter 5 by Lorraine Eden and Stewart Miller, in this volume, very few potential problems are currently unanticipated by existing laws and regulations. Furthermore, if one is prepared to take a longer-run perspective, the few potential problems that are not obviously addressed by existing laws and regulations will be mitigated by the continued economic integration between developed and developing countries.

NOTES

*   This chapter was prepared in the context of the Deloitte–Vale Columbia Center on Sustainable International Investment project on "Is the US ready for FDI from China?" The authors thank Karl P. Sauvant for helpful comments on an earlier draft and Yao Tang for research assistance. Copyright © 2009 by Columbia University. All rights reserved.

1.   The CEO of Abu Dhabi National Energy Co. indicated in 2008 that it is targeting Canada for takeovers in the oil and gas sector because of its political stability and its location next to the United States, a market in which it would like to participate but in which it perceives Middle Eastern investment being frustrated by tight rules; see Cattaneo (2007). It should be noted that in 2008 the Canadian government introduced legislation making national security grounds for rejecting foreign investments. National security concerns are likely to pertain to investments by SOEs.

2.   For a discussion of the ambivalent United States attitude toward foreign investment from China, see He and Lyles (2008).

3.   Concern is also being expressed in the United States and elsewhere about equity investments made in those countries by sovereign wealth funds headquartered in China and other emerging markets. See, for example, Davis (2007).

4.   There have, however, been calls for reviewing all foreign investments by SOEs, as well as by government-owned investment funds (Scannell 2007).

5.   This cell may also include contractual strategic alliances in which the foreign investor has no equity ownership in an alliance but, rather, contracts with a domestic partner to carry out specific activities; however, we do not consider this a foreign investment.

6.   It is relevant to note that most FDI now occurs via cross-border mergers and acquisitions (M&As). However, less well known is that M&A of this low-control type accounts for about 16 percent of total M&A and about 12 percent of total FDI (Brakman et al. 2006).

7.   This statement might be qualified to include only the largest Chinese companies, which have been the most widely studied, but not perhaps the most representative (Yeung and Liu 2008).

8.   In this respect, the global expansion plans of Chinese companies are similar to those of Indian companies. Pradhan and Alakshendra (2006) show that acquisitions are a preferred mode of FDI for Indian pharmaceutical companies.

9.   Kang and Liu (2007) and Deng (2007) assert that government sponsorship and funding support may be offered by the Chinese government for overseas investments that are deemed by the government to be in China's national interest. We shall consider the relevance of this phenomenon from the US host country perspective in a later section.

10. Recent evidence suggesting that this is the case for emerging market acquisitions in the US is provided by Chari et al. (2009).
11. In contrast, Huttunen (2007) found for a sample of Finnish establishments that foreign acquisitions resulted in a decreased share of highly educated workers in a plant's employment.
12. Many studies of SOEs use multiple measures of enterprise performance. Hence, we use the generic term "performance" when a study reports several different measures and the results are consistent. When a study uses only one measure, we identify that measure.
13. It is relevant to note in this regard, that several proposed Chinese investments in Australia's mining sector, including the Aluminum Corporation of China's investment in Rio Tinto PLC, triggered reviews by Australia's Foreign Investment Review Board, even though they were not takeover investments. See Bell (2009).
14. Another US company, Iomega Corp., agreed to a stock-swap agreement with a unit of China Electronics Corp. owned by the Chinese government. The investment resulted in China Electronics Corp. owning about 27 percent of Iomega. The chief executive officer (CEO) of Iomega said the deal will help Iomega build a foothold in the Chinese market where it has no presence to date. See Clark (2007).

REFERENCES

Aivazian, Varouj, Ying Ge and Jiaping Qiu (2005). "Can Corporatization Improve the Performance of State-Owned Enterprises Even Without Privatization?" *Journal of Corporate Finance*, 11, pp. 791–808.

Asia Pacific Foundation of Canada (2005). "China Goes Global Survey," www.asiapacific.ca.

Asia Pacific Foundation of Canada (2006). "China Goes Global Survey II," www.asiapacific.ca.

Barkley, Tom (2008). "Code Is Set for State-Run Funds," *Wall Street Journal*, March 21, p. A4.

Bell, Stephen (2009). "China Deals Scrutinized in Australia," *Wall Street Journal*, March 20, p. B4.

Bertrand, Oliver, Katarina Hakkala and Pehr-Johan Norback (2007). "Cross-Border Acquisition or Greenfield Entry: Does it Matter for Affiliate R&D?" Stockholm: Research Institute of Industrial Economics, Working Paper No. 693.

Blomstrom, Magnus, Ari Kokko and Mario Zejan (2000). *Foreign Direct Investment: Firm and Host Country Strategies*, New York: St Martin's Press.

Blonigen, Bruce and Matthew Slaughter (2001). "Foreign Affiliate Activity and US Skill Upgrading," *Review of Economics and Statistics*, 83 (2), pp. 362–376.

Brakman, S., H. Garretson and C. van Marrewijk (2006). "Cross-Border M&A: The Facts as a Guide for International Economics," CESifo Working Paper 1823.

Brouthers, Keith and Jean-François Hennart (2007). "Boundaries of the Firm: Insights from International Entry Mode Research," *Journal of Management*, 33 (3), pp. 395–425.

Carney, Michael, Daniel Shapiro and Yao Tang (2009). "Business Group Performance in China: Ownership and Temporal Considerations," *Management and Organization Review*, 5 (2), pp. 167–193.

Cattaneo, Claudia (2007). "Abu Dhabi National Targets Canadian Oil and Gas Growth", *National Post*, August 17, p. 5.

Chari, Anusha, Wenjie Chen and Kathryn Dominguez (2009). "Foreign Ownership and Firm Performance: Emerging Market Acquisitions in the United States," National Bureau of Economic Research, Working Paper 14786, mimeo.

Chen, Gongmeng, Michael Firth and Oliver Rui (2006). "Have China's Enterprise Reforms Led to Improved Efficiency and Profitability?," *Emerging Markets Review*, 7 (1), pp. 82–109.

Chen, Gongmeng, Michael Firth and Liping Xu (2009). "Does the Type of Ownership Control Matter? Evidence from China's Listed Companies," *Journal of Banking and Finance*, 33 (1), pp. 171–181.

Chung, Wilbur (2001). "Mode, Size and Location of Foreign Direct Investments and Industry Markup," *Journal of Economic Behaviour and Organization*, 45, pp. 185–211.

Claeys, Sophie and Christa Hainz (2006). "Acquisition versus Greenfield: The Impact of the Mode of Foreign Bank Entry on Information and Bank Lending Rates," Working Paper Series No. 653.

Clark, Don (2007). "Iomega Seeks Chinese Foothold With Excelsior Deal," *Wall Street Journal*, December 13, p. B4.

Davis, Bob (2007). "How Trade Talks Could Tame Sovereign Wealth Funds," *Wall Street Journal*, October 29, p. A2.

Deitz, Meagan, Gordon Orr and Jane Xing (2008). "How Chinese Companies Can Succeed Abroad," *The McKinsey Quarterly*, May, pp. 1–9.

Deng, Ping (2007). "Investing for Strategic Resources and Its Rationale: The Case of Outward FDI from Chinese Companies," *Business Horizons*, 50, pp. 71–81.

Dollar, David and Shang–Jin Wei (2007). "Das (Wasted) Kapital: Firm Ownership and Investment Efficiency in China," NBER Working Paper No. 13103.

Dong, Li and Keith Glaister (2007). "National and Corporate Culture Differences in International Strategic Alliances: Perceptions of Chinese Partners," *Asia Pacific Journal of Management*, 24, pp. 191–205.

Estrin, Saul, Jan Hanousek, Evzen Kocenda and Jan Svejnar (2007). "Effects of Privatization and Ownership in Transition Economies," *International Policy Center Working Papers Series*, June 4, number 30.

Girma, Sourafei, Yundan Gong and Holger Gorg (2006). "Can You Teach Old Dragons New Tricks? FDI and Innovation Activity in Chinese State–Owned Enterprises," IZA Discussion Paper 2267, Bonn: IZA.

Globerman, Steven and Daniel M. Shapiro (2005). "Assessing International Mergers and Acquisitions as a Mode of Foreign Direct investment," in Lorraine Eden and Wendy Dobson (eds). *Governance, Multinationals and Growth*, Cheltenham, UK and Northampton, MA: Edward Elgar, pp. 68–100.

Goergen, Marc (2007). "What Do We Know about Different Systems of Corporate governance?," European Corporate Governance Institute, Finance Working Paper No. 163/2007.

He, Wei and Marjorie Lyles (2008). "China's Outward Foreign Direct Investment," *Business Horizons*, 51, pp. 485–491.

Hemerling, Jean, Holger Michaelis and David Michaels (2006). "China's Global Challengers: The Strategic Implications of Chinese Outbound M&A," Cambridge: Boston Consulting Group.

Heyman, Frederic, Frerik Sjoholm and Patrik Tingvall Gustafson (2004). "Is There Really a Foreign Ownership Wage Premium? Evidence from Matched Employer–Employee Data," Stockholm: European Institute of Japanese Studies, mimeo.

Hong, E. and L. Sun (2004). "Go Overseas via Direct Investment: Internationalization Strategy of Chinese Corporations in a Comparative Prism," Centre for Financial and Management Studies, University of London, mimeo.

Hovey, Martin and Tony Naughton (2007). "A Survey of Enterprise Reforms in China: The Way Forward," *Economic Systems*, 31, pp. 138–156.

Huttunen, Kristiina (2007). "The Effects of Foreign Acquisitions on Employment and Wages: Evidence From Finnish Establishments," *Review of Economics and Statistics*, 89 (3), pp. 497–509.

Jefferson, Gary, Bai Huamao, Guan Xiaojing and Yu Xiaoyun (2006). "R&D Performance in Chinese industry," *Economics of Innovation and New Technology*, 15 (4–5), pp. 345–366.

Kang, C.S. Eliot (1997). "US Politics and Greater Regulation of Inward Foreign Direct Investment," *International Organization*, 51 (2), pp. 301–333.

Kang, Yuanfei and Wengang Liu (2007). "Internationalization Patterns of Chinese Firms: Entry Mode, Location, and Government Influence," *International Journal of Business Strategy*, September, http://findarticles.com/p/articles/mi_6766/is_3_7/ai_n28516705, accessed March 9, 2009.

Li, Peter Ping (2007). "Toward an Integrated Theory of Multinational Evolution: The Evidence of Chinese Multinational Enterprises as Latecomers," *Journal of International Management*, 13 (93), pp. 296–318.

Li, Shaomin and Jun Xia (2008). "The Roles and Performance of State Firms and Non-State Firms in China's Economic Transition," *World Development*, 36 (1), pp. 39–54.

Ma, Xufei, Youmin Xi and Xiaotao Yao (2006). "Business Group Affiliation and Performance in the Transition Economy: A Focus on the Ownership Voids," *Asia-Pacific Journal of Management*, 23 (4), pp. 467–484.

Mata, Jose and Pedro Portugal (2000). "Closure and Divestiture by Foreign Entrants: The Impact of Entry and Post-Entry Strategies," *Strategic Management Journal*, 20 (5), pp. 549–562.

Mathews, John. A (2002). "Competitive Advantages of the Latecomer Firm: A Resource-Based Account of Industrial Catch-up Strategies," *Asia Pacific Journal of Management*, 29, pp. 467–88.

Mathieu, Edouard (2006). *Investments From Large Developing Economies in France and Europe*, Paris: Invest in France Agency.

McCloughan, Patrick and Ian Stone (1998). "Life Duration of Foreign Multinational Subsidiaries: Evidence from UK Northern Manufacturing Industry 1970–93," *International Journal of Industrial Organization*, 16 (6), pp. 719–747.

Meyer, Klaus, Saul Estrin, Sumon Kumar Bhaumik and Mike Peng (2009). "Institutions, Resources and Entry Strategies in Emerging Economies," *Strategic Management Journal*, 30, pp. 61–80.

Nee, Victor, Sonja Opper and Sonia Wong (2007). "Developmental State and Corporate Governance in China", *Management and Organization Review*, 3 (1), pp. 19–53.

Nocke, Volker and Stephen R.R. Yeaple (2008). "An Assignment Theory of Foreign Direct Investment," *Review of Economic Studies*, 75 (2), pp. 529–557.

Organisation for Economic Co-operation and Development (OCED) (2007). *Trends and Recent Developments in Foreign Direct Investment*, Paris: OECD.

Pradhan, Jaya Prakash and Abhinav Alakshendra (2006). "Overseas Acquisition versus Greenfield Foreign Investment: Which Internationalization Strategy is Better for Indian Pharmaceutical Enterprises?," New Delhi: Institute for Studies in Industrial Development, mimeo.

Raff, Horst, Michael Ryan and Frank Staehler (2005). "Asset Ownership and Foreign Market Entry," CESifo Working Paper No. 1676, Kiel, mimeo.

Ralston, David A., Jane Terpstra-Tong, Robert H. Terpstra, Xueli Wang and Carolyn Egri (2006). "Today's State-Owned Enterprises of China: Are they Dying Dinosaurs or Dynamic Dynamos?" *Strategic Management Journal*, 27 (9), pp. 825–843.

Scannell, Kara (2007). "Cox Cites Concerns Over Sovereign Funds", *Wall Street Journal*, October 26, p. A8.

Shiu, Alice (2002). "Efficiency of Chinese Enterprises," *Journal of Productivity Analysis*, 18 (3), pp. 255–267.

Slangen, Arjen and Jean-François Hennart (2007). "Greenfield or Acquisition Entry: A Review of the Empirical Foreign Establishment Mode Literature," *Journal of International Management*, 13 (4), pp. 403–429.

UNCTAD (2000). *World Investment Report 2000: Cross-Border Mergers and Acquisitions and Development*, New York and Geneva: United Nations.

UNCTAD (2008). *World Investment Report 2008: Transnational Corporations, and the Infrastructure Challenge*, New York and Geneva: United Nations.

Woo, Yuen Pau and Kenny Zhang (2006). "China Goes Global: The Implications of Chinese Outward Direct Investment for Canada," Vancouver: Asia-Pacific Foundation of Canada, mimeo.

World Bank (2006). *Held by the Visible Hand*, Washington, DC: World Bank.

Wu, Friedrich (2005). "The Globalization of Corporate China," *National Bureau of Asian Research*, 16 (3), pp. 5–29.

Yeung, Henry Wai-chung and Weidong Liu (2008), "Globalizing China: The Rise of Mainland Chinese Firms in the Global Economy," *Eurasian Geography and Economics*, 49 (1), pp. 59–86.

Zhou, Changhui and Jing Li (2008), "Product Innovations in Emerging Market–Based International Joint Ventures: An Organizational Ecology Perspective," *Journal of International Business Studies*, 39, pp. 1114–1132.

3. The US regulatory and institutional framework for FDI

David N. Fagan*

INTRODUCTION

In May 2007, President George W. Bush issued a statement on United States policy toward foreign investment, termed by the administration as a statement on "open economies." The statement was spurred by a desire to affirm to the world that the United States remained open to foreign direct investment (FDI) – a task made essential by the highly politicized reaction of the US Congress in 2006 to the proposed investment in US port operations by Dubai Ports World. The statement also anticipated the more balanced action taken by Congress later in 2007 to adopt reasonable reforms to the primary legal mechanism for vetting FDI, the Exon–Florio Amendment to the Defense Production Act. Importantly, though, President Bush's statement was not centered only on promoting foreign investment. Rather, it sought a balance between maintaining an open environment for investment and preserving important security interests, as follows:

> A free and open international investment regime is vital for a stable and growing economy, both here at home and throughout the world. The threat of global terrorism and other national security challenges have caused the United States and other countries to focus more intently on the national security dimensions of foreign investment. While my Administration will continue to take every necessary step to protect national security, my Administration recognizes that our prosperity and security are founded on our country's openness.
>
> As both the world's largest investor and the world's largest recipient of investment, the United States has a key stake in promoting an open investment regime. The United States unequivocally supports international investment in this country and is equally committed to securing fair, equitable, and nondiscriminatory treatment for US investors abroad. Both inbound and outbound investment benefit our country by stimulating growth, creating jobs, enhancing productivity, and fostering competitiveness that allows our companies and their workers to prosper at home and in international markets.[1]

President Bush's statement affirming the importance of foreign investment to the United States was not ground-breaking. On the contrary, it followed a long line of administration policy pronouncements expressing openness to foreign investment.[2] The significance of President Bush's statement on "open economies" was that it explicitly linked the policy of open investment to US national security interests. This basic policy framework – recognizing the benefits of open investment, but also emphasizing the importance of national security – is especially important when considering FDI from China. Indeed, not by coincidence, the issues presented by FDI from China in many respects embody the balance set forth in the Bush administration's statement on "open economies."

China has the potential to be a tremendous source of FDI for the United States. At the same time, the history of Chinese investments in the United States tells us that, from the perspective of US regulators and policy-makers, Chinese FDI can present unique considerations, especially in the area of national security. As described further below, of the United States' ten largest trading partners, China is the only one not considered an ally;[3] key institutions, including the Department of Defense, the US intelligence and law enforcement agencies, and Congress view certain Chinese investments with great suspicion; and US concerns over the unlicensed transfer of dual-use technologies are especially acute with China. In fact, the only transaction ever formally blocked under Exon–Florio was an investment by a Chinese company.[4] In early 2008, the US private equity firm Bain Capital Partners and the Chinese technology firm Huawei Technologies were forced to drop their bid for the US computer communications equipment manufacturer 3Com Corp. after they were unable to address the national security concerns of the United States government.[5] Sensitivities over Chinese investment can extend to the state level as well, as demonstrated when the 1990s sale of the Indiana-based magnet company Magnaquench to an investment group that included Chinese state-owned companies belatedly became a political issue in the 2008 Democratic Party primary campaign in Indiana.[6]

In this context, the question of whether the United States is ready, from a regulatory and institutional perspective, for mergers and acquisitions (M&As) from China takes on added significance. Whether Chinese FDI in the US will increase substantially, and the US in turn will receive the attendant benefits of this investment after years of outward investment flowing to China, depends on whether US laws and institutions can treat Chinese investors at least approximately like other investors, that is, whether Chinese investors can approach the US market with some degree of certainty with respect to process, timeframes and, ultimately, results on the regulatory and political fronts – and whether the United States, at the same time, can preserve its legitimate non-economic interests.

Before addressing this subject more fully, it should be emphasized that the discussion herein is not legal advice. As noted, the applicability of particular laws, whether federal, state or local, to any given transaction will depend highly on the facts and circumstances of that transaction. Elements of the US legal and institutional framework addressed in this chapter will not be applicable in every case of foreign investment, or even necessarily in the majority of them. Rather, the chapter is intended to provide a general overview of the framework for cross-border M&As, with a more detailed focus on Exon–Florio, the potential political challenges that Chinese investors can face in Congress and potential strategies to mitigate regulatory and political risk for investment from China. *Moreover, the discussion of existing laws in this chapter is based on the status of the laws at the end of 2008. With this in mind, investors would be prudent to consult with US counsel on any particular investment to ensure that all relevant laws and regulatory requirements – at the federal, state and local levels – are identified and addressed.*

3.1   THE US REGULATORY LANDSCAPE FOR FDI FROM CHINA AND CONSIDERATIONS FOR INVESTORS

The legal and corporate due diligence evaluation for any particular investment can be a complex exercise, touching on a wide range of laws, regulations and other issues. On the legal side alone, a due diligence review typically will encompass, among other elements, a review of material contracts, supply and licensing agreements, pending and ongoing litigation, intellectual property portfolios and potential liabilities, labor and employment issues, insurance coverage and environmental issues. Such a due diligence review also must encompass three fundamental issues: (1) What, if any, regulatory compliance issues will be implicated by the investment? (2) What, if any, regulatory approvals are required to complete the investment? (3) What other stakeholders, such as legislative bodies or other third parties, may be interested in the transaction? For certain foreign investors, including in particular Chinese investors, there is an additional consideration that pervades each of these issues: whether the transaction implicates – in fact or in perception – US national security considerations.

These due diligence-related factors and their impact on strategic considerations for an investment are discussed in depth below. As the following due diligence and strategy flow chart in Figure 3.1 demonstrates, and as described more fully herein, the answers to these fundamental questions and how they interact with US national security considerations directly bear on the appropriate strategy for addressing regulatory and political risk for foreign M&A transactions in the United States.

3.1.1 Ongoing Regulatory Compliance Considerations

As an initial matter, a thorough due diligence review of a potential acquisition target should assess not only current liabilities that have been identified, but also ongoing compliance issues that arise from a foreign acquisition. Two ongoing compliance issues, in particular, need to be identified and evaluated for foreign investment from China: foreign trade control compliance and compliance with the Foreign Corrupt Practices Act of 1977 (FCPA).[7]

Foreign trade controls compliance
Compliance with US laws and regulations governing foreign trade controls laws is particularly important in the context of Chinese M&A activity in the United States because of prominent reported cases of Chinese violations of these provisions. An example of such reported cases is included in the discussion in section 3.4, below. These cases have arguably contributed to a perception among US regulatory officials, whether accurate or not, of heightened risk with respect to foreign trade controls compliance when Chinese companies or partners are at issue. They have also resulted in stricter licensing requirements for the export of products or technologies that could make a contribution to, or be destined for end use by, the Chinese military.[8]

The unlicensed physical export of controlled US products or technologies is not the only compliance risk that should be understood and mitigated by a Chinese investor. Potential acquirors of US companies as well as Chinese companies evaluating greenfield investments also should understand and be prepared to implement compliance programs for US foreign trade controls governing not only access to and transfers of controlled technologies to foreign nationals in the United States, but also compliance with US trade embargoes. This section summarizes only briefly these US programs which have far-reaching implications for owners of US businesses.

There are three programs that principally comprise the US foreign trade controls regime.[9]

US Regulatory Due Diligence and Strategy Framework for FDI

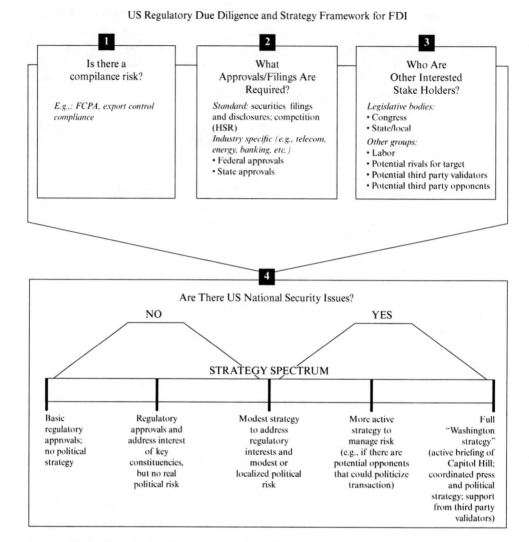

Figure 3.1   US regulatory and strategic due diligence flow chart

First, US Commerce Department regulations, known as the Export Administration Regulations (EAR), apply to so-called "dual-use items" – that is, products and technologies that may have both military and commercial applications. The EAR specifically provide restrictions on the export of commercial products (including software) and technologies from the United States and on the re-export between foreign countries of US-origin (including foreign-made items with more than *de minimis* US-origin content) commercial products (including software) and technologies.[10] The degree to which a particular item is controlled (for example, whether export or re-export is prohibited or subject to specific licensing requirements) under the EAR depends upon:

(1) the technical capabilities and performance specifications of the product, software or technology involved (according to a classification list maintained by the Commerce Department); (2) the country of destination; and (3) in certain circumstances, the actual end-user and end-use of the item.

Second, the State Department administers the International Traffic in Arms Regulations (ITAR),[11] which control the export or foreign transfer of any defense article or service. In general, defense articles are products, software or technical information that are specially designed, modified or configured for military or intelligence uses, as defined on the US Munitions List.[12] Defense services include any support or training for design, production, repair or use of defense articles, whether in the US or abroad.[13] The State Department requires specific licensing authorization for the export of all defense articles and services to virtually any country. Under current US legislation, export or re-export to China of US Munitions List products, software or technical information subject to the ITAR is prohibited.

Third, the US Treasury Department's Office of Foreign Assets Control (OFAC) administers certain sanctions programs that generally preclude export–import transactions and other business and financial dealings with targeted countries (for example, Cuba and Iran) and parties (for example, terrorist organizations and drug kingpins and narco-traffickers) for US national policy and security reasons. These restrictions apply quite broadly to US persons, which include not only entities organized under the laws of the United States but, depending on the program, also their foreign subsidiaries (for example, Cuba). In addition, "US person" includes any individual or legal entity physically in the United States or any US citizen or permanent resident wherever located or employed.[14] Thus, no foreign national in the United States and no US citizen located abroad, including as an employee of a foreign company, may take action to facilitate trade or other financial transactions with an OFAC-sanctioned country or party.

Each of these foreign trade controls programs provides for civil penalties, including substantial fines, for violations and criminal penalties for willful violations. In this regard, it is worth highlighting one aspect of US foreign trade controls that can pose particularly challenging ongoing compliance issues – namely, the restrictions on "deemed exports" or technology transfers inherent in the Commerce Department and State Department regulations. As explained by the Commerce Department:

> [T]echnology is 'released' for export when it is available to foreign nationals for visual inspection (such as reading technical specifications, plans, blueprints, etc.) even if such release occurs in the United States. This same interpretation applies to technology that is exchanged orally with a foreign national or technology that is made available by practice or application under the guidance of persons with knowledge of the technology.[15]

This broad restriction encompasses information necessary for the "development," "production" or "use" of a product. When such technology – or certain kinds of software source code – is released to a foreign national in the United States, it is deemed to be exported and, therefore, such release may require prior authorization from the Commerce Department. A similar requirement obtains with respect to technology retransfers abroad – namely, if State or Commerce Department-controlled technology is approved for export or otherwise transferred abroad and then, in turn, proposed for transfer to an individual from a third country that would require licensing for direct US exports, the additional retransfer without a license would be a violation of Commerce Department regulations.[16] Likewise, with respect to defense articles, the State Department requires an export license "for the oral, visual, or documentary transmission of technical data by US persons to foreign persons, by such means as in-person or telephone discussions and written correspondence including electronic messages, even when they are in the United States."[17] Like the Commerce Department, the State Department applies retransfer controls for "deemed" exports that occur outside the United States.

For Chinese investors who may wish to access US technology in connection with their investments, it is especially important to be aware of the US restrictions on deemed exports and to plan for ongoing compliance mechanisms to ensure that the acquired entity and existing and future employees act in compliance with applicable US foreign trade control restrictions. In particular, prospective Chinese owners of US businesses need to evaluate whether limitations on access to certain technology may interfere with managing their investment.

FCPA

The FCPA is a broad anti-corruption statute with both criminal and civil provisions that address bribery directly (corrupt offers, payments, gifts, and so on, in exchange for a quid pro quo) and via provisions focused on accounting and internal controls that hide corrupt transactions.[18] (See also the chapter by Lorraine Eden and Stewart Miller in this volume.) Like the US foreign trade control regimes, the FCPA is nuanced; a thorough discussion of its provisions, the various permutations in which it may apply, and the potential pitfalls for US firms and others is beyond the scope of this chapter. For present purposes, the pertinent point with respect to the FCPA is that while the statute typically addresses activities of US firms and nationals abroad (indeed, it was adopted in response to Congressional findings in the 1970s that US firms "were routinely making payments to foreign officials in exchange for business favors"[19]), it also has relevance as an ongoing compliance matter for foreign investors in the United States.

The FCPA in particular can have special relevance for Chinese firms for several reasons. First, the anti-bribery provisions are not limited to gifts or other graft provided to employees of state agencies; they also can reach state-owned companies or quasi-private entities serving state functions.[20] Second, the statute's bribery prohibitions apply not only to all US companies and persons, but also to any foreign national in the United States who violates the Act "by use of the mails or any means or instrumentality of interstate commerce."[21] Thus, for example, a Chinese employee from a Chinese company doing business in the United States who, while in the US, arranges for a gift to be made to an officer or an employee of a Chinese state-owned entity to obtain an advantage with that entity in a business matter, could face criminal liability under the FCPA.

Given the potential scope of the FCPA and its tripwires for liability, it would be prudent for a Chinese investor to plan and implement a strong FCPA compliance program (if one does not already exist) in connection with acquisitions in the United States. Likewise, investors should be aware that, as with other compliance issues, a US counterparty may seek certain FCPA-related representations or disclosures from the investor.

3.1.2   Required Regulatory Approvals

The second fundamental regulatory issue that foreign companies examining potential targets for acquisition or investment in the United States should consider is what regulatory approvals are required. On this issue, the conceptual framework can be broken down further as: (1) Are there any standard regulatory approvals or disclosures that are required for the transaction based on certain general characteristics, such as the value of the transaction and whether it involves any publicly listed entities? (2) Are there specific approvals that are required because of the nature of the assets, which would encompass approvals that are specific to certain industries?

Standard approvals and disclosures
Foreign M&A activity in the United States may implicate at least two standard regulatory approval and compliance matters depending on the specific transaction's terms: namely, whether there are any required filings with securities regulators and exchanges in the United States, which turns on whether the US target or foreign entity is publicly listed in the United States; and whether there are any antitrust-related notifications and reviews required.

   In terms of US securities laws and regulations, there are several requirements that may be imposed on either the US target company or the foreign investor. Again, the federal securities laws are detailed and nuanced, and the full range of rules and requirements cannot be covered here. However, the following is a non-exhaustive list of the types of filings and disclosures that may be required as a result of an investment or merger involving entities that are registered with the Securities and Exchange Commission (SEC) in the United States:

- Registered US entities must make Form 8-K filings with the SEC to provide prompt disclosure of certain events, which would include a change of control of the entity and any material definitive merger, asset purchase or other business combination agreements.[22]
- Persons who acquire beneficial ownership interest of more than 5 percent of a class of voting equity securities registered under the Securities Exchange Act of 1934 must file with the SEC a form addressing, among other things, the shareholder's intent with respect to the target (including plans or proposals with regard to future actions), the percentage of ownership, the source and amount of any financing and an explanation of the transaction.[23]
- For exchange offers, issuers must submit a form addressing, among other things, the bidder's financial condition and results of operations, the reasons for the transaction, the shareholder's financing and prior material contacts with the company being acquired.[24]
- Tender offers for publicly held stock must comply with the SEC's tender offer rules, which include filing a schedule with the SEC describing the tender offer and providing substantive disclosures.[25]
- Shareholder votes required under state corporate law or stock exchange rules for mergers, asset sales, issuances of stock or similar transactions involve the filing of a preliminary proxy statement with the SEC followed by a definitive proxy statement when it is delivered to shareholders.[26]

The SEC will review, and may provide comments on, certain of these filings, and the parties will not be permitted to complete the transaction until the SEC confirms that it has no further comments on such filings.

In addition to these federal filing requirements, the various exchanges (NYSE, AMEX, Nasdaq) have certain requirements, such as disclosure and notification requirements for material events that may affect the value of a company's stock.[27] Many states also have anti-takeover laws that govern acquisitions of stock of companies incorporated in their jurisdictions. These state laws may impose requirements for shareholder or board approval for acquisitions of stock above a certain threshold (for example, 10 or 15 percent).[28]

In addition to securities-related disclosures and filings, the other standard federal review in connection with M&A activity is a competition review conducted by the US Federal Trade Commission (FTC) and the Department of Justice (DOJ). The US antitrust laws prohibit acquisitions of interests or assets of a party engaged in interstate commerce where the "effect of such acquisition may be substantially to lessen competition" in a relevant US product market.[29] To provide the FTC and DOJ with an opportunity to review proposed acquisitions in advance, the Hart–Scott–Rodino Antitrust Improvements Act of 1976 (HSR)[30] requires parties to submit a premerger notification for most significant acquisitions. The HSR notification requirements apply if the transaction meets certain thresholds based on the value of the transaction and the parties' sizes, or if, regardless of the parties' sizes, the transaction will result in the acquiror receiving at least certain thresholds[31] of the target's interests and assets (the threshold values may vary annually).

Upon receipt of the HSR notification, the FTC and DOJ have a 30-day "waiting period" to investigate the transaction to determine whether there is any potential harm to competition. If the FTC and DOJ believe that the transaction warrants closer scrutiny, they can further delay the transaction pending their review. Ultimately, if the agencies conclude that the acquisition would substantially lessen competition, they may seek a court injunction prohibiting the transaction. Notably, even if the FTC or DOJ do not act during the HSR waiting period, the transaction is not exempt from US antitrust laws, and is subject to later challenge by the FTC and DOJ, state enforcement officials, and even private parties.

Industry-specific requirements

Depending on the particular sector and assets at issue in an M&A, the transaction parties may be required to seek additional approvals from US federal or state officials before consummating the transaction. Thus, in addition to potential securities-related filings (for publicly traded companies), a federal competition review (depending on the size of the transaction) and national security review (discussed below), Chinese firms looking to acquire control of a US target must also consider what, if any, industry-specific federal and state regulatory approval processes they will confront. While it is not possible here to address in depth the various industry regulatory regimes in the United States, two sectors provide useful illustrations of the potential additional federal and state approvals required for M&A activity: telecommunications and banking.

First, with respect to transactions in the telecommunications sector, Section 310 of the Communications Act of 1934 restricts foreign ownership of broadcast, common carrier and aeronautical radio station licensees. Section 310 expressly prohibits a foreign corporation or "alien" from holding any broadcast, common carrier or aeronautical radio station license, but, as interpreted by the Federal Communications Commission (FCC), it does not prohibit indirect foreign control of certain licensees.[32] Section 310 also prohibits foreign governments, individuals and corporations from owning more than 20 percent of the stock of a broadcast, common carrier, or aeronautical radio station licensee. Yet, as the FCC has noted, most foreign investments occur through intermediate companies organized in the United States. Section 310 provides a presumptive 25 percent ownership limitation for foreign investment in entities that in turn control US broadcast, common carrier and aeronautical radio licensees. However, Section 310 also grants the FCC discretion to allow higher levels of foreign ownership at the holding company level unless it finds that such ownership is inconsistent with the public interest. Thus, foreign entities may acquire, directly or indirectly, up to 100 percent of the stock of a US company owning or controlling an FCC licensee if the FCC does not find the foreign ownership to be inconsistent with the public interest.[33] Although the FCC has frequently exercised its discretion under Section 310 to permit foreign investment in excess of the 25 percent limitation with respect to non-broadcast licensees, historically it has declined to do so in the broadcast context.

In addition, acquisitions of telecommunications providers may require approval by state public utility commissions, which typically have jurisdiction over transfers of control of state-issued telecommunications authorizations and also may have authority to review M&As for their competitive effects on the local market and impact on customers' rates, terms and conditions of service. Transactions in the US telecommunications sector, therefore, may require both FCC approval for the transfer of federal authorizations to a foreign acquirer, and approvals of state authorities based on a review of the qualifications of the acquiror and the competitive effects of the proposed controlling acquisition.

Second, with respect to banking transactions, the US system of financial institution regulation involves multiple regulators, including at the federal and state level, and in turn may require multiple approvals for M&A transactions. As presently constituted, commercial banking in the United States is principally overseen by four primary federal regulators – the Federal Reserve Board, the Federal Deposit Insurance Corporation, the Office of the Comptroller of the Currency, and the Office of Thrift Supervision. In addition, states have laws and regulations that govern the business of banking within the state, including in some cases mergers and acquisitions. Most foreign banks elect to enter the United States through the establishment of their own branches or other offices in the US;[34] however, the federal and state regulators have ample authority to review M&A activity, whether it is the initial avenue for a foreign bank to enter the US market or involves a foreign bank that already has existing branches in the United States.

In particular, at the federal level, the federal Bank Holding Company Act (BHC Act) requires the Federal Reserve Board to review and either approve or disapprove any proposed transaction that would result in any company, foreign or domestic, acquiring control of a banking holding company or certain types of banks. This includes, among other things, the acquisition of 25 percent or more of any class of voting securities of a bank or bank holding company. The Federal Reserve also can find control where an investment would result in a lower percentage (down to 5 percent) of ownership over voting securities, if other indicia of control are also present. In considering whether control is present, the Federal Reserve:

considers the size of the investment, the involvement of the investor in the management of the bank or bank holding company, any business relationships between the investor and the bank or bank holding company, and other relevant factors indicating an intent or ability to significantly influence the management or operations of the bank or bank holding company.[35]

Commercial banking in the United States is principally overseen by various primary federal regulators. Notably, in order for a foreign bank to make an acquisition in the United States, the BHC Act also requires the Federal Reserve to assess a number of other factors, including the supervision exercised by home country authorities. Foreign entrance into the US market may not be permitted if the Federal Reserve does not determine that home country regulators exercise comprehensive consolidated supervision (CCS).

3.1.3   Other Interested Stakeholders

In addition to identifying regulatory compliance issues and assessing what regulatory approvals will be required for foreign M&As, a critical due diligence consideration for certain foreign investments is an assessment of how other interested stakeholders may align on the transaction. This, in part, is an assessment of how controversial a transaction will be – and that is particularly relevant to foreign investors from potentially sensitive countries, like China. Specific considerations may include whether a transaction will be welcomed by the employees of the target; whether there are any highly organized political groups, such as unions, that may be interested in the transaction and how it may affect their constituencies; whether there are rival bidders who could seek to interfere in the transaction; and what other third parties will be oriented either in favor of or against the transaction.

As Figure 3.1 demonstrates, national security considerations overlay each of these fundamental due diligence issues, especially with respect to M&A activity from China: reputation for ongoing compliance matters, such as export control and anti-corruption compliance, can impact the trustworthiness and determination of a foreign acquiror for US national security purposes (see section 3.4); prior approval of the Committee on Foreign Investment in the United States (CFIUS), which assesses the impact on US national security of mergers, acquisitions and investments that result in foreign control, may be the most significant regulatory approval for certain foreign investments (see section 3.2); and if there are national security implications of an investment, the existence of other interested stakeholders and their orientation toward a transaction becomes amplified in importance. In particular, with respect to the last point, because national security considerations can generate political interest in a transaction, they can provide greater leverage to potential opponents to create controversy and, in turn, may require more active outreach to potential supporters to head off such controversy. In turn, the combination of national security with the fundamental due diligence questions – compliance, approvals and stakeholders – that accompany cross-border M&As activity should help determine transaction parties' ultimate strategy for securing approval within the US regulatory and institutional framework.

   With this background in mind, the remainder of this chapter will focus in greater depth on the challenging US regulatory and institutional issues associated with Chinese investment in particular: national security reviews undertaken by CFIUS; the role that the US Congress can play in Chinese transactions; certain characteristics of Chinese investment that can make such transactions challenging for the US system; and, finally, strategies that Chinese firms can deploy to manage regulatory and political risk.

3.2 NATIONAL SECURITY: CFIUS REVIEWS UNDER EXON–FLORIO/FINSA

Mergers and acquisitions of US businesses that may implicate national security are required to receive closer regulatory scrutiny from CFIUS. Of all potential investors, Chinese M&As are among the most likely to receive the greatest scrutiny. In fact, there have been several potential transactions involving Chinese firms that were abandoned after initial consultations with CFIUS or to avoid a potential negative Presidential decision.[36] In addition, the only divestment of an acquisition ever formally ordered by a President under Exon–Florio involved China – namely, President George H.W. Bush's order in 1990 requiring China National Aero Tech to divest MAMCO Manufacturing, Inc., an aerospace company based in Washington state.[37] Accordingly, as part of assessing the US regulatory framework for investment from China, this section provides a more detailed discussion of the CFIUS process and the statute that controls the CFIUS process – historically known as the Exon–Florio Amendment.

3.2.1 Overview of Exon–Florio

The principal US statute governing regulatory reviews of certain types of FDI is Section 721 of the Defense Production Act of 1950. Section 721 is known as the Exon–Florio Amendment after the original amendment to the Defense Production Act, which was adopted in 1988 amidst concerns over Japanese investment.[38] The Exon–Florio Amendment provided the President with express authority to review the national security effects of foreign acquisitions, mergers and takeovers.[39] The law was recently amended by the Foreign Investment and National Security Act of 2007 (FINSA).[40] FINSA left intact the essential elements of Exon–Florio, while also adopting amendments that provide for greater clarity on process, additional factors related to national security reviews under the statute, greater accountability among the agencies charged with implementing the statute, and enhanced Congressional oversight. The amended law as well as the implementing Executive Order and final regulations are provided as annexes.

Under the statute as amended by FINSA, CFIUS, as the President's designee, has authority to review "any merger, acquisition, or takeover . . . by or with any foreign person which could result in foreign control of any person engaged in interstate commerce in the United States."[41] The purpose of the review is to determine the effects of a transaction on US national security. CFIUS then must investigate any transaction that: (1) threatens to impair the national security of the United States, if the threat has not been mitigated during the initial review period; (2) would involve control by a foreign government;[42] or (3) would result in foreign control of US critical infrastructure, if such control threatens to impair US national security and the threat is not mitigated during the initial review period. The President ultimately has authority to suspend or prohibit any transaction that threatens to impair the national security if, after a full investigation is completed, "there is credible evidence that leads the President to believe that the foreign interest exercising control might take action that threatens to impair the national security," and other laws, except for the International Emergency Economic Powers Act,[43] "do not in the President's judgment provide adequate and appropriate authority for the President to protect the national security in the matter before the President."[44]

When Exon–Florio became law, President Reagan delegated his initial review and decision-making authorities, as well as his investigative responsibilities, to CFIUS,[45] an inter-agency body that President Gerald Ford originally established via Executive Order in 1975 to monitor and evaluate the impact of foreign investment in the United States.[46] Since the original adoption of Exon–Florio, CFIUS has been chaired by the Secretary of the Treasury. The fact that the Treasury Department, the most naturally pro-investment of all executive agencies, chairs a national security review process is both a symbolic and a practical nod to the importance of foreign investors and the open investment regime of the United States. The precise membership of the other CFIUS agencies has evolved since the original enactment. Under FINSA and its implementing Executive Order, CFIUS is comprised, in addition to the Treasury Department, of eight other voting members (the departments of Commerce, Defense, Homeland Security, Justice, State and Energy; the US Trade Representative; and the White House Office of Science and Technology); two permanent non-voting members (the Director of National Intelligence and the Department of Labor); and several other White House offices that act as observers and, on a case-by-case basis, participate in CFIUS reviews.[47]

By statute, CFIUS is authorized to review a transaction either upon a voluntary filing by either party to the transaction, or upon initiation of the committee. By regulation, CFIUS historically has also provided for any committee member to issue its own notice to the full committee requesting a review of a particular transaction.[48] The Treasury Department, as chair of CFIUS, also has considerable discretion on whether to accept a notice for review. Thus, for example, while the statute and regulations indicate a single party to a transaction may file a voluntary notice, it is extremely rare for the Treasury to deem a notice containing information and responses from only one party to a transaction sufficient to initiate a review.

Once CFIUS has sufficient information from both parties to begin a review, the statutorily mandated timetable for the review and "investigation" process is as follows:

- Initial 30-day review following receipt of notice.
- Forty-five-day "investigation" period for transactions deemed to require additional review following the initial 30-day period, including foreign government-controlled transactions.
- Formal report to the President at the end of the 45-day investigation period.
- Presidential decision within 15 days of receiving the formal report.

Notwithstanding these statutorily prescribed time-frames for reviews, there is no statute of limitations on the inherent Presidential authority in Exon–Florio (Box 3.1). The President can act at any point, even after a transaction has closed. Moreover, the President's decision is not subject to judicial review by US courts.[49] However, once a transaction has undergone a review, it receives a form of safe harbor: FINSA and the

---

BOX 3.1   EXON–FLORIO AND GREENFIELD FDI

The Exon–Florio law does not provide a mechanism for the Executive Branch to review greenfield investment in the United States. There are sound policy reasons for this distinction. First, by their nature, such investments at the outset will not involve contracts or assets that are inherently central to national security. By comparison, an existing business may have contracts with the US government or access to sensitive or classified information; it is much more difficult to implement measures to guard against potential foreign ownership threats once such assets and contracts exist than it is not to grant the contract or provide access to sensitive information in the first instance. Second, there are likely to exist adequate laws to address any national security risks posed by a greenfield investment. For example, if foreign investors wish to establish new communications lines, they would be subject to licensing authority from the Federal Communications Commission,[a] which in turn would seek input from the Department of Defense, Department of Justice, Federal Bureau of Investigation, and the Department of Homeland Security on the national security and law enforcement issues raised by the potential grant of such authority. Given these other controls on national security risks and the potential economic benefits that greenfield investments can present, the balancing of economic and security interests in the context of greenfield investments weighs strongly in favor of a lighter regulatory touch.

[a]   Communications Act of 1934, Section 214.

---

implementing Executive Order provide that the committee can unilaterally initiate another review only if certain limited circumstances are met – such as: the initial review was based on false or materially misleading information, or material omitted information, or if there has been an intentional material breach of a mitigation agreement upon which approval was originally conditioned.[50]

3.2.2   Exon–Florio in Practice

CFIUS is a unique regulatory body insofar as it operates by consensus[51] and includes multiple agencies with viewpoints that reflect their distinct missions and equities. There is an inherent tension between the security agency members of CFIUS, with their focus on defense, homeland security, counter-intelligence and law enforcement, and the economic agencies, which are more focused on trade and investment.[52] This tension is purposeful: having a consensus-based, confidential process that requires input from cabinet agencies with differing equities is intended to facilitate careful, objective determinations that permit investments where possible but without sacrificing important national security interests.

At the same time, one consequence of having a consensus-based, confidential process that involves so many agencies and with limited information flow to the regulated parties is that the process itself can be opaque. In turn, much in CFIUS practice turns not only on what is set forth in the statute and regulations, but on understanding which agencies have particular interests in a transaction, who the key decision-makers will be at those agencies, and what questions or considerations are likely to be of principal concern to those decision-makers. Particularly for the hardest cases, understanding the idiosyncrasies of agency interests and perspectives and what issues will matter to the key decision-makers is more a regulatory art than a science. Added to this mix is the fact that prominent transactions, especially those involving FDI from China, can attract media and political attention. (See in this context also Chapter 4 by Timothy Frye and Pablo Pinto in this volume.)

Accordingly, investors and US parties alike are well advised to understand and anticipate CFIUS's analysis and considerations before launching into transactions that might require a CFIUS review. This is particularly true for investments from China, which for reasons described below are more likely to raise both strategic and political issues. The critical threshold questions for a CFIUS review are: (1) whether there is foreign control over a US business; (2) if there is foreign control, whether the transaction may present any significant national security issues; and (3) if there are national security concerns, whether they can be mitigated through contractual commitments from the transaction parties or other permissible means. For additional data on CFIUS reviews, see Committee on Foreign Investment in the United States Annual Report to Congress – Public Version (December 2008).

Control over US business

The threshold question for any CFIUS review is whether there is a transaction that presents a foreign person[53] with "control" over a US business. Where there is potential foreign government ownership or influence, the control analysis is applied twice: first, in assessing whether a foreign entity will be controlling a US business; and second, in assessing whether in fact that foreign entity is itself controlled by a foreign government.

The definition of "control" in the CFIUS regulations is quite broad. "Control" means:

> [T]he power, direct or indirect, whether or not exercised, through the ownership of a majority or a dominant minority of total outstanding voting interest in an entity, board representation, proxy voting, a special share, contractual arrangements, formal or informal arrangements to act in concert, or other means, to determine, direct, or decide important matters affecting an entity.[54]

In practice, "control" is very much a functional definition. The amount of share interests and the right to board seats, for example, are highly relevant to finding control, but they are not necessarily determinative. Rather, CFIUS will take into consideration all relevant factors of a foreign person's ability to determine, direct or decide important matters affecting a US business. Among other things that CFIUS will consider are the right to direct or determine certain extraordinary corporate actions such as the sale of all assets or dissolution of an entity, as well as other "matters," such as approval over major expenditures, closing or relocation of facilities, the appointment or dismissal of managers and officers, and how non-public information is treated.[55] At the same time, certain standard minority economic protections – including certain negative rights and anti-dilution rights – may not, by themselves, confer control.[56]

In addition, there must be control over a US business. There are two important points with respect to the term "US business." First, CFIUS's jurisdiction extends only to the extent that a business undertakes activities in interstate commerce in the United States.[57] Thus, for example, in the case of a foreign acquisition of a Canadian company that has a sales office in the United States, CFIUS's jurisdiction would only extend to the sales office and its business in the United States. Second, a transaction does not necessarily have to involve an investment into or acquisition of a legally organized entity to trigger CFIUS's jurisdiction. For example, the sale of a business unit or of assets in the United States that includes customer lists, intellectual property and employees (that is, elements of a going concern) could be a covered transaction.[58]

National security analysis
FINSA formally requires CFIUS to conduct a risk-based analysis, informed by an analysis performed by the Director of National Intelligence, of the national security risk posed by any transaction.[59] This new statutory requirement simply codifies CFIUS's existing practice with respect to how it analyzes transactions.

Specifically, for every transaction, CFIUS engages in a three-part analysis comprised of: (1) a threat assessment focused on national security issues associated with the buyer; (2) a vulnerability assessment focused on national security issues associated with the US assets and business at issue; and (3) an assessment of the potential consequences that results from the "interaction between threat and vulnerability."[60]

What constitutes "national security" for CFIUS purposes – and, in turn, what might inform the threat and vulnerability assessments – is not defined precisely. Prior to FINSA, the Exon–Florio statute asked that the President assess the potential effects of a proposed transaction on:

- Domestic production needed for projected national defense requirements.
- The capability and capacity of domestic industries to meet national defense requirements, including the availability of human resources, products, technology, materials, and other supplies and services.
- The control of domestic industries and commercial activity by foreign citizens as it affects US capability and capacity to meet national security requirements.
- The sales of military goods, equipment or technology to a country that supports terrorism, or proliferates missile technology or chemical and biological weapons.
- US technological leadership in areas affecting US national security.[61]

These criteria focused primarily on protecting the defense industrial base and US technological leadership, which reflected Congress's preoccupation with two transactions: Fujitsu's potential takeover of Fairchild (which was deemed to threaten technological leadership), and an attempted takeover of Goodyear Tire and Rubber (a key defense contractor) by the British corporate raider Sir James Goldsmith.[62] However, Congress purposely did not adopt an exclusive list of national security considerations, instead indicating that the term "national security" is "to be read in a broad and flexible manner."[63] CFIUS, in turn, has never formally defined the term.

FINSA attempted to provide additional indicia of the meaning of "national security" in the CFIUS context – or at least to codify CFIUS's existing practice with respect to considering those factors. First, the amendments stated that "national security": "shall be construed so as to include those issues relating to homeland security, including its application to critical infrastructure."[64] This reflects the practice of CFIUS, at least since September 11, 2001, and in particular since the Department of Homeland Security was added to CFIUS in 2003, to examine transactions in sectors that relate to "critical infrastructure." CFIUS has defined "critical infrastructure" to mean "in the context of a particular transaction, a system or asset, whether physical or virtual, so vital to the United States that the incapacity or destruction of the particular system or asset . . . over which [foreign] control is acquired . . . would have a debilitating impact on national security."[65] Under this definition, not every foreign investment occurring in a critical infrastructure sector will be covered by CFIUS. Rather, it is the particular character of the assets and business at issue in the particular transaction that matters for CFIUS's purposes.

Second, FINSA codified many of the factors already discussed as additional indicia for the President to consider in assessing the national security impact of a transaction. Specifically, it added the following factors for the President to consider:

- The potential national security-related effects on United States critical infrastructure, including major energy assets.
- The potential national security-related effects on United States critical technologies (which means "critical technology, critical components, or critical technology items essential to national defense," subject to regulations issued by CFIUS).[66]
- Whether the covered transaction is a foreign government-controlled transaction.
- For transactions involving foreign government control that result in an investigation, whether the host country adheres to non-proliferation regimes, whether the host country presents any risk of transshipment of export and military-controlled items, and the relationship of the host country to US counterterrorism efforts.
- The long-term projection of United States requirements for sources of energy and other critical resources and material.[67]

Third, FINSA required CFIUS to issue guidance on the types of transactions that the committee has reviewed and that have presented national security considerations. This includes transactions that may constitute covered transactions that would result in control of critical infrastructure relating to United States national security by a foreign government or an entity controlled by or acting on behalf of a foreign government. However, in providing this guidance, CFIUS was also obligated to preserve the statutory confidentiality afforded. To strike this balance, the guidance issued by CFIUS ultimately offered a measure of additional clarity in identifying transactions that present "national security considerations," while also largely repeating the aforementioned statutory factors for national security and the information requests contained in the CFIUS regulations.[68]

Beyond the guidance and an enhanced number of information requests in the final regulations under FINSA, there are other unidentified factors that CFIUS will consider in its national security analysis. A more analytical list of factors that CFIUS considers is provided below at Table 3.1. In section 3.4, this chapter will examine how characteristics of Chinese FDI relate to some of these factors, including the connection of a foreign company to its home country government; its reputation for compliance on regulatory issues related to national security, such as export control laws; the perception of a

Table 3.1   Factors considered by CFIUS in national security analysis

Foreign acquiror	US company
• The acquiror's reputation for compliance with laws and regulations, with a particular focus on export control compliance and/or prior commitments to CFIUS. • The reputation of the acquiror's home country for cooperating on important US national security policy objectives, including non-proliferation and counter-terrorism matters. • The reputation of the acquiror's management, including whether the acquiror's officers and directors have any past or current connection to the home country's military or intelligence agencies. • The reputation of the acquiror's home country for commercial or state espionage. • Whether the acquiror does business in countries subject to US embargoes (e.g., Iran, Democratic People's Republic of Korea, Sudan, Cuba). • Whether the transaction could aid the military or intelligence capabilities of a foreign country with interests adverse to those of the United States. • Whether the acquiror is likely to move critical technology or key products offshore. • Whether a foreign government exercises control or influence over the acquiror. • How the acquiror is financing the transaction, and whether the financing would give any other party, including a foreign government, control over the aquiror or the transaction.	• The assets of the US target company, including whether those assets themselves are part of US critical infrastructure, supply US critical infrastructure, or otherwise could be a threat (e.g., are assets or materials that could be used for terrorist purposes). • Government customers of the US company, including in the first instance defense customers but also including non-defense and intelligence customers. • Access of the US company to government systems. • Access to US government classified information (and, in turn, the existence of a US government approved facility security clearance). • The importance of the US assets to US law enforcement interests. • The importance of the US assets or technology to the defense supply chain. • What other assets or businesses are located near the US company. • What existing security procedures the US business has in place. • Whether US management will remain in place, and whether US citizens will occupy important security-related positions after the transaction. • The existence of sensitive technology, including export controlled technology. • The record of the US company on compliance issues, including in particular export control compliance. • The non-government customer base of the US company (i.e., whether the US company supplies a customer base that is critical to homeland or national security). • The level of competition in the applicable marketplace and, in particular, whether the US company occupies a dominant position in a market that involves important strategic products, services or technologies.

military rivalry with the foreign country; and the foreign country's reputation for commercial and state espionage.

Mitigation

If CFIUS – specifically, the agency or agencies with the primary security equities presented by a transaction – determines that a particular transaction presents national security risks, it will seek to mitigate the perceived threats by imposing conditions and/or extracting commitments from the parties to a transaction. Such conditions and commitments may take the form of a signed agreement with agreed-upon penalties between the transaction parties, on the one hand, and the relevant security agencies, on the other. Alternatively, parties have been requested to provide somewhat more informal "assurances" via a letter from the principals of the parties to the applicable agencies.

The types of commitments and assurances sought by CFIUS can vary. At the most basic level, they can be straightforward assurances that the foreign acquiror does not intend to change continued production levels, facilities in the United States or participation in certain US government programs. Such assurances also can include concomitant record-keeping and reporting obligations. On the other end of the spectrum, certain mitigation agreements impose various governance requirements and more costly and onerous security measures, including technical and physical security requirements, US government access to systems and personnel, testing and screening of personnel, and third-party auditing. The most extreme agreements also can limit a foreign acquiror's decision-making authority and access to the US company.

In adopting FINSA, the US Congress sought to clarify that mitigation agreements should only be adopted when: (1) the transaction causes an incremental increase in the risk to national security; (2) existing regulatory authority is not adequate to address the incremental risk; and (3) a "risk-based analysis" of the threat to national security has been performed and approved by the committee. Specifically, FINSA states that a mitigation agreement "may" be imposed "in order to mitigate any threat to the national security of the United States that *arises as a result of the covered transaction*" and that such an agreement "shall be based on a risk-based analysis . . . of the threat to national security of the covered transaction."[69]

The reports of the US House of Representatives and Senate that accompanied the Act reinforce Congress's intent that mitigation agreements should be used only where existing legal authorities are inadequate to protect national security. For example, the House report states:

> The Committee believes that mitigation agreements should address national security threats that arise *as a result of the covered transaction, when those threats cannot be adequately addressed by other areas of law or regulation.* The Committee believes that an important principle in the original Exon–Florio Amendment with respect to Presidential action should also apply to mitigation agreements. Specifically, *mitigation agreements should not be considered the first line of defense in addressing general national security concerns and should be focused on threats that arise directly from the transaction when other areas of law or regulation can not adequately mitigate those threats.*[70]

CFIUS has described its process for developing mitigation agreements in light of the FINSA amendments, as follows:

First, before CFIUS may pursue a risk mitigation agreement or condition, the agreement or condition must be justified by a written analysis that identifies the national security risk posed by the covered transaction and sets forth the risk mitigation measures that the CFIUS member(s) preparing the analysis believe(s) are reasonably necessary to address the risk. CFIUS must agree that risk mitigation is appropriate and must approve the proposed mitigation measures. Second, CFIUS may pursue a risk mitigation measure intended to address a particular risk only if provisions of law other than [Exon–Florio] do not adequately address the risk.[71]

Finally, while CFIUS agencies can bargain for various penalties, including agreed-upon damages figures, FINSA also makes clear that CFIUS can reopen a transaction for a material breach of a mitigation agreement if there is a finding of intentional breach by the lead agency and a finding by all of CFIUS that no other remedies are available.[72]

While the CFIUS process focuses on a specific class of transactions – that is, those that may raise legitimate national security issues – it can entail significant costs for FDI in certain types of US businesses, including ongoing compliance costs with mitigation commitments to which investors must agree to receive CFIUS approval.[73] In the most extreme cases, the Exon–Florio statute, as amended by FINSA, can serve as an absolute bar to certain acquisitions that present national security issues. As evidenced by the experience of Huawei Technologies, the risk of investment screening and the potential costs related to CFIUS is greater for Chinese investors. Accordingly, as part of any due diligence exercise that Chinese companies undertake when considering an acquisition or significant investment in a US business – and, likewise, as part of the US business's consideration of Chinese investment – it would be prudent to assess fully the risks and costs associated with a potential CFIUS review and to plan appropriately for addressing those risks. The concluding section of this chapter sets forth certain strategies and steps that Chinese investors can take to help manage such risks.

3.3 THE US POLITICAL LANDSCAPE FOR CHINESE INVESTMENT

Apart from CFIUS and other regulatory approvals, the US Congress can take an active interest in FDI and be an important institution for investors to consider and engage in the context of specific transactions. (See also Chapter 4 by Timothy Frye and Pablo Pinto in this volume.) This is particularly true for investments that present national security issues. In that regard, Congress's interest and attempted intervention in foreign investments has not been circumscribed to Chinese investment. A Japanese investment in Fairchild and a proposed British takeover of Goodyear Tire & Rubber Company originally led to the adoption of Exon–Florio. In 2000, members of Congress expressed concern over the sale of Silicon Valley Group, a semiconductor equipment manufacturer, to the Dutch company ASML Holding N.V., and in 2006 Congress famously intervened in the sale of US port terminals to the Emirati firm Dubai Ports World.[74]

There is no question, however, that Congress will likely to continue to be a more important institutional consideration for investments from China than it will be for FDI from virtually any other country. Indeed, in 2000, Congress created a bipartisan committee, the United States–China Economic and Security Review Commission (USCC), specifically "to monitor, investigate, and report to Congress on the national security implications of the bilateral trade and economic relationship between the United States and the People's Republic of China."[75] The USCC must submit an annual report to Congress, which includes recommendations for legislative and administrative action. In 2005, Congress directed the USCC to focus its work and study on proliferation practices, economic transfers, energy, US capital markets, regional economic and security impacts, US–China bilateral programs, World Trade Organization (WTO) compliance, and the implications of restrictions on speech and access to information in China.[76]

The experience of a number of Chinese companies – which can be defined broadly to encompass Hong Kong (China)-based companies as well – has proven the impact that Congress can have directly on individual transactions involving Chinese investors. These case studies include the transfer of port operations in Long Beach, California, to China Ocean Shipping Company (COSCO); the Hong Kong (China)-based company Hutchison Whampoa's acquisition of rights to operate the Panama Canal; China National Offshore Oil Corporation's (CNOOC) bid for Unocal; and, more recently, the proposed investment by Huawei Technologies (Huawei) in 3Com.

As described further below, these case studies demonstrate that Congress is an important consideration for FDI from China. However, as also described below, Congress does not always intervene in even high-profile transactions from China, and even if some members express concern over a particular investment – which is likely to be the case in any high-profile investment from China – that does not in all cases mean the transaction is politically doomed.

3.3.1   COSCO's Port Operations in Long Beach

The transfer of a former military base in Long Beach, California, to COSCO in 1997 provoked considerable criticism in Congress. Although several administration officials and a few members of Congress stated that the transaction posed no security concerns, the weight of the political response was negative, focusing on an alleged connection between COSCO and the People's Liberation Army (PLA) and the threat posed by having China operate the former naval station.

Rep. Duncan Hunter, one of the most vocal critics of the transaction, summarized the arguments of the opponents:

> COSCO is not a private enterprise. It is an arm of the Chinese government and an auxiliary to the People's Liberation Army . . . Chinese control of a 135-acre terminal in Long Beach would pose a number of security threats to the United States. The terminal obviously would become a center for Chinese espionage on the West Coast. And it also would give the Chinese a stable, high-powered listening post for the interception of communications throughout California and beyond. The Chinese would know every move the US military makes and could monitor training exercises as well as operational deployments. Beijing also could develop ways to interrupt, neutralize or mislead the command, control and communications networks upon which our military operations depend.[77]

However, the Pentagon and at least two members of Congress publicly stated that the deal posed no national security threat. Pentagon spokesperson Kenneth Bacon said: "There are no national security concerns attendant to expanding COSCO's presence in the United States."[78] Representatives Steve Horn and David Dreier wrote in a joint letter to their colleagues that, based on intelligence briefings from the Central Intelligence Agency (CIA), Office of Naval Intelligence, Coast Guard and Bureau of Customs: "there is no evidence that the agreement between the City and Port of Long Beach and the China Ocean Shipping Company is a national security issue."[79]

Nevertheless, Congress incorporated into the Defense Authorization Act for fiscal year 1999 restrictions that prohibited "any funding to be used to enter into or renew a contract with any company owned, or partially owned, by the People's Republic of China."[80] Long Beach and COSCO worked around the restriction by having other port tenants use the new facilities, with COSCO picking up the areas vacated by those tenants.[81]

3.3.2 Hutchison Whampoa Panama Canal Ports Acquisition

Two years after the uproar over COSCO, there was a similar Congressional reaction to Hutchison Whampoa's winning bid to acquire the rights to operate Atlantic and Pacific entrances to the Panama Canal. A number of Congressional leaders and retired military officers expressed concern over the transaction, with criticism centered on an alleged relationship between Hutchison Whampoa and the PLA, the strategic importance of the canal to US interests and the bidding process instituted by Panama:

- Sen. Trent Lott (R-MS) stated that Panama's decision to let Hutchison Whampoa operate ports at both ends of the canal meant: "the Chinese Communist Party will gain an intelligence information advantage by controlling this strategic chokepoint."[82]
- The former Chairman of all Joint Chiefs of Staff, Adm. (Ret.) Thomas Moorer, also weighed in, stating: My specific concern is that Beijing, operating through this company, has virtually achieved, without a single shot being fired, not just a beachhead but a stronghold at the Panama Canal."[83]
- Former Secretary of Defense Caspar Weinberger seemed to concur, stating: "The biggest threat to the canal is that in 1997 Panama granted a subsidiary of Hong Kong-based Hutchison Whampoa Ltd. a 25-year concession to operate the canal's Atlantic and Pacific entrances at Balboa and Cristobal."[84]
- Resolutions were introduced in both the House and the Senate calling for the Clinton administration to request that Panama investigate corruption charges related to the award of the port concessions to Hutchison Whampoa and nullify the concessions if corruption was found.[85]

However, Congress never took any formal action to block the Hutchison Whampoa deal in Panama, and other military leaders, administration officials and at least one senator viewed the transaction less critically and as motivated by commercial interests.

- Ambassador Peter F. Romero, Acting Assistant Secretary of State, Bureau of Western Hemisphere Affairs in the State Department stated in Congressional testimony: "We have concluded that the presence of Hutchison Whampoa in the ports of Balboa and Cristobal does not represent a threat to Canal operations or to US interests in Panama."[86] He explained that: "the process leading to the award to

Hutchison Whampoa has been reviewed by, inter alia, a Senate Foreign Relations Committee staff delegation and the Federal Maritime Commission. These studies concluded that though the bidding process was at best unorthodox, there did not appear to be discrimination against US companies."[87] He further emphasized that he had "asked the intelligence community to use all sources to look at any threats to the canal and where those threats might be coming from," and a classified report concluded that the "particular business arrangement of Hutchison-Whampoa, does not constitute a threat to canal operations."[88]

- Assistant Secretary of Defense Brian Sheridan noted similar conclusions in his Congressional testimony: "Our analysts have no evidence to suggest that China, through Hutchison Whampoa or any other firm, has the capability, the desire or the wherewithal to seek to control the Panama Canal after its transfer to Panama on 31 December 1999. Our analysts believe that . . . Hutchison Whampoa's motivations are commercial."[89]
- US Secretary of State Colin Powell similarly stated: "I have not found that the so-called 'presence' in the form of shipping companies and the like have created any danger to the Panamanian people, the Panamanian government, or to the canal itself. Our interests are served . . . I don't see anything that should cause . . . any great distress."[90]
- The US Ambassador to Panama, William Eaton, stated the US view of the Chinese interest in the canal as being "purely economic."[91]
- Sen. Carl Levin (D-MI) was one of the few members of Congress to challenge those who were opposed to the transaction, saying: "I would . . . note a statement of Henry Kissinger's that would be wise advice for us to follow, and at least I'm going to try to follow it, that in the domestic debate that we should not invent imaginary dangers of foreign influence threatening the security of the canal."[92]

3.3.3 CNOOC's Proposed Bid for Unocal

Graham and Marchick (2006, pp. 128–136) comprehensively reviewed the political firestorm that erupted over CNOOC's bid for Unocal in 2005. They identified five arguments put forth by opponents to the transaction: (1) the transaction put global energy sources at risk, due to the possibility of CNOOC hoarding Unocal's reserves for China's exclusive use, thereby compromising US national security interests that depend on secure supplies of oil and gas; (2) the CNOOC bid was an attempt by the Chinese government to control critical oil and gas supplies, and the control and accompanying revenues would strengthen China's government; (3) CNOOC's bid relied upon preferential loans from Chinese state-owned banks and CNOOC's state-owned parent, which put US companies at a competitive disadvantage; (4) CNOOC's acquisition of Unocal would have potentially facilitated the transfer of sensitive technologies to China; and (5) because the Chinese would never allow a US company to acquire a major Chinese oil company, based on reciprocity, the United States should not allow the transaction.[93]

Notwithstanding sound counter-arguments from supporters of the transaction, politics carried the day and overwhelmed CNOOC's bid. Congress's actions, which were detailed at length in Graham and Marchick, included the following:

- Multiple letters were written by Members of Congress to Cabinet-level officials in the Bush administration expressing concern over the transaction. More than three dozen members of Congress wrote to then Treasury Secretary John Snow asking that the potential transaction "be reviewed immediately to investigate the implications of the acquisition of US energy companies and assets by CNOOC and other government-controlled Chinese energy companies."[94] Senators Kent Conrad (D-ND) and Jim Bunning (R-KY) complained to US Trade Representative Rob Portman and Secretary of Commerce Carlos Gutierrez that CNOOC's bid was "inconsistent with China's WTO commitments," citing the financing terms for CNOOC as evidence that: "The proposed acquisition is not being conducted on commercial terms and has little commercial justification."[95]
- The House of Representatives was active in passing legislation expressing opposition to the CNOOC bid. It overwhelmingly (by a vote of 333 to 92) passed a bill prohibiting the Treasury Department's use of funds for recommending approval of the sale of Unocal to CNOOC.[96] It also approved, by a vote of 398 to 15, a non-binding resolution urging an Exon–Florio review of the bid.[97]
- The House Armed Services Committee held a hearing on the CNOOC–Unocal transaction on July 13, 2005.

Ultimately, Congress provided the death knell for CNOOC's bid by adopting an amendment to an energy bill requiring that the Secretaries of Energy, Defense and Homeland Security conduct a study of China's growing energy requirements and the implications of "such growth on the political, strategic, economic, or national security of the United States."[98] The amendment would have prohibited CFIUS from completing any review of a CNOOC–Unocal transaction for 141 days, which is 51 days longer than the maximum of 90 days established by the Exon–Florio Amendment – thereby greatly increasing the cost of the CNOOC bid. Faced with this pressure, CNOOC withdrew its bid.

3.3.4 Huawei's Proposed Investment in 3Com

In 2007 to 2008, Huawei's proposed joint investment with Bain Capital Partners in the telecommunications firm 3Com elicited concern from Congress. According to public filings by 3Com, Bain Capital Partners and Huawei:

> agreed to purchase 3Com . . . for $2.2 billion. Bain Capital will control 83.5 percent of the voting shares. Bain Capital will appoint 8 of 11 board members. Huawei will acquire a minority interest of 16.5 percent. Huawei will appoint 3 of 11 board members. Huawei can increase its equity by up to 5 percent (but no more), based on certain performance criteria, but cannot gain additional seats on the board or gain any measure of additional operational control.[99]

The Congressional response included the following actions and statements:

- A small group of principally Republican members of the House of Representatives introduced a proposed resolution opposing the transaction. Reciting a litany of alleged espionage-related activities attributed to China, Huawei's alleged ties to the PLA and other publicly reported concerns over Huawei's business, the proposed resolution specifically stated that the transaction "threatens the national security of the United States" and called on CFIUS to reject the transaction.[100]

- Sen. John Kyl (R-AZ), joined by 13 other senators, sent a letter to the Treasury Department urging that the transaction be closely reviewed under FINSA. The letter stated the senators' belief that: "Huawei has built and currently maintains most of the PLA's telecommunications backbone systems and is the Chinese military's preferred provider for a wide variety of telecommunications products." The letter went on to say that: "because of this long-standing and apparently deeply-engrained relationship between Huawei Technologies and the PLA, we are concerned about the national security implications of this acquisition for the United States."
- Senator Chris Bond (R-MO), the ranking Republican on the Senate Select Committee on Intelligence, stated: "It is troubling to me that a foreign military organization with interests in communications might obtain access to our security systems."[101]
- Representatives Peter Hoekstra and Duncan Hunter wrote to Treasury Secretary Paulson formally requesting CFIUS review of the transaction regardless of whether it was submitted for examination by the parties.[102] The letter stated in part: "This review should be conducted, and a determination made, as to whether this sale will in any way impact the national security of the United States or increase the vulnerability of US computer networks and telecommunications systems to Chinese intrusion." In an interview, Rep. Hoekstra (R-MI) said: "There is no doubt as to why the Chinese want a partnership with 3Com. They look at this as a key connection to stealing additional secrets from US corporations and from our national security apparatus."[103]
- The House of Representatives Committee on Energy and Commerce, chaired by Representative John Dingell (D-MI) and led on the Republican side by Ranking Member Joe Barton (R-TX), wrote to the Treasury Department on January 31, 2008 – in the middle of the investigation by CFIUS – that it intended independently to investigate the transaction, and requested that CFIUS respond to certain questions. The letter cited "growing apprehension" among Members of Congress over the deal and stated that concerns over national security "are more than justifiable, especially in light of recent increases in attacks on government and private networks [by Chinese military hackers]."[104]
- Representative Thaddeus McCotter (R-MI) made repeated statements, including on the House floor, calling on CFIUS to block the investment by Huawei.

On February 20, 2008, 3Com, Bain Capital and Huawei announced that they had withdrawn the transaction from CFIUS following their failure to reach a mitigation agreement that adequately addressed CFIUS's concerns.[105] On March 20, 2008, Bain Capital announced its intent to terminate the merger agreement with 3Com.[106]

3.3.5 The Political Environment Going Forward

The experiences of COSCO, Hutchison Whampoa, CNOOC and Huawei demonstrate that Congressional reaction to a potential investment is a factor that Chinese investors would be wise to consider and to strategize for. To be sure, the potential for a Chinese investment to become highly politicized – to the point that it might not be feasible – is significant. However, not all FDI from China has been subject to the same degree of Congressional scrutiny, and Chinese investors should not necessarily anticipate a Congressional environment that will always be as hostile as in the CNOOC case.

For example, the political reaction to Lenovo's acquisition of IBM's personal computer division was relatively mild. In that case, three Republican members of Congress – Henry Hyde, then chair of the House International Relations Committee; Don Manzullo, then chair of the House Small Business Committee; and Duncan Hunter, then Chair of the House Armed Services Committee – requested that CFIUS investigate the national security ramifications of the Lenovo–IBM deal. They warned that the sale could result in corporate assets and technology with military uses being passed to the Chinese, and the Chinese could use its new acquisition to conduct espionage activities in the United States. Representatives Hyde, Manzullo and Hunter indicated, however, that they were not necessarily opposed to the transaction going forward, so long as a proper review was undertaken. After the extended review by CFIUS that resulted in approval of the transaction, Congressional criticism was muted.

Other financial investments, while eliciting some concern on Capitol Hill, have also been less politicized. Senator Jim Webb (D-VA) expressed concern over CIC's minority investment in the US private equity company Blackstone,[107] but he was relatively isolated in making an issue of that investment. The Congressional reaction to CIC's investment in Morgan Stanley was even more muted. CITIC's proposed investment in the subsequently defunct Bear Stearns likewise caught the attention of Congress at the time but no Member issued exceptionally critical statements. Even in the case of 3Com-Huawei, the Congressional reaction arguably was milder than prior Chinese transactions, such as CNOOC.

The political environment for investment from China likely will remain dynamic for the foreseeable future, dependent upon tangential factors that may rise or fall quickly as well as the particular facts of a transaction and transaction timing. Those factors may include the overall health of the US economy, broader US–China trade balance issues, attention by the press and human rights groups on Tibet, debate in the US on sovereign investment, prominent press articles regarding potential Chinese espionage, and US sensitivities to energy prices and consumption. Election cycles also may contribute to the politicization of certain investments.

Yet, there also is arguably a stronger overall sense today among leadership and rank-and-file members of Congress that, for transactions that undergo a CFIUS review, the CFIUS process should be permitted to play out before even broaching the possibility of any Congressional intervention. In this regard, FINSA's increased accountability and reporting mechanisms and the additional formal role of the intelligence community in the CFIUS process may enhance the faith of US politicians in the CFIUS process and tamp down instincts to intervene.

3.4 SPECIAL CONSIDERATIONS OF CHINESE INVESTMENT

Why is certain M&A activity from China likely to attract greater scrutiny from CFIUS and perhaps be prohibited outright? What factors about particular Chinese transactions may present other institutional challenges, including creating greater political risk? Apart from certain interest groups and geopolitical issues, including human rights, there are at least six factors that may be presented by Chinese FDI that can present challenging national security and political issues: (1) the predominance of state ownership and the perceived ties of Chinese companies to the Chinese military; (2) the use of state subsidies to assist Chinese investors; (3) a perceived risk of espionage presented by a transaction; (4) the regulatory compliance record, including in particular export control compliance record, of Chinese companies; (5) the other markets in which the Chinese company may do business; and (6) a perceived rivalry between the US military and the Chinese military.

3.4.1 State Ownership and Control

As noted, FINSA formalizes a presumption of investigation in the CFIUS process where an acquiror is foreign government-controlled. Given the landscape of the Chinese economy and the strong history of Chinese companies being at least partly owned by the government, this issue of state control, and whether an entity is acting on the basis of commercial concerns or on behalf of government interests, may result in increased scrutiny when a Chinese company is involved.[108]

A 2008 US State Department report noted that the state-owned sector accounts for approximately 40 percent of China's (gross domestic product) GDP.[109] Indeed, as of 2008, the ten largest multinational enterprises in China were all state-owned enterprises (SOEs).[110] Most large publicly traded SOEs remain subject to substantial state control due to restrictions on the transfer of state-owned shares, which constitute a majority of shares issued by listed companies,[111] as well as state approval over officers in management positions.[112]

Many of the largest SOEs are also owned by the State-owned Assets Supervision and Administration Commission (SASAC), which has control over the budgets of the SOEs and has ultimate authority over approving M&As.[113] In addition, publicly listed firms have a parallel structure to their board – the firm's Party Committee, chaired by the Party Secretary, who reports to the Communist Party of China's Organizational Department. According to one study, the CEOs of the 53 largest SOEs in China are appointed directly by the Communist Party of China's Organizational Department.[114] Local governments or the Communist Party also can exercise control by informally influencing the composition of corporate boards and the corporation's management team.[115]

From the perspective of US government officials and politicians evaluating Chinese investment, even publicly traded Chinese companies that otherwise look and feel like Western companies not affiliated with the state may present government control issues. Ministries and agencies within China have served as incubation grounds for companies that were later spun off privately. The fact that the founders of these companies have their origins with the Chinese government can contribute to a view of the companies as government-affiliated or controlled. Furthermore, the Chinese government often retains shares in publicly traded company.

That even publicly listed Chinese companies can have ownership interests held by the government or be aligned in some way with the government even when there is no apparent state ownership (for example, if officials are tied to the government) is significant from the perspective of the US regulatory and political environment. SOEs comprise a high share of China's outward-bound FDI. Of the 30 Chinese companies that are the largest outward investors, only one – the Lenovo Group – is not officially state controlled.[116] Indeed, ten of these companies accounted for approximately 84 percent of all outward FDI from China between 2004 and 2006.[117] With this background, the US officials involved in the CFIUS process may start with the presumption that all Chinese companies seeking to invest in the United States are controlled by the Chinese government – and it will be left to the Chinese company to convince the US government otherwise.

3.4.2 State Subsidies

As the CNOOC experience with Unocal indicates, the funding that Chinese companies rely upon in making investments in the United States may be an important regulatory and political factor. First, on the regulatory front, such funding can be indicative of state control. As Graham and Marchick noted, one of the factors that CFIUS considers to determine government control is "contractual arrangements" and the "pledge or other transfer of any or all of the principal assets of the entity." As a contract, a loan agreement likely could be considered to meet these terms if it included a "pledge" of certain of the acquirer's assets as collateral.[118] Further, if an entity appears to be making an investment on non-market terms, CFIUS may question whether the transaction is purely a commercial transaction or, instead, reflects state-related interests and direction. In this regard, it is significant that four state-controlled banks – the Bank of China, the Industrial and Commercial Bank of China, the China Construction Bank, and the Agricultural Bank of China – are responsible for a sizeable portion of all commercial loans in China.[119] Financing from such state-controlled entities may impact CFIUS's threat assessment of the transaction.

State subsidies also can present policy questions that garner attention from Congress. For example, CNOOC reportedly received two low- or no-interest loans totaling $7 billion from its state-owned parent to make its bid for Unocal.[120] In response, members of Congress, in a joint letter to the President, expressed concern about the appropriateness of states subsidizing investment transactions to acquire scarce natural resources that are in high demand. They observed that, when government subsidies are directed toward such highly demanded and scarce resources: "any ensuing market distortions should be of particular concern . . . [because] [s]uch subsidies may facilitate the allocation of scarce resources to inefficient or less-efficient producers."[121] The OECD has noted that large Chinese SOEs:

> have inherent advantages in undertaking large foreign investments since they enjoy formal as well as informal support from the government in the area of finance, networking, information access, and administrative procedures. They can also rely on monopolistic power in their respective subsector in the domestic market which has been protected by the government.[122]

More to the point, state subsidies to Chinese companies can easily translate into political concerns over the impact of FDI from China on small and medium-sized US businesses. Indeed, in its 2007 report to Congress, the USCC claimed that subsidies from the Chinese government negatively impact market conditions for US companies, stating that:

"China's unfair trade practices, including . . . illegal subsidies for Chinese exports," harm small and medium-sized US manufacturers.[123]

Another policy concern related to state subsidies is that they obscure inherent inefficiencies or other weaknesses in SOEs. These weaknesses can include, for example, a high cost of production, inefficient capital–labor combinations and artificially determined product mixes and technology.[124] In the context of Chinese investment, subsidies to SOEs can raise questions, whether fair or not, about the SOE's ability to make efficient decisions and be a beneficial investor for the US company.

3.4.3 Commercial and State Espionage

Chinese FDI in certain sectors – in particular defense, aerospace, telecommunications and information technology – also can present regulatory and political challenges because of US concerns over Chinese commercial and state espionage. The US intelligence community has characterized the Chinese intelligence services as "among the most aggressive in collecting against sensitive and protected US targets,"[125] and the Department of Justice "consider[s] China to be one of [its] top counter-intelligence priorities."[126] The USCC claims: "Chinese espionage in the United States . . . comprises the single greatest threat to US technology," and "is straining the US counterintelligence establishment."[127]

According to the US government, China's intelligence-gathering is more complicated than traditional state espionage because it is decentralized, involving data collection through Chinese students, scientists, researchers and other visitors to the United States.[128] US officials have publicly claimed that there are over 3000 Chinese "front companies" operating in the United States whose purpose is to gather intelligence and technology.[129] While that may have been an exaggerated number, in response to the threat, the FBI reportedly increased the number of counter-espionage agents assigned to China from 150 in 2001 to more than 350 in 2007.[130] One-third of all economic espionage matters being actively pursued by the FBI in 2007 were reportedly tied to China.[131] Since the beginning of 2007, there have been at least a dozen guilty pleas or criminal charges resulting from alleged Chinese espionage activity in the United States.[132]

A frequently reported target of commercial and state espionage is the US technology sector. For example, according to a report to Congress, China accounted for almost half of the illicit attempts in the United States to obtain space-related technology between 1997 and 2005.[133] Concerns over Chinese industrial espionage in the technology sector also have not been limited to the United States. A senior official in Germany's domestic intelligence agency identified China as the most frequent source of industrial espionage against German companies, noting that: "China is intensively collecting information around the world – political, military and scientific data, and company strategies in order [to] close the gap in their [sic] technology developments as quickly as possible."[134]

The implications of these concerns over Chinese espionage are two-fold. First, Chinese FDI in defense, aerospace, telecommunications, IT and other high-technology sectors will face very close scrutiny from CFIUS and may not be permitted; if it is permitted, it would likely only be on the basis of an entirely passive investment and/or considerable mitigation commitments. Second, as the proposed Huawei–3Com transaction makes clear, the potential nexus between an individual investment from China and broader concerns over Chinese espionage will remain a focus for Congress.

3.4.4   Regulatory Compliance

A fourth special consideration for FDI from China is the issue of regulatory compliance by Chinese companies, including in particular with US export control laws. The importance of export controls as an ongoing compliance matter is described in section 3.1 above. However, the issue of export control compliance also may have a broader regulatory and political impact on the ability of Chinese firms to make investments in the first instance. As noted, under FINSA, CFIUS must formally consider compliance with the US export control regime when investigating a transaction that involves foreign government ownership. And, as noted, the US government believes that China focuses industrial espionage on the technology sector, with the purpose of obtaining cheap and easy access to technologies that might be restricted for transfer to China. Moreover, the US government has adopted stricter licensing requirements for export to China. Specifically, under the so-called "China Rule," items controlled on the Commerce Control List will generally be denied for export if they would "make a direct and significant contribution to Chinese military capabilities" or otherwise would be destined for "military end-use" in the People's Republic of China, even if such items would not need an export license in typical circumstances.[135]

Compliance with US export controls has taken on significance for certain Chinese investments in part because of the prevalence of reported violations involving Chinese nationals and firms. For example, the US has imposed sanctions against several Chinese companies for violating embargoes to sanctioned countries, including against Norinco, China's largest military conglomerate, for transshipments to Iran.[136] As a result of this history – and virtually irrespective of the compliance record of the particular Chinese firm at issue in a transaction before it – CFIUS will apply additional scrutiny to transactions involving Chinese investment in US companies possessing export-controlled technology.

Another compliance factor that may impact the regulatory and political environment for Chinese investment is the reputation of both the foreign investor and the US party for compliance with anti-bribery laws. As with export controls, ongoing compliance with the Foreign Corrupt Practices Act[137] is discussed in section 3.1 (and in the chapter by Lorraine Eden and Stewart Miller in this volume). And, as with export controls, the broader issue of FCPA compliance may be relevant to the ability of Chinese firms to invest in the United States.

First, as a political matter, ties between Chinese firms and the Chinese government and, in turn, any connection with public corruption, whether real or alleged, can be exploited politically by opponents of any particular investment.

Second, because so many Chinese firms are state-owned, there can be particular challenges for US firms dealing with Chinese business partners, even when the dealings occur in the United States. For example, a US firm may be interested in a particular investment from a Chinese firm because the partnership could also help open markets in China. However, in assessing that investment, the record and reputation of US management for regulatory compliance and the Chinese firm with respect to its own compliance can impact the trustworthiness analysis conducted by CFIUS. In particular, CFIUS may consider compliance with the FCPA and the corruption reputation of the buyer when performing its analysis. Thus, in part because of the state ownership characteristics of Chinese investors, the general compliance record of both the Chinese firm and the US firm in an M&A transaction – in particular, their respective reputations for export control and anti-bribery compliance – can take on added significance in the regulatory and political risk calculus associated with that transaction.

3.4.5   Investments in Other Markets

Closely related to concerns that US authorities may have over export control risks associated from Chinese investment are concerns over the markets in which a Chinese investor conducts business. In particular, US government authorities and Congress are focused on Chinese investment in countries subject to US sanctions, such as Iran, the Sudan and the Democratic People's Republic of Korea, as well as other countries where the US has proliferation concerns. Thus, for Chinese investors, CFIUS will consider the potential threat posed by the transaction for controlled materials and technology, including dual-use technology relevant to nuclear and missile proliferation, to be transshipped to countries such as Iran, Pakistan and the Democratic People's Republic of Korea.

In addition, given the level of Chinese energy-related investment in Iran and the Sudan, investments by the major Chinese energy SOEs in the US in particular may be more difficult politically. In 2005, CNOOC did not have major concessions in Iran or the Sudan; however, other large Chinese SOEs, Sinopec and China National Petroleum Corporation, had investments in Iran and the Sudan that contributed to the politically charged nature of CNOOC's bid for Unocal.

3.4.6   Military Rivalry

Finally, the United States' view of the Chinese military as an emerging strategic threat impacts the US regulatory and institutional environment for Chinese FDI. The National Defense Authorization Act for Fiscal Year 2000 required the US Department of Defense to issue an annual report to Congress on Chinese military power and strategy.[138] In its 2008 annual report, the Pentagon noted an increased "pace and scope of China's military transformation," "fueled by continued high rates of investment in its domestic defense and science and technology industries, acquisition of advanced foreign weapons, and far reaching reforms of the armed forces."[139] The report stated that, while "China's ability to sustain military power at a distance remains limited," China "has the greatest potential to compete militarily with the United States and field disruptive military technologies that could over time offset traditional US military advantages."[140]

The Pentagon's concerns over Chinese military objectives and strategic behavior are important for Chinese FDI for three reasons. First, to the extent Chinese FDI involves a state-owned company or CFIUS has questions about the connection of a Chinese investor to the Chinese government or military, CFIUS will assess the Chinese investment in terms of how it might strengthen the Chinese military or reduce the strategic standing of the United States military. This may well be a significant factor given that many of the largest Chinese SOEs have been involved in the production of military items.[141] Second, in turn, Chinese investments in the technology sector as well as in the energy or natural resource sectors will receive even greater scrutiny from the Defense Department – and the other CFIUS agencies likely will provide great deference to the DOD's interests in such transactions. Third, as CNOOC and Huawei Technologies experienced, the perceived threat of the Chinese military is an issue that resonates with Congress, and Chinese investments that arguably might benefit the Chinese military or have some connection to the military – even remotely – stand the greatest likelihood of becoming highly politicized.

3.5 CONCLUSIONS: STRATEGIC MEASURES FOR CHINESE FDI

Notwithstanding that Chinese SOEs and other investors may have inherent characteristics that, at least in the United States, raise their regulatory and, in particular, political risk profile, there are a number of practical measures that Chinese investors can take to help manage these risks and enhance the prospects of regulatory approval without political interference.

First, investors should understand the potential risks associated with any investment and be strategic about the sectors and US businesses in which to invest. The recent experience of Bain Capital, 3Com and Huawei Technologies reflects the perils of potentially underestimating the risk inherent in Chinese investments in certain sectors. Based upon the public statements of the transaction parties, it would appear from the outside that, to varying degrees, they may have underestimated the degree to which Huawei's proposed 16 percent interest in 3Com and minority representation in 3Com's Board would jangle regulatory and political nerves.[142]

This is not to argue that Bain Capital and Huawei Technologies should have refrained from pursuing the investment in 3Com, or that the decision by CFIUS to block the transaction was the right result. Outsiders to any transaction cannot know exactly the considerations that factored into the respective analyses of the transaction parties or CFIUS. However, the 3Com case does exemplify the importance for Chinese investors to conduct an informed regulatory and political risk analysis in connection with the due diligence evaluation of potential investments in the United States. In this regard, Chinese investors should be aware that certain US businesses, including those in the defense, aerospace, telecommunications, information technology and, to a lesser degree, energy sectors, will present considerable regulatory and/or political risk and may not be realistic transaction targets. Other assets may still be subject to CFIUS review but potentially will be less sensitive, such as chemicals and certain infrastructure (for example, sea ports). Even with these assets, however, political risk may remain high. And still other assets, such as real estate and manufacturers of consumer retail products, may present minimal regulatory and political hurdles even for Chinese investors. In each asset class, though, the same lesson remains: be smart about the investment and conduct a full risk analysis before proceeding.

Second, in connection with a long-term strategy to develop and grow their position in the US marketplace, investors from potentially sensitive regions and countries, including China, often are wise to initiate their entrance into the US merger market by picking up "low-hanging fruit" with their initial investments. This may mean taking a minority share in a non-sensitive US business with another US partner holding the majority share. It also could mean exploring greenfield investments, if those make economic sense.

Or, it may mean making a relatively easy acquisition that is likely to receive CFIUS approval. The benefit of the latter approach is that the investor becomes a known quantity to CFIUS, including through a full intelligence analysis by the Director of National Intelligence. Having this first-time review occur in the depressurized context of a non-sensitive transaction can help reduce questions and establish a better environment for larger transactions down the road.

Third, along similar lines, establishing a strong record of business in the United States can be helpful to ease concerns and address questions from certain regulatory bodies like CFIUS. Indeed, in virtually every CFIUS review, it is helpful, albeit far from dispositive, for the transaction parties to be able to note that the foreign investor is already selling products into the US market and has an established record of doing business in the US – the point being that the investment should not present any additional threat.

Fourth, measures to enhance corporate transparency of Chinese investors are important both for the CFIUS process and to help pre-empt potential criticisms from Congress. As described more fully above, among the characteristics that can make Chinese investment challenging for CFIUS and contribute to political risk are the perceived opacity of corporate governance structures and the belief that Chinese investors may benefit from government subsidies when making their investments. There is no magic bullet for any Chinese investor to address completely US government concerns over the investor's ties, perceived or actual, to the Chinese government. However, as a regulatory matter, CFIUS seeks to probe ownership structures, examine management of the foreign investor, understand business lines and practices, and examine the financing for transactions. In this regard, there are certain fundamental steps that Chinese companies can take to address these questions and create greater confidence that they are acting on commercial grounds. These include publishing annual reports with standard financial disclosures, briefing reporters and financial analysts on commercial strategies, using Western financial advisors and financing transactions solely on commercial terms, and in certain circumstances, offering briefings to CFIUS agencies regarding business plans and product developments.

Fifth, given the potential post-transaction compliance concerns that are frequently attributed to Chinese investment, being able to demonstrate a strong compliance program and culture to US authorities is another important measure to enhance prospects for successful investment in the United States. For example, having sound written policies and procedures for export control compliance and anti-corruption compliance, including training materials for employees, would reflect an understanding of US regulatory interests and enhance the reputation for the Chinese investor.

Sixth, in certain transactions, the Chinese investor may wish to join with a well-known and reputable US partner to pursue an investment or to defer to the US party on the opposite side of a transaction to take the lead in public statements and political strategy. Having a US partner obviously will not equate to a successful and quiet investment in all circumstances – after all, Huawei Technologies was the minority partner to Bain Capital's predominant position in the failed 3Com transaction. However, US parties will often be able to deliver political supporters, and involving US citizens in a transaction, in turn, may be prudent politically. The IBM–Lenovo transaction is one that demonstrates the potential import of having a strong US party to a given transaction. In that case, IBM, with its virtually unparalleled reputation both in the Executive Branch and in Congress, provided a strong voice to the rationale for the transaction. Lenovo, to its credit, exercised discipline and enabled IBM to take the higher profile publicly in the transaction. By comparison, executives from CNOOC and Huawei each made public comments that hurt their cause and contributed to political controversy. Huawei's chief marketing officer famously called US concerns over the transaction "bullshit."[143]

Seventh, it is important for all investors, including especially Chinese firms, to understand how business outside the United States can impact the ability to make investments in the United States. In particular, transacting business with and having significant investments in countries subject to US sanctions, including Iran, Sudan, the Democratic People's Republic of Korea and Cuba, can present regulatory compliance challenges as well as political risks for investments in the United States. Some potential investors may conduct a cost–benefit analysis of business opportunities in these sanction countries and conclude the risks, including risks of impact on US opportunities, outweigh the potential rewards. Others may reach the opposite conclusion. In all events, for those firms that seek to invest in the United States and that also conduct business in such sanctioned markets, it is imperative that they be thoughtful about how their various investments are structured and who is involved, to avoid legal minefields of US sanctions laws.

Eighth, and finally, Chinese firms potentially contemplating major acquisitions in the United States may wish to develop a comprehensive strategy – well before any investment is made – to help manage political risk, especially in Washington. Such a "Washington strategy" might include: a communications effort intended to help lay the groundwork for future investment and improve the investor's reputation among key Washington institutions; efforts to make the Chinese investor more transparent publicly as well as to key agencies and members of Congress, including by providing briefings to these audiences; and establishing a framework of third-party validators – that is, well-respected third parties who, when asked to comment about the Chinese firm, will be favorably inclined. Such a "Washington strategy" may also involve participating in the larger Washington policy-related environment outside the context of any particular transaction – such as by participating in events hosted by trade organizations and think-tanks and potentially even seeking opportunities to participate in certain industry organizations.

None of these measures is necessarily easy to implement. Even with the best intentions, Chinese firms may face resistance in pursuing certain of these measures – for example, certain members of Congress may not wish to meet directly with a Chinese firm, and other parties may be wary about being publicly associated with a prominent Chinese investor. Nor would these measures collectively insulate all Chinese firms against political and regulatory risk for all types of transactions. In the end, there will remain investments in certain US assets that may be entirely off-limits to Chinese companies because of regulatory considerations (that is, CFIUS would not approve the transaction), political considerations (the US Congress or state or local officials would interfere to the point of killing the transaction), or both.

Nevertheless, the United States maintains an official policy of welcoming investment. The challenge for Chinese investors, therefore, is to find the right transactions that enable them to invest in the US market without incurring regulatory or political trouble. This is the aim of the foregoing recommendations: namely, to help provide Chinese investors with a broad roadmap to lessen regulatory and political risk and avail themselves of the open investment environment in the United States.

NOTES

*   This chapter was prepared in the context of the Deloitte–Vale Columbia Center on Sustainable International Investment project on "Is the US ready for FDI from China?" For their insights and guidance throughout this project, I would especially like to thank Karl Sauvant, Clarence Kwan, Wendy Cai-Lee and Kris Knutsen, as well as the other authors in the project. I owe a special gratitude for the support and guidance of Mark Plotkin, and for the opportunity provided to me in this chapter by David Marchick. Finally, my love to Marnie, Chloe and Ian for tolerating the late nights and much more. Copyright © 2009 by Columbia University and Deloitte Development LLC. All rights reserved.
1.   President George W. Bush Statement on Open Economies (May 10, 2007), available at http://www.white house.gov/news/releases/2007/05/20070510-3.html.
2.   In 1977, the Carter administration had issued a policy statement recognizing that: "international investment will generally result in the most efficient allocation of economic resources if it is allowed to flow according to market forces," and "the United States has an important interest in seeking to assure that established investors receive equitable and nondiscriminatory treatment from host governments" Jackson (2007, p. 6) (internal citation omitted). In 1983, President Reagan issued a statement welcoming foreign investment, and clarifying the US government's "neutrality" position on international investment to include three objectives: liberalization of barriers to international investments abroad, encouraging FDI to assist in the economic development of developing countries and maintaining an open US economy to contribute to FDI. *Id*. p. 7 (internal citation omitted). The administration of George H.W. Bush then issued a statement promoting foreign investment in 1991. The Clinton administration, while not formally adopting a policy statement, sought the development of a Multilateral Agreement on Investment (MAI) among OECD countries that would have formally addressed various issues that hamper the free flow of investments, such as discriminatory treatment and creating dispute settlement mechanisms. *Id*. (internal citation omitted).
3.   Graham and Marchick (2006).
4.   See *infra* note 37 and accompanying text.
5.   See *infra* notes 105–106 and accompanying text.
6.   Hillary Clinton Press Release, "Hillary Clinton Promotes Plan for Strong Defense and Good Jobs in Indiana," Apr. 12, 2008 (claiming that Indiana lost 225 jobs when "Chinese investors moved the operations of Magnaquench to China" and, as a result, "today the US military buys 'neo' magnets from China."); see also Tapper (2008).
7.   15 U.S.C. §§ 78m, 78dd.
8.   Department of Commerce (2007).
9.   For a thorough overview of the basics of the US foreign trade control regime, see Flanagan and Brown (2003); see also GAO (2006).
10.   15 C.F.R. Parts 730 to 774.
11.   22 C.F.R. Parts 120-130.
12.   22 C.F.R. Pt. 121.
13.   Flanagan and Brown (2003), pp. 15–16.
14.   The restrictions are even broader with respect to the Cuba embargo, which applies to "persons subject to the jurisdiction of the United States" – a term that can mean even foreign affiliates are subject to control of a US party and, in turn, the Cuba embargo.
15.   US Department of Commerce Bureau of Industry and Security, "Deemed Export Questions and Answers," available at http://www.bis.doc.gov/deemedexports/deemedexportsfaqs.html#1 (citing 15 C.F.R. § 734.2(b)(3)). For additional background on deemed export control rules, see Christensen (2001).
16.   *Id*.
17.   GAO (2006), p. 8.
18.   For a thorough overview of the FCPA's criminal provisions and pitfalls, see Wolff and Clarke (2007).
19.   *Id*. at 13. FCPA also applies to "issuers" of registered securities in the United States, which can include foreign companies that trade American Depository Receipts in US financial markets.
20.   *Id*. at 15 (citing 15 U.S.C. § 78dd-1(f)(1) and *U.S. v. DPC (Tianjin) Co. Ltd*, No. 05 Cr. 282 (C.D. Cal. May 20, 2005)).
21.   *Id*. (quoting 15 U.S.C. § 78dd-3(a)).
22.   Levin at ¶ 503.3.2.1 (2007).

23. *Id.* at ¶ 503.3.2.2; see also Tafara (2008).
24. See Form F-4, Registration Statement Under the Securities Act of 1933, available at http://www.sec.gov/about/forms/formf-4.pdf.
25. Levin (2007) at ¶ 503.3.2.4.
26. *Id.* at ¶ 503.3.2.7.
27. *Id.* at ¶ 503.2.1.
28. *Id.* at ¶ 503.3.3.
29. 15 U.S.C. § 18.
30. 15 U.S.C. § 18a.
31. Figure current as of 2008.
32. FCC (2007) (hereinafter "FCC Guidelines").
33. *Id.* at 10.
34. Felsenfeld (2006).
35. Alvarez (2008).
36. Graham and Marchick (2006), p. 102.
37. President Bush's order is available at http://www.presidency.ucsb.edu/ws/index.php?pid=18108.
38. In particular, Fujitsu's attempted acquisition of an 80 percent interest in the US semiconductor manufacturer Fairchild prompted a backlash on Capitol Hill that ultimately led to the adoption of Exon–Florio. See *infra* note 62 and accompanying text.
39. Omnibus Trade and Competitiveness Act of 1988, § 5021, Pub. L. 100-418 (1988), codified at 50 U.S.C. App. § 2170. The original authorization was scheduled to expire in 1991, but was made permanent by Section 8 of Defense Production Act Extension and Amendments of 1991, Pub. L. 102-99 (1991).
40. Pub. L. 110-49 (2007) (FINSA).
41. *Id.* § 2(a)(3) (codified at 50 U.S.C. App. § 2170(a)(3)).
42. An investigation of such transactions is not required if the Secretary or Deputy Secretary of the Treasury, and an equivalent official at the "lead" CFIUS agency, determine that the proposed transaction will not impair national security. The concept of a "lead" CFIUS agency is discussed further below. For those acquisitions by state-owned enterprises that reach the investigation stage, the law requires an assessment of the foreign country's compliance with US and multilateral counter-terrorism, nonproliferation and export control regimes.
43. 50 U.S.C. §§ 1701–1706.
44. FINSA, § 6 (codified at 50 U.S.C. App. § 2170(d)).
45. Executive Order 12661 (1988).
46. Executive Order 11858 (1975).
47. Executive Order 13456, Further Amendment of Executive Order 11858 Concerning Foreign Investment in the United States § 3 (2008) (hereinafter "FINSA Executive Order"). The additional White House offices are the Office of Management and Budget, the Council of Economic Advisers, the Assistant to the President for National Security Affairs, the Assistant to the President for Economic Policy, and the Assistant to the President for Homeland Security and Counterterrorism.
48. 31 C.F.R. § 800.401.
49. FINSA, § 6 (codified at 50 U.S.C. App. § 2170(e)).
50. FINSA, § 2 (codified at 50 U.S.C. App. § 2170(b)(1)(D)); FINSA Executive Order § 7(f).
51. The drive toward a consensus reflects the desire among CFIUS members to avoid sending a transaction to the President, if at all possible. Thus, there is internal pressure among the CFIUS cabinet membership to form a consensus view on every transaction. In the rare instance when a transaction does proceed all the way to the President for a decision, the reports prepared for the President by the member agencies of CFIUS can reflect differing views.
52. Graham and Marchick (2006), pp. 34–35.
53. While perhaps less significant for purposes of this chapter – given its focus on inward-bound investment – it is important to note that for CFIUS persons, "foreign person" includes any foreign national, foreign government, or entity over which "control" is exercised by a foreign national, foreign government, or another foreign entity. Thus, controlling acquisitions of US businesses by US subsidiaries of foreign companies fall within the jurisdiction of CFIUS if they potentially impact US national security.
54. 31 C.F.R. § 800.204(a).
55. *Id.*
56. *Id.* at § 800.204(c).
57. *Id.* at § 800.226.
58. *Id.* at § 800.301(c)(Examples 6 and 7).
59. Pub. L. No. 110-049, §§ 2,5, 50 U.S.C. App. §§ 2170(b)(4), (*l*)(1)(B).
60. Department of Treasury, Guidance Concerning the National Security Review Conducted by the

Committee on Foreign Investment in the United States, 73 Fed. Reg. 74567, 74569 (Dec. 8, 2008) (CFIUS Guidance).

61. 50 U.S.C. App. § 2170(f).
62. Alvarez (1989); Graham and Marchick (2006), p. 41.
63. Statement of Senator Exon, Congressional Record 134 (April 25, 1988): S 4833.
64. FINSA § 2, 50 U.S.C. App. § 2170(a)(5).
65. 31 C.F.R. § 800.208.
66. A working group of US government agencies, chaired by the Department of Treasury, has identified 14 sectors in which critical technologies arise: advanced materials and processing; chemicals; advanced manufacturing; information technology; telecommunications; microelectronics; semiconductor fabrication equipment; military-related electronics; biotechnology; professional and scientific instruments; aerospace and surface transportation; energy; space systems; and marine systems. See Report to Congress on Foreign Acquisition of and Espionage Activities Against US Critical Technology Companies (Unclassified) 9-10 (Sept. 2007).
67. FINSA § 4; 50 U.S.C. App. § 2170(f)(6)-(10).
68. That information focuses on certain obvious national security criteria, including whether the US company has any contracts with US defense or intelligence agencies or defense contractors, whether the US company has technology that is controlled under export control laws, whether a foreign government controls or directs the foreign acquiror, and what the foreign acquiror's intentions are for the US operations. 31 C.F.R. § 800.402(c).
69. FINSA § 5, 50 U.S.C. App. § 2170(l)(1)(A)-(B) (emphasis added).
70. H.R. Rep. No. 110-24, at 16 (Feb. 23, 2007) (emphasis added).
71. CFIUS Guidance, op. cit, 73 Fed. Reg. at 74568.
72. FINSA § 2, 50 U.S.C. App. § 2170(b)(1)(D).
73. In addition to the investment review provided by CFIUS, it should be noted that the Department of Defense, US intelligence agencies, the Department of Energy, and the Nuclear Regulatory Commission have independent authority to review and restrict investments into companies that, as contractors to those agencies, possess US government classified information. These authorities are less likely to be relevant to Chinese investors; it would be extremely unlikely for a Chinese company to be permitted to acquire outright – or even to make an investment that would be deemed "controlling" – in a business that is part of the defense industrial base or that possesses any classified contracts with the US government.
74. Graham and Marchick (2006), pp. 124–125.
75. Floyd D. Spence National Defense Authorization Act for 2001 § 1238 (codified at 22 U.S.C. § 7002).
76. Pub. L. No. 109-108.
77. Hunter (1997).
78. Kreischer (1997).
79. March 25, 1997 Dear Colleague letter quoted in CRS study on "Long Beach: Proposed Lease by China Ocean," 97-476 (June 3, 1998).
80. Department of Defense Appropriations Act of 1999, Pub. L. 105-262, § 8060, 112 Stat. 2311 (Oct. 17, 1998).
81. "The town the Navy left behind: Long Beach reinvents itself as tourist, shipping port of call," CNN.
82. Leavitt et al. (1999), quoting letter from Sen. Lott to then Defense Secretary Cohen.
83. "Impact of transfer of Panama Canal: Hearing before the House Banking and Financial Services Domestic and International Monetary Policy", 106th Cong., 1st Sess. 5 (1999) (testimony of Admiral Thomas Moorer).
84. Weinberger (1999).
85. Senate Concurrent Resolution 61, "Expressing the Sense of the Congress Regarding a Continued United States Security Presence in Panama," 145 Cong. Rec. S12841 (daily ed.) 106th Cong., 1 Sess. (1999); House Concurrent Resolution 186, "Expressing the Sense of the Congress regarding a continued United States security presence in the Panama Canal Zone," 145 Cong. Rec. H8385 (daily ed.), 106 Cong., 1st Sess. (1999).
86. "To Receive an Update on Selected Regional Issues to Include: Colombia and US Policy; Legislative Elections in Haiti and US Troop Withdrawal; Status of Counterdrug Forward Operating Locations; US Cuba Counter-Narcotics Cooperation Proposal; Chinese Influence in the Panama Canal; Political Events in Venezuela; and Status of US Property Claims in Nicaragua," 106 Cong., 1st Sess. 11 (1999) (testimony of Peter Romero).
87. *Id.*
88. *Id.*
89. "Panama Canal Security: Panel Two of a Hearing of the Senate Armed Services Committee," 106th Cong., 1st Sess. (1999) (testimony of Brian Sheridan).
90. Gertz (2001).

91. Hirsch (2006).
92. "Panama Canal Security: Panel One of a Hearing of the Senate Armed Services Committee," 106th Congress, 1st Sess. (1999).
93. Graham and Marchick (2006), p. 120.
94. Letter to Treasury Secretary John W. Snow from Representative William J. Jefferson et al. (undated).
95. Letter to the Honorable Carlos M. Gutierrez and Ambassador Rob Portman from Senators Kent Conrad and Jim Bunning (July 11, 2005), available at conrad.senate.gov.
96. H. Amdt. 431 offered to HR 3058 by Rep. Carolyn Kilpatrick of Michigan, approved in roll-call vote no. 353, 109th Congress, 1st sess., 151 *Congressional Record* H5515 (daily ed. June 30, 2005).
97. 109th Congress, "Expressing the Sense of the House of Representatives that a Chinese State-Owned Energy Company Exercising Control of Critical United States Energy Infrastructure and Energy Production Capacity Could Take Action That Would Threaten to Impair the National Security of the United States," (1st sess., 151 *Congressional Record* H194 (daily ed. January 25, 2005): § 1, 4). The resolution was offered by Rep. Pombo and approved in roll call vote no. 360.
98. Energy Policy Act of 2005, § 1837, Public Law 109-58, US Statutes at Large 119, 594.
99. 3Com 8-K, filed Oct. 11, 2007.
100. H. Res. 730, 110th Cong., 1st Sess. (introduced Oct. 10, 2007).
101. "GOP Urges Probe in China Firm Deal," *Washington Times*, Oct. 4, 2007.
102. Id.
103. *Id.*
104. "Letter to Secretary of Treasury Henry Paulson from Chairman Dingell, Ranking Member Barton, and Representatives Rush and Whitfield," January 31, 2008, available at http://energycommerce.house.gov/Press_110/110-ltr.013108.DOTreasury.CFIUS.pdf.
105. 3Com Press Release, "3Com and Bain Capital Partners Announce Mutual Withdrawal of CFIUS Application," February 20, 2008.
106. 3Com Press Release, "3Com Announces Intent to Pursue Break-up Fee from Bain Capital," March 20, 2008.
107. "Senator Raises China Concerns on Blackstone," Reuters, June 21, 2007, available at http://www.cnbc.com/id/19322421.
108. Graham and Marchick (2006), pp. 105–106.
109. US Department of State, Background Note: China (April 2008), available at http://www.state.gov/r/pa/ei/bgn/18902.htm.
110. OECD (2008) (hereinafter "Draft OECD Report on China OFDI").
111. Kwan (2006), Graham and Marchick (2006), pp. 106–107.
112. Of nearly 1400 publicly listed Chinese companies at the end of 2005, nearly two-thirds of the outstanding shares were non-tradeable. Morck et al. (2007). More than half of the non-tradeable shares were owned directly by governmental entities, and the remainder were owned principally by other large SOEs or state-managed investment funds (*Id.*).
113. Hemerling et al. (2006); Draft OECD Report on China OFDI, op. cit., ¶ 104.
114. Morck et al. (2007), p. 13.
115. Graham and Marchick (2006), p. 107.
116. Morck et al. (2007), at 6.
117. Draft OECD Report on China OFDI, op. cit., ¶ 33 (internal citation omitted).
118. Graham and Marchick (2006), p. 116.
119. Morck et al. (2007), p. 14.
120. Sloan (2005).
121. Grassley and Baucus (2005); Graham and Marchick (2006), p. 116.
122. Draft OECD Report on China OFDI, op cit., ¶ 35.
123. United States–China Economic and Security Review Commission, Executive Summary: Annual Report to Congress 3 (2007), available at http://www.uscc.gov/annual_report/2007/executive_summary.pdf.
124. Eckaus (2004); Boardman (2001).
125. Statement of John Negroponte, Director of National Intelligence, Before the Senate Select Committee on Intelligence, January 11, 2007.
126. Testimony of Alberto Gonzalez, Attorney General, Before the House Judiciary Committee, April 6, 2006.
127. USCC Executive Summary for 2007 Report, op. cit., p. 6.
128. Report of the House of Representatives Select Committee on US National Security and Military/Commercial Concerns with the People's Republic of China, Chapter 1: Commercial and Intelligence Operations – PRC Acquisition of US Technology, at 2, 19, H. Rep. 105-851 (105th Cong. 2d Sess.) ("Cox Report"); Central Intelligence Agency and Federal Bureau of Investigation Report to Congress on Chinese Espionage Activities Against the United States (1999).

129. "FBI Spy Chief asks Public for Help," CNN.com, Feb. 10, 2005, available at http://www.cnn.com/2005/US/02/10/fbi.espionage/index.html.
130. Lynch (2007).
131. *Id.*
132. Warrick and Johnson (2008), p. A1.
133. Annual Report to Congress on Foreign Economic Collection and Industrial Espionage 12 (2005), available at http://www.fas.org/irp/ops/ci/docs/2005.pdf.
134. "Foreign intelligence services spy on German companies," DW-World.DE, November 11, 2007, available at http://www.dw-world.de/dw/article/0,2144,2879734,00.html (last accessed August 28, 2008).
135. Department of Commerce (2007).
136. Graham and Marchick (2006), p. 110.
137. 15 U.S.C. §§ 78dd-1, et seq.
138. Pub. L. 106-65, § 1202 (2000).
139. US Department of Defense (2008), p. I.
140. *Id.* (internal quotation and citation omitted).
141. Graham and Marchick (2006), pp. 114–115.
142. In a supplemental to a proxy statement issued by 3Com in February 2008, the company disclosed: "The Board of Directors considered Huawei's participation in the proposed transaction as a factor in their recommendation of the Merger. The Board believed that Huawei's participation increased deal certainty." 3Com Corporation, Proxy Statement Pursuant to Section 14(a) of the Securities Exchange Act of 1934 (Feb. 19, 2008).
143. Parker and Taylor (2008).

REFERENCES

106th Congress, "Expressing the Sense of the Congress Regarding a Continued United States Security Presence in Panama," (145 Cong. Rec. S12841 (daily ed.), (1st Sess. 1999)).

106th Congress, "Expressing the Sense of the Congress Regarding a Continued United States Security Presence in the Panama Canal Zone," (145 Cong. Rec. H8385 (daily ed.), (1st Sess. (1999)).

106th Congress, "Panama Canal Security: Panel One of a Hearing of the Senate Armed Services Committee," (1st Sess. (1999)).

109th Congress, "Expressing the Sense of the House of Representatives that a Chinese State-Owned Energy Company Exercising Control of Critical United States Energy Infrastructure and Energy Production Capacity Could Take Action That Would Threaten to Impair the National Security of the United States," (1st Sess., 151 *Congressional Record* H194 (daily ed. January 25, 2005)).

Alvarez, Jose E., "Political Protectionism and United States International Investments Obligations in Conflict: The Hazards of Exon Florio," (30 *Virginia Journal of International Law*, 1, 101 (1989)).

Alvarez, Scott, "Testimony Before the Senate Committee on Banking, Housing, and Urban Affairs," (Apr. 24, 2008).

Boardman, Harry G., "The Business(es) of the Chinese State," (Blackwell Publishers 2001).

Central Intelligence Agency and Federal Bureau of Investigation Report to Congress on Chinese Espionage Activities Against the United States (1999) available at http://www.fas.org/irp/threat/fis/prc_1999.html.

Christensen, Larry E., "Technology and Software Controls," in *Coping with US Export Controls* (Practicing Law Institute 2001).

CNN.com, "The Town the Navy Left Behind: Long Beach Reinvents Itself as Tourist, Shipping Port of Call," available at http://www.cnn.com/SPECIALS/cold.war/experience/the.bomb/route/08.long.beach/ (accessed November 19, 2007).

Committee on Foreign Investment in the United States Annual Report to Congress – Public Version (December 2008).

Department of Commerce, Bureau of Industry and Security, Revisions and Clarification of Export and Reexport Controls for the People's Republic of China (PRC); New Authorization Validated

End-User; Revision of Import Certificate and PRC End-User Statement Requirements, 72 Fed. Reg. 33646 (June 19, 2007).

Eckaus, Richard S., "China's Exports, Subsidies to State Owned Enterprises and the WTO," (MIT Dept. of Economics Working Paper No. 04-35 (2004)) available at http://papers.ssrn.com/sol3/papers.cfm?abstract_id=611941.

FCC, Foreign Ownership Guidelines for FCC Common Carrier and Aeronautical Radio Licenses, (Nov. 17, 2007).

Felsenfeld, Carl, *Banking Regulation in the United States* (Second Edition), (Juris Publishing 2006).

Flanagan, Peter L. and Eric D. Brown, "Foreign Trade Controls," E-Commerce Law and Business (Plotkin, Wells, and Wimmer, eds, Aspen 2003).

GAO, "Export Controls: Agencies Should Assess Vulnerabilities and Improve Guidance for Export-Controlled Information at Universities," (Dec. 2006) available at http://www.gao.gov/new.items/d0770.pdf (hereinafter "GAO Report on Export Controls").

Gertz, Bill, "Powell: China Poses no Danger in Canal," (*Washington Times*, Feb. 7, 2001).

Graham, Edward M. and David M. Marchick, *US National Security and Foreign Direct Investment* (Institute for International Economics 2006).

Grassley, Charles E. and Max Baucus, "Grassley, Baucus Express Concern over Potential CNOOC–Unocal Deal," (press release, July 13, 2005) available at http://grassley.senate.gov.

Hemerling, Jim, David C. Michael, and Holger Michaelis, "China's Global Challengers: The Strategic Implications of Chinese Outbound M&A," (The Boston Consulting Group 2006).

Hirsch, Steve, "Panama Canal expansion seen as positive," (*Washington Times*, Oct. 24, 2006).

House of Representatives Select Committee on US National Security and Military/Commercial Concerns with the People's Republic of China, Chapter 1: Commercial and Intelligence Operations – PRC Acquisition of US Technology, H. Rep. 105-851 (105th Cong. 2d Sess.).

Hunter, Duncan, "US Turns a Blind Eye as China Hits the Beach," (*Insight on the News*, Apr. 21, 1997).

Jackson, James, "Foreign Direct Investment: Current Issues," Congressional Research Service Report to Congress (Apr. 27, 2007).

Kreischer, Otto, "Navy sees no national security threat in Cosco lease," (*Copley News Service*, April 1, 1997).

Kwan, Chi Hung, "Who Owns China's State-owned Enterprises? Toward Establishment of Effective Corporate Governance," (*China in Transition* July 28, 2006) available at http://www.rieti.go.jp/en/china/06072801.html.

Leavitt, Paul, K. Kiely and J. Drinkard, "Lott Concerned by China's possible Influence over Canal," (*USA Today*, August 13, 1999).

Levin, Jack, "Structuring Venture Capital, Private Equity, and Entrepreneurial Transactions," (Ginsburg and Rocap, eds, Aspen 2007).

Lynch, David J., "FBI Goes on Offensive against China's Tech Spies," (*USA Today*, July 23, 2007) available at http://www.usatoday.com/money/world/2007-07-23-china-spy-2_N.htm (last accessed November 20, 2007).

Marchick, David, "Swinging the Pendulum Too Far: An Analysis of the CFIUS Process Post-Dubai Ports World", (National Foundation for American Policy 2007).

Moorer, Thomas, "Impact of Transfer of Panama Canal: Hearing before the House Banking and Financial Services Domestic and International Monetary Policy," (106th Cong., 1st Sess. 5 (1999)).

Morck, Randall, Bernard Yeung and Minyuan Zhao, "Perspectives on China's Outward Foreign Direct Investment," (Working Paper Aug. 2007).

OECD, Directorate for Financial and Enterprise Affairs, "Draft report: China's outward foreign direct investment," DAF/INV/WD(2008) at 9933-35 (Feb. 22, 2008).

Parker, Andrew and Paul Taylor, "Huawei rails at 3Com deal security concerns," (*Financial Times*, Feb. 12, 2008).

Report to Congress on Foreign Acquisition of and Espionage Activities Against US Critical Technology Companies (Unclassified) (Sept. 2007).

Romero, Peter (testimony), "To Receive an Update on Selected Regional Issues to Include:

Colombia and US Policy; Legislative Elections in Haiti and US Troop Withdrawal; Status of Counterdrug Forward Operating Locations; US Cuba Counter-Narcotics Cooperation Proposal; Chinese Influence in the Panama Canal; Political Events in Venezuela; and Status of US Property Claims in Nicaragua," (106 Cong., 1st Sess. 11 (1999)).

Sheridan, Brian (testimony), "Panama Canal Security: Panel Two of a Hearing of the Senate Armed Services Committee," (106th Cong., 1st Sess. (1999)).

Sloan, Allan, "Lending a Helping Hand: The Math behind CNOOC's Rich Offer to Buy out Unocal," (*Newsweek*, July 18, 2005).

Tafara, Ethiopas, Testimony Before the Senate Committee on Banking, Housing, and Urban Affairs (Apr. 24, 2008).

Tapper, Jake, "Hoosier Responsible? Clinton Decries China's Acquisition of Indiana Company – Ignoring Her Husband's Role in the Sale," (ABCNews.com, Apr. 30, 2008) available at http://abcnews.go.com/Politics/Vote2008/story?id=4757257.

Tse, Tomoeh Murakami, "Chinese Firm to Buy Big Stake in Bear Stearns," (*Washington Post*, Oct. 23, 2007).

US Department of Defense, Annual Report to Congress: Military Power of the People's Republic of China (2007).

US Department of Defense, Annual Report to Congress: Military Power of the People's Republic of China (2008).

Warrick, Joby and Carrie Johnson, "Chinese Spy 'Slept' in US for 2 Decades," (*Washington Post*, Apr. 3, 2008).

Weinberger, Caspar W., "Panama, the Canal and China," (*Forbes*, Oct. 4, 1999).

Wolff, Jacqueline C. and Jessica A. Clarke, "Liability Under the Foreign Corrupt Practices Act," 40 *Review of Securities and Commodities Regulation* 13 (Jan. 17, 2007).

4. The politics of Chinese investment in the US

Timothy Frye and Pablo M. Pinto*

INTRODUCTION

Why are economic policies that are widely believed to improve social welfare often not adopted? A consensus reigns among economists that restrictions on the free flow of foreign investment impair social welfare and that economies as a whole would grow larger where those restrictions are lifted. Yet, countries often raise barriers to the free flow of capital and goods, to their economic detriment. Chinese investment in the US illustrates this more general puzzle. For example, while Chinese companies have made several high-profile investments in the US in the last decade (for example, IBM), other efforts have failed (for example, Maytag, Unocal). Whether additional barriers will be placed on investment from China in the future is very much an open question.[1]

This chapter maps the landscape of stakeholders involved in policy decisions over Chinese foreign direct investment (FDI) in the United States, with the larger goal of identifying the political dynamics motivating support for and opposition to FDI from China. We analyze both the political demand and the supply of politics on this issue. On the demand side, we identify the power and preferences of major stakeholders in decision-making, including business lobbies, labor organizations and the mass public. Which groups are most active and successful in lobbying for and against easier access for Chinese investment? In addition, we explore how interest groups and foreign policy elites may shape public debate on investment from China. In seeking to justify their positions, do they refer primarily to economic consequences, such as loss/gain of jobs, or prospects for reciprocal investment opportunities in China? Do they frame their arguments in terms of human rights and democratization? Do they invoke national security concerns? Moreover, is there a systematic pattern of support for, and opposition to, Chinese FDI and mergers and acquisitions (M&As)? Last, is this pattern rooted in sectoral or geographic considerations?

Identifying individual and group preferences is not enough to explain (and forecast) policy outcomes. Policies are the output of the political process – hence they are shaped by the intersection of demand and supply conditions in policy-making. Political institutions mediate political demands and thereby determine the nature of policy-making. Indeed, because political institutions privilege some groups at the expense of others, policies are often only a reflection of the power and preferences of different stakeholders in civil society. What are the preferences of political representatives on easing access of FDI from China? How do political institutions aggregate and constrain these preferences? How does policy-making in the US privilege some groups and disadvantage others? What political coalitions are forming on the issue of Chinese FDI? Do we expect legislators in safe seats or in marginal seats to be more important on this issue?

In assessing the prospects for FDI from China, we take both the demand and supply sides into account by examining voting patterns in Congress. We find preliminary evidence that both material and non-material ideological factors influence voting behavior in the House of Representatives. For example, economic ties with China shape the policy position of Congress members. Representatives from states with more employment in finance and professional activities whose economic links to China have increased in recent years, and those from states with more exports to China, tend to adopt a relatively pro-China stance. Representatives from states whose firms compete with Chinese imports or have large manufacturing sectors tend to cast anti-China votes on key legislative issues identified for our analysis. Representatives with links to the security community and those concerned about China's rise as a military power are associated with a more negative disposition toward China as well.

Moreover, our analysis shows that ideology and the distribution of employment and trade with China are also good predictors of membership in the US–China Working Group (USCWG) and in the Congressional China Caucus (CCC), the two groups associated with pro-China and anti-China attitudes in the House.[2] Our case study analysis also suggests that, at the local level, the motivation and form of entry by Chinese firms seem to affect the disposition of economic and political actors toward Chinese investment. These factors can mitigate negative sentiments associated with national security, strategic and other ideological concerns. At the national level, however, the public continues to express generally negative attitudes toward economic cooperation with China, due to concerns about the employment and wage effects of trade with China, and a general concern with the rise of China as a strategic competitor.

Our analysis suggests that investment from China in the United States is as much a political as an economic issue. Investments that make economic sense may run into difficulties where they cut against important political and national security interests. Recognizing that "politics matters" is an important step, but it is important to identify which aspects of politics are especially important. First, investors need to find ways to navigate the committee network in Congress and the Executive. Second, they need to recognize that preferences are partly determined by local interests and constituencies. Hence, it is very important to cultivate local interests and engage local politicians. Potential investors need to invest in learning about the political game, be part of that game and monitor key players.

In the ensuing sections we begin with the demand side of politics by examining the preferences of interest groups and the mass public on the issue in sections 4.1.1 and 4.1.2, before turning to the supply side and a focus on political institutions in section 4.1.3. We then examine the impact of demand-side factors on a roll call vote on issues related to Chinese FDI in section 4.2. We present two brief case studies of attempts by Chinese firms to invest in the US in section 4.3, before concluding.

4.1   THE DEMAND AND SUPPLY RISKS OF POLICY-MAKING

In order to understand the demand side of politics we start by identifying the sources of individual preferences toward foreign investment and explore how these preferences get activated politically, that is, which groups are more likely to become influential.[3] We can treat their preferences as a function of income and ideology. Income effects are associated with the net welfare and distributive consequences of trade, investment and other eco-nomic interactions with a foreign country and its nationals. Ideational interests, on the other hand, are those related to nationalism and strategic concerns associated with the political externalities of economic relations and economic externalities of political rela-tions. One key question in this analysis is: how orthogonal the material and ideational dimensions are, i.e., how much do material interests (usually derived from individuals' position in the economy and/or ownership of assets affected by economic interactions with China) determine attitudes toward China?

4.1.1 Preferences and the Demand Side of Policy-Making

What drives preferences towards foreign investment? We can identify two different sources: material and economic interests, related to the effect of investment on the well-being of the economy and individuals; and non-material interests and ideological interests associated with nationalistic, security and cultural concerns. Material and non-material interests can, in turn, be classified as supporting or opposing closer economic relations with China. One potential material and economic source of conflict on the politics of inward investment is the technological relationship that determines the degree of complementarity and substitutability in production between foreign investment and factors of production owned by domestic actors in the host country. Where foreign investment complements local factors of production, stakeholders in the host country may be especially supportive. For example, where labor is plentiful, but local capital is scarce, local stakeholders and workers in particular may welcome foreign investment. In contrast, where foreign investment substitutes for local factors of production, one might expect opposition from host country producers to be especially fierce. For example, where foreign investors seek to build firms from scratch that compete directly against local firms, local opposition from owners of capital is likely (Pinto 2004; Pinto and Pinto 2008).

More generally, foreign investment could affect the demand and relative prices paid to owners of capital and labor in the host country, creating incentives for these actors to try to influence government to adopt their preferred policies.[4] Moreover, even though business owners irrespective of their nationality share an interest in creating a more favorable business environment, domestic investors who are likely to have better access to the policy-making process would prefer restricting inflows of foreign investment that are likely to compete away their rents.[5] This would result in a direct economic incentive for agents to organize politically in support of, or opposition to, initiatives to prevent the acquisition of domestic assets by certain types of investors. Thus, the distributional consequences of FDI may motivate conflict.[6]

In addition, non-economic concerns may lead to opposition to FDI. For example, a disposition toward more permissive or restrictive investment policies could be driven by an actor's sensitivity to security and political externalities associated with the type of investment, which in turn could depend on the sector, nationality and nature of the investor.[7] The political and economic consequences of foreign investment are likely to resonate in the politics of investment, and consequently may be reflected in legisla-tive and regulatory activity around the issue, creating one of the sources of "liability of foreignness" faced by foreign investors.[8] The academic literature has also analyzed the effect of politics on investment decisions within an individual industry (Levy and

Spiller 1994; Henisz and Zelner 2001; Henisz 2002, among others), but there is limited work on industries that may create national security concerns.

Some individuals and groups who advocate economic nationalism, and hence restrictive policies, are confronted with a trade-off that Harry Johnson (1965) eloquently described:

> it is quite possible that the psychic enjoyment that the mass of the population derives from the collective consumption aspects of nationalism suffices to compensate them for the loss of material income imposed on them by nationalistic economic policies, so that nationalistic policies arrive at a quite acceptable result from the standpoint of maximizing satisfaction. (Johnson 1965, p. 184).[9]

The existence of this trade-off at the individual and group level has important implications for coalition formation: some individuals might be willing to embrace economic nationalism purely on grounds of self-interest (reflected in the commercial manipulation of the CFIUS process identified by Graham and Marchick 2006), yet others will be forced to trade off material (net welfare and individual-level losses) and ideological preferences when supporting a national industry.

Economic and security concerns with foreign direct investment originating in China are likely to differ depending on the form of entry (whether greenfield investment creating new facilities or acquisitions of existing assets),[10] the characteristics of the sector and of the firm, and an investor's relationship to other public and private actors.[11] Hence we should expect attitudes toward Chinese investment in the US to vary depending on the instrument of choice: government bonds and greenfield investment are likely to be less sensitive than M&As and more easily tolerated, whereas sensitivity to political externalities and security concerns may make the public less likely to support investments in natural resources and technology.[12] The perceived driving force behind Chinese investment into a developed country like the United States is likely to be access to technology and skills-intensive goods and services, but also natural resources, as the Lenovo–IBM and China National Offshore Oil Corporation (CNOOC)–Unocal cases illustrate. This motivation might increase the strategic concern among individuals and leaders alike.[13] Yet the Haier–Maytag and Huawei–Com cases suggest that the response could also result from manipulation of the legislative and regulatory process even when strategic concerns are low.

The vehicle through which investment occurs is likely to affect the disposition of individual and collective political actors. Investment by a foreign state-owned enterprise (SOE) or by foreign government-controlled firms could be more salient and sensitive. Ownership and governance structure of the parent is important in the case of Chinese investment as China recently created the China Investment Corporation, a sovereign wealth fund (SWF) worth over $200 billion, to purchase assets abroad. Such SWFs have raised concerns that certain investments may have a political rather than an economic goal, particularly since most SWFs offer little information about their investments.[14] Political responses in the US could be different if China funneled its investment through an investment agency, like Singapore or Dubai, and when sensitive assets in the US are sheltered from direct foreign control.[15]

Thus, individual and group responses toward Chinese FDI may be shaped by a variety of factors, including: whether the investment is a substitute or complement of local factors of production; commercial linkages with economic actors in China and the region; the extent to which it raises concerns for national security; whether it is a greenfield investment or an acquisition of an existing asset; and the property type of the organization making the investment.

The combination of material and non-material interests could result in a coalition of strange bedfellows around the politics of regulating investment in general, and Chinese acquisition of US assets in particular. Identifying individual and collective actors' preferences is key for understanding their political motivations and activity, and the stances of those political agents who aim at representing these groups.

4.1.2 Individual and Group Attitudes toward Chinese Investment

In this section, we explore the positions toward China of key stakeholders in the United States. For presentational purposes, we classify these stakeholders depending on their stance (pro or anti-China) and the motivation for their stance (economic or ideological/strategic). Table 4.1 presents a synopsis of this classification. One problem with this preliminary classification of material interests is that, on the economic dimension, we cannot separate whether the attitudes are driven by trade or investment concerns. However, we believe that both trade and investment are closely related in individuals' and groups' assessments of the benefits of engaging China.[16]

Among economically motivated groups in the pro-China camp we find business associations, such as the Business Roundtable, which includes a broad coalition of chief executive officers aimed at promoting a pro-business regulatory environment, and the

Table 4.1   *American stakeholders' position on economic liberalization towards China*

	General attitude	
	Relatively pro-China	Relatively anti-China
Economic motivation	Financial firms (private equity, M&A players) Business associations (Business Roundtable, Financial Services Forum) Liberal think-tanks (IIE; OFFI) Congress: US–China Working Group US states actively seeking foreign investment The public: richer, more educated people who value cosmopolitanism	Labor leaders and unions Conservative think-tanks (American Enterprise Institute; Heritage Foundation) Labor-affiliated think-tanks Congress: Congressional China Caucus House membership The public: anti-globalization and concerned about trade with China and "US jobs"; human rights advocates
Nationalistic/ strategic	"Panda huggers" in defense community	US military; security community Congress: Congressional China Caucus The public: slight tendency to be wary of China for people concerned about US military superiority

Financial Services Forum, which brings together the chief executive officers of 21 leading financial institutions.[17] The Business Roundtable and the Financial Services Forum had been staunch supporters of Treasury Secretary Paulson's US–China Strategic Economic Dialogue, and strong advocates in public fora of initiatives aimed at "engaging" China.[18]

Among political groupings in Congress that support closer economic ties with China, we find the US–China Working Group (discussed in section 4.1.3), and political leaders from states actively seeking Chinese investment, such as Washington and North Carolina.[19] Liberal think-tanks, such as the Organization for International Investment and the Peterson Institute for International Economics, have adopted either a pro-China or a neutral stance.[20] Among the public, surveys show that richer, more educated people tend to support economic liberalization in general, and opening to China in particular. This group is usually associated with a more cosmopolitan attitude.

Among those holding a relatively anti-China stance based on economic interests, we find labor leaders and other individuals and groups who tend to oppose economic liberalization due to concerns about jobs.[21] The pharmaceutical, software and entertainment industries have adopted a negative stance toward Chinese investment in order to force the Chinese government to crack down on piracy and enforce property rights protection. Big businesses in the auto, steel and furniture sector oppose investment by Chinese firms in their sector out of self-interest: their biggest motivation is curbing competition from China and preventing Chinese firms from making further inroads to the domestic market. The labor-affiliated Economic Policy Institute is a key anti-China advocate; its motivations are mostly driven by the effects of Chinese imports on wages. Economic ideology associated with government intervention in the economy, lax property rights protection and restriction on market forces is the core motivation of the anti-China stances of the conservative Heritage Foundation, and of the American Enterprise Institute, a normally pro-business think-tank.

Among those adopting anti-China attitudes for nationalistic and strategic concerns, we find members of the US Armed Forces and the defense community. The overall consensus of the defense community around the adoption of a hawkish stance toward China is driven by concern over China's rise and the potential for conflict resulting from the US commitment to protect Taiwan Province of China.[22] Members of the Congressional China Caucus and large sectors of the public who are concerned about US military superiority and are wary of China's ascent as a regional and world power, have expressed similar concerns.[23]

The Appendix provides survey data on attitudes among the mass public and selected elite groups in the US toward trade and investment in general, and economic interactions with China in particular. The surveys were conducted by the Chicago Council on Global Affairs (CCGA) and provide some interesting information about factors influencing individual attitudes toward China. The 2004 Global Views Survey shows strong support for trade with China. Yet the pattern of support varies across groups of individuals and leaders according to their ideology, and it reveals varied attitudes toward security and economic issues. Respondents who believe that US military superiority is important are slightly less likely to favor trade with China. Similarly, but in a more pronounced fashion, the importance of protecting US jobs makes respondents less likely to favor trade with

China. For instance, 62 percent of those believing that jobs are "very important" favor trade with China. But support for trade is slightly higher (71 percent) among those who believe it is only "somewhat important." Interestingly, strategic supremacy plays a modest role in respondents' attitudes toward trade with China. Among those who believe that it is important to make active efforts to "ensure no other superpowers," only a minority (32.8 percent) oppose trade with China. The figure only falls to 31.3 percent opposing trade among those not so concerned about preventing other superpowers. Higher levels of education are associated with respondents favoring trade with China more (74.2 percent of college and graduate school-educated, versus 55.8 percent for those with high school education or less).

On the more fundamental issue of diplomatic relations with China, higher income results in sharply greater support for diplomatic relations. Income also has a comparable effect on respondents' tendency to favor trade with China. This result firmly dovetails with economic expectations that trade with China hurts unskilled workers. Party identification also has an arguable association with attitudes toward trading with China. Right-wingers seem slightly more likely to oppose trade with China than left-wingers. Strong Republicans, for instance, oppose trade by 40.7 percent, versus 29.2 percent of strong Democrats. The individual level results from the CCGA surveys seem to confirm the existence of the two different dimensions that determine how attitudes toward China are formed: economic and ideological. However, it is worth noting that individuals tend to be more favorably predisposed toward trade with China in general, which may reflect the fact that they privilege in their responses their role as consumers who are more likely to benefit from the gains from trade through lower prices and a larger variety of products. Yet, to reiterate, individual preferences are not necessarily translated into policy outcomes. Some individuals find it worthwhile spending time and resources to organize politically in defense of their interests, but most do not. Political outcomes are, thus, more likely to reflect the preferences of those that turn their preferences into political influence. Hence, we need to analyze the preferences of politically active groups as well as the attitudes of the mass public.

The CCGA Survey for 2004 also compiled the views of elites across various fields, from policy-makers to business people to academics and labor representatives. Support for trade with China among the elites is even stronger than among the public. In contrast to the public at large, political leanings have little impact on stances toward trade with China. In a similar vein, the Republicans surveyed were only slightly more prone to oppose trade with China (9 percent of Republican versus 8 percent of Democrats). Across categories of elites, it is obvious that labor leaders are more hesitant to embrace freer trade with China. Only 66 percent of labor leaders favor trade with China, a stark contrast to the other categories. (Business leaders, for instance, are 92 percent in agreement for freer trade.) Finally, House respondents displayed a slight inclination to oppose trade with China versus their Senate counterparts (9 percent versus 3 percent, respectively). Looking more in depth at parties across Congress, the bulk of opposition to China trade seems to reside almost exclusively in the House. In fact, only one Senate respondent, a Democrat, opposed trade. In the House, Democrats were actually slightly more prone to favor trade with China (94 percent versus 87 percent for House Republicans).[24]

The Appendix presents some general figures from the Chicago Council on Global

Affairs surveys across time. Looking at results since 1990, it is apparent that more US respondents thought China's potential world-power status was critical in 1994 and 1998 than in the latest 2006 results (57 percent thought so in 1994 and 1998, versus only 36 percent in 2006). The tables in the Appendix also suggest the existence of a somewhat increasing resentment against China. First, there is a slight increase over time in respondents who oppose freer trade with China. Meanwhile, there is a slight decrease in those who favor US–China diplomatic relations at all. Moreover, more US respondents in 2006 expressed the belief that China practices unfair trade (58 percent agreed this was the case) than the earlier respondents of 2002 or 2004. In terms of Chinese FDI, US respondents worry about it, but only slightly more than, say about Indian or Republic of Korea direct investment in the US.

The survey provides an interesting snapshot of the different attitudes that the public and elites hold regarding China. Yet it does not allow us to analyze whether these attitudes are driven by self-interest, altruistic or national security concerns. We have to be careful in our analysis of how much can be attributed to foreign investment, particularly to M&As, since recent scandals surrounding Chinese products, and negative attitudes toward Chinese exports in general, may influence people's views.[25] We also reproduce a series of cross-tabs obtained from survey data on individual (and elite) attitudes toward trade with China as a function of income, education and degree of concern with national security and strategic issues.[26] These results provide a snapshot of the attitudes at a particular time and in a particular context, which may differ from the more recent political environment where sensitivities toward China seem to have intensified. This snapshot does not allow us to assess how individuals and leaders might react to a changing environment and different plausible scenarios in US–China relations, nor does it allow us to estimate the degree to which actors might be willing to forego economic and material benefits for ideational and other non-material concerns, including national security.

In sum, we find that, while interest groups focused on the economy are active on both sides of the issue, groups opposing easy access for FDI from China benefit from a natural alliance with groups focused on national security issues. The mass public generally recognizes the importance of China as a rising player on the global stage and tends to favor trade with China despite concerns about unfair trade practices and the possibility of job losses. Of course, the mass public is often removed from policy-making on narrow issues such as FDI from China leaving well-organized interest groups as the most important influences on policy.

4.1.3   Political Institutions and the Supply Side of Policy

Identifying interest group and individual motivations toward FDI is an essential first step. But to understand and predict policy outcomes we must also examine how the policy-making process and political institutions aggregate these preferences. Because political institutions privilege some groups at the expense of others, they often have an independent impact on policy choices. We begin with the assumption that politicians want to maximize the probability of retaining office, but that they do so in different ways in different political settings. In the US Congress, representatives are elected in single-member districts, and therefore place special weight on delivering benefits to their constituents in the district. The President is elected from the nation as a whole and therefore is often seen as being less responsive to narrow concerns. These simple assumptions combine with four other features of the supply side of policy-making in the US that are pertinent to foreign investment.

Weak political parties

First, consider the implications of weak parties. In the US, representatives often self-nominate, raise their own funds to run for office, and develop their campaign strategies with little help from political parties. In office, members of Congress can often vote against the wishes of the party as a whole without suffering great costs. Indeed, legislators frequently depict themselves as defenders of local priorities. Politicians retain office not by toeing the party line as they do in most parliamentary systems, but by delivering benefits to their constituents. But they cannot deliver benefits to their constituents on their own. They must instead build legislative majorities by gaining the votes of other members who are also interested in delivering benefits to their districts. To persuade other members to vote for so-called "pork-barrel projects" in their district, a representative must often pledge to vote for pork-barrel projects in other districts.

This is complicated because bills that provide mutual benefits are often voted on sequentially. Legislators can seek to build a coalition by promising to vote for other members' pet projects, but once a legislator gets their pet project approved, they have little incentive to vote in favor of pet projects in other districts because their constituents will bear some of the costs for these projects without getting any benefits. Because other legislators can anticipate this defection they may be reluctant to consent to vote for another legislator's pet project in the first place.

In countries with strong parties, party leaders can compel members to vote for pet projects in other districts, but in a weak party system like in the US, members must build an individual reputation for being a trustworthy member of a voting coalition.[27] Ultimately, the legislative deals that bring benefits to constituents rely on the ability of lawmakers to build a reputation among their colleagues for being trustworthy partners. The importance of having a good reputation gives greater power to representatives from safe districts than to representatives from competitive districts (McGillivray 2004). Because legislators from safe districts are expected to be in office for a long time, they are likely still to be in office when they vote for a member's pet project. This makes them especially attractive members for a potential coalition. While one might think that legislators in marginal seats have greater influence over policy, given that parties would want to protect them against the possibility of losing the seat to the rival party, it is often the legislators in safe seats who can more reliably deliver their votes and thereby gain greater benefits for their district.

This has three implications for the case of Chinese investment in the United States. First, it is critical to identify the preferences of constituents in particular legislative districts to determine their stance on the issue. For example, members from high-tech industrial districts are likely to be especially strong supporters of closer economic ties with China (for example, Washington state, the research triangle in North Carolina), while members from districts whose industries compete with Chinese firms directly or indirectly may be less supportive. Second, it is important to determine whether representatives reside in safe or marginal seats. Long-serving members of Congress facing little electoral threat are likely to be especially influential. And last, in order to signal their preferences to their constituents and enhance their reputation as trustworthy coalition partners, Congress members create and participate in informal groups aimed at advancing their political agenda on specific issues.

As discussed in section 4.1.1, economic considerations associated with the consequences of trade with China and Chinese investment on the well-being of their constituencies are not the sole force motivating legislators. Representatives from districts with strong military components may emphasize the security aspects of closer economic relations with China. By playing on fears of Chinese government-controlled companies gaining access to assets that may have dual-use capabilities, legislators can build support within the district. Lawmakers' positions on the issue of foreign investment can be couched in a variety of terms for political purposes, such as national security, human rights or economic benefits; yet the underlying issue is likely to be constituency support.

The two dimensions driving individual attitudes toward China identified in section 4.4.1, material and ideational, are also likely to be reflected in the formation of Congressional coalitions on China.[28] Two groupings within Congress are especially relevant to the issue at hand: the Congressional China Caucus (CCC) and the US China Working Group (USCWG), with interests based on strategic concerns and economic links with China, respectively. The Caucus's stated goal is to "investigate China's global reach and the consequences of its growing international, economic and political influence on US interests."[29] The Caucus is chaired by Randy Forbes (R-VA) and Madeleine Z. Bordallo (D-Guam),[30] two representatives with strong constituencies in the armed services. Representatives from Southern states are a prominent group within the China Caucus, such as Spencer Bachus (R-Al). Other key members of this group include: Ike Skelton (D-MO), chair of the Armed Services Committee in the 110th Congress and a 16-term veteran; Gary Miller (R-CA), the assistant Republican whip; and Tim Ryan (D-OH), member of the Democratic Steering and Policy Committee and of the Taiwan Caucus. The Caucus has 34 members with 9 Democrats and 25 Republicans, including 14-term veterans Duncan Hunter of California and Frank Wolf of Virginia. On average, CCC members have served five terms in Congress. A cursory examination of several press releases, working papers, reports and Congressional testimony provided by Caucus members and staff reveals a critical and cautious view of China. The focus seems to be primarily security-related, with relatively fewer pieces on economic issues.

A second important organization in Congress is the relatively pro-China US China Working Group. Mark Kirk (R-IL) and Rick Larsen (D-Washington) co-chair the Working Group which has 40 members in total as of April 2008. The US–China Working Group's expressed purpose is: "to build diplomatic relations with China and to make the Congress more aware of US–China issues."[31] Contrary to the Caucus, the USCWG expresses relatively favorable opinions of China. Most of its members are moderate and tend to come from the coastal areas of the US.

Republicans are a majority in the CCC (73.53 percent), and a minority in the USCWG (42.50 percent). Both parties are about evenly split with members who straddle both coalitions, that is, who are members of the CCC and the USCWG. But pure-CCC members are overwhelmingly Republican (86.96 percent). DW-nominate scores[32] for the first dimension (liberal conservative) are on average much higher (more conservative) for pure-CCC members than for mixed or pure-USCWG members.[33] The scores for pure-CCC members also feature less dispersion. Irrespective of party affiliation, USCWG members tend to be more moderate[34] and have served 4.7 terms in Congress, on average.[35]

When looking across the largest industries in terms of job contribution in the districts of coalition members, there seem to only be slight differences. For instance, 13.8 percent of pure-USCWG members belong to districts in which manufacturing contributes the most jobs, while the same goes for 17.4 percent of pure-CCC members. In terms of occupation, members of the USCWG have a larger proportion of professionals and scientists in their districts. Madeleine Bordallo and Randy Forbes, co-chairs of the CCC, both have the defense industry (miscellaneous defense) among their top five campaign-contributing industries. Further, Ike Skelton, an original founder of the CCC, along with Forbes, has defense-related industries as three out of five of his top contributing industries. Meanwhile, neither Mark Kirk nor Rick Larsen, co-chairs of the USCWG, have defense-related contributions in their top five contributing industries. Instead, among Kirk's top five contributing industries we find securities and investments, while Larsen has information technology and computers among his biggest supporters.[36]

Next, we examine what types of representatives are likely to join the Congressional China Caucus, a group generally skeptical of closer ties between the US and China. Table 4.2, column 1 presents a probit analysis of CCC membership for the 109th Congress. We find that, controlling for other factors, representatives from states with stronger ties to China, particularly those exporting large volumes to China, are more likely to belong to the CCC. In addition, representatives from states with more workers in the "professions and science" are more likely to be members of the CCC. Partisanship does not seem to affect CCC membership: Republicans are no more likely than Democrats to join the Caucus. However, there is an ideological dimension at work. Right-wing representatives are more likely to join than left-wing representatives as indicated by the coefficient on ideology. In addition, we can explore the relationship between committee membership and the likelihood of joining the CCC. Members of the House Armed Services Committee were especially likely to join the CCC. This suggests a national security dimension to the decision to sign up for the CCC and echoes findings from the Congressional debates on the issue: CCC members tend to be more conservative and hawkish.

Membership in the USCWG is also positively associated with state exports to China, and negatively related to Chinese imports and to manufacturing employment (Table 4.2). The positions adopted by the USCWG and its members systematically emphasize economic opportunities and do not dwell on national security issues. This is reflected in the vote on House Resolution 344 of June 2005, which called for the President to "initiate immediately a thorough review of the proposed acquisition, merger or takeover" if Unocal accepted CNOOC's bid. The resolution passed by a margin of 398 to 15.[37] The USCWG accounted for 8 of the 15 "nays" for House Resolution 344.[38] Note that none of the "nays" came from the Congressional China Caucus (the "anti"-China group). Looking at the "nays," it is apparent that Washington State Democrats are an important subgroup, accounting for 6 of the 15 votes (no other state–party combination rivals this contribution).

That the relatively pro-labor Democrats were not against the CNOOC deal dovetails with economic theory, insofar as representatives of labor would tend to see Chinese capital as a complement and not a substitute (Pinto and Pinto 2008). As for the fact that the state of Washington features so prominently, there are indications that the state

Table 4.2 *Probit analysis of group membership*

Dependent variable	CCC membership	USCWG membership
Trade with China (2004)		
Ln Exports	0.546**	0.523**
	(0.25)	(0.21)
Ln Imports	−0.728*	−1.059***
	(0.42)	(0.32)
Partisanship		
Republican	−0.546	1.405
	(0.58)	(0.65)
Ideology (DW nominate score)		
First dimension	1.103*	−1.093
	(0.60)	(0.67)
Regional dummies		
Northeast	−0.225	1.162***
	(0.44)	(0.40)
West	−0.459	1.273***
	(0.31)	(0.37)
Midwest	0.049	0.441
	(0.39)	(0.42)
Constant	1.628	4.756*
	(2.48)	(2.68)
House Committee dummies	Yes	Yes
State employment dummies	Yes	Yes
Observations	437	437
Wald χ^2 (N)	66.32 (22)	52.14 (22)
Prob $>\chi^2$	0.0000	0.0000
Log pseudolikelihood	−83.1	−69.88
Pseudo R^2	0.2077	0.2244

Notes:
Robust standard errors in parentheses.
*** $p < 0.01$, ** $p < 0.05$, * $p < 0.1$.

has an active interest in Chinese investment. One prominent Washington body is the Washington State China Relations Council, whose membership includes companies in finance (Bank of America, United Commercial Bank), consumer goods (Costco), aerospace technology (Boeing) and several law firms. Its expressed goal is "promoting stronger commercial, educational, and cultural relations between the state of Washington and the People's Republic of China."[39]

Why is Washington state so overwhelming pro-China? One reason provided by the Washington State China Relations Council is based on the economic advantages provided by the state's proximity to China: the Council is the principal voice for promoting Washington State as the leading gateway to China. Due to its proximity to China, Washington State is in a unique position to take advantage of the growing Chinese economy. In 2002, Washington's trade with China totaled well over $15 billion, ranking second only to California in state exports to China.

In sum, one dimension of the conflict over Chinese investment in the US appears to pit districts with strong national security interests against those in which high-tech industries with interests in China are especially prevalent.

Committee dominance

Second, policy-making is marked by the significant role played by committees in the US Congress. As one former House member noted: "Congress is a collection of committees that come together periodically to approve one another's actions" (Cox and McCubbins 2007, p. 1). Given constraints on time, resources and expertise, members of Congress often do not have the luxury of scrutinizing in great detail legislation outside of their committee assignments. This gives committees a near monopoly in their particular area of policy. In addition, members often choose to serve on committees that are especially likely to deliver benefits to their constituents (see also Cox and McCubbins 1993). Legislators from agricultural states are most likely to serve on the Agriculture Committee and members from states with military bases are likely to serve on the Military Affairs Committee. This suggests that policy can veer from the interests of the average voter or average member of Congress.

Within committees, members from both parties iron out differences over policy and bills are then presented to the Congress as a whole for a floor vote. Given that most controversial issues are resolved within committees before a bill reaches the floor, it is not surprising that many bills pass with overwhelming bipartisan support.

In the case at hand it is critical to identify the preferences of the members of the Congressional committees responsible for passing legislation related to Chinese investment. This is complicated as several committees may claim jurisdiction over the issue. The House Ways and Means Committee and its Subcommittee on Trade are central players on the issue of US–China economic relations. In addition, the House Armed Services Committee and the House Energy and Commerce Committee also weighed in on the Unocal case (see CRS 2006). In the Senate, the Finance Committee is central to trade issues with China, particularly with respect to the difficult issue of currency regulation.[40]

The 2006 elections removed several prominent Republican China skeptics from positions of authority on committees within the House of Representatives, including Henry Hyde of Illinois, the former chair of the International Relations Committee; Duncan Hunter of California, the former chair of the House Armed Services Committee; and Richard Pombo of California, the former chair of the House Resources Committee. As Chevron's headquarters are in Mr Pombo's district, it is no surprise that he was an especially outspoken critic of CNOOC's offer to Unocal.

The Democrats who assumed leading positions on foreign policy committees in the House in 2006 are somewhat more supportive of closer ties with China, but express strong reservations about China's intentions nonetheless. The head of the powerful House Ways and Means Subcommittee on Trade, Sander Levin, a Democrat from Michigan, has long been a critic of China's currency policy, trading relationships and violations of human rights, but did vote to grant China permanent normal trade status in 2000.[41] John Dingell (D) Michigan, the chair of the House Energy and Commerce Committee and currently the longest-serving member of the House, voted against granting permanent normal trade relations with China. Finally, Ike Skelton (D) Missouri, the head of the House Armed Services Committee and member of the Congressional China

Caucus, voted in favor of granting China permanent normal trade status in 2000, but was a vocal critic of the CNOOC's bid to take over Unocal. Thus, the composition of relevant committees in the US House are not especially likely to support easy access for Chinese direct investment in the US.[42]

The executive branch

Thus far the analysis has focused on political parties and Congress, but the Executive Branch is also a key player in formulating policy. Indeed, given the difficulty of building coalitions to pass legislation, Congress has at times delegated considerable policy-making authority to the Executive. Congress may do so to shift the political costs of taking a policy decision that will benefit the broad public interest, but hurt narrow and powerful constituencies. The President is elected based on support from the electoral college and therefore has an interest in retaining support across a range of states. Thus, his constituency of supporters is broader than that of any particular member of Congress whose primary responsibility is to their electoral district.[43] As such, the Executive Branch has generally been more supportive of free trade and investment than has Congress (Baldwin 1985; Milner 1988; Bailey et al. 1997; Lohmann and O'Halloran 1994).

The Executive has in principle supported foreign investment from China in recent administrations. For example, while President Clinton campaigned on a platform of revoking China's "most-favored-nation" trading status, he became a supporter of closer economic relations with China after assuming office. More recently, Secretary of the Treasury Henry Paulson is on record as supporting investment from China, noting: "I very much welcome investment in our country by all foreign nations, including China" (Reuters, October 16, 2007). Paulson was the promoter of the US–China Strategic Dialogue Initiative, and took the lead on policies aimed at punishing Chinese trade and currency practices. In response to legislation designed to impose tariffs across the board on China unless it revised its currency policy, he noted: "When we look at taking unilateral actions aimed at another nation, this can have enormous repercussions to our economic well-being. You know we are playing with fire" (*China Daily*, September 11, 2007).

At the same time, the White House has had to balance economic gains from investment from China with national security concerns. As Commander in Chief, the President is responsible for national defense. Given these competing obligations, President Bush adopted a "wait-and-see" attitude toward the purchase of Unocal, stating that he would be guided by the decisions of the Department of the Treasury's Committee on Foreign Investment in the United States (CFIUS).[44]

The Executive is however, more than just the President, as agencies and committees located within the Executive also shape policy on many issues. For example, CFIUS was created in 1975 by an Executive Order of the President to determine the national security impact of specific foreign investments (CRS 2007). The committee determines whether a foreign investment is a sufficient threat to national security to warrant an investigation. If so, the CFIUS investigates and submits a report and a recommendation to the President who can then decide whether to block the investment. (See Chapter 3 by David Fagan in this volume.)

As the deliberations of the CFIUS are confidential, it is difficult to know its inner workings. Among recent Chinese investment activity in the US, the sale of the personal computer division of IBM to Lenovo was less controversial than the proposed sale of Unocal, given that the assets involved in the deal were low-tech, and the technology ubiquitous.[45] Nonetheless, there was Congressional activity aimed at blocking the deal, particularly from lawmakers in the Foreign Affairs and Armed Forces committees who raised espionage and security concerns. Don Manzullo (R-IL), ranking member of the House International Relations Committee (now Foreign Affairs) and member of the Congressional–Executive Commission on China (created in October 2000 to monitor human rights in China), Henry Hyde (R-IL), chair of the House International Relations Committee at the time, and Duncan Hunter (R-CA), then chair of Armed Services Committee, sent a letter to the Treasury Secretary asking that the Treasury representatives at CFIUS conduct a full investigation of the sale of IBM's personal computer (PC) unit to Lenovo. The plans received clearance from the FTC on January 10, 2005, on grounds that it did not violate antitrust regulations.[46] The deal ultimately received CFIUS approval on March 9, 2005, after a series of concessions from Lenovo aimed at pleasing US lawmakers and regulators.[47]

The proposed Unocal–CNOOC deal ended with a different result. CNOOC withdrew its bid before it was reviewed by CFIUS. CNOOC stated that it was prepared to undergo the review and "address concerns relating to energy security and ownership of Unocal assets located in the US" (CRS 2007, p. 14). It also promised to retain the jobs of almost all Unocal employees and to continue selling almost all of the oil and gas from Unocal's US properties in US markets; this promise was arguably aimed at sweetening the deal on economic grounds to gain support from local economic actors. Thus, even without a formal review, CFIUS can shape transactions involving foreign investment in the US.

On the heels of the political controversy over the Dubai Ports sale and the proposed Unocal–CNOOC merger, Congress has been active in trying to regulate inward FDI. In the 109th Congress, lawmakers introduced at least two dozen measures that addressed foreign investment (see Corr 2007). These measures tended to broaden the definition of national security and enhance the power of CFIUS.

In October 2001 Congress created the US China Economic and Security Review Commission (USCC), made up of private sector appointees (the Floyd D. Spence National Defense Authorization Act for 2001). The legislative mandate of the USCC is to monitor the national security implications of US trade and investment relations with China.[48] The USCC, which harbors stronger anti-China sentiment, has played a prominent role in public debates on Chinese investment in the US.[49] Immediately after CNOOC announced its plans to acquire Unocal, Richard D'Amato, former chair and current commissioner of the USCC, expressed the Commission's position against the deal.[50] The Commission has also been vocal in the recent bid by the Bain Capital group in association with Chinese Huawei Technologies to merge with 3Com, the Massachusetts-based disk drives and computer network equipment producer.[51]

Congress recently passed new legislation regulating FDI (Corr 2007). The Foreign Investment and National Security Act (FINSA) (which came into effect October 24, 2007) builds on existing legislation governing CFIUS, but also expanded reviews to include investments "critical to US infrastructure" added representatives from the Energy Department and the Labor Department to CFIUS, and required CFIUS to notify Congress about each transaction it considers. In addition, the new legislation makes it more difficult for government-owned entities to invest in the US – a clause that will certainly be of interest to a number of investors from China. (See David Fagan, Chapter 3 in this volume.)

Multiple veto points

Finally, policy-making in the United States is marked by multiple veto points. Congress has two chambers, each of which can block legislation. Given that representation in the House is based on population, while the representation in the Senate is based on geography, lobby groups tend to be strong in one chamber or the other, but not in both (McGillivray 2004). Much of Chinese investment in the US has been in natural resources, which tend to be concentrated in specific electoral districts.[52] This may help in the House, where representatives tend to back local interests, but not in the Senate where lobby groups need to create broad coalitions across many states to pass legislation. Over-representation in the Senate of sparsely populated states, usually those relatively better endowed with natural resources, on the other hand, could grant additional political clout to investors in those states. However, as noted above, opposition to trade with China has been far more pronounced in the House than in the Senate, thanks to a convergence of interests between legislators in districts with a strong national security constituency and those fearing job losses in manufacturing.

The Executive Branch provides another potential veto point, and its position is particularly relevant during periods of divided government when one party controls the presidency and another controls at least one House of Congress. The Executive has generally been supportive of free trade and closer economic relations with China, but in recent years it has also been cross-pressured by concerns over national security and human rights. Within the Executive, CFIUS makes recommendations to the President on the advisability of specific investments. The composition of CFIUS ensures that several different agencies are positioned to weigh in on the national security dimension of foreign investment.

The federal structure of the US government provides an additional layer of influential political actors. States can pass legislation that makes investment from abroad more or less attractive. Moreover, states often compete fiercely for FDI that can provide jobs and tax revenue, but they also face the possibility of opposition from narrow groups likely to be adversely affected by the investment. At the state level, Attorneys General usually have the right to challenge mergers to ensure that potential investors comply both with federal regulators and with the demands and preferences of state politicians. In the case of Chinese investment, for example, the Attorneys General of California, Texas, Montana and New Mexico wrote to Unocal to express their opposition to the deal on the grounds that it would "adversely affect the environment, the health of their citizens and the solvency of their state treasuries" (Thomson 2005, p. 6). These multiple veto points make it difficult to move policy dramatically and quickly from the status quo.

In sum, political institutions in the US provide a number of means of entry for groups to exert influence in support of policies that they favor, and at the same time allow pivotal actors to obstruct the passage of new legislation of their disliking.

4.2 CONGRESSIONAL VOTING PATTERNS: THE INTERSECTION OF SUPPLY AND DEMAND

Throughout the previous sections, we have made the case that policy outcomes are determined by the intersection of demand and supply conditions in politics. But it is hard to assess how lobbying, constituency pressure and the personal preferences of members of Congress affect their activity and votes because most contentious issues are worked out in committees before they reach the floor. However, we have identified two roll call votes in the House of Representatives in the 109th Congress on two different issue dimensions associated with US–China relations. The statistical analyses on these two votes allows us to assess our predictions about the role of material and ideational motivations in regulating US–China relations. The first vote is House Resolution 344 (roll call vote 360 of June 20, 2005), a motion expressing the House's opposition to CNOOC's attempt to acquire Unocal, and instructing the President to block the deal at CFIUS. The motion passed by a large margin: 398 to 15.[53] The second vote is on H.R. 3100 (roll call vote 374), a failed motion associated with the passage of the East Asia Security Act of 2005, which sought to authorize the President to adopt measures to deter arms transfers by foreign countries to China. This motion failed to get the two-thirds majority necessary to suspend rules and pass the East Asia Security Act.

In section 4.1.3, we discussed the characteristics of the 15 representatives adopting a relatively more pro-China stance. In this section, we conduct a more systematic analysis of the determinants of the vote by fitting a probit model where the binary dependent variable takes a value of 1 if a representative voted in favor of this resolution, that is, took an anti-China stance, and 0 if the representative voted against the resolution, that is, a pro-China stance. Table 4.3 presents the results of roll call analyses on H. Res. 344, opposing the CNOOC deal. The explanatory variables include proxies for characteristics of the constituencies, including commercial links with China (imports and exports measured at the state level due to data limitations) and employment. We also add variables aimed at measuring the characteristics of the representatives, such as ideology and partisanship, and Congressional Committee assignments.[54] One of our key explanatory variables is membership in the two China groups in the House (CCC and USCWG). Despite the limited number of "no" votes (pro-China), the results are quite compelling. Membership of USCWG is strongly associated with a pro-China vote (a negative coefficient on the USCWG dummy variable): the change in the predicted probability of voting "no" is minus 13 percentage points for members of this group.[55] CCC membership, on the other hand, has no discernible effect on the probability of voting "aye" in Roll Call 360.

The results also suggest that trade with China and sectoral employment at the state level affect the probability of casting a pro-China vote. Higher exports to China, and a higher ratio of employment in finance and professional and scientific activities at the state level are negatively correlated with an "aye" vote, while representatives from states with higher levels of Chinese import penetration and those with a higher ratio of employment in mining are more likely to vote "aye." For a Republican representative from the West, for instance, the predicted probability of voting "No" increases 66 percentage points when the value of exports moves from the mean to the maximum level in the sample, holding the rest of the variables constant at their means, except for the dummy variables which are set to zero. The confidence interval on the change of the predicted probability is, however, wide: it ranges from −95 to −26 percentage points.[56] A change in the ratio of employment in professional and scientific activity from the minimum to the maximum value in the sample is associated with a −24 percentage point change in the probability of voting "aye." Committee membership, on the other hand, has no significant effect on voting in the CNOOC case.

Investing in the United States

Table 4.3 *Probit analysis: 109th Congress–vote on H. Res 344 (Roll Call 360)*
          (dependent variable: 1 = "Aye")

	Model (1)	Model (2)	Model (3)	Model (4)
Congressional groups				
USCWG member	−1.06***	−1.06***	−1.06***	−1.00**
	(0.40)	(0.40)	(0.41)	(0.46)
CCC member	0.56	0.57	0.58	0.04
	(0.51)	(0.52)	(0.51)	(0.55)
Trade with China (2004)				
Ln Imports	1.97***	2.00***	2.03***	2.58***
	(0.43)	(0.43)	(0.46)	(0.58)
Ln Exports	−1.52***	−1.54***	−1.56***	−2.12***
	(0.36)	(0.37)	(0.39)	(0.50)
Employment (ratio of state employment)				
Finance	−33.62*	−34.03*	−35.96*	−9.96
	(18.58)	(18.80)	(19.47)	(21.00)
Prof. and scientific	−30.28***	−30.98***	−32.20***	−34.52***
	(11.47)	(11.21)	(11.60)	(12.48)
Mining	49.70**	50.76***	50.19***	64.86***
	(19.67)	(18.07)	(18.81)	(24.51)
Ideology (DW nominate score)				
First dimension		−0.15	−0.46	−0.23
		(0.37)	(1.36)	(0.38)
Second dimension				2.11***
				(0.52)
Partisanship				
Republican	−0.10		0.33	
	(0.30)		(1.25)	
Regional dummies				
West	−0.77	−0.75	−0.76	−0.39
	(0.49)	(0.50)	(0.49)	(0.60)
Midwest	−1.14	−1.13	−1.16	−1.06
	(0.75)	(0.74)	(0.76)	(0.80)
South	−0.94*	−0.89	−0.84	−1.02
	(0.56)	(0.55)	(0.53)	(0.64)
Constant	−2.87	−3.06	−3.37	−4.66
	(3.21)	(3.00)	(2.82)	(3.36)
Observations	413	413	413	413
Wald χ^2 (N)	74.13 (11)	75.27 (11)	77.97 (12)	49.61 (12)
Prob > χ^2	0.0000	0.0000	0.0000	0.0000
Log pseudolikelihood	−41.00	−40.93	−40.86	−34.06
Pseudo R^2	0.3638	0.3649	0.3661	0.4715

Notes:
Robust standard errors in parentheses.
*** $p < 0.01$, ** $p < 0.05$, * $p > 0.1$.

The previous results seem to confirm our intuition that positive economic links with China at the constituency level and membership in a pro-China group in Congress (which we have also shown to be associated with those economic interactions) are associated with a pro-China vote even in the highly controversial CNOOC case.

Next, we move to the analysis of the vote on the East Asia Security Act of 2005 (H. Res. 3100). Here our aim is to explore whether economic motivations affect the disposition of Congress members in the security realm. Table 4.4 reproduces the results from a series of statistical analyses of the probability of voting "aye" on H. Res. 3100. Despite differences in the details of the two pieces of legislation, we find some similar patterns in the vote on Roll Call 374. Membership in the two main China-focused organizations in the House is related to voting patterns. Members of the USCWG were significantly less likely to support the bill, and members of the Congressional China Caucus were significantly more likely to favor the bill, than were the majority of House members who belonged to neither group. This pattern is expected as opponents of the bill felt that it was prejudicial to business interests working with Chinese counterparts. In addition, representatives from states with a greater volume of exports to China were significantly less likely to vote for the bill, while their counterparts from states importing more goods from China were more likely to support it. Again, party membership has little impact on vote choice.

Congress is a critical arena for economic relations between the US and China, because here we see the intersection of both demand- and supply-side factors. Economic factors, such as trade links with China, were important predictors of voting patterns, as was membership in the congressional groups related to China. Membership of the CCC, a group of representatives concerned with the strategic implications of China's rise, is associated with a more negative disposition toward China in general. The membership of USCWG is driven by strong economic ties to China, and is correlated with a more positive disposition aimed at "engaging" China through economic integration and stronger diplomatic interactions. It is important to note that these results hold when controlling for a range of other factors, including party membership, region and the ideology of representatives. Party membership and region were generally unrelated to voting patterns or membership in the two China-related groups in the House. These results suggest that both political demand- and supply-side factors shape the behavior of House members on economic relations with China.

Examining roll call votes and the membership of China-related organizations in Congress allows us to analyze how different features of representatives and their constituents shape policy choices, but it does not allow us to explore how specific features of specific foreign investments might influence their success. In the next section, we briefly present two case studies that highlight how the motivations of foreign investors and local conditions influence attempts by Chinese companies to invest in the United States.

4.3 INVESTMENT STRATEGIES AND LOCAL POLITICS: THE LAIWU STEEL AND WANXIANG GROUP EXPERIENCES IN THE MIDWEST

Case studies are not a good tool to generalize about investment from China as they may be driven by factors idiosyncratic to the particular investment, but they do allow us to

Investing in the United States

Table 4.4   Probit analysis: 109th Congress – vote on H.Res 3100 (Roll Call 374)
(dependent variable: 1 = "Aye")

	(1)	(2)	(3)	(4)	(5)
Congressional groups					
USCWG member	−0.546*	−0.533*	−0.498*	−0.563*	−0.368
	(0.29)	(0.29)	(0.30)	(0.29)	(0.31)
CCC member	0.539**	0.531**	0.484*	0.598**	0.573**
	(0.27)	(0.27)	(0.27)	(0.29)	(0.29)
Partisanship					
Republican	0.053	−0.27	0.086	0.090	0.288
	(0.13)	(0.39)	(0.42)	(0.43)	(0.43)
Ideology (DW nominate score)					
First dimension		0.361	0.082	0.024	−0.091
		(0.41)	(0.44)	(0.44)	(0.45)
Second dimension			0.449**	0.403**	0.616***
			(0.20)	(0.20)	(0.21)
Trade with China (2004)					
Ln Imports	0.283*	0.293**	0.323**	0.243	0.311**
	(0.15)	(0.15)	(0.15)	(0.23)	(0.16)
Ln Exports	−0.270***	−0.274***	−0.275**	−0.211	−0.280**
	(0.10)	(0.10)	(0.11)	(0.13)	(0.11)
Employment (ratio of state employment)					
Administrative				7.362	
				(4.91)	
Finance				−4.54	
				(10.80)	
Manufacturing				5.565	
				(3.68)	
Mining				−3.93	
				(14.20)	
Prof. and scientific				−4.484	
				(5.71)	
Retail				1.228	
				(10.70)	
Constant	−0.657	−0.603	−1.05	−1.235	−0.672
	(1.25)	(1.26)	(1.31)	(3.30)	(1.37)
House Committee dummies	No	No	No	No	Yes
Regional dummies	Yes	Yes	Yes	Yes	Yes
Observations	418	418	418	418	418
Wald χ^2 (N)	17.51 (7)	18.18 (8)	23.42 (10)	31.71 (16)	43.49 (2)
Prob > χ^2	0.0144	0.0199	0.0093	0.0109	0.0027
Log pseudolikelihood	−280.6	−280.2	−277.3	−271.6	−265.4
Pseudo R^2	0.0308	0.0322	0.0424	0.0619	0.0834

Notes:
Robust standard errors in parentheses.
*** $p < 0.01$, ** $p < 0.05$, * $p > 0.1$.

examine some specific features of an investment in greater detail.[57] We begin by presenting a "most likely" case of a successful investment: the purchase of the Eveleth mine in the Minnesota iron range by Laiwu, a large Chinese steel and metals firm, and Cleveland Cliffs, an Ohio-based supplier of iron ore pellets. The new company, United Taconite, was founded in December 2003. The Eveleth mine opened in 1963, but after years of poor performance finally went bankrupt in May 2003, a casualty of the decline of steel production in the US and heightened competition from foreign producers. The local economy is highly dependent on mining. Over the past 25 years, the number of jobs in mining declined from about 16,000 to 4000. The need for new capital was pressing. Hence the investment from China complemented local factors of production and was largely well received in the community because it promised to boost employment.

The politics of the case were quite favorable. Congressman Jim Oberstar (D), who represented the district in which the Eveleth mine is located, and Minnesota Governor Timothy Pawlenty (R), both strongly supported the investment and helped to broker the deal. Representative Oberstar traveled to Jinan, China, the home base of Laiwu Steel Group and wrote glowingly about the trip on his Congressional Website. Governor Pawlenty also backed the deal, noting:

> There is also a big benefit [from foreign investment] to our natural resources areas. For example our major iron-ore and taconite industries in northeastern Minnesota had been pretty much on the decline. But because of the world demand for steel that has been driven by China, and China now investing in a taconite plant in Minnesota, the industry is rebounding at a remarkable rate.[58]

In 2005, Governor Pawlenty launched the Minnesota–China Partnership, and led a trade mission to Shanghai, Beijing and Hong Kong with hopes of attracting further investment.[59]

The Laiwu Steel Group is state-owned and some observers have been skeptical of the extent to which firms owned by the Chinese government will maximize profits rather than political goals. In this case, however, state ownership did not raise strong objections, and three factors may have dampened this concern. First, the investment in the Eveleth mine was not seen as a potential threat to national security or strategic holdings, unlike the CNOOC merger or, to some observers, the 3-Com and IBM cases. Second, Laiwu partnered with Cleveland Cliffs, an Ohio-based company that is the largest supplier of iron ore pellets to the steel industry in North America. In addition, Laiwu took a minority position. It held 30 percent of the shares and Cleveland Cliffs owned the rest. Moreover, it signed a ten-year contract for 30 percent of the mine's pellets which indicated a long-term commitment to the project.

In contrast, the Wainxang Group's investment experience in the US has been more difficult, in part because of its plans for the firms and because its investments are generally substitutes rather complements to local industry. The Wainxang Group is a private enterprise based in East China's Zhejian Province and is the largest auto parts supplier in China with roughly US$1.3 billion in annual sales. Its principal owner and founder, Lu Guanqiu, is reported to be one of China's ten richest men (Bloomberg 2006). The group has holdings in Latin America and Europe, but its main foreign focus is the United States. Wainxang America manages the Wanxiang Manufacturing Fund of more US$100 million and has stakes in a variety of enterprises.[60] Its main form of business in the US is the sale and distribution of auto parts that are largely imported from its Chinese factories. Its centerpiece in the US is a 168,000 square foot warehouse in Elgin, Illinois.

Wainxang's experience of investing in the US has been more controversial than Laiwu Steel's. In part this is related to the Wainxang's initial decision to cut costs and its decision to move jobs and equipment back to China. In 1998, it sought to take over a cash-strapped engine parts maker in Muskegeon, Michigan, but the deal fell apart when the company's union rejected the reduced employment benefits offer by Wainxang.[61] According to one source, the local government in Michigan backed the deal in hopes of creating more jobs, but failed to convince the union to accept the offer (*Wall Street Journal*, November 26, 2004). In 2001, Wainxang purchased the NASDAQ-listed brake supplier, Universal Automotive Industries, but the firm was soon delisted and subsequently liquidated. In 2003, it took over DriveLine Rockford Powertrain; while it helped to reduce costs, it also cut employment by more than one-third and experienced a walkout by 280 employees during a contract dispute. Even the management of DriveLine Rockford Powertrain noted "major quality issues" with Wainxang's products after the takeover (*Wall Street Journal*, November 26, 2004).

Yet, the group has had more success with Rockford's DriveLine Systems, an axle-maker purchased in 2002. In this case, the Wainxang Group did not cut jobs and the company has prospered. In recent years it has continued to expand. For example, in January 2008 it concluded a memorandum of understanding with Ford to buy the drive-shaft division of Ford's Automotive Components Holding. Recognizing the difficulties of moving equipment and jobs to China while becoming a more important player in the US auto parts market, Liu noted: "The key question to get right now is how much activity to leave in the US and how much to bring to China."[62]

These two cases underscore the political importance and saliency of the motivation, form of entry and timing of an investment. Laiwu Steel's investment in Minnesota minimized local backlash by engaging key political actors and reassuring the community using a strategy aimed at reducing its control over the firm, securing employment levels, increasing exports to China and revitalizing a sector that was in dire straits prior to the firm's entry. The Wainxang Group's strategy was bound to create political backlash; the auto industry in the US is undergoing a major overhaul, which may lead to a significant downsizing of the sector. Makers of auto parts feel the competitive pressure of foreign imports and fear the rise of Chinese parts makers as much as they dreaded competition from Japan and the Republic of Korea in the 1980s and 1990s. The Wainxang Group's motivation to acquire technology and equipment that could be shipped back to China was a source of conflict with the labor union, while an increase of imports from the parent company channeled through US affiliates placed the company at odds with domestic producers. The negative political disposition toward the company in Michigan is a clear reflection of this strategy

4.4   SUMMARY AND CONCLUSION

We began by noting the puzzle that easing access for FDI is generally thought to increase social welfare, but restrictions on the movement of investment capital abound. We examined a variety of political factors that help shed light on this puzzle. The case study analysis suggested that the motivations of the foreign investor and the local economic conditions help shape the likelihood of success. Where FDI serves as a complement to local factors of production, then the politics of FDI can be quite consensual. In addition, firms committed to retaining jobs are likely to face less resistance, even if the companies are state-owned. Yet, investor motivation may also affect the politics of investment negatively, particularly when the objective is controlling assets or acquiring sensitive technologies, which are likely to motivate policy-makers to block investments for strategic considerations.

We find that mass public opinion has generally not been an especially significant barrier to closer economic relations with China, although more recent data may paint a somewhat different picture. National security concerns have generally been less important than concerns about jobs as a reason for opposing closer economic ties with China, and a majority of Americans believe that China practices unfair trade. Trade relations with China compete with a host of other issues for the public's attention, and it is difficult to mobilize public support for or opposition to trade relations with China.

Finally, and most importantly, we examined how the factors of supply and demand intersect in the policy process within Congress. We find that constituent features shape the policy preferences of representatives on economic policies toward China. Representatives from states with a strong presence in finance and with high levels of exports to China are especially likely to support closer economic relations with China. In addition, supply-side factors, such as the ideology of the representatives and national security concerns, also play a significant role. Representatives with strong military presence in their district have played a leading role in the Congressional China Caucus, a key anti-China group in Congress. Indeed, one lesson from the failure of the proposed Unocal–CNOOC merger is that few representatives in the House are prepared to back high-profile investments that are even indirectly related to national security concerns.

All this suggests that FDI from China in the United States is as much a political as an economic issue. Investments that make economic sense may run into difficulties where they cut against important political and national security interests. Recognizing that "politics matters" is an important step, but it is also important to identify which aspects of politics are especially important. Party allegiance appears to have a rather weak influence on preferences toward economic relations with China. Among the mass public, party membership is not an especially good guide to attitudes toward economic relations with China. Moreover, among members of Congress, party membership is a poor predictor of voting behavior on key economic issues related to China. Democratic representatives are just as likely as Republican representatives to cast anti-China votes. Unlike many issues, politics toward economic relations with China have not been driven by party competition.

While public opinion has been important on some international economic issues (witness the public debate on the North American Free Trade Agreement NAFTA), in the case of Chinese investment, public opinion toward economic ties with China has not proven to be an insuperable barrier, with the possible exception of high-profile investments with national security implications.

Three other political factors, however, have been especially important to our analysis. First, the distributional consequences of trade are an important obstacle to easing access for Chinese firms in the US market. While in general the mass public does not object to economic relations with China, representatives from states with constituencies expected to be harmed by greater trade and investment from China have been well placed to block legislation promoting closer economic ties with China. In addition, representatives from states with a large presence of military bases or defense contractors who may benefit from concerns about China as a strategic rival are also an important constituency against expanding access for Chinese firms to the US market. This alliance is emerging as a formidable obstacle to improving economic relations with China. This suggests that improved relations with China on other matters, such as national security and human rights, may help to lower the costs to politicians of supporting closer economic ties with China.

Second, it is critical to understand how the demand for policies as revealed by interest group and constituent preferences shapes policy, but it is equally important to understand how the supply side of politics influences policy as well. Political institutions mediate constituent demand and interest group pressures in ways that influence policy outcomes systematically. Simply identifying which interest groups are active on economic relations between the US and China is a necessary step, but since powerful groups have emerged on both sides of the issue, it is difficult to predict which groups will be most important without taking into account how the policy-making process privileges some groups at the expense of others. For example, while the Executive Branch and the Senate have generally been more supportive of trade given their larger constituencies, the House of Representatives has been a bigger hurdle to closer economic relations with China as members of the House answer to narrower constituencies. This suggests that efforts to improve the climate for investment from China to the US should pay special attention to the House of Representatives.

Third, the nature of the investment itself helps to shape outcomes. Investments that complement local factors of production are likely to be easier to conclude than those that substitute for local factors of production. In addition, investments that maintain employment allow local politicians to claim credit for protecting constituent interests and can be valuable tools for local politicians. Firms from China that invest in the US are likely to gain reputations based on the previous investments in the US. Thus, firms that threaten local jobs with their current investments may heighten local opposition to their future investments.

NOTES

*   This chapter was prepared in the context of the Deloitte–Vale Columbia Center on Sustainable International Investment project on "Is the US ready for FDI from China?" The authors are grateful to Alan Wiseman, Karl P. Sauvant, Kris Knutsen and participants in the Columbia University Workshop "Is the US ready for FDI from China?" for very helpful comments, and to Gustavo de las Casas and Boliang Zhu for research assistance. Copyright © 2009 by Columbia University and Deloitte Development LLC. All rights reserved.

1.   A *New York Times* Op-ed from August 4, 2005 titled "No way to treat a dragon," concluded: "The Congressional hysteria over the CNOOC bid demonstrates that only too well. It is a sad example self-interested pandering for votes and contributions – with little regard for the dangerous dynamic it could set in motion."

2.   CCC membership, for instance, is positively associated with support for the East Asia Security Act, arguably an anti-China vote.

3.   The first step in the process is identifying individuals' objective functions, that is, what they are trying to maximize. We assume that individuals prefer more, rather than less income, and that they are willing to trade off part of that income for non-material, ideological or psychological benefit.

4. The consequences of restricting capital mobility are discussed in Quinn and Inclan (1997), Quinn (1997), Alfaro (2004) and Alesina and Tabellini (1989); these four papers focus on capital controls, but make contrary predictions. See also Alesina et al. (1994). On the causes and consequences of foreign investment see Hymer (1976), Dunning (1989), Caves (1996), Feliciano and Lipsey (1999), Henisz (2000), Lipsey (2001) and Janeba (2001).

5. The role of material and ideological concerns at the individual level have been the subject of a large body of literature analyzing the politics of trade and integration. See, among others, Herrmann et al. (2001), Mansfield and Mutz (2006), Mayda and Rodrik (2005), Scheve and Slaughter (2001a, 2001b) and Hiscox (2006).

6. Trade relations could also predispose political actors positively or negatively toward China. Regions that are net exporters to China, for instance, are likely to support friendly Sino–US relations, while individuals displaced by Chinese imports might harbor anti-China sentiment. Moreover, the distributive consequences of FDI inflows might be attenuated or magnified by trade linkages. Depending on its entry strategy and linkages with the local economy, a Chinese affiliate may reduce pressure on local competitors by selling its output back to the parent company or its affiliates abroad, help local businesses place their products in Chinese markets or it might increase import competing pressures when procuring directly from China. Given the dearth of micro-level data on Chinese investment at the state level in the US, this trade–investment linkage is a key in our strategy to identify connections to China in the roll-call analyses conducted in section 4.2. There is a vast body of literature on the distributive consequences of trade: see Stolper and Samuelson (1941), Rogowski (1989), Hiscox (2002), Wood (1991, 1994, 1995) among others.

7. Security concerns in the regulation of FDI in the US are far from new as reflected in the 1917 Trade with the Enemy Act discussed elsewhere in this volume. The source of the concern is different today: in the early 1900s foreign investors dominated critical sectors and technologies that were not available to indigenous firms. The intent of the policy-makers was to guarantee access to that technology and know-how, and develop domestic firms that could master them to reduce foreign dependence (Graham and Krugman 1995; Graham and Marchick 2006, p. 28). Today, the source of the strategic concern is that foreign powers (China in particular) could come to use M&As to acquire sensitive or dual-use technologies not previously available to them. This is the rationale behind the Exon–Florio Amendment of 1988, and the Byrd Amendment of 1991.

8. See Lorraine Eden and Stewart Miller, Chapter 5 in this volume.

9. Johnson defined nationalism as: " a state of social psychology or political sentiment that attaches value to having property in this broad sense physical and financial assets, plus rights to certain kinds of jobs owned by members of the national group" (Johnson 1965, p. 176). However, economic nationalism should not be confounded with protectionism, since under some circumstances the national interest could be better served by promoting foreign investment, exports and imports and integrating with the world economy (Helleiner 2002; Pickel 2003). The conditions under which we would expect economic nationalism to be associated with a particular investment (and trade) policy orientation depend on the nature and characteristics of the investor (including nationality and other strategic considerations), target sector and assets, and on the size, location, level of investment resource endowment and other characteristics of the economy.

10. See Chapter 2 by Steven Globerman and Daniel Shapiro in this volume.

11. There have been around 900 Chinese investments in small and medium-sized firms in the US, worth approximately $1 billion according to a Hildebrandt International report (Graham and Marchick 2006, p. 101).

12. The timing of decision of the Chinese government to encourage Chinese firms to "go out" (in the 10th 5-year Plan of 2001) is also a critical factor, since the US government has tended to impose higher restrictions of inward investment and multinational enterprises (MNEs) activity in times of international conflict and heightened insecurity.

13. It is worth noting that of the top ten largest US economic partners, China is the only one that is not considered an ally (Graham and Marchick 2006, p. 102).

14. See Teslik (2008) for a discussion of sovereign wealth funds.

15. Note, however, that ownership and form of entry are conditional on the effect that the investment has on different actors in the economy: policy-makers' disposition toward sovereign wealth funds, for instance, varies depending on the assets targeted by those funds. Despite strong rhetoric against sovereign wealth funds and SOEs in the US in 2006 aimed at blocking the Dubai Ports deal, Senator Schumer was a supporter of the Abu Dhabi Investment Authority acquisition of a 4.9 per cent stake in Citigroup and Singapore's state-run Temasek Holdings purchase of $5 billion of Merrill Lynch stocks. Bob Davis and Dennis K. Berman, "Lobbyists smoothed the way for a spate of foreign deals." *Wall Street Journal*, January 25, 2008, p. A1. Schumer said in support of the Citigroup deal: "It seemed to me that this is good for Citigroup, it's good for jobs in New York. It bolsters their capital position, allows what is fundamentally a very strong company to weather a difficult time," Heather Timmons and Julia Werdigier, "For Abu Dhabi and Citi, credit crisis drove deal", *New York Times*, November 28, 2007. Wall Street firms are a key constituency of Schumer's, who is also the chair of the Senate Banking Committee.

16. Investment activity by Chinese firms in the United States is likely to be associated with higher trade with China, irrespective of the motivation of that investment. Tariff jumping investment will create similar effects on product markets to Chinese imports, yet different effects on factor markets, since it could lead to higher demand for the factor that complements the Chinese firm in production. Resource and technology-seeking foreign investment, on the other hand, are likely to lead to higher exports to China. This differential effect is central in the two case studies discussed in section 4.3.

17. The Business Roundtable places emphasis on US–China trade relations and proposes a more conciliatory language aimed at promoting US exports. The group has taken positions against Congressional activity aimed at imposing tariffs on Chinese imports to force China to revalue its currency, in favor of easing technology export controls, and reforming CFIUS to promote Chinese investment aimed at protecting jobs at home and creating opportunities abroad. See http://www.businessroundtable.org/newsroom/index.aspx. The Financial Services Forum is a strong advocate of the free flow of capital and investment that would increase the demand for US assets. Robert Nichols, FSF's President and Chief Operating Officer, testified before the House Financial Services Committee on February 7, 2007 in favor of CFIUS reform. See http://financialservices.house.gov/pdf/HTNichols020707.pdf. Nichols argued that the vast majority of inward investment has no bearing on national security and advocated a complete overhaul of CFIUS, with special emphasis on reducing the scope of investment initiatives subject to review.

18. The Financial Business Forum is a member of the Engage China Coalition, an association of nine associations in the financial sector; see http://www.engagechina.com/.

19. Several Washington state Democrats who voted "nay" for HR Resolution 344 regarding the CNOOC deal belong to this group.

20. See Edward M. Graham, and David M. Marchick, "A misplaced curb on investment," *Financial Times*, October 5, 2005.

21. For a review of debate on the effect of trade on wages and inequality see Wood (1994), Lawrence and Slaughter (1993), Freeman (1995), Slaughter (1999) and Bhagwati and Dehejia (1994).

22. This concern is reflected in the academic community in the work of Aaron Friedberg, a Princeton professor, who is currently serving as Vice-President Cheney's national security advisor between 2003 and 2005, and Thomas Christensen, another Princeton faculty member, currently serving as Deputy Assistant Secretary of State for East Asian and Pacific Affairs. See Friedberg (1993, 2005) and Christensen (2002).

23. These views are also present in the press. Bill Gertz, from the *Washington Times* and *The Gertz File* (http://www.gertzfile.com/gertzfile/), and William C. Triplett II, a prominent conservative pundit, usually stress in their columns and blogs the security concerns and blackmail potential associated with Chinese investment and the "China threat."

24. In the roll-call vote analyses presented in section 4.2, we find that representatives from states that are net importers of Chinese goods and services are associated with a more negative disposition toward China.

25. See David Barboza, "An export boom suddenly facing a quality crisis," *New York Times*, May 18, 2007; Davide Barboza, "China steps up its safety efforts," *New York Times*, July 6, 2007. Louise Story and David Barboza, "Mattel recalls 19 million toys sent from China," *New York Times*, August 15, 2007. A recent public opinion poll reported in the *New York Times* shows that US consumers view Chinese imports as more dangerous than imports from other countries, yet concern about product quality is not limited to China. Steven Weisman and Marjorie Connelly, "Americans are open to Chinese goods, poll finds," *New York Times*, October 22, 2007.

26. The survey was run by the Chicago Council on Global Affairs in 2004.

27. In the US system, then, protection to key industries can arise from two different routes: a universalistic log-rolling of interests, or preferential access to policy-makers in key Congressional positions. In proportional representation systems with party control over the ballots, on the other hand, where parties are strong, representatives typically owe their seat to party leaders and are often more responsive to the party than to voters. The electoral system hence provides incentives for parties to cater to the party's core constituents (McGillivray 2004, pp. 19, 53).

28. Membership in Congressional Committees and leadership positions correspond to those of the 110th Congress.

29. See http://forbes.house.gov/Biography/chinacaucus.htm.

30. By convention, we identify legislators by their party R stands for Republican, and D for Democrat), and their state.

31. For USCWG membership see: http://www.house.gov/kirk/uscwg.shtml.

32. DW-nominate scores are estimates that compute the ideological position of policy-makers in two dimensions based on their votes in Congress: liberal-conservative and North–South/social.

33. Lewis and Poole (2004). See http://voteview.com/dwnomin.htm.

34. We coded as moderate if the Congress-member is a Democrat and member of the Blue Dog Coalition (right-center Democrats) or a Republican and member of the Republican Main Street Partnership (moderate Republican).

35. With 16 terms in office, Norm Dick (D-WA) is the longest serving member of the USCWG.
36. Data on industry and occupation in Congressional districts were obtained from the US Census Bureau's Fast Facts from the Congress site (http://fastfacts.census.gov/home/cws/main.html). Data on contributions were obtained from http://www.opensecrets.org.
37. In Table 4.3 we present a statistical analysis of the determinants of the roll-call vote that led to the passage of H. Res. 344.
38. H.Res. 344, is a non-binding resolution adopted by the House on June 30, 2005 declaring: "that a Chinese state-owned energy company exercising control of critical United States energy infrastructure and energy production capacity could take action that would threaten to impair the national security of the United States." http://clerk.house.gov/evs/2005/roll360.xml.
39. See: http://www.wscrc.org/default.cfm.
40. Senator Charles Schumer (D-NY) and Senator Lindsey Graham (R-SC) introduced legislation calling for a 27 percent tariff on Chinese goods to persuade China to revalue its currency. It is interesting to note that Schumer, who has been harsh critic of China's currency policy and trade practices, did not oppose the Unocal/CNOOC merger. *New York Times*, August 3, 2005. See also note 15.
41. For example, see http://www.cecc.gov/pages/hearings/092403/levin.php and http://www.cecc.gov/pages/hearings/020702/levin.php?PHPSESSID=a6fcdc1627ac5864bd77e8ba4c8d72c8.
42. Control by the Democratic Party over Congress strengthened after the 2008 election.
43. Of course, some states are more influential than others in the presidential election. Witness President Bush's decision to levy tariffs on steel imports to offer protection to firms in swing states in the Upper Midwest prior to the election of 2004.
44. Congressional Research Service (CRS) (2006, p. 15).
45. Otis Bilodeau, "US begins inquiry into Lenovo–IBM deal," *International Herald Tribune*, January 31, 2005.
46. Ibid.
47. Stephanie Kirchgaessner, Richard Waters and Simon London, "IBM deal with Lenovo cleared," *International Herald Tribune*, March 9, 2005.
48. Note on US–China Economic and Security Review Commission, http://www.uscc.gov/.
49. *Financial Times*, August 4, 2005 "China group sees its influence grow in Washington."
50. D'Amato is a long-term adviser to Senator Robert Byrd (D-WV), a prominent member of the anti-China coalition in Congress. In an interview with the *LA Times* D'Amato said: "When we're so dependent on foreign suppliers, giving away American sources of petroleum and hydrocarbons does not make much sense to me, *Los Angeles Times*, June 23, 2005, "Chinese oil firm bids for Unocal."
51. The evolution of the debate around the 3Com deal is particularly interesting due to the active participation of private actors such as Seagate and Cisco, which played an instrumental role in raising economic and national security concerns. See John Markoff, "Chinese seek to buy a US maker of disk drives," *New York Times*, August 25, 2007; Laurie J. Flynn and Keith Bradsher, "Bain and Chinese company to acquire 3Com," *New York Times*, September 29, 2007. In October 10, 2007, eight representatives sponsored House Resolution 730 that states: "As currently structured, the proposed transaction involving Huawei threatens the national security of the United States and should not be approved." One of the co-sponsors of resolution 730 was Rep. Thad McCotter (R-MI), a CCC member, and supporter of the interests of the IT industry. On Oct. 19, 2007, Senators John Kyl (R-AZ) and 13 other senators wrote a letter to the Executive Branch requesting a rigorous review of the 3Com deal. For information on this bill, see GovTrack.us. H. Res. 730-110th Congress (2007). In the end CFIUS decided to block the deal; see Steven R. Weisman, "US security concerns block China's 3Com deal," *New York Times*, February 21, 2008.
52. China expert Nicholas Lardy noted: "Whether it is phosphates in Florida, iron-ore deposits in the Upper Midwest, timber cutting rights in the Pacific Northwest – most of it [Chinese Investment] has been in the natural resources area" (Baxter 2005).
53. Voting in non-binding resolutions such as H.Res. 344 are associated with what Mayhew (1974) classifies as "position-taking," namely activities performed by re-election-driven incumbents aimed at signaling to their constituents their policy preferences. Votes on procedure, such as H.R. 3100, on the other hand are equivalent to votes for final passage of the bill, and hence more likely to be cast on partisan lines.
54. Unfortunately we were not able to obtain data on the geographic and sectoral allocation of Chinese investment in the US, which would have allowed us to assess the relative influence of the presence of Chinese firms at the district or state levels. The export data used in our analysis, on the other hand, could be considered as a broad proxy for the importance of economic ties with China (note 16). Trade data are only available at the state level, and were obtained from the US–China Economic and Security Review Commission (ww.uscc.gov). Import data were allocated to states according to each state's share of US population. Employment data come from the US Census Bureau. The variables used for the analysis are the proportion of the state totals. As a measure of ideology, we use the first dimension of the DW Nominate score, obtained from past votes (Lewis and Poole 2004; see note 32). We use the scores for the 108th Congress

for those representatives who moved on to Congress 109th, and the score for the 109th Congress for those who were not in the 108th Congress. While this is in principle problematic, since the scores for the 109th voted used RC 360 and 374 to estimate the ideal points, dropping these observations makes no substantive difference to our analysis. Regional dummies, partisanship and committee membership were coded by the authors using Congressional records.

55. Results obtained using Clarify 2.1 (King et al. 2000; Tomz et al. 2003) with parameters from model 1, setting the rest of the covariates to their means, and the partisan dummy to Republican. Note that trade with China has two effects on a representative's vote on this issue: one is direct, and the other one indirect, through CCC and USCWG membership (Table 4.2).
56. Results obtained with Clarify using the coefficients from model (4).
57. It should be noted that neither of the case studies is from industries which raise concerns for national security. Thus, the politics that underpin these cases are quite different from the proposed Unocal–CNOOC merger.
58. http://www.forbes.com/home/feeds/afx/2005/11/14/afx2336515.html.
59. http://www.governor.state.mn.us/priorities/initiatives/TradeMission/index.htm; http://www.governor.state.mn.us/journal/missiontochina/index.htm.
60. Peter Wonacott, "Shopping for China: a scourge of the rust belt offers some hope there too," *Wall Street Journal*, November 26, 2004.
61. *Financial Times*, December 12, 2006.
62. Ibid.

REFERENCES

Alesina, A., V. Grilli and G.M. Milisi-Fereeti (1994). "The political economy of capital controls," in Leonardo Leiderman and Assaf Razin, eds., *Capital Mobility: The Impact on Consumption, Investment, and Growth* (New York: Cambridge University Press), pp. 289–321.

Alesina, A. and G. Tabellini (1989). "External debt, capital flight and political risk," *Journal of International Economics*, 27 (3–4), pp. 199–220.

Alfaro, Laura (2004). "Capital controls: a political economy approach," *Review of International Economics*, 12 (4), pp. 571–90.

Bailey, Michael, Judith Goldstein and Barry Weingast (1997). "The institutional roots of American trade policy," *World Politics*, April, pp. 309–38.

Baldwin, Richard (1985). *The Political Economy of US Import Policy* (Cambridge, MA: MIT Press).

Baxter, Annie (2005). "Minnesota eager for Chinese Investment," Minnesota Public Radio, November 21, 2005.

Bhagwati, Jagdish and Vivek Dehejia (1994). "Free trade and wages of the unskilled: is Marx striking again?" in Jagdish Bhagwati and Marvin Kosters, eds, *Trade and Wages: Leveling Wages Down?* (Washington, DC: AEI Press), pp. 36–75.

Bloomberg (2006). Cheng, Allen T. "Paper Tycoon becomes 1st Woman to Top China Rich List", (update 4), http://www.bloomberg.com/apps/news?pid_en&sid=asySLLXOSolg (accessed October 11, 2006).

Caves, Richard E. (1996). *Multinational Enterprise and Economic Analysis* (Cambridge, UK and New York, USA: Cambridge University Press).

Christensen, Thomas (2002). "Deterring a Taiwan conflict: the contemporary security dilemma," *The Washington Quarterly*, 25 (4), pp. 7–21.

Corr, Christopher (2007). "FINSA: raising the risks for foreign investment in the US," White and Case, Washington, DC, August 3.

Cox, Gary W. and Mathew D. McCubbins (1993). *Legislative Leviathan: Party Government in the House*, California Series on Social Choice and Political Economy, (Berkeley, CA: University of California Press).

Cox, Gary W. and Mathew D. McCubbins (2007). *Legislative Leviathan: Party Government in the House* (New York: Cambridge University Press).

CRS, Dick K. Nanto, James K. Jackson and Wayne M. Morrison (2006). Report for Congress,

"China and the CNOOC bid for Unocal: issues for Congress," Congressional Research Service, Washington, DC, February 23.

CRS and James K. Jackson (2007). Report for Congress, "The Committee on Foreign Investment in the United States (CFIUS)," Congressional Research Service, Washington, DC, July 23.

Dunning, John H. (1989). *International Production and Multinational Enterprise* (New York: Allen & Unwin).

Feliciano, Z. and R. Lipsey (1999). "Foreign ownership and wages in the United States, 1987–1992". NBER Working Paper No. w6923. Cambridge, MA: National Bureau of Economic Research.

Freeman, Richard B. (1995). "Are your wages set in Beijing?" *Journal of Economic Perspectives*, 9 (3), pp. 15–32.

Friedberg, Aaron L. (1993). "Ripe for rivalry: prospects for peace in a multipolar Asia," *International Security*, 18 (3), pp. 5–33.

Friedberg, Aaron L. (2005). "The future of US–China relations is conflict inevitable?" *International Security*, (Fall 2005) Vol. 30 (2), pp. 7–45.

Graham, Edward and Paul K. Krugman (1995). *Foreign Direct Investment in the United States*. 3rd ed. (Washington, DC: Institute for International Economics).

Graham, Edward M. and David M. Marchick (2006). *US National Security and Foreign Direct Investment* (Washington, DC: Institute for International Economics).

GovTrack.us. H. Res. 730–110th Congress (2007). "Expressing the sense of the House of Representatives regarding the planned acquisition of a minority interest in 3Com by affiliates of Huawei." GovTrack.us (database of federal legislation), http://www.govtrack.us/congress/bill. xpd?bill=hr110-730 (accessed December 15, 2007).

Helleiner, Eric (2002). "Economic nationalism as a challenge to economic liberalism? Lessons from the 19th century," *International Studies Quarterly*, 46 (3), pp. 307–29.

Henisz, Witold J. (2000). "The institutional environment for multinational investment," *Journal of Law, Economics, and Organization*, 16 (2), pp. 334–64.

Henisz, Witold J. (2002). "The institutional environment for infrastructure investment," *Industrial and Corporate Change*, 11 (2), pp. 355–89.

Henisz, Witold J. and O. Williamson (1999). "Comparative economic organization: within and between countries," *Business and Politics*, 1 (3), pp. 261–76.

Henisz, Witold J. and Bennet A. Zelner (2001). "The institutional environment for telecommunications investment," *Journal of Economics and Management Strategy*, 10 (1), p. 123.

Herrmann, Richard K., Philip E. Tetlock and Matthew N. Diascro (2001). "How Americans think about trade: reconciling conflicts among money, power, and principles," *International Studies Quarterly*, 45, pp. 191–218.

Hiscox, Michael J. (2002). *International Trade and Political Conflict: Commerce, Coalition, and Mobility* (Princeton, NJ: Princeton University Press).

Hiscox, Michael J. (2006). "Through a glass darkly: attitudes toward international trade and the curious effects of framing," *International Organization*, 60, pp. 755–80.

Hymer, Stephen (1976). *The International Operations of National Firms: A Study Direct Foreign Investment* (Cambridge, MA: MIT Press).

Janeba, Eckhard (2001). "Global corporations and local politics: a theory of voter backlash". NBER Working Paper No. w8254. Cambridge, MA: National Bureau of Economic Research.

Johnson, Harry G. (1965). "A theoretical model of economic nationalism in new and developing states," *Political Science Quarterly*, 80 (2), pp. 169–85.

King, Gary, Michael Tomz and Jason Wittenberg (2000). "Making the most of statistical analyses: improving interpretation and presentation," *American Journal of Political Science*, 44 (2), pp. 347–61.

Lawrence, Robert Z. and Matthew Slaughter (1993). "International trade and American wages in the 1980s: giant sucking sound or small hiccup?" *Brookings Papers on Economic Activity. Microeconomics*, pp. 162–226.

Levy, Brian and Pablo T. Spiller (1994). "The institutional foundations of regulatory commitment: a comparative analysis of telecommunications regulation," *Journal of Law, Economics, and Organization*, 10 (2), pp. 201–46.

Lewis, Jeffrey B. and Keith T. Poole (2004). "Measuring bias and uncertainty in ideal point estimates via the parametric bootstrap," *Political Analysis*, 12, pp. 105–27.

Lipsey, Robert E. (2001). "Foreign direct investment and the operations of multinational firms: concepts, history, and data". NBER Working Paper No. w8665. Cambridge, MA: National Bureau of Economic Research.

Lohmann, Susanne and Sharyn O'Halloran (1994). "Divided government and US trade policy," *International Organization*, 48 (4), pp. 595–632.

Mansfield, Edward D. and Diana Mutz (2006). "Public support for free trade: self-interest or sociotropic politics." Paper presented at the Annual Meeting of the American Political Science Association. September, Philadelphia, PA.

Mayda, Anna Maria and Dani Rodrik (2005). "Why are some people (and countries) more protectionist than others?" *European Economic Review*, 49 (6), pp. 1393–430.

Mayhew, David R. (1974). *Congress: The Electoral Connection* (New Haven, CT: Yale Press).

McGillivray, Fiona (2004). *Privileging Industry: The Comparative Politics of Trade and Industrial Policy* (Princeton, NJ: Princeton University Press).

Milner, Helen (1988). *Resisting Protectionism: Global Industries and the Politics of International Trade* (Princeton, NJ: Princeton University Press).

Pickel, Andreas (2003). "Explaining, and explaining with, economic nationalism," *Nations and Nationalism*, 9 (1) pp. 105–27.

Pinto, Pablo M. (2004). "Domestic coalitions and the political economy of foreign direct investment". PhD dissertation, Department of Political Science, University of California, San Diego, CA.

Pinto, Pablo M. and Santiago M. Pinto (2008). "The politics of investment: partisanship and the activity of multinational corporations," *Economics and Politics*, 20 (2), pp. 216–54.

Quinn, Dennis (1997), "The correlates of change in international financial regulation," *American Political Science Review*, 91 (3), pp. 531–51.

Quinn, Dennis P. and Carla Inclan (1997). "The origins of financial openness: a study of current and capital account liberalization," *American Journal of Political Science*, 14 (3): pp. 771–813.

Rogowski, Ronald (1989). *Commerce and Coalitions: How Trade Affects Domestic Political Alignments* (Princeton, NJ: Princeton University Press).

Scheve, Kenneth F. and Matthew J. Slaughter (2001a). "What determines individual trade-policy preferences," *Journal of International Economics*, 54, pp. 267–92.

Scheve, Kenneth F. and Matthew J. Slaughter (2001b). *Globalization and the Perceptions of American Workers* (Washington, DC: Institute for International Economics).

Slaughter, Matthew J. (1999). "Globalization and wages: a tale of two perspectives," *World Economy*, 22 (5), pp. 609–30.

Spiller, P.T. and M. Tommasi (2003). "The institutional foundations of public policy: a transactions approach with application to Argentina," *Journal of Law Economics and Organization*, 19 (2), pp. 281–306.

Stolper, Wolfgang F. and Paul A. Samuelson (1941). "Protection and real wages," *Review of Economic Studies*, 9 (1), pp. 58–73.

Teslik, Lee Hudson (2008). "Sovereign Wealth Funds: Backgrounder," http://www.cfr.org/publication/15251/, accessed January 25, 2008.

Thomson, Elspeth (2005). "The Unocal bid and free-market principles," *Perspectives* 6 (December 31), pp. 4–8.

Tomz, Michael, Jason Wittenberg and Gary King (2003). CLARIFY: Software for Interpreting and Presenting Statistical Results. Version 2.1. Stanford University, University of Wisconsin, and Harvard University. January 5. Available at http://gking.harvard.edu/.

Williamson, Oliver E. (1985). *The Economic Institutions of Capitalism: Firms, Markets, Relational Contracting* (New York: Free Press).

Wood, Adrian (1991). "How much does trade with the south affect workers in the north?" *World Bank Research Observer*, 6 (January), pp. 19–36.

Wood, Adrian (1994). *North–South Trade: Employment and Inequality* (Oxford: Clarendon).

Wood, Adrian (1995). "How trade hurts unskilled workers," *Journal of Economic Perspectives*, 9 (3), pp. 57–80.

APPENDIX

Table 4A.1a   Attitudes toward China: individuals

Q120 Whether Favor/Oppose Engaging In Trade With: "China"

	Military superiority		
	Very important	Somewhat important	Not important
Yes, favor trade	376	321	54
(%)	62.4	66	66.1
No, oppose trade	196	142	25
(%)	32.5	29.1	30.1

Source: Chicago Council on Global Affairs (Global Views Survey) 2004.

Q120 Whether Favor/Oppose Engaging In Trade With: "China"

	Protect US jobs		
	Very important	Somewhat important	Not important
Yes, favor trade	581	158	15
(%)	62	71	81.6
No, oppose trade	309	51	3
(%)	33.01	22.8	14.8

Source: Chicago Council on Global Affairs (Global Views Survey) 2004.

Q120 Whether Favor/Oppose Engaging In Trade With: "China"

	Ensure no other superpowers	
	Make active efforts	Not make active efforts
Yes, favor trade	392	333
(%)	62.7	67.5
No, oppose trade	205	154
(%)	32.8	31.3

Source: Chicago Council on Global Affairs (Global Views Survey) 2004.

Q120 Whether Favor/Oppose Engaging In Trade With: "China"

	Education summary		
	Total college grad	Total college	HS or less
Yes, favor trade	214	433	324
(%)	74.21	70.41	55.8
No, oppose trade	67	156	209
(%)	23.1	25.4	36.1

Source: Chicago Council on Global Affairs (Global Views Survey) 2004.

Q345 Feeling Towards Having Diplomatic Relations with China

	Income						
	<$15K	15–24.9K	25K–34.9K	35K–49.9K	50K–99.9K	100K–149.9K	150K
Favor	108	128	114	206	268	54	16
(%)	58.7	71.6	76	79	79.8	76.5	95.9
Oppose	45	36	25	37	51	11	1
(%)	24.4	20.4	16.6	14.4	15.2	15.7	4.1

Source: Chicago Council on Global Affairs (Global Views Survey) 2004.

Q120 Whether Favor/Oppose Engaging In Trade With: "China"

	Income						
	<$15K	15–24.9K	25K–34.9K	35K–49.9K	50K–99.9K	100K–149.9K	150K
Yes, favor trade	107	97	102	173	214	50	14
(%)	58.2	54.3	67.6	66.6	63.7	71.7	83.7
No, oppose trade	59	61	44	73	109	17	3
(%)	31.8	34.3	29.4	27.9	32.5	24.8	16.3

Source: Chicago Council on Global Affairs (Global Views Survey) 2004.

Q120 Whether Favor/Oppose Engaging In Trade With: "China"

	Party ID						
	Strong Rep	Not strong Rep	Lean Rep	Pure Ind	Lean Dem	Not strong Dem	Strong Dem
Yes, favor trade	83	74	48	180	65	150	157
(%)	54.5	65.6	67.9	59.5	56.8	70.7	68.1
No, oppose trade	62	34	20	91	38	52	68
(%)	40.7	30.5	28.5	30.2	33.7	24.4	29.2

Source: Chicago Council on Global Affairs (Global Views Survey) 2004.

Table 4A.1b   Attitudes toward China: elites

Q120 Whether Favor/Oppose Engaging In Trade With: "China"

	Conservative	Middle-of-the-Road	Liberal
Yes, favor trade	86	120	157
	90%	91	91
No, oppose trade	7	10	14
	8%	7	8

Source: Chicago Council on Global Affairs (Global Views Survey) 2004.

Q120 Whether Favor/Oppose Engaging In Trade With: "China"

	Republican	Independent	Democrat
Yes, favor trade	85	88	172
	89%	93	91
No, oppose trade	8	5	15
	9%	6	8

Source: Chicago Council on Global Affairs (Global Views Survey) 2004.

Q120 Whether Favor/Oppose Engaging In Trade With: "China"

	Leader category						
	Religious	Business	Labor	Special interest	Foreign policy	Senate	House
Yes, favor trade	45	35	21	22	28	19	40
	88%	92%	66%	88%	97%	94%	90%
No, oppose trade	4	3	11	2	1	1	4
	8%	8%	34%	8%	3%	3%	9%

Source: Chicago Council on Global Affairs (Global Views Survey) 2004.

Q120 Whether Favor/Oppose Engaging In Trade With: "China"

Base: Senate	Republican	Independent	Democrat
Yes, favor trade	11	5	13
	100%	100%	87%
No, oppose trade	0	0	1
	–	–	6%
Base: House	Republican	Independent	Democrat
Yes, favor trade	20	5	34
	87%	71%	94%
No, oppose trade	2	2	2
	9%	29%	6%

Source: Chicago Council on Global Affairs (Global Views Survey) 2004.

Table 4A.2   Attitudes toward China as a world power, various years

3/2. The development of China as world power   (N = 1195)

Year	Critical (%)	Important but not critical (%)	Not important (%)	Not sure/ decline (%)	Total (%)
1990	40	43	9	8	100
1994	57	32	5	6	100
1998	57	32	6	5	100
2002 (telephone)	56	34	8	2	100
2004 (telephone)	40	39	16	5	100
2004 (internet)	33	54	10	2	100
Change in % points 2002–04	−16	+5	+8	+3	100

Source: Chicago Council on Global Affairs (Global Views Survey), various years.

2006 Results
3/1. The development of China as world power

	Critical (%)	Important but not critical (%)	Not important (%)	Not sure/ decline (%)	Total (%)
US	36	54	8	2	100
China	n/a	n/a	n/a	n/a	
India	43	31	18	9	100
South Korea	49	42	8	1	100
Australia	25	52	22	1	100

Source: Chicago Council on Global Affairs (Global Views Survey), 2006.

120/4. China   (N = 1195)

Year	Yes, favor trade (%)	No, oppose trade (%)	Not sure/ decline (%)	Total (%)
2002 (telephone)	71	26	3	100
2004 (internet)	63	31	6	100

Source: Chicago Council on Global Affairs (Global Views Survey), 2006.

345/4. China   (N = 1195)

Year	Yes, favor trade (%)	No, oppose trade (%)	Not sure/ decline (%)	Total (%)
2002 (telephone)	80	18	2	100
2004 (internet)	75	17	8	100

Source: Chicago Council on Global Affairs (Global Views Survey), various years.

2002–04 Results
140/4. China   (N = 1195)

Year	Practice fair trade (%)	Practice unfair trade (%)	Not sure/ decline (%)	Total (%)
2002 (telephone)	32	53	15	100
2004 (internet)	36	51	13	100

Source: Chicago Council on Global Affairs (Global Views Survey), various years.

2006 Results
202/4. China

	Practice fair trade (%)	Practice unfair trade (%)	Not sure/ decline (%)	Total (%)
US	31	58	12	100
China	n/a	n/a	n/a	
India	34	36	30	100
South Korea	44	54	2	100
Australia	n/a	n/a	n/a	

Source: Chicago Council on Global Affairs (Global Views Survey), 2006.

2006 Results
Question 245 (1–6): In your opinion, should companies from the following countries generally be allowed or not allowed to purchase a controlling interest in [survey country] companies:

245/1. EU countries

	Should be allowed (%)	Should not be allowed (%)	Not sure/ decline (%)	Total (%)
US	39	55	5	100
China	50	33	17	100
India	48	34	18	100
South Korea	34	64	2	100
Australia	n/a	n/a	n/a	

Source: Chicago Council on Global Affairs (Global Views Survey), 2006.

245/3. China

	Should be allowed (%)	Should not be allowed (%)	Not sure/ decline (%)	Total (%)
US	24	71	5	100
China	n/a	n/a	n/a	100
India	48	36	16	100
South Korea	31	68	2	100
Australia	n/a	n/a	n/a	

Source: Chicago Council on Global Affairs (Global Views Survey), 2006.

245/4. Japan

	Should be allowed (%)	Should not be allowed (%)	Not sure/ decline (%)	Total (%)
US	28	66	5	100
China	43	38	19	100
India	n/a	n/a	n/a	
South Korea	33	65	2	100
Australia	n/a	n/a	n/a	

Source: Chicago Council on Global Affairs (Global Views Survey), 2006.

245/5. India

	Should be allowed (%)	Should not be allowed (%)	Not sure/ decline (%)	Total (%)
US	28	66	5	100
China	43	38	19	100
India	n/a	n/a	n/a	
South Korea	33	65	2	100
Australia	n/a	n/a	n/a	

Source: Chicago Council on Global Affairs (Global Views Survey), 2006.

245/6. South Korea

	Should be allowed (%)	Should not be allowed (%)	Not sure/ decline (%)	Total (%)
US	27	67	5	100
China	51	31	18	100
India	43	32	25	100
South Korea	n/a	n/a	n/a	
Australia	n/a	n/a	n/a	

Source: Chicago Council on Global Affairs (Global Views Survey), 2006.

5. Revisiting liability of foreignness: socio-political costs facing Chinese multinationals in the United States

Lorraine Eden and Stewart R. Miller*

Alien status always imposes some penalty on managerial effectiveness. (Caves 1971, p. 6)

INTRODUCTION

China's gaze is now looking outward. With over $1 trillion in foreign exchange reserves at the beginning of 2008, the Chinese government encourages domestic firms to engage in a strategy of outward direct investment – "Going Global." In addition, the China Investment Corporation (CIC), the new state agency inaugurated in October 2007 with a registered capital base of $200 billion, has been set up to make its own overseas investments (*China Business* 2007). In 2006, Chinese outward foreign direct investment (FDI) flows had reached $18 billion, for a stock of $82 billion (Kekic and Sauvant 2007). Firms are expanding abroad – and one of their primary destinations (as so many firms before them) is the United States of America.

As Chinese investment into the United States increases, one cause for concern for Chinese executives is liability of foreignness (LOF), which refers to the added costs, specifically socio-political costs, faced by the foreign affiliate of a multinational enterprise (MNE) that are not incurred by domestic firms in the host country (Zaheer 1995). In this chapter, we ask what kinds of LOF costs face affiliates of these new Chinese multinationals when they come to the United States. Our study focuses on LOF costs to both Chinese parent firms and their US affiliates.

We begin by discussing liability of foreignness and focus on the key driver of the level of LOF – differences in the institutions of two countries (that is, institutional distance). We explore three types of institutions (regulatory, normative, cognitive) and argue that both the difference between, and the level of, institutions matter when a foreign firm enters a host country. We then link LOF to the institutional distance between China and the United States as we highlight the principal legal and non-legal costs that may arise after a Chinese firm establishes a US affiliate. Lastly, we outline possible strategies that Chinese MNEs can use to cope with these socio-political costs.

5.1 LIABILITY OF FOREIGNNESS AND INSTITUTIONAL DISTANCE

5.1.1 Liability of Foreignness

The costs of doing business abroad measure all the costs faced by a home country firm associated with its activities in a foreign country, over and above the costs faced by a local firm conducting similar activities. These costs can be separated into activity-based costs and liability of foreignness (Eden and Miller 2004). Liability of foreignness manifests itself as unfamiliarity costs, discriminatory costs and relational costs.

Unfamiliarity costs reflect a foreign MNE's lack of host country knowledge compared to domestic firms in the host country. Discriminatory costs reflect the differential treatment of foreign MNEs by producers, consumers, factors and governments in the host country (Balabanis et al. 2001; Henisz and Williamson 1999; Sumner 1906), including both formal and informal discriminatory treatment.[1] Relational costs represent the additional administrative costs of managing relationships at a distance, for example between a parent firm and its foreign affiliate or between the two partners if the affiliate is constituted as a joint venture with another firm (Buckley and Casson 1998; Henisz and Williamson 1999). Relational costs include both the managerial information-processing demands of managing highly complex internationally diversified firms and the negotiating, monitoring and dispute settlement costs of dealing with foreign partners. One set of costs could influence the other; for example, discriminatory treatment by a host government might encourage a domestic licensee or joint venture partner to become more opportunistic in its dealings with a multinational, so that political discrimination encourages interorganizational relational costs (Henisz and Williamson 1999).

What causes liability of foreignness? Why do foreign firms face additional costs not faced by domestic firms in a host country? We argue that institutional distance is the cause.

Institutions
In order to understand institutional distance, we must first understand institutions. Nobel laureate Douglass North defined institutions as: "the rules of the game in a society" (1990 p. 3). Institutions can be formal constraints (for example, laws) as well as informal constraints (codes of behavior) that underlie or supplement formal rules (North 1990). These classifications coincide well with research that has emphasized regulatory, normative and cognitive pillars of institutions (Scott 1995, p. 33), in that formal constraints are shaped by regulatory institutions while informal constraints are shaped by normative and cognitive institutions.

The regulatory pillar deals with "existing laws and rules in a particular national environment which promote certain types of behaviors and restrict others" (Kostova 1997, p. 180). It outlines prescriptive ("may") and proscriptive ("may not") behaviors, and applies rewards and sanctions for compliance with these pre/proscriptions. The regulatory pillar is perhaps the easiest for foreign MNEs to observe, understand and correctly interpret because host country regulatory institutions tend to be codified and formalized in rules and procedures.

The normative pillar consists of "social norms, values, beliefs, and assumptions about human nature and human behavior that are socially shared and are carried by individuals" (Kostova 1997, p. 180). The normative pillar is "rooted in societal beliefs and norms" (Xu and Shenkar 2002, p. 610) about how things should and should not be done. Such informal prescriptions and proscriptions are often culturally driven, and therefore difficult for outsiders to see and interpret (Kostova and Zaheer 1999).

The cognitive pillar affects the "schemas, frames, and inferential sets, which people use when selecting and interpreting information" (Kostova 1997, p. 180). Cognitive institutions affect "the way people notice, characterize, and interpret stimuli from the environment" (Kostova 1999, p. 314) in terms of national symbols, stereotypes, key sectors, and so on.

In sum, as Eden and Miller (2004) concluded, the regulatory pillar defines what organizations and individuals "may or may not do" (where "may" implies permission), the normative pillar defines what they "should or should not do", and the cognitive pillar defines what "is or is not true" and what "can or cannot be done" (where "can" implies ability). Thus, the three pillars are akin to three verb tenses: may/may not (regulatory), should/should not (normative) and can/cannot (cognitive).

Institutional distance
The institutional distance between two countries is the degree of difference/similarity between the regulatory, cognitive and normative institutions of two countries (Kostova 1997). Institutional distance can be different for each of the three institutional pillars: regulatory, normative and cognitive. In all three cases, we argue that greater institutional distance increases the liability of foreignness and the need for foreign MNEs to be locally responsive to host country institutions.

Regulatory institutional distance measures the difference between home and host countries in terms of the setting, monitoring and enforcement of rules. Within developed countries, regulatory frameworks have become more homogeneous due to globalization pressures, regional integration schemes and international institutions such as the World Trade Organization and the Organisation for Economic Co-operation and Development (OECD). As a result, regulatory distance between OECD member countries has been falling for many years, and in most industries may now be considered minimal.

Even in the emerging economies of Asia, Latin America and the former USSR, the ability of governments to force unilateral policy changes on MNEs has been substantially curtailed by the web of bilateral investment and double taxation treaties, membership in international organizations, and structural adjustment constraints imposed by the World Bank and International Monetary Fund (Ramamurti 2001). In addition, almost all national policy changes affecting MNEs since the early 1990s have been liberalizing (UNCTAD 2007); as a result, the regulatory institutional distance between OECD and emerging economies has been falling. We therefore conclude that regulatory distance, for most industries and countries, is low and therefore is no longer a primary driver of LOF for MNEs entering most (but not all) industries in most (but not all) host countries.[2]

Normative institutional distance is generated by differences across countries in societal beliefs about how things should and should not be done. Because norms are typically informal and tacit, foreign firms are likely to have great difficulty understanding host country institutional guidelines, which increases the likelihood of discriminatory treatment (Kostova and Zaheer 1999). Moreover, with high levels of normative distance, it is more difficult for a parent firm to transfer organizational practices to an acquired local affiliate, especially when the practices of local firms are institutionalized in the host country environment. This difficulty in transferring practices within a MNE group raises the intra-relational costs of managing operations at a distance. Therefore, we expect unfamiliarity, discriminatory and inter- and intra-relational costs all to increase with normative distance.

Cognitive institutional distance facing the MNE is caused primarily by differences among countries in their national symbols and stereotypes. Cognitive institutions represent "the way people notice, characterize, and interpret stimuli from the environment" (Kostova 1999, p. 314). Cognitive institutions are affected by the way domestic firms and consumers interact with, and how they view, foreigners. Kostova and Zaheer (1999) suggested that foreign firms can incur stereotyping by host country institutions and organizations due to their unfamiliarity with outsiders. For example, industries with strong national symbolism (such as the petroleum industry in Mexico) typically have low penetration rates by foreign firms due to substantive host country regulations restricting foreign equity ownership. When cognitive distance is high, acquisitions are viewed as "takeovers" and a "blow to national sovereignty" from the local market's perspective (Xu and Shenkar 2002, p. 613).

Institutional levels versus institutional distance

Emerging economies in Asia and Latin America tend to have weak formal institutions and are therefore more likely to rely on informal institutional enforcement procedures such as networks, *guanxi* and family conglomerates. When an MNE moves from a country with high-quality, well-developed institutions (for example, the United States) to an emerging economy where the institutions are less developed, clearly there is institutional distance between the two countries.

In addition to the distance between the two countries, there is the issue of whether it is easier for the firm to move from low to high levels of institutions (for example, from China to the United States) or from high to low levels of institutions (vice versa). Emerging market firms that engage in foreign direct investment in a developed economy are typically moving from low- to high-level institutions, that is, from institutional voids to well-developed, market-based and more formalized institutions. We hypothesize that the costs of moving from a country with low-quality or missing institutions to a country with high-quality institutions should be larger than the reverse, in the same way that it is harder to walk upstairs than it is to walk down (the "stair-climbing" problem). Thus, the institutional distance between a developed market and an emerging economy is exacerbated when the firm involved is moving upwards in term of institutions.

Coping with liability of foreignness

We start from the premise that, holding revenues constant, the multinational enterprise wants to minimize the additional costs of doing business abroad – that is, the sum of activity-based costs, unfamiliarity costs, discriminatory costs, and intra- and interrelational costs. The greater the institutional distance, the greater the liability of foreignness faced by a foreign MNE in a host country. In order to be successful in the host country, the MNE must engage in activities (that is, select one or more strategies) to minimize or offset these LOF costs.[3]

The typical strategies for coping with liability of foreignness are designed to offset the three types of institutional distance: regulatory, normative and cognitive. As we have explained above, differences in regulatory institutions are easier for an MNE to understand since regulatory institutions tend to be more formalized in rules and procedures. In addition, differences in regulations affecting FDI flows and foreign ownership between countries have been falling for several years (with some exceptions, notably Venezuela). On the other hand, normative and cognitive institutions are more problematic since they tend to be tacit and opaque. A common strategy for coping with liability of foreignness is to take on a foreign partner ("put a local face" on the MNE in the host country), as explored in Eden and Miller (2004).

Let us now apply our LOF institutional distance framework to the case of Chinese multinationals entering the United States.

5.2　CHINESE MULTINATIONALS: SAME OR DIFFERENT?

Are US affiliates of Chinese firms different from US affiliates of other emerging-market firms or from non-US affiliates of Chinese firms? We argue that there are some key differences.

First, Chinese multinationals are latecomer MNEs, recent entrants to the world of outward FDI flows. Starting from almost zero in 1980, Chinese outward FDI flows have grown to more than $16 billion in 2006. While an impressive growth rate, China's FDI stock represented less than 0.6 percent of the 2005 world FDI stock (Morck et al. 2008). Latecomer status is likely to have both benefits and costs for Chinese MNEs. There is the opportunity to learn (the demonstration effect) from first- and second-mover foreign MNEs that entered a host country market earlier than Chinese firms, thus helping them to avoid mistakes in location choice, mode of entry and so on. As a result, liability of foreignness arising from unfamiliarity costs may be smaller for latecomers. Prior entrants may also help reduce discriminatory LOF for latecomer entrants if stereotyping and "fear of the foreigner" hazards have been overcome by prior entrants. However, competition in the host country should be harsher and the barrier to success higher due to the larger number of foreign-based competitors.

Second, multinationals in China that locate their investments in developed market economies face the "stair-climbing" problem we identified earlier. Moving from a country with weak institutions, particularly regulatory institutions, to OECD countries such as the United States with much stronger regulatory institutions, imposes unique LOF costs in addition to their latecomer status.

Third, historically, foreign investments by state-controlled firms have generally been treated with extra suspicion by local residents due to concerns about extraterritoriality (Vernon 1971; Marchick 2007). In China, as in many transition economies, many if not most of the largest multinationals are state-controlled. Moreover, many publicly traded Chinese firms have a high degree of state ownership (Miller et al. 2008). As a result, traditional concerns about loss of sovereignty, Trojan horses and so on accompany FDI by state-controlled MNEs. These concerns may have grown more pronounced as the number of state-controlled firms coming from emerging economies in Asia, Latin America and the former Soviet Union has surged and these firms have begun to invest in OECD countries (Vernon 1998).

Lastly, investment pools funded by foreign governments, sovereign wealth funds, are now making substantive passive investments in US firms without any large public outcry (Davis and Berman 2008). Chinese foreign investments are supported by a large investment pool, the China Investment Corporation, created by the Chinese government in 2007. The fund has designated one-third of its $200 billion reserves for overseas investments (Weisman 2008). Unlike US affiliates of other emerging-market firms, Chinese enterprises now have substantial financial resources to make inroads into the US economy. This could and has created public concerns over foreign takeovers of US assets. In response, Lou Jiwei, chairperson of the China Investment Corporation, recently promised US government officials that: "China had no intention of gaining controlling interest in any companies, and that it would be a 'good corporate citizen' and not invest in companies that damage the environment, waste energy or produce tobacco" (Weisman 2008).

5.3 CHINESE MULTINATIONALS AND US REGULATORY INSTITUTIONS

As we have argued above, Chinese multinationals entering the United States face two types of regulatory barriers: the institutional distance between US and Chinese regulations, and the difference in the levels of institutions between the two countries. Chinese firms come from a much weaker home base, one that is both emerging (poor, dynamic, fast-growing) and in transition (a mixture of communist, socialist and market institutions). Thus, the regulatory distance between China and the United States is higher than for most foreign firms entering the United States, and liability of foreignness should therefore be higher.

In this section, we discuss several laws and regulations and their implications for the US affiliates and their Chinese parent headquarters – violations of which would hold the US affiliates accountable, and violations of which would hold the parent firms and their employers accountable. These regulations apply to both domestic (US) firms and foreign firms in the United States. A comprehensive analysis of every law is not feasible in this chapter. Instead, we discuss regulations that may affect both the US affiliate of a Chinese organization and its parent (the Foreign Corrupt Practices and the Sarbanes–Oxley Acts) and then highlight other regulations with implications for the US affiliate of the Chinese organization.[4]

5.3.1 Foreign Corrupt Practices Act

The Foreign Corrupt Practices Act (FCPA) is a law, passed by Congress in 1977, intended to punish and eliminate bribes paid by US firms to influence the acts and/or decisions of foreign officials (15 U.S.C. §§ 78dd-1, et seq.). The FCPA was amended in 1988 and again in 1998. The 1998 amendment sought to: (1) strike a balance between combating illicit practices while facilitating the international competitiveness of US firms; and (2) provide more extensive reach in terms of those accountable under the Act to include foreign nationals and corporations. The FCPA's anti-bribery clause applies to issuers, domestic concerns and other persons. Domestic concerns are defined as:

any individual, who is a citizen, natural or resident of the US and any corporation, partnership association joint-stock company, business trust, unincorporated organization, or sole proprietorship which has as its principal place of business in the US, or which is organized under the laws of a state of the United States, or a territory, possession, or commonwealth of the United States. (15 U.S.C.A. 78dd-2(h))

The amended FCPA, therefore, applies to officers, directors, employees, or agents of an issuer (that is, a firm that lists its stock on a US stock exchange) or domestic concern.

As a result of the above definitions, a Chinese firm that lists its stock on a US exchange must comply with FCPA and Sarbanes–Oxley (described below) as well as with the Security Exchange Commission's disclosure requirements. In this case, the parent firm can be held accountable for violations of the FCPA, even if the US affiliate was uninvolved. For example, SEC officials and the Department of Justice announced that Statoil, Norway's largest oil company, would pay $21 million, as part of its penalty for FCPA violations; however, Statoil agreed to settle for $10.5 million (Taub 2006). The Securities and Exchange Commission and Department of Justice have jurisdiction over Statoil's conduct because the company's securities – American Depository Receipts (ADRs) – are traded on the New York Stock Exchange. For an ADR-issuing firm, the applicability of FCPA to the parent firm is straightforward, regardless of whether the Chinese firm has a US affiliate. In sum, the FCPA applies to Chinese firms that issue securities and thus cross-list on a US exchange.

For Chinese firms that are not listed on a US exchange, the applicability of the FCPA depends on a number of factors. The major issue has to do with whether the US affiliate of a Chinese firm is a "domestic concern." In this chapter, we use "affiliate" to encompass a range of organizational forms such as subsidiaries or branch offices. However, it is necessary to distinguish between these two types of affiliates to understand the conditions in which the affiliate is classified as a domestic concern.[5]

There is no federal legal requirement in most situations for a foreign investor to conduct business in the United States via a separately established subsidiary. For banks and other financial institutions, a branch is the preferred method of doing business, if permitted by the regulators, since it costs less capital to operate through a branch. For some specific industries, there is a legal requirement to operate through a subsidiary rather than a branch – for example, many states require insurance operations within their territories to use subsidiaries. The issue is generally regulated by states (not the federal government, except for some financial institutions) on an industry-by-industry basis. A separately established US subsidiary of a Chinese parent firm is clearly a "domestic concern" for FCPA purposes, as explained below.

For example, if a Chinese company establishes a US-incorporated subsidiary, then bribes to non-US officials – by that subsidiary or by an officer, director, employee or agent of that subsidiary, or by a shareholder of that subsidiary (that is, the parent) acting on behalf of that subsidiary – would trigger application of the FCPA to the person or entity making the corrupt payment. Bribes by a shareholder of that subsidiary (that is, the parent) to a non-US official, but not acting on behalf of that subsidiary, would not trigger application of the FCPA. Hence, if the parent Chinese firm bribed a foreign non-US official in a matter involving the parent firm's subsidiary in a third country but not involving its US subsidiary, the FCPA would not apply.

If a Chinese firm establishes a US affiliate as a branch office (rather than a separately incorporated subsidiary), then that branch might easily be deemed to be an "unincorporated organization," which has its principal place of business in the United States (within the meaning of the definition of "domestic concern" noted above; also see 15 U.S.C.A. § 78dd-2: Prohibited foreign trade practices by domestic concerns). Accordingly, a bribe to a non-US official paid by that branch office or by an officer, director, employee or agent of that branch office or by a shareholder of that branch office acting on behalf of that branch office could trigger application of the FCPA. Thus, it would be poor advice to a foreign investor in the United States to suggest that its conduct within the United States could fall outside the FCPA just by using a branch rather than formally incorporating a subsidiary.

Corporate directors of a subsidiary are usually at the same time officers of the parent firm. If a director of a domestic concern is involved in bribery covered by the FCPA, then there is a high likelihood that the Department of Justice could form a case against the parent firm based on conspiracy or aiding and abetting. The same point often applies to senior executives of a subsidiary, who may simultaneously hold officer positions in the subsidiary and the parent firm. The parent firm may contend that the director's or senior executive's actions were not authorized by the parent firm; however, the Department of Justice tends to resist these types of arguments.

It is also important to recall that any individual who is a citizen, national, or resident of the United States will be subject to the FCPA, regardless of the nature of legal organization or nationality of their employer or indeed their own nationality (for definitions see 15 U.S.C.A.§ 78dd-2h). That clause includes officers and employees of a Chinese enterprise in the United States, unless the individual is only an occasional visitor to the United States.[6]

Finally and importantly, the FCPA is a federal criminal statute. If a Chinese individual or company not based in the United States (for example, the Chinese parent firm or a China-based executive of the parent firm) improperly cooperates with a "domestic concern" or US person in bribing a non-US official, then that non-US individual or company (that is, the parent firm or its executive) may be separately covered by the federal criminal laws for conspiracy to violate federal law, by federal aiding and abetting laws or the Racketeer Influenced and Corrupt Organizations Act. None of those criminal statutes is limited in scope to "domestic concerns." Instead, those federal criminal statutes cover all persons and entities subject to the jurisdiction of the United States fully permitted by the due process clause of the US Constitution.

5.3.2 Sarbanes–Oxley Act

In 2002, the Sarbanes–Oxley Act (SOX) came into effect and brought with it substantial changes to regulation of corporate governance and financial practices (Pub. L. No. 107-204, 116 Stat. 745). The parent firms and US affiliates of cross-listed firms are required to comply with the Sarbanes–Oxley Act. As part of Sarbanes–Oxley, executives of US listed firms must attest via signature that they have reviewed the financial statements. Moreover, they must attest to the accuracy of the financial statements. Sarbanes–Oxley penalizes executives of these firms that incur accounting improprieties.

Although only firms publicly traded on US exchanges must comply with these rigorous accounting standards, Chinese firms that cross-list via American Depository Receipts

incur extremely high costs of compliance because the integrity of Chinese financial statements is subject to debate. Ambiguous accounting practices and poor enforcement have
resulted in unreliable financial statements. As such, parent firms of Chinese firms that
cross-list (including Chinese-owned firms in the United States that issue equity in the
United States) must incur disclosure costs (that is, providing additional financial information) and potential penalties (i.e., exposing executives to the consequences of SOX
violations).

5.3.3   Transfer Pricing Regulations

An important issue for MNEs is transfer pricing, particularly the tax aspects under
Section 482 of the US Internal Revenue Code (Eden 1998). China's deficiency with
respect to accounting standards and enforcement becomes a concern for US government
officials when assessing transfer pricing of Chinese firms. Chinese firms with US affiliates
may exploit transfer prices such that US taxes are avoided or underreported. US officials,
aware of the less-than-transparent accounting environment in China, may be more likely
to pay attention to these firms. While China has had transfer pricing regulations in place
for a few years now, and these rules are based on the OECD's Transfer Pricing Guidelines
(OECD 1995), the regulations in China are much weaker than those in the United States.
The ability of the Chinese government to enforce these regulations is also at question
since enforcement in the first place takes place at the state level with local tax inspectors.
Weak administrations, corruption and lax enforcement suggest that Chinese firms in the
United States must learn to deal with a much more regulated environment. Moreover,
since Chinese firms are only now adopting international accounting principles, and only
starting to employ the Big Four accounting firms, this is an area where the potential for
disputes is high.[7]

5.3.4   Other US Regulatory Institutions

As we noted above, Chinese organizations may vary in their exposure to the FCPA and
SOX. The Chinese organizations with the greatest level of exposure to US regulatory
institutions – both in the United States and throughout the world – are firms listed on
a US stock exchange. There are other regulations, however, that influence only the US
affiliates of Chinese firms. Again, we point out that this section in not intended to be
a comprehensive list. Rather, our intent is to heighten awareness of some of the more
salient US regulations.

One important act is the Currency and Foreign Transactions Reporting Act, also
known as the Bank Secrecy Act (BSA), and its implementing regulation 31 CFR 103.
The US Congress enacted the BSA to prevent banks and other financial service providers
from being used as intermediaries for, or to hide transfers or deposits of money derived
from, criminal activity. This Act was amended to facilitate the prevention, detection
and prosecution of international money laundering and financing terrorism as part of
revisions to the US Patriot Act.

The Arms Export Control Act (AECA; 22 U.S.C. § 2778(a)(2)) authorizes the export
and temporary import control activities of the Department of State. The AECA is the
basic authority for the Directorate of Defense Trade Controls to issue regulations and

administer and enforce export and temporary import controls for national security and foreign policy reasons.

The Trading with the Enemy Act (TWEA; 12 U.S.C. § 95a) restricts trade and attempts to trade:

> either directly or indirectly, with, to, or from, or for, or on account of, or on behalf of, or for the benefit of, any other person, with knowledge or reasonable cause to believe that such other person is an enemy or ally of enemy, or is conducting or taking part in such trade, directly or indirectly, for, or on account of, or on behalf of, or for the benefit of, an enemy or ally of enemy.

The International Emergency Economic Powers Act (IEEPA) grants the President emergency powers to respond to a threat to US national security, foreign policy or the economy from abroad. The IEEPA (50 U.S.C. §1701 et seq.) grants the President authority to "investigate, regulate, or prohibit" certain activities and transactions such as "the importing or exporting of currency and securities" (50 U.S.C. §1702).

The Occupational Safety and Health Act of 1970 (OSHA) is a federal statute designed to regulate employment conditions relating to occupational health and safety (29 U.S.C. 651, et seq.), which may potentially affect Chinese-owned affiliates in the United States.

During the mid-1970s the United States adopted two laws that seek to counteract the participation of US citizens in other nations' economic boycotts or embargoes. These "anti-boycott" laws are the 1977 amendments to the Export Administration Act (EAA; PL 96-72) and the Ribicoff Amendment to the 1976 Tax Reform Act (TRA; *Pub.L.* 94-455).

In sum, our overview of US regulatory institutions that could affect Chinese MNEs with operations in the United States is not exhaustive. Rather, our intent was to make salient the formal rules established by US regulatory institutions and identify some regulations that may be problematic for Chinese firms and their US affiliates. Next, we turn to the informal rules, which are captured by normative and cognitive institutions.

5.4 CHINA MULTINATIONALS AND US NORMATIVE INSTITUTIONS

Normative institutional distance arises from differences in societal beliefs about how things should and should not be done, that is, what is the best or most appropriate way to accomplish a particular task, what activities are prescribed or proscribed, what are inappropriate ways to tackle problems, and so on. Because "should/should not" norms of behavior are culturally derived and often tacit, foreign entrants (both individuals and firms) are likely to make mistakes. Therefore, unfamiliarity, discriminatory and relational components of liability of foreignness should all increase with normative distance.

Do Chinese MNEs face unique challenges in terms of normative distance when entering the US market, relative to other foreign entrants or relative to Chinese firms entering other developed market economies? We argue that the Chinese experience with US normative institutions should be similar to those of other Asian firms entering the United States. This suggests that Chinese MNEs can learn from the entry experiences of earlier

Asian entrants from Japan, the Republic of Korea, Hong Kong (China) and Taiwan Province of China into the US market.

Moreover, issues associated with normative distance are likely to occur in other societies with which China experiences substantial cultural differences. Thus, there may be nothing particularly unique about Chinese entries to the US market, in terms of normative institutions, that do not also characterize Chinese entries to other OECD markets.

5.5   CHINESE MULTINATIONALS AND US COGNITIVE INSTITUTIONS

Cognitive institutional distance is caused primarily by differences between countries in national symbols and stereotypes, the way domestic firms and consumers interact and how domestic actors (households, firms, government) view foreigners. The degree of stereotyping of foreigners depends partly on the level of ethnocentrism in the host country (Balabanis et al. 2001). Ethnocentrism reflects an unfavorable perception of outsiders and favorable perception of insiders (Sumner 1906). High levels of ethnocentrism result in stronger, more intense stereotyping against outsiders (or favoritism of insiders) and are associated with higher discriminatory LOF costs.

The size of an MNE may be important here. Firm size provides advantages such as financial strength, market power and strong reputation that should lower discriminatory costs and encourage an MNE to opt for a wholly owned subsidiary. On the other hand, as a firm's size increases, it becomes more visible in the host country. As such, there is a greater likelihood of being targeted by special interest groups, making it more difficult for the MNE to maintain external legitimacy (Kostova and Zaheer 1999).

The mix of foreign to local firms in a host country can also affect cognitive institutional distance. As Anderson and Gatignon (1986) argued, the presence of foreign MNEs encouraged local workers to "obtain a business education abroad, which in turn, can reduce problems associated with sociocultural distance and reduce the level of ethnocentrism in the host country" (Eden and Miller 2004, p. 200). As the number of foreign firms in a host country increases, the host country has more information by which to evaluate new entrants so unfamiliarity and discriminatory costs, from the host country perspective, should be lower. However, as the proportion of foreign to domestic firms rises in a politically salient industry (for example, petroleum, autos, banking), further entry can cause a backlash against foreign firms because of the perceived violation of national symbols and national security.

For many years, China has been the subject of controversy in the United States on topics such as human rights violations, insider trading (in Chinese financial markets), questionable accounting practices, intellectual property protection, international trade, undervalued exchange rates and even the loss of US manufacturing jobs (King et al. 2005; Knowledge@Wharton 2005; Marchick and Graham 2006). Exposures of tainted food products and lead paint in toys coming from China have only exacerbated these negative views of Chinese products among US consumers and firms. For example, a 2007 poll found that 52 percent of the US general public and 65 percent of US business leaders strongly agreed with the statement that: "Chinese food contamination cases have reduced your confidence in products made in China" (Committee of 100 2007). As a result, the

US public tends to regard Chinese imported products with suspicion. This stereotyping should spill over over to US affiliates of Chinese multinationals, particularly in the distribution sector where their primary function is to distribute imported Chinese goods.

For Chinese firms operating in the United States, country-of-origin effects should vary over time, reflecting swings in public opinion stemming from nationalistic views associated with US–China economic and political relations. The US–China trade imbalance, for example, which has received considerable attention from the US press, can raise tensions about Chinese imports, US manufacturing job losses to China and other controversial legal issues mentioned above. Reports that a Chinese firm engaged in bribery with a non-US official may trigger negative spillover effects to US affiliates, even though the US affiliates were uninvolved in or not found guilty of a violation. In a related example, US consumers boycotted French-made products (especially French wines) in response to the oil-for-food scandal, which implicated French, Iraqi and United Nations officials (www. boycottwatch.org; Gatti 2005).

There has been a surge in research on non-government organizations (NGOs), namely activist groups. China has been a target of criticism with respect to Tibet, human rights and child labor. The Chinese government has been able to deflect much of the criticism at home with the state-owned media and large ownership stakes in many publicly traded firms (Miller et al. 2008); however, Chinese state-ownership of a US affiliate can be a lightning rod for any country-specific or firm-specific actions perceived by NGOs.

Furthermore, NGOs receive considerable attention – whether warranted or unwarranted – from the US media, most of which are not state-owned (though a few receive some state funding). The US media, unlike its counterpart in China, can choose what information to report, how to report it, as well as what information to ignore. For Chinese firms, the NGOs, via the US media, can paint a very negative view of actions undertaken by the Chinese government, even though the actions under scrutiny have occurred outside of the United States. Such NGO actions that target the Chinese government may spill over such that US affiliates of Chinese firms serve as a focal point of the NGO allegations for US consumer and stakeholders. Therefore, the US affiliate of a Chinese firm may need to incur public relations costs on behalf of the headquarters in order to diffuse or redirect attention from home country issues.

5.6 CHINESE STRATEGIES FOR COPING WITH LIABILITY OF FOREIGNNESS

5.6.1 Strategies to Overcome Regulatory LOF

The above discussion of US regulations that affect Chinese firms and their US affiliates suggests that Chinese firms may incur additional litigation costs (in the event of violations), as well as compliance, training and recruiting costs (to reduce the likelihood of future violations). In the United States, foreign firms are sued more frequently than domestic firms (Mezias 2002) and, thus, the legal costs for representation and settlement may be substantial. Strategically, these acts may require substantial changes to an organization's value chain, resulting in higher coordination costs.

Although we expect the costs of compliance with US regulations to be higher for foreign firms, these costs may be even higher for US affiliates of Chinese firms because of China's less-than-favorable reputation regarding human rights and worker conditions. In order to overcome the home country stigma regarding employee rights and to be perceived as legitimate in the eyes of US employees and US regulators, Chinese firms will need to incur training costs to overcome unfamiliarity with US employee laws, and they are likely to endure ongoing scrutiny by OSHA officials.

Compliance training

To minimize the likelihood of violating US laws and the associated legal costs, Chinese MNEs in the United States should undergo extensive compliance training. We contend that a firm needs to view this training as an "investment" rather than an "expense," in order to underscore the seriousness of violating US laws due in part to the regulatory distance between China and the United States. As Chinese firms increase their presence on the global stage, especially in countries with stringent regulatory institutions, it is imperative for Chinese firms and their executives to improve standards not just in the United States, but also in other countries in which they operate – especially the home market. The stigma associated with Chinese firms' questionable business practices requires a proactive approach to a long-term commitment to adopting a corporate culture that encourages compliance and discourages corruption and illicit payments at home and abroad, not just a short-term public relations campaign (Bartlett et al. 2006). In doing so, Chinese firms will derive long-term benefits.

Taking on a local partner

Perhaps the most common strategy for coping with liability of foreignness is to take on a local partner – either as a joint venture or an acquisition – in the host country (Kostova and Zaheer 1999; Eden and Miller 2004). The local partner better understands the host country institutions (regulatory, normative and cognitive) and provides a "local face" for the firm in its dealings with local stakeholders.

However, a key worry for Chinese multinationals entering the United States since the 1990s has been the public outcry over Chinese full or partial acquisitions of US firms. Moreover, CFIUS can be triggered by acquisitions above a certain size or percentage of ownership.[8] As a result, Chinese firms are wary of crossing these thresholds, preferring minority stakes in US firms (Davis and Berman 2008). China's $3 billion investment in the US private equity firm Blackstone Group, for example, underscores the sensitivity of Chinese investment in the United States. China Investment Corporation requested no voting rights or influence in Blackstone's decision-making, and appears to have preempted criticism about foreign-government ownership in the event of lay-offs at any of the Blackstone acquisitions. Nevertheless, this approach seems to sidestep the LOF challenges facing Chinese organizations. Moreover, this approach presents a major obstacle to accumulating market knowledge in the United States, and thus reinforces short-term benefits with long-term costs.

In cases in which a Chinese firm does partner with a US firm, relational costs are an important consideration (Eden and Miller 2004). US firms may choose not to form alliances with firms unfamiliar with US regulations, to reduce the likelihood of legal missteps, or with firms that do not offer complementary resources. For instance, a Chinese partner's local market knowledge may be important for a US firm entering in China;

however, this knowledge is not transferable. Further, stigmas about US jobs lost to China may produce some spillover effect as well. A US firm may not want to associate with a Chinese firm for fear of perceptions of contributing to the job loss issue. That said, intra-relational costs might arise between a US affiliate and its Chinese parent, as well as interrelational costs between the US affiliate and Chinese suppliers. These costs may stir tensions between a US affiliate and its Chinese parent, increase coordination costs and present transfer pricing issues.

5.6.2 Strategies to Overcome Normative and Cognitive LOF

How can Chinese MNEs in the United States reduce their non-regulatory (normative and cognitive) costs? An obvious strategy is to partner with local firms, which we have discussed above. We discuss alternative strategies below.

Social embeddedness: becoming an "insider"
Social embeddedness reflects the degree to which economic transactions take place through social relationships and networks of relationships that use social and non-commercial criteria to govern business dealings (Marsden 1981). A key premise of social embeddedness is the importance of "in-group" affiliations that, in turn, may lead to differential treatment and perceptions of outsiders (Tajfel and Billig 1974). Granovetter (1973) found that tight relationship ties between host country insiders led to exclusion of organizations that were unable to establish comparable ties. High embeddedness of local firms increases the distinction between insiders and outsiders that, in turn, raises cognitive institutional distance and increases discriminatory costs. Local embeddedness can also be a barrier to the sharing of information, increasing unfamiliarity costs for foreign firms. Whereas for developed market firms operating abroad, it has been hypothesized that a higher degree of social embeddedness of local firms is associated with greater cognitive institutional distance and higher LOF (Eden and Miller 2004).

Scholars have suggested that trust in cross-border business relationships is especially prevalent in Oriental cultures, which tend to exhibit high collectivism and long-term orientation that, in turn, is integrated into managerial decision-making and affects the business environment (Hofstede 1980). As a result, social embedded ties between Chinese organizations are quite common (Egelhoff 1984; Ouchi 1980). An MNE accustomed to building trust in business relationships at home is more inclined to understand information-sharing in order to operate more effectively abroad.

For US affiliates of Chinese firms, this relationship may be different if the firm through its affiliate employs a strategy that involves serving ethnic customers. For Chinese firms that follow this strategy, the US affiliate can become socially embedded within the ethnic community, resulting in enhanced information sharing and reduced unfamiliarity costs. Domestic firms (or in the present context, US firms) may be unable to achieve social embeddedness in these ethnic communities, especially when normative distance is high. Several Chinese banking executives have suggested that it takes more than using bilingual signs to gain the trust of Chinese consumers in the United States. Within a local Chinese community, liability of foreignness falls dramatically and in fact becomes a benefit for US affiliates of Chinese firms that adhere to a strategy that focuses on ethnically similar customers. Moreover, consumer ethnocentrism is dampened for firms that emphasize a local ethnic strategy.

Social embeddedness by Chinese firms operating in the United States can also be useful for US firms seeking to gain access to the Chinese market. A US affiliate of a Chinese multinational can draw upon its social network in China to provide services to US firms. For this niche strategy, it is less critical to become social embedded with host country firms and institutions. Thus, a US affiliate of a Chinese firm can attenuate some pressures to achieve external legitimacy by serving US customers seeking expertise on expanding into China.

Clustering with ethnically similar customers and competitors
Foreign firms tend to establish affiliates near ethnically similar populations (Shaver and Flyer 2000). As such, large local Chinese populations within the United States are likely to be able to support high local density of US affiliates of Chinese firms. In these environments, Chinese business practices become legitimized. Moreover, unlike US affiliates of firms from other developed countries, US affiliates of Chinese firms are likely to emphasize competition, which underscores the notion of strength in numbers – firms operate in a network of interdependent relationships developed through collaboration with the objective of deriving mutual benefits (Lado et al. 1997). A limitation of this "location" strategy is that legitimacy remains a problem in local markets with a low density of US affiliates of Chinese firms – that is, in the long term there may be constraints to this strategy. As a result, Chinese MNEs need to consider other actions to temper Chinese-specific LOF in the United States. One means of addressing this concern is to contribute to the local community.

Contributing to the local community
Often, multinational enterprises make local contributions because of government pressure, as a means to gain acceptance in the host country, to show corporate goodwill, or all of the above. These contributions may ameliorate host country concerns about foreigners exploiting the local market and increase the foreign firm's legitimacy in the host country. Eventually, such contributions might turn outsiders into insiders (Eden and Molot 1993). Japanese auto multinationals, for example, became successful insiders in the Canadian auto industry through their contributions to the Canadian economy (Eden and Molot 2002). Local contributions, however, do not always guarantee that the local affiliate of a foreign MNE will be accepted unconditionally by the local community. For example, Unocal built schools and hospitals in Myanmar and still faced substantial criticism from non-governmental organizations and other stakeholders.

Building schools and hospitals may be suitable acts of goodwill by MNEs operating in emerging markets; however, the nature of contributions in a developed market requires careful thought. One possibility is to establish university scholarships for less affluent US citizens, or make unconditional contributions to charities such as the Salvation Army, United Way or the American Heart Association, or perhaps to worthy youth organizations such as the Boy Scouts and Girl Scouts of America. These actions are likely to be viewed favorably by US citizens.

Building US–China relations
Another coping strategy for Chinese MNEs is to develop industry associations and lobby groups within the United States to help build US–China economic relations. Examples

are the Committee of 100, made up of US and Chinese business and government leaders, and the US–China People's Friendship Association. These business associations are similar to the government-to-government associations, such as the US–China Joint Commission on Commerce and Trade (JCCT). Such groups can help overcome liability of foreignness and change the perception of Chinese firms from "outsiders" to "insiders" (Eden and Molot 1993, 2002). These associations can also address US perceptions of Chinese trade and FDI irritants. [9]

Another coping strategy could be to focus on Chinese parent MNE's activities at home. Chinese MNEs might also seek, with the help of the Chinese government, to address US human rights concerns about China, especially labor conditions in Chinese factories. Chinese firms could lobby for lowering (or speeding up the reduction of) entry barriers for US products and firms into China. Improved enforcement of Chinese laws (for example, against counterfeiting) where violations have adversely affected multinational firms operating in China would also be welcome in the United States. These gestures are likely to have positive spillover effects that can reduce some of the negative stereotypes and perceptions of Chinese firms held by the US public.

Learning from early entrants to the US market

We have argued above that Chinese MNEs are latecomers to the US market. Particularly in terms of cognitive institutional distance, Chinese MNEs are now facing barriers similar to those faced by earlier Asian entrants from Japan, the Republic of Korea and elsewhere. Therefore, studying the problems faced by earlier Asian entrants, their strategies, and their successes and failures can be useful learning tools for coping with LOF costs (for details, see Curtis Milhaupts, Chapter 7 in this volume).

Can Chinese executives learn anything from the US experiences of Japanese firms during the 1970s and 1980s? The answer is yes; however, there were both successful and unsuccessful Japanese operations in the United States. In terms of successful operations, Honda used sequential investment to pave the way for US expansion. First, Honda made a small investment – building a motorcycle production facility in Marysville, Ohio, "as an experiment to see if the company could eventually produce autos in North America" (Koenig and Ohnsman 2008). The MNE accumulated local market knowledge in the United States and then proceeded to increase investment with a large-scale auto production facility. Even though Honda's North American motorcycle production is now being discontinued, its Greenburg, Indiana, auto plant – its sixth vehicle assembly plant and thirteenth plant of any type in North America – began production in November 2008.

Despite many successes, some prominent Japanese firms encountered difficulties with their US operations. For example, Sony acquired Columbia Pictures (ICMR 2004). Financial analysts criticized Sony's venture into the movie business for a lack of synergies. In 1994, Sony reported a $2.7 billion write-off of this investment. Another firm that failed with its US operations is the Mitsubishi Estate Company, which purchased the Rockefeller Center in New York City. In 1995, a bankruptcy law filing by the Rockefeller Center enabled the Japanese firm to avoid additional cash infusions into the property although Mitsubishi Estate Company still owned $190 million in tax obligations (Hansell 1995; Strom 1995).

A second example is Toyota, which produced its first US-made vehicle at the New United Motor Manufacturing Inc. (NUMMI) plant in a joint venture with General

Motors. The MNE used this joint venture as a means to gather valuable knowledge about labor unions and US suppliers, not only as a mean to produce cars. Toyota has achieved success in the US market, and has contributed a great number of jobs and $14 billion in wages to the US economy in 2003 (Hill 2005).[10] Long seen as a successful example of Japanese entry into the US market, the expected closing of NUMMI shows that even long-term positive relationships can go sour.[11]

Although some academic scholars have proposed "springboard" approaches for emerging-market firms as a means to catch up to rivals operating in the United States (Luo and Tung 2007), the Honda and Toyota examples illustrate that a sequential or incremental approach can produce favorable results with less risk. Our discussion of two failed acquisitions is not an attempt to dissuade Chinese firms from using acquisitions as a mode of entry, but rather to underscore that the challenges involved in making large-scale acquisitions involve many issues, such as exploiting synergies between the acquiring firm and a target firm, and overpaying for a target firm, in addition to potential obstacles stemming from integration, institutional distance and cultural distance, among others (Morck et al. 2008).

5.7 CONCLUSIONS

In this chapter, we have explored the socio-political costs that Chinese multinationals face when engaging in foreign direct investment in the United States. Our framework under-scores the LOF challenges facing many Chinese investors. Some firms may have avoided issues raised in our framework by taking very small stakes in a number of publicly traded firms rather than controlling stakes or acquisitions of Chinese and foreign companies (US–China Economic and Security Review Commission Hearing, July 5, 2007). In effects, their investments are so small they are invisible to federal authorities, reducing their firms' LOF costs.

Our interest lies with those Chinese firms that make investments (whether *de novo* or through mergers or acquisitions of US firms) satisfying the minimum 10 percent thresh-old to qualify as foreign direct investment in the United States. Where Chinese invest-ments do qualify as FDI, the entering firm faces an array of socio-political costs, known as liability of foreignness, that raise the costs of doing business abroad for Chinese MNEs. These higher costs, unless offset through proactive strategies by the MNE parent and/or its US affiliate, will reduce profitability and could impair long-run survivability of the US affiliate. In sum, we have sought to link socio-political costs and institutional distance between the United States and China, and outlined some strategies that Chinese MNEs can use to offset these costs. Our work is preliminary and somewhat speculative. We hope that it encourages executives and other scholars to dig deeper into both the costs and successful coping strategies that Chinese firms face in the United States.

NOTES

*   This chapter was prepared in the context of the Deloitte–Vale Columbia Center on Sustainable International Investment project on "Is the US ready for FDI from China?" The authors have benefited from the research assistance of Kehan Xu and helpful discussions with David Fagan, James Groff, Mark Kantor, Kris Knutsen and Karl P. Sauvant. Copyright © 2009 by Columbia University. All rights reserved.

1. "National treatment" means that foreign investments and investors receive the same treatment inside a country as do local investors and investments. Chapter 11 of the North American Free Trade Agreement (NAFTA), for example, guarantees national treatment to investors and investments within North America.

2. There are, of course, exceptions, most notably the forced expropriation of foreign-owned petroleum assets in Venezuela. Vernon (1998) was perhaps the first international business scholar to foresee the rise in anti-FDI sentiment in Latin American economies in the early years of the twenty-first century. See also the 2007 *World Investment Report* (UNCTAD 2007).

3. We assume an intermediate ownership strategy (for example, equity joint venture) involves a local partner.

4. Chinese organizations investing in the US need to seek counsel in the United States to have a full understanding of the regulatory requirements in the US. Note that our analysis does not cover US regulations related to imported products from China (for example, US anti-dumping and countervailing duties, health regulations, safeguards, trade with state-owned enterprises and WTO commitments). Note also that not all US regulatory institutions raise costs for Chinese entrants. For example, the federal EB-5 Immigrant Investor program offers foreign investors who locate in poverty-stricken areas of the United States an opportunity to get permanent residency for entrepreneurs and their family members (Jordan 2007).

5. We provide a more detailed discussion in our analysis of the Foreign Corrupt Practices Act; however, this distinction is also relevant to the applicability of the other laws to the US affiliate and/or the Chinese parent firms.

6. That also includes US citizens living abroad, even if they are employed by non-US organizations.

7. In fact, the fastest-growing locations for transfer pricing professionals are Shanghai and Hong Kong (China).

8. See Chapter 3 by David Fagan in this volume.

9. The USTR's annual report to Congress on Chinese barriers facing US products and firms provides a useful summary of trade and investment irritants from the US perspective (USTR 2007). The Congressional Record Service report (CSR 2007) also provides useful background on US–China trade issues, along with several GAO reports.

10. Toyota Motor North America, Inc. commissioned the Center for Automotive Research, a non-profit research group, to complete an assessment of its economic and workforce contributions in the United States.

11. For an article on NUMMI closing see http://www.businessweek.com/autos/autobeat/archives/2009/08/nummi_to_close.html.

REFERENCES

Anderson, E. and Gatignon, H. (1986). "Modes of foreign entry: a transaction cost analysis and propositions," *Journal of International Business Studies*, 17, pp. 1–26.

Balabanis, G., Diamantopoulos, A., Mueller, D.R. and Melewar, T.C. (2001). "The impact of nationalism, patriotism and internationalism on consumer ethnocentric tendencies," *Journal of International Business Studies*, 32, pp. 157–175.

Bartlett, C., Ghoshal, S. and Beamish, P. (2006). *Transnational management*, 5th edition (Burr Ridge, IL: Irwin).

Boycottwatch.org (2004). http://www.boycottwatch.org/misc/france-04.htm.

Buckley, P. and Casson, M. (1998). "Analyzing foreign market entry strategies: extending the internalization approach," *Journal of International Business Studies*, 29, pp. 539–562.

Caves, R. (1971). "International corporations: the industrial economics of foreign investment," *Economica*, 38, pp. 1–27.

China Business (2007). "China's trillion-dollar kitty is ready," October 2.

Committee of 100 (2007). "Hope and fear: full report of C-100's survey on American and Chinese attitudes toward each other," report available at: http://www.americans-world.org/digest/regional_issues/china/china12.cfm.

Congressional Research Service (CRS) (2007). "CRS report for Congress: China's trade with the United States and the World," Report No. RL31403 (Washington, DC: US Congressional Research Services).

Davis, B. and Berman, D.K. (2008). "Lobbyists smoothed the way for a spate of foreign deals," *Wall Street Journal*, January 25, p. A1.

Eden, L. (1998). *Taxing Multinationals: Transfer Pricing and Corporate Income Taxation in North America* (Toronto: University of Toronto Press).

Eden, L. and Miller, S.R. (2004). "Distance matters: liability of foreignness, institutional distance and ownership strategy," *Advances in International Management*, 16, pp. 187–221.

Eden, L. and Molot, M.A. (1993). "Insiders and outsiders: defining 'Who Is Us?' in the North American auto industry," *Transnational Corporations*, 2 (3), pp. 31–64.

Eden, L. and Molot, M.A. (2002). "Insiders, outsiders and host country bargains," *Journal of International Management*, 8 (4), pp. 359–433.

Egelhoff, W. (1984). "Patterns of control in US, U.K. and European multinational corporations," *Journal of International Business Studies*, 15, pp. 73–83.

Gatti, C. (2005). "Oil-for-food inquiry looks to the French connection," *Financial Times*, April 28.

Granovetter, M. (1973). "The strength of weak ties," *The American Journal of Sociology*, 78, pp. 1360–1380.

Hansell, S. (1995). "Rockefeller Center filing may mean big tax bill," *New York Times*, May 13.

Henisz, W. and Williamson, O. (1999). "Comparative economic organizations: within and between countries," *Business and Politics*, 1, pp. 261–276.

Hill, K. (2005). "Contribution of Toyota to the economies of fourteen states and the United States in 2003," Economic and Business Group – Center for Automotive Research.

Hofstede, G. (1980). *Culture's Consequences, International Differences in Work-Related Values* (Beverly Hills, CA: Sage Publications).

ICMR (2004). "Sony-Columbia Pictures: lessons from a cross border acquisition," http://www.icmrindia.org.

Jordan, M. (2007). "Got $500,000? The US awaits. Government's EB-5 program offers foreign investors green cards for job creation," *Wall Street Journal*, November 2, p. B1.

Kekic, Laza and Sauvant, Karl P., eds (2007). *World Investment Prospects to 2012: Foreign Direct Investment and the Challenge of Political Risk* (London: Economist Intelligence Unit).

King, N., Hitt, G. and Ball, J. (2005). "Bid for power: oil battle sets showdown over China; CNOOC's offer for Unocal raises stakes in conflict over Sino–US ties; threat, rival, or vast market?" *Wall Street Journal*, June 24, p. A1.

Knowledge@Wharton. (2005). "Is CNOOC's bid for Unocal a threat to America?" http://knowledge.wharton.upenn.edu/article.cfm?articleid=1240.

Koenig, W. and Ohnsman, A. (2008). "Honda to end motorcycle output at first US plant (update3)," http://www.bloomberg.com, February 27.

Kostova, T. (1997). "Country institutional profiles: concept and measurement," *Academy of Management Best Paper Proceedings*, pp. 180–189.

Kostova, T. (1999). "Transnational transfer of strategic organizational practices: a contextual perspective," *Academy of Management Review*, 24 (2), pp. 308–324.

Kostova, T. and Zaheer, S. (1999). "Organizational legitimacy under conditions of complexity: the case of the multinational enterprise," *Academy of Management Review*, 24 (1), pp. 64–81.

Lado, A., Boyd, N. and Hanlon, S. (1997). "Competition, cooperation, and the search for economic rents: a syncretic model," *Academy of Management Review*, 22, pp. 110–141.

Luo, Y. and Tung, R. (2007). "International expansion of emerging market enterprises: a springboard perspective," *Journal of International Business Studies*, 38, pp. 481–498.

Marchick, D. (2007). "The extent of the government's control of China's economy, and its impact on the United States," Testimony before the US–China Economic and Security Review Commission, May 25.

Marchick, D. and Graham, E. (2006). "How China can break down American's wall," *Far East Economic Review*, 169 (6), pp. 10–14.

Marsden, P. (1981). "Introducing influence processes into a system of collective decisions," *American Journal of Sociology*, 86, pp. 1203–1235.

Mezias, J. (2002). "Identifying liabilities of foreignness and strategies to minimize their effects: the case of labor lawsuit judgments in the United States," *Strategic Management Journal*, 23 (3), pp. 229–244.

Miller, S.R., Li, D., Eden, L. and Hitt, M.A. (2008). "Insider trading and the valuation of international strategic alliances in emerging stock markets," *Journal of International Business Studies*, 39 (1), pp. 102–117.

Morck, R., Yeung, B. and Zhao, M. (2008). "Perspectives on China's outward foreign direct investment," *Journal of International Business Studies*, 39, pp. 1–14.

North, D.C. (1990). *Institutions, Institutional Change and Economic Performance* (Cambridge: Cambridge University Press).

OECD (1995). *Transfer Pricing Guidelines* (Paris: OECD).

Ouchi, W. (1980). "Markets, bureaucracy, and clans," *Administrative Science Quarterly*, 25, pp. 129–141.

Ramamurti, R. (2001). "The obsolescing 'bargaining model'? MNC host-developing country relations revisited," *Journal of International Business Studies*, 32, pp. 23–39.

Scott, W.R. (1995). *Institutions and Organizations* (Thousand Oaks, CA: Sage).

Shaver, J.M. and Flyer, F. (2000). "Agglomeration economies, firm heterogeneity, and foreign direct investment in the United States," *Strategic Management Journal*, 21, pp. 1175–1193.

Strom, S. (1995). "Rockefeller Center forced to file for bankruptcy by Tokyo owner," *The New York Times*, May 12.

Sumner, W. (1906). *Folkways: The Sociological Importance of Usages, Manners, Customs, Mores and Morals* (New York: Ginn & Co.).

Tajfel, H. and Billig, M. (1974). "Familiarity and categorization in intergroup behavior," *Journal of Experimental Social Psychology*, 10, pp. 159–170.

Taub, S. (2006). "SEC settles bribery charges with Statoil," *CFO.com*, October 16.

UNCTAD (2007). *World Investment Report 2007: Transnational Corporations, Extractive Industries and Development* (New York and Geneva: UNCTAD).

US–China Economic and Security Review Commission Hearing, July 5, 2007.

USTR (2007). *2007 National Trade Estimate Report on Foreign Trade Barriers* (Washington, DC: United States Trade Representative), http://www.ustr.gov/Document_Library/Reports_ Publications/2007/2007_NTE_Report/Section_Index.html.

Vernon, R. (1971). *Sovereignty at Bay* (New York: Basic Books).

Vernon, R. (1998). *In the Hurricane's Eye: The Troubled Prospects of Multinational Enterprises* (Cambridge, MA, USA and London, UK: Harvard University Press).

Weisman, S.R. (2008). "Official says China is not after individual companies," *The New York Times*, February 1, p. C2.

Xu, D. and Shenkar, O. (2002). "Institutional distance and the multinational enterprise," *Academy of Management Review*, 27, pp. 608–618.

Zaheer, S. (1995). "Overcoming the liability of foreignness," *Academy of Management Journal*, 38 (2), pp. 341–363.

6. International investment law protections for Chinese investment into the US

Mark Kantor*

INTRODUCTION

Under US bilateral investment treaties (BITs) and the investment chapters of US free trade agreements (FTAs; collectively, "US international investment agreements" or US IIAs), the investors and investments covered by those agreements are normally entitled to a number of important substantive protections, among them: (1) compensation at fair market value for expropriation; (2) treatment in accordance with minimum international standards (including "fair and equitable treatment," "full protection and security" and a prohibition on "denial of justice"); (3) national treatment; (4) most-favored-nation treatment; (5) protection against trade-related investment measures like "local content" requirements; (6) free transferability and convertibility of funds transfers related to investments into and out of the US; and (7) the right to select senior management for the US investment. Investors may enforce their claims directly by means of a claim for damages in investor–state arbitration.

Today, China and the United States are not mutual parties to any bilateral or multilateral international investment agreements. However, the protections afforded by US IIAs may still be available to Chinese enterprises investing in the US if the Chinese enterprise invests through an intermediate operating company having the nationality of a third country, so long as that third country is a party to such an international instrument with the US. That process is often called "treaty-shopping."

Moreover, following 17 months of exploratory talks between the two countries, China and the US began negotiation of a BIT in the context of the regular trade discussions held between the two countries in mid-2008.[1] The negotiations were initiated under the Bush Administration which was seeking to reinvigorate and expand the US network of BITs. The new Obama Administration has decided to conduct a review of the US Model Bilateral Investment Treaty (BIT), the template that the US uses as a starting point when contemplating the negotiation of a new bilateral investment treaty. As part of this process, the US State Department and the Office of the United States Trade Representative are seeking input from the private sector, including by inviting a report from a private sector advisory subcommittee formed under the State Department's Advisory Committee on International Economic Policy. Negotiation of a US China BIT has slowed during the Obama Administration's general review of the trade and investment policy it inherited from the Bush Administration. While that review has not yet concluded, perhaps a small signal of the approach the US will take may be gleaned from a speech by Ambassador Ron Kirk, the new US Special Trade

Representative, before the US–China Business Council on June 2, 2009. In that speech, Amb. Kirk said:

> Our approach to China will involve both direct diplomacy and strong enforcement of America's rights in the global trading system. USTR's preferred instruments are those of engagement with China, through dialogue, ongoing efforts to negotiate a bilateral investment treaty, and coordinated efforts with like-minded trading partners.

China, of course, has recently entered into new-format BITs with Germany and other countries that contain protections found in investment treaties commonly employed by Organisation for Economic Co-operation and Development (OECD) countries.[2] According to press reports, a BIT between Canada and China is also close to finalization. Consequently, the prospects for an eventual BIT between China and the US should remain on any potential investor's radar screen. However, the text of China's recent generation of BITs differs significantly (both substantively and procedurally) from the approach taken by the US in its recent generation of investment agreements, and indeed the US may be changing its approach as a result of the transition from the Bush Administration to the Obama Administration.

Whatever the new template may be, the US in the past has been quite firm in refusing to depart significantly from its model – witness the refusal by the US to sign the Energy Charter Treaty, as well as the suspension of BIT talks between the US and Pakistan, free trade agreement talks between the US and South Africa and free trade agreement talks between the US and Thailand. The US approach now seeks to balance investor protections with the regulatory interests of the host state, while also establishing transparency and accountability in a fashion somewhat similar to that found in the US courts. China's recent BITs do not strike the same balance. Therefore, US–China negotiations may be quite protracted even apart from the obvious political difficulties facing such talks. Moreover, the US political climate for significant new trade and investment agreements with China and other countries remains difficult, and may prove even more difficult now that the results of the November 2008 US general election have become clear.

In addition to investor protections afforded to Chinese investors by investment agreements, both the US and China are, as discussed more fully in section 6.2 below, bound by a "most-favored-nation" (MFN) provision in the General Agreement on Trade in Services (GATS). The GATS contains a variety of protections for foreign companies that supply services through a "commercial presence" in the host country, which includes investment vehicles like subsidiaries. Accordingly, to the extent the US has granted investment-related protections to services and services suppliers of another country, then China may assert that its own enterprises are directly entitled by operation of the MFN provision in the GATS to treatment no less favorable than the US grants to services and services suppliers of that other country. The extent to which this MFN obligation results in Chinese services suppliers obtaining the substantive and procedural benefits of a US IIA with a third country is simply untested as this book goes to point. Investors should be aware that rights under the GATS may be enforced only by China itself (not the Chinese investor) in state–state dispute proceedings under the WTO Dispute Settlement Understanding. It is therefore also unclear whether a Chinese investor asserting IIA rights by operation of the MFN obligation in the GATS will be entitled to enforce these rights directly in investor–state arbitration.

The protections afforded to Chinese investors by US domestic law and the US court system are considerable, and in many respects more protective than international investment law. For example, the Administrative Procedures Act (at the US federal level) and equivalent legislation at the US state level offer significant procedural due process assurances in regulatory proceedings. The Administrative Procedures Act and case law interpreting it provide detailed transparency, impartiality and "level playing field" protections, with far more clarity than the somewhat analogous international law principles of "fair and equitable treatment" and "denial of justice" found in IIAs.

Similarly, the "Takings Clause" of the Fifth Amendment to the US Constitution (and similar provisions of US state constitutions) guarantees full compensation for expropriations (including regulatory takings) of investments by the US, whether the taking affects property of US nationals or foreign investors. The US Congress has for a very long time maintained a "standing appropriation" for successful "takings" claims against the federal government, so no additional legislative act is required to obtain moneys ordered by a US court to be paid on account of a taking of property (an expropriation) by the US government.

The "anti-discrimination" portions of international investment law (most-favored-nation and national treatment) also have their analogue in the Equal Protection Clause of the US Constitution. The Equal Protection Clause is commonly understood to prevent improper discrimination on the basis of national origin. However, legislative "Buy America" requirements have routinely survived challenges under the Equal Protection Clause, so MFN and national treatment commitments in IIAs remain the only source today of barriers to such conduct by US authorities.

6.1   INTERNATIONAL INVESTMENT AGREEMENTS

In this section, I will first review the opportunity for a Chinese enterprise to obtain the benefits of US investment treaties by sourcing its investment through a third country, where that third country is a treaty partner with the US (so-called "treaty-shopping"). For example, a Chinese-controlled enterprise located in Mexico would generally be entitled to the benefits of the North American Free Trade Agreement (NAFTA). Then, I will explain the common international investment law protections afforded by those treaties. Finally, I will review important exceptions in these treaties, including the "essential security interests" exception. In summary:

- Today, Chinese investors may employ an intermediate company in a third country that is a US treaty partner to obtain international investment protections (for example, using a Mexican or Canadian intermediary company to obtain benefits under Chapter 11 of NAFTA). However, that intermediate company should itself have significant business authority in that third country.
- The substantive investment protections of US IIAs include: compensation at fair market value for expropriations; "fair and equitable" treatment; national treatment; most-favored-nation treatment; protection against many "local content" and similar trade-related investment measures; free transferability and convertibility of funds transfers into and out of the US; and the right to select management for the US investment without regard to nationality.

- Investors may directly enforce these rights through investor–state arbitration. The ordinary remedy is to compensate injured investors for the damages they have suffered.
- By virtue of the "essential security" exclusion in US IIAs, arbitral panels established pursuant to the latest generation of US treaties will not be able to review measures that the US considers necessary to protect its essential security interests, regardless of the measures' impact on an investment.

For ease of analysis, I will employ the provisions of the 2004 US Model Bilateral Investment Treaty (2004 US Model BIT) to illustrate these concepts.[3] I caution, however, that US international investment instruments are not identical. Consequently, the particular terms of the relevant treaty must be carefully reviewed to determine the rights actually afforded to investors by that instrument.

6.1.1 Nationality of the Investor

The protections of the 2004 US Model BIT and investment chapters of recent US IIAs are available to an "investor of a Party [that is, China or the US]" and to investments made by such an investor in the territory of the other party. The term "investor of a Party" means:

> a Party or state enterprise thereof, or a national or an enterprise of a Party, that attempts to make, is making, or has made an investment in the territory of the other Party; provided, however, that a natural person who is a dual national shall be deemed to be exclusively a national of the State of his or her dominant and effective nationality. (2004 US Model BIT, Art. 1)

Based on this definition, an investing enterprise organized under the laws of, say, Mexico or Canada is an investor of Mexico or Canada, respectively, and thus covered by the NAFTA, even if it is wholly owned and controlled by a Chinese enterprise. A similar result will occur under other US IIAs, for example the US–Singapore Free Trade Agreement.

As is clear from the specific reference to "state enterprises" in the above definition of "investor," ultimate government ownership or control of the investor by China or a Chinese provincial or municipal authority does not operate to exclude the investor from the protections of a US IIA.

> The term "investor" as used in US IIAs includes state enterprises.

As of January 1, 2008, the US had IIAs in full force and effect with about 60 states. In addition, the US had executed FTAs awaiting ratification with Colombia, the Republic of Korea and Panama. As discussed in section 6.3 below, the US is also party to older Friendship, Commerce and Navigation (FCN) treaties that remain effective with a number of states. However, FCN treaties do not provide for enforcement of investor protections through investor–state arbitration. Most US BITs are based on the older and far less detailed 1994 US Model BIT, not the updated provisions of the 2004 US Model BIT. The investment chapters of recent US FTAs, however, are generally based on the 2004 US Model BIT. Prospective investors should therefore carefully review the actual text of the relevant BIT, rather than assuming that each treaty offers identical substantive and procedural protections.

> A "national" of a US treaty partner is entitled to the protections of the investment treaty unless it has "no substantial business activities" in the territory of that treaty partner. Therefore, a Chinese enterprise may obtain the benefits of a US investment treaty by sourcing its investment through an intermediate business entity located in a treaty partner, so long as that intermediate entity conducts significant business activities within the country where it is located.

The US, like many other countries, is concerned that its treaty partners not become "flags of convenience" for investors engaged in treaty-shopping. For that reason, Article 17.2 of the 2004 US Model BIT and similar provisions in other US IIAs entitle a party to deny the benefits of the investment agreement to investors having "no substantial business activities" in its treaty partners:

> A Party may deny the benefits of this Treaty to an investor of the other Party that is an enterprise of such other Party and to investments of that investor if the enterprise has no substantial business activities in the territory of the other Party and persons of a non-Party, or of the denying Party, own or control the enterprise.

There is currently no arbitral award or definitive US commentary on the meaning of the phrase "no substantial business activities." For Chinese investors seeking to use an intermediate company in a third country like Mexico or Singapore as their "investor" entity, the question is: what quantity or nature of business activities is sufficient to avoid denial of benefits under this provision? It seems clear that a special-purpose holding company with no other business activities will be at risk of denial of benefits. Less clear, however, are situations involving intermediate holding companies established in the US treaty partner State for bona fide purposes, when the intermediate entity has investments in several jurisdictions or is a company engaged in operating business activities itself. Moreover, there is also no authority to guide us regarding situations where, for example, a Chinese enterprise holds a non-controlling ownership interest in a Mexican or Singaporean single-purpose holding company, with the remaining ownership interests held by non-Chinese entities.

In light of the foregoing, a Chinese enterprise may be able to obtain the protections of a US IIA by sourcing its investment through an investing enterprise having the nationality of a third state that is an IIA treaty partner with the US, so long as that investing enterprise conducts substantial business activities within that third state. To increase the likelihood of treaty coverage, however, Chinese investors should utilize only intermediate business entities with a substantial operating track record unrelated to the US investment.

6.1.2 Substantive IIA Protections

I will briefly review below eight core investment protections commonly found in US IIAs: national treatment; most-favored-nation treatment; minimum standard of treatment; expropriation and compensation; protection for funds transfers; protection against performance requirements like "local content" mandates; protection for appointment of senior management and boards of directors; and publication of laws and decisions respecting investment. Each of these protections can be enforced by a foreign investor through investor–state arbitration under US IIAs. Damages are the principal remedy available to the investor for breach by the host country of its IIA obligations. In contrast, other substantive provisions in US IIAs, such as the obligations respecting protection of the environment and labor rights, are either enforceable only through state–state dispute resolution or are not subject to binding dispute resolution at all, depending on the text of the particular IIA.

US IIAs investment protections take the form of general obligations, with the only exceptions to these general obligations being found in detailed schedules annexed to the IIA. Therefore, to understand properly the scope of a substantive protection found in a US IIA, it is also necessary to review the annexed schedules for mutually agreed exceptions. Most importantly, there are a number of scheduled exceptions to the national treatment and most-favored-nation protections discussed in section 6.2.2 below.

National treatment

> US IIAs provide "national treatment" protection – treatment no less favorable than the US provides, in like circumstances, to its own investors and investments. However, a number of exceptions are specifically listed in each IIA.

Article 3 of the 2004 US Model BIT obligates the parties to provide both investors and covered investments with "national treatment" protection, that is, treatment no less favorable than the host country, in like circumstances, provides to its own investors and investments. A Chinese investor who is covered by a US IIA is therefore generally protected from improper US discrimination in favor of US companies, subject only to specific listed exceptions in the IIA. BITs extend this national treatment obligation beyond the US federal government to cover conduct by regional and local levels of government as well. Very few exceptions exist for non-conforming measures of the US federal government. However, it is common in US IIAs to include a general exclusion for existing non-conforming measures of US states. The effect, therefore, is to grandfather existing non-conforming measures of the 50 US states, but to prohibit the introduction by US states of most new or additional non-conforming measures. Article 3 states:

Article 3: National Treatment
1. Each Party shall accord to investors of the other Party treatment no less favorable than that it accords, in like circumstances, to its own investors with respect to the establishment, acquisition, expansion, management, conduct, operation, and sale or other disposition of investments in its own territory.

2. Each Party shall accord to covered investments treatment no less favorable than that it
    accords, in like circumstances, to investments in its territory of its own investors with
    respect to the establishment, acquisition, expansion, management, conduct, operation, and
    sale or other disposition of investments.
3. The treatment to be accorded by a Party under Paragraphs 1 and 2 means, with respect to
    a regional level of government, treatment no less favorable than the treatment accorded, in
    like circumstances, by that regional level of government to natural persons resident in and
    enterprises constituted under the laws of other regional levels of government of the Party
    of which it forms a part, and to their respective investments.

The national treatment provisions of a US IIA are more detailed than similar provisions found in BITs of other OECD countries. The 2004 US Model BIT specifies the types of activities to which the national treatment obligation applies: "establishment, acquisition, expansion, management, conduct, operation, and sale or other disposition of investments." Of considerable significance, US IIAs grant a "right of establishment" (that is, a market access commitment). Most IIAs of other countries, in contrast, only grant national treatment protection to investments once they are established, but do not contain the market-opening guarantee of the right of establishment. Therefore, investors from US treaty partners are guaranteed a right of market access unless their proposed activities fall within one of the specific exceptions listed in the annex to the relevant IIA.

In addition, US IIAs limit the national treatment protection only to foreign investors and their US investments "in like circumstances" with US investors and their US investments. The nature of this comparison has been the subject of several arbitration awards under Chapter 11 of NAFTA, including the *S.D. Myers*, *Pope & Talbot* and *Methanex* decisions:

> While the scope of comparison to determine "in like circumstances" remains unsettled, two
> common approaches are often argued by, respectively, the claimant investor and the respond-
> ent Party. In *S.D. Myers v. Canada*, a NAFTA tribunal held that the primary indicator of a
> breach of the national treatment commitment was the effect on the claimant, not the motive
> (protectionist or otherwise) of the host State.[4]

The *Methanex* v. *US* case illustrates that IIA "national treatment" standards may differ from the national treatment obligation in the WTO and other "trade in goods" treaties. The claimant in that case argued that a California prohibition on the use of the additive methanol in gasoline was inconsistent with the state's permission for the use of the additive ethanol, when both additives had the same purpose. To make that argument, Methanex looked to WTO jurisprudence treating the phrase "in like circumstances" as equivalent to "like products." If ethanol is a "like product" to methanol because they are both gasoline additives, then ethanol producers were, said Methanex, "in like circumstances" to methanol producers. The *Methanex* NAFTA tribunal rejected that argument, holding that the proper comparison was US methanol producers and Canadian methanol producers, not US ethanol producers and Canadian methanol producers.[5]

A second area of controversy is whether the "no less favorable" standard requires the host state to accord foreign investors and investments the best treatment offered to locals, the average treatment offered to locals or the lowest level of lawful treatment offered to locals. In *Pope & Talbot Inc.* v. *Canada*, another NAFTA tribunal concluded that the phrase "no less favorable" meant "equivalent to, not better or worse than, the best treatment accorded to the comparator."[6] Moreover, the *Pope & Talbot* tribunal rejected Canada's argument that a breach of the national treatment standard only occurred upon proof of disproportionate disadvantage to the foreign investor. That tribunal stated:

> as a first step, the treatment accorded a foreign owned investment protected by Article 1102(2) [the NAFTA national treatment obligation] should be compared with that accorded domestic investments in the same business or economic sector. However, that first step is not the last one. Differences in treatment will presumptively violate Article 1102(2), unless they have a reasonable nexus to rational government policies that (1) do not distinguish, on their face or *de facto*, between foreign-owned and domestic companies, and (2) do not otherwise unduly undermine the investment liberalizing objectives of NAFTA.[7]

International arbitration awards, however, do not create binding precedent. Consequently, these issues will remain live until a string of consistent awards settles the interpretive questions.

A handful of existing US statutes would be inconsistent with this national treatment obligation unless exempted. For that reason, annexes to US IIAs will contain a schedule of excluded industries and activities. Because these regulatory measures are listed as "national treatment" exemptions in US IIAs, the US is entitled to continue to discriminate in favor of US companies under the specific enactments. Appendix 6.1 below contains, illustratively, the items excluded by the US from the national treatment protections of the US–Singapore FTA (other US IIAs contain virtually identical exclusions). An exception in that treaty for "all existing non-conforming measures" of the 50 US states has the effect of grandfathering current state and local, but not federal, discriminatory measures (for example, local content requirements and local residency requirements). Most other countries, of course, maintain a much longer list of exclusions from their national treatment obligations than the US.

US IIAs do not in general permit a treaty partner to add unilaterally to its list of excluded items or subsequently to impose more stringent limits on foreign investors for activities included in the list of excluded matters. As a result, the schedule of excluded items appended to a US IIA represents a ceiling. Unless specifically provided otherwise, only liberalizing steps are permitted in the future.

Most-favored-nation treatment

> US IIAs provide "most-favored-nation" protection – treatment no less favorable than the US provides, in like circumstances, to investors and investments from other countries. However, a number of exceptions are specifically listed in each IIA.

Article 4 of the 2004 US Model BIT establishes most-favored-nation treatment for investors and covered investments, again subject to an annexed schedule of exclusions. A Chinese investor who is covered by a US IIA is generally protected from improper US discrimination in favor of companies from other countries, subject only to specific listed exceptions in the IIA. Article 4 provides:

Article 4: Most-Favored-Nation Treatment
1.   Each Party shall accord to investors of the other Party treatment no less favorable than that it accords, in like circumstances, to investor of any non-Party with respect to the establishment, acquisition, expansion, management, conduct, operation, and sale or other disposition of investments in its territory.
2.   Each Party shall accord to covered investments treatment no less favorable than it accords, in like circumstances, to investments in its territory of any non-Party with respect to the establishment, acquisition, expansion, management, conduct, operation, and sale or other disposition of investments.

By virtue of this MFN provision, covered Chinese investors and investments in the US by Chinese investors would be entitled to treatment that is no less favorable than the treatment the US grants to investors and investments from other countries "in like circumstances." Just as is the case for the national treatment obligation, the US MFN obligation covers market access – the right of establishment. Similarly, crucial interpretive issues include: (1) the meaning of the phrase "in like circumstances;" and (2) whether the guaranteed treatment is the best available to any third-country investor or covered investment, the average treatment available or the lowest level of lawful treatment. The principles employed by arbitral tribunals to resolve these issues are likely to be similar to those discussed above to resolve the similar national treatment issues.

The schedule of MFN exclusions by the US that is appended to the US–Singapore FTA contains a number of items (Appendix 6.2, below). Like the case of items listed as exceptions from national treatment, the US is entitled to discriminate in favor of companies from other countries under these specific enactments because these items are listed as MFN exemptions in US IIAs.

Minimum standard of treatment

US IIAs guarantee investors a minimum standard of treatment for US legislation, regulatory and judicial actions, including the obligations of "fair and equitable treatment," "full protection and security" and a prohibition on "denial of justice." The scope of these protections is ambiguous. The US takes the position that the questioned government conduct must amount to a gross denial of justice or manifest arbitrariness to fall below this standard. Some arbitral tribunals, however, set the standard substantially higher.

The national treatment and MFN obligations in IIAs prohibit improper discriminatory conduct by the US. While a covered foreign investor or investment is entitled under those obligations to be treated no less favorably than a US or third-country investor or investment in like circumstances, a covered foreign investor or investment is not by operation of those commitments entitled to better treatment. However, US IIAs (like IIAs with the UK, other Western European countries, Canada and many other states) also contain a number of important absolute international standards – standards that the US may not fall below in its treatment of foreign investors and investments regardless of whether the US grants such treatment to its own nationals. One such set of those standards is found in

Article 5 of the 2004 US Model BIT, which covers the so-called "international minimum standard of treatment."

Among the protections the US considers to be encompassed within this minimum level of treatment mandated by international law are the obligations to afford "fair and equitable treatment" (including the obligation "not to deny justice" in adjudicatory proceedings) and the obligation to provide "full protection and security." Therefore, a Chinese investor covered by a US IIA may bring an investor–state arbitration claim against the US if the investor believes US legislative, regulatory or juridical measures violate the international law standards requiring "fair and equitable" treatment or "full protection and security" or constitute a "denial of justice." However, the exact definition of these absolute international standards is unclear.

The relevant portion of the text of Article 5 reads as follows:

Article 5: Minimum Standard of Treatment[8]
1. Each Party shall accord to covered investments treatment in accordance with customary international law, including fair & equitable treatment and full protection and security.
2. For greater certainty, paragraph 1 prescribes the customary international law minimum standard of treatment of aliens as the minimum standard of treatment to be afforded to covered investments. The concepts of "fair & equitable treatment" and "full protection and security" do not require treatment in addition to or beyond that which is required by that standard, and do not create additional substantive rights. The obligation in paragraph 1 to provide:
   (a) "fair & equitable treatment" includes the obligation not to deny justice in criminal, civil, or administrative adjudicatory proceedings in accordance with the principle of due process embodied in the principal legal systems of the world; and
   (b) "full protection and security" requires each Party to provide the level of police protection required under customary international law.

As the United Nations Conference on Trade and Development (UNCTAD) has pointed out: "[a]lthough clauses providing foreign investment with fair and equitable treatment are widespread in IIAs, the standard itself lacks a precise meaning."[9] The US takes the position that the "fair and equitable treatment" commitment in its treaties is co-extensive with the customary international law obligation to treat the investment in accordance with the international minimum standard. Thus, the US has stated in a recent submission in the *Glamis Gold* dispute under NAFTA Chapter 11 that the "fair and equitable treatment" commitment is breached only if the regulatory conduct of the host state constitutes a "gross denial of justice or manifest arbitrariness:"

The tribunal in *International Thunderbird Gaming Corp. v. United Mexican States*, for example, remarked that "the threshold for finding a violation of the minimum standard of treatment still remains high." That tribunal held that mere "arbitrary" conduct by an administrative agency is insufficient to constitute a breach of Article 1105(1); rather, the regulatory action must amount to a *"gross denial of justice* or *manifest arbitrariness* falling below international standards" in order to breach the minimum standard of treatment. In that case, the tribunal acknowledged that the administrative proceedings in question "may have been affected by certain procedural irregularities," but that the record did not establish that "the proceedings were "arbitrary or unfair, *let alone so manifestly arbitrary or unfair as to violate the minimum standard of treatment.*"[10]

The US takes the position that this is the proper interpretation for the "fair and equitable treatment" commitment in all of its recent generation of IIAs. In those IIAs, the US has been careful to specify that "fair and equitable treatment" is a part of the customary international law minimum standard, not an independent treaty standard. Moreover, the text of the recent generation of US IIAs specifically limits the "denial of justice" commitment (but not the broader "fair and equitable treatment" commitment) to judicial and administrative adjudicatory proceedings, rather than the broader sweep of all regulatory and legislative conduct. Similarly, in the texts of recent US IIAs, the "full protection and security" obligation focuses on "the level of police protection required under customary international law," not a broader regulatory commitment.

The specificity of the recent generation of US IIAs contrasts with investment treaties negotiated by other countries (apart from Canada), as well as the earlier generation of US BITs. Those treaties are far less detailed, and do not delimit these absolute standards in the manner of the recent generation of US IIAs. Under third-country investment treaties, as well as under NAFTA, investors argue for broader protection than the position taken by the US. Common positions taken by investors include arguing that: (1) the "fair and equitable treatment" commitment protects foreign investors from regulatory conduct of the host country that improperly interferes with the investor's "legitimate expectations;" (2) the "full protection and security" obligation covers regulatory misconduct by the host country improperly failing to protect the interests of the investor, not just police conduct; and (3) the obligation not to deny justice encompasses regulatory and legislative conduct, not just adjudicatory proceedings. Moreover, investors assert that the international minimum standard is an "evolving" standard, which must take account of the significant changes in the world of government and business affairs since the nineteenth century.

The disagreement between investors and the US on the scope of these protections will continue to play out in future investor–state arbitrations. Nevertheless, even under the less protective "minimum standard" espoused by the US government in the *Glamis Gold* case, a Chinese investment having the benefit of a US IIA may have a claim directly against the US government for manifestly arbitrary US regulatory conduct.

Expropriation and compensation
US IIAs also set an absolute standard with respect to compensation for expropriations.

> US IIAs assure investors of compensation for expropriations, including regulatory takings that are equivalent in effect to expropriations. However, recent US treaties make clear that non-discriminatory regulatory actions designed and applied to protect public heath, safety, the environment, and other legitimate public welfare objectives are not generally expropriations. The treaties require the US to pay compensation for expropriation at fair market value calculated as of the date of expropriation.

A Chinese investor who is covered by a US IIA will be entitled to compensation at fair market value if its investment is expropriated by the US. Article 6 of the 2004 US Model BIT requires a host country to pay fair market value compensation for lawful expropriations. That compensation is to be calculated as of the date of expropriation and to be paid in a fully realizable and freely transferable currency. The relevant provisions of Article 6 are as follows:

Article 6: Expropriation and Compensation[11]
1. Neither Party may expropriate or nationalize a covered investment either directly or indirectly through measures equivalent to expropriation or nationalization ("expropriation"), except:
   (a) for a public purpose;
   (b) in a non-discriminatory manner;
   (c) on payment of prompt, adequate, and effective compensation; and
   (d) in accordance with due process of law and Article 5 [Minimum Standard of Treatment] (1) through (3).
2. The compensation referred to in paragraph 1(c) shall:
   (a) be paid without delay;
   (b) be equivalent to the fair market value of the expropriated investment immediately before the expropriation took place ("the date of expropriation");
   (c) not reflect any change in value occurring because the intended expropriation had become known earlier; and
   (d) be fully realizable and freely transferable.

Recent US IIAs have been careful to specify that the test for whether a Party's conduct constitutes expropriation is to be determined in accordance with principles of customary international law. (See Annex B, Paragraph 1, of the 2004 US Model BIT.) US IIAs require the host country to compensate for lawful expropriations, whether the expropriation was effected directly or indirectly. Indirect expropriations, often referred to as regulatory expropriations, raise difficult political and factual issues involving the proper scope of a host country's regulatory conduct. The US has tried, therefore, to describe with some specificity in its IIAs the standard for determining when regulatory conduct constitutes an indirect expropriation. Moreover, the US also sets out in its recent IIAs the circumstances under which legitimate regulatory conduct of the host country does not constitute indirect expropriation. Unlike NAFTA and earlier US IIAs, Paragraph 4(a) of Annex B to the 2004 US Model BIT describes the elements to be considered in deciding whether state action constitutes indirect expropriation:

4. The second situation addressed by Article 6 [Expropriation and Compensation](1) is indirect expropriation, where an action or series of actions by a Party has an effect equivalent to direct expropriation without formal transfer of title or outright seizure.
   (a) The determination of whether an action or series of actions by a Party, in a specific fact situation, constitutes an indirect expropriation, requires a case-by-case, fact-based inquiry that considers, among other factors:
      (i) the economic impact of the government action, although the fact that an action or series of actions by a Party has an adverse effect on the economic value of an investment, standing alone, does not establish that an indirect expropriation has occurred;
      (ii) the extent to which the government action interferes with distinct, reasonable investment-backed expectations; and
      (iii) the character of the government action.

Then, Paragraph 4(b) of Annex B seeks to preserve the host country's "regulatory space" for legitimate regulatory conduct, as follows:

(b) Except in rare circumstances, non-discriminatory regulatory actions by a Party that are designed and applied to protect legitimate public welfare objectives, such as public health, safety, and the environment, do not constitute indirect expropriations.

It is noteworthy that the elements to be considered under the US 2004 Model BIT, as described above, are taken directly from US Supreme Court practice in applying the "Takings Clause" of the Fifth Amendment to the US Constitution, which prohibits the US government from taking private property without compensation. Consequently, US Supreme Court interpretations of the "Takings Clause" may play a role in setting parameters for the protections in US IIAs against expropriations.[12] Unlike recent US (and Canadian) IIAs, BITs entered into by other OECD countries do not seek to define indirect or regulatory expropriations with any specificity.

Article 6 of the US Model BIT only addresses "lawful" expropriations. According to Article 6, to be lawful an expropriation must be: (1) for a public purpose; (2) effected in a non-discriminatory manner; (3) accompanied by prompt and effective compensation (that is, compensation at fair market value); and (4) effected in accordance with due process of law and the international minimum standard prescribed by Article 5 of the US Model BIT. If an expropriation is not "lawful" within the meaning of the IIA, then practice in international arbitral awards suggests that the injured investor may be entitled to additional remedies, potentially including restitution of the expropriated investment or an increase in compensation to include the amount of any appreciation in value of the expropriated investment between the date of the expropriation and the date of the arbitration award.[13]

Transfers

Consistent with current US law, US IIAs also guarantee that all transfers of funds related to a covered investment may freely be made into and out of the US. Therefore, a Chinese investor covered by a US IIA will be entitled to unrestricted transferability and unrestricted convertibility of its funds transfers into the US (for example, contributions of capital and loan disbursements) and its funds transfers out of the US (e.g., profits, dividends and distributions, proceeds of sale of the investment and payments of principal and interest on loans). Those guarantees have not been the subject of any investment treaty arbitrations with the US. Nevertheless, the assurance that repatriation of interest payments and principal payments on loans, dividends, profits, royalties, sales proceeds and other transfers will be permitted in a freely usable currency at market exchange rates is a crucial investment undertaking. Article 7 of the 2004 US Model BIT contains the following commitments:

Article 7: Transfers
1. Each Party shall permit all transfers relating to a covered investment to be made freely and without delay into and out of its territory. Such transfers include:
   (a) contributions to capital;
   (b) profits, dividends, capital gains, and proceeds from the sale of all or any part of the covered investment or from the partial or complete liquidation of the covered investment;
   (c) interest, royalty payments, management fees, and technical assistance and other fees;
   (d) payments made under a contract, including a loan agreement;

(e)   payments made pursuant to Article 5 [Minimum Standard of Treatment] (4) and (5) and Article 6 [Expropriation and Compensation]; and

(f)   payments arising out of a dispute.

2.   Each Party shall permit transfers relating to a covered investment to be made in a freely usable currency at the market rate of exchange prevailing at the time of transfer.

Some of the US's treaty partners have negotiated for modifications to these guarantees, to provide for themselves flexibility to impose exchange control regulations in foreign exchange crises. However, those provisions are all one-sided in favor of the non-US party; the US does not seek similar exclusions for its own exchange control regulations. Annex 15A of the US–Singapore FTA, for example, contains an exclusion in the following terms.

Where a claimant submits a claim alleging that Singapore has breached an obligation under Section B [substantive protections], other than Article 15.4 [national treatment and MFN], that arises from its imposition of restrictive measures with regard to outward payments and transfers, Section C [investor–state arbitration] shall apply except as modified below:

(a)   A claimant may submit the claim under Article 15.15 [submission of claim to arbitration] only after one year has elapsed since the measure was adopted.

(b)   If the claim is submitted under Article 15.15.1(b) [submission by investor on behalf of local enterprise], the claimant may, on behalf of the enterprise, only seek damages with respect to the shares of the enterprise for which the claimant has a beneficial interest.

(c)   Paragraph 1(a) shall not apply to claims that arise from restrictions on:

    (i)   payments or transfers on current transactions, including the transfer of profits and dividends of foreign direct investment by investors of the United States;

    (ii)   transfers of proceeds of foreign direct investment by investors of the United States, excluding investments designed with the purpose of gaining direct or indirect access to the financial market; or

    (iii)   payments pursuant to a loan or bond regardless of where it is issued, including inter- and intra-company debt financing between affiliated enterprises, when such payments are made exclusively for the conduct, operation, management, or expansion of such affiliated enterprises, provided that these payments are made in accordance with the maturity date agreed on in the loan or bond agreement.

(d)   Excluding restrictive measures referred to in paragraph 1(c), Singapore shall incur no liability, and shall not be subject to claims, for damages arising from its imposition of restrictive measures with regard to outward payments and transfers that were incurred within one year from the date on which restrictions were imposed, provided that such restrictive measures do not substantially impede transfers.

(e)   Claims arising from Singapore's imposition of restrictive measures with regard to outward payments and transfers shall not be subject to Article 15.24 [consolidation of similar arbitration claims] unless Singapore consents.

2.   The United States may not request the establishment of an arbitral panel under Chapter 20 (Administration and Dispute Settlement) [state–state arbitration] relating to Singapore's imposition of restrictive measures with regard to outward payments and transfers until one year has elapsed since the measure was adopted. In determining whether compensation is owed or benefits should be suspended, or the level of such compensation or suspension, pursuant to Article 20.6 (Non-Implementation), the aggrieved Party and the panel shall consider whether the restrictive measures were implemented at the request of the International Monetary Fund (IMF).

The US–Peru and US–Colombia Trade Promotion Agreements also include a number of provisions limiting the impact on Peruvian or Colombian sovereign indebtedness of the substantive protections of the investment chapters in those FTAs.[14] Again, the US does not seek similar limitations with respect to its own sovereign debt.

Investment-related performance requirements

The 2004 US Model BIT contains an extensive section limiting the ability of the treaty partners, in connection with investment activities, to require that foreign investors comply with minimum export requirements, domestic content requirements, technology transfer requirements, and similar investment-related performance requirements. The US, therefore, has only limited ability to impose "local content" and similar requirements on a Chinese investment in the US. The very detailed text of Article 8 of the 2004 US Model BIT contains these restrictions. The provisions of Article 8 are more protective of investors than the similar restrictions found in the TRIMS agreement. Like national treatment and MFN treatment, accompanying annexes list items excluded by the US from this commitment.

Senior management and boards of directors

> Unlike investment treaties of other countries, US IIAs prohibit the US from imposing nationality requirements for senior management positions and limit nationality requirements for board of director positions.

By virtue of commitments in US IIAs, a Chinese investor covered by a US IIA will generally be entitled to choose Chinese nationals to manage its investment. The 2004 US Model BIT prohibits nationality requirements for senior management positions at covered investments. With respect to the board of directors of a covered investment, however, the Model BIT does permit the US to require that a majority of the board, or any committee of the board, be of a particular nationality or be a resident of the US, provided that the nationality or residency requirement with respect to the board of directors does not materially impair the investor's control of the covered investment. Article 9 of the 2004 US Model BIT sets out these limitations in the following terms:

Article 9: Senior Management and Boards of Directors
1. Neither Party may require than an enterprise of that party that is a covered investment appoint to senior management positions natural persons of any particular nationality.
2. A Party may require that a majority of the board of directors, or any committee thereof, of an enterprise of that Party that is a covered investment, be of a particular nationality, or resident in the territory of the Party, provided that the requirement does not materially impair the ability of the investor to exercise control over its investment.

Publication of information

> US IIAs obligate the US to make publicly available all legislation, regulatory measures and judicial decisions respecting matters covered by the treaty.

US IIAs obligate the treaty parties to publish or make publicly available all laws, regulations, procedures, administrative rulings of general application, and adjudicatory decisions respecting any matter covered by the IIA. Article 10 of the 2004 US Model BIT provides for this publication requirement in the following manner:

Article 10: Publication of Laws and Decisions Respecting Investment
1. Each Party shall ensure that its:
   (a) laws, regulations, procedures, and administrative rulings of general application; and
   (b) adjudicatory decisions
   respecting any matter covered by this Treaty are promptly published or otherwise made publicly available.
2. For purposes of this Article, "administrative ruling of general application" means an administrative ruling or interpretation that applies to all persons and fact situations that fall generally within its ambit and that establishes a norm of conduct but does not include:
   (a) a determination or ruling made in an administrative or quasi-judicial proceeding that applies to a particular covered investment or investor of the other Party in a specific case; or
   (b) a ruling that adjudicates with respect to a particular act or practice.

Investor–state arbitration

Most importantly, a Chinese investor covered by a US IIA is entitled itself to enforce each of the preceding substantive IIA protections in investor–state arbitration.

> Covered investors are entitled under US IIAs to enforce these treaty protections against the US by means of investor–state arbitration. However, at the time of writing this chapter, no claim against the US under NAFTA or any other US IIA has yet been successful.

By virtue of access to investor–state arbitration, a Chinese investor will not need to rely directly on the US court system. Moreover, a Chinese investor will be able to enforce these protections by itself, rather than needing to have the Chinese government agree to bring the claim as claimant. Under US IIAs, investors, on their own behalf or on behalf of their investment enterprise in the host country, may bring a claim in arbitration against the host country for breach of: (1) any of the foregoing IIA obligations; (2) an "investment authorization" issued by the host country's "foreign investment authority;" or (3) an "investment agreement" between the investor and a "national authority" of the host country with respect to natural resources, the supply of public services or infrastructure projects. Note that the above right of an investor to bring an arbitration claim against the US for breach of an "investment authorization" is an empty right, since (as recent US IIAs expressly acknowledge) the US does not have a "foreign investment authority."

Moreover, the right of an investor to bring an arbitration claim against the US for breach of an "investment agreement" is limited in recent US IIAs solely to agreements with an authority at the federal level of the US government (a "national authority"), not US state, regional or local authorities. However, the right to bring a claim against the US for breach of one of the substantive treaty obligations described above is a formidable entitlement, leading thus far to at least 13 NAFTA Chapter 11 arbitrations against the US (one of which involves dozens of individual claimants).[15]

Under US IIAs, an investor may elect to bring the arbitration claim: (1) in an administered arbitration proceeding under the ICSID Convention (the World Bank-related Convention on the Settlement of Investment Disputes between States and Nationals of Other States) if both the US and its IIA treaty partner are parties to the ICSID Convention; (2) in an administered arbitration proceeding under the ICSID Additional Facility Rules if one state is an ICSID party but the other relevant state is not; (3) in an ad hoc arbitration proceeding under the UNCITRAL Arbitration Rules; or (4) pursuant to any other arbitration procedures if the investor and the host country mutually agree. The investor–state arbitration provisions of recent US IIAs are quite complex, and I refer readers to Section B of the 2004 US Model BIT. To date, a number of arbitration claims have been brought against the US under Chapter 11 of NAFTA, but thus far under no other US IIAs. None of those claims has yet been successful.

6.1.3 General Exclusions from the Substantive Protections of US IIAs

In addition to schedules of particular excluded items, US IIAs contain several important general exclusions. Several of those general exclusions may be of particular interest to Chinese investors.

Denial of benefits for investments controlled by certain third-country persons

> US IIAs permit the US to deny treaty protections to a covered investment if: (1) that investment is owned or controlled by nationals of a third country; and (2) the US either does not maintain diplomatic relations with that country or imposes economic sanctions against that third county prohibiting the transaction. Therefore, enterprises from the Democratic People's Republic of Korea, Cuba, Sudan and Iran (among others) may not control a Chinese business seeking to obtain US treaty benefits.

US IIAs permit a state to deny the benefits of the investment treaty to an enterprise of the other State if: (1) that enterprise is owned or controlled by nationals of a third country; and (2) the denying state either does not maintain diplomatic relations with that third country or imposes sanctions against the third country prohibiting transactions with the relevant enterprise. Thus, if a North Korean, Cuban, Sudanese or Iranian entity (for example) controlled a Chinese enterprise, that Chinese enterprise could not rely on the provisions of a US IIA to make a protected investment in the US in circumvention of current US trade embargoes against those states. Article 17.1 of the 2004 US Model BIT provides as follows:

Article 17: Denial of Benefits
1. A Party may deny the benefits of this Treaty to an investor of the other Party that is an enterprise of such other Party and to investments of that investor if persons of a non-Party own or control the enterprise and the denying Party:

(a) does not maintain diplomatic relations with the non-Party; or
(b) adopts or maintains measures with respect to the non-Party or a person of the non-Party that prohibit transactions with the enterprise or that would be violated or circumvented if the benefits of this Treaty were accorded to the enterprise or to its investments.

Financial services

Notwithstanding any investment protections in a US IIA, the treaty also preserves the ability of US banking and securities regulators to impose financial services regulatory measures for prudential reasons. Similarly, US IIAs exempt non-discriminatory measures of general application in pursuit of monetary or related credit or exchange policies. The latter exemption cannot, however, be used to expressly nullify or amend contractual provisions specifying the currency of denomination or the rate of exchange between currencies. Article 20 of the 2004 US Model BIT provides in pertinent part:

Article 20: Financial Services
1. Notwithstanding any other provision of this Treaty, a Party shall not be prevented from adopting or maintaining measures relating to financial services for prudential reasons, including for the protection of investors, depositors, policy holders, or persons to whom a fiduciary duty is owed by a financial services supplier, or to ensure the integrity and stability of the financial system.[16] Where such measures do not conform with the provisions of this Treaty, they shall not be used as a means of avoiding the Party's commitments or obligations under this Treaty.
2. (a) Nothing in this Treaty applies to non-discriminatory measures of general application taken by any public entity in pursuit of monetary and related credit policies or exchange rate policies. This paragraph shall not affect a Party's obligations under Article 7 [Transfers] or Article 8 [Performance Requirements].[17]
    (b) For purposes of this paragraph, "public entity" means a central bank or monetary authority of a party.
3. Where a claimant submits a claim to arbitration under Section B [Investor–state Dispute Settlement], and the respondent invokes paragraph 1 or 2 as a defense, the following provisions shall apply:
    (a) The respondent shall, within 120 days of the date the claim is submitted to arbitration under Section B, submit in writing to the competent financial authorities[18] of both Parties a request for a joint determination on the issue of whether and to what extent paragraph 1 or 2 is a valid defense to the claim. The respondent shall promptly provide the tribunal, if constituted, a copy of such request. The arbitration may proceed with respect to the claim only as provided in subparagraph (d).
    (b) The competent financial authorities of both Parties shall make themselves available for consultations with each other and shall attempt in good faith to make a determination as described in subparagraph (a). Any such determination shall be transmitted promptly to the disputing parties and, if constituted, to the tribunal. The determination shall be binding on the tribunal.
    (c) If the competent financial authorities of both Parties, within 120 days of the date by which they have both received the respondent's written request for a joint determination under subparagraph (a), have not made a determination as described in that subparagraph, the tribunal shall decide the issue left unresolved by the competent financial authorities. The provisions of Section B shall apply, except as modified by this subparagraph.
        (i) In the appointment of all arbitrators not yet appointed to the tribunal, each disputing party shall take appropriate steps to ensure that the tribunal has expertise or experience in financial services law or practice. The expertise of particular candidates with respect to financial services shall be taken into account in the appointment of the presiding arbitrator.

(ii)   If, before the respondent submits the request for a joint determination in conformance with subparagraph (a), the presiding arbitrator has been appointed pursuant to Article 27(3), such arbitrator shall be replaced on the request of either disputing party and the tribunal shall be reconstituted consistent with subparagraph (c)(i). If, within 30 days of the date the arbitration proceedings are resumed under subparagraph (d), the disputing parties have not agreed on the appointment of a new presiding arbitrator, the Secretary-General, on the request of a disputing party, shall appoint the presiding arbitrator consistent with subparagraph (c)(i).

(iii) The non-disputing Party may make oral and written submissions to the tribunal regarding the issue of whether and to what extent paragraph 1 or 2 is a valid defense to the claim. Unless it makes such a submission, the non-disputing Party shall be presumed, for purposes of the arbitration, to take a position on paragraph 1 or 2 not inconsistent with that of the respondent.

(d)   The arbitration referred to in subparagraph (a) may proceed with respect to the claim:

(a)   10 days after the date the competent financial authorities' joint determination has been received by both the disputing parties and, if constituted, the tribunal; or

(b)   10 days after the expiration of the 120-day period provided to the competent financial authorities in subparagraph (c).

4.   Where a dispute arises under Section C and the competent financial authorities of one Party provide written notice to the competent financial authorities of the other Party that the dispute involves financial services, Section C shall apply except as modified by this paragraph and paragraph 5.

(a)   The competent financial authorities of both Parties shall make themselves available for consultations with each other regarding the dispute, and shall have 180 days from the date such notice is received to transmit a report on their consultations to the Parties. A Party may submit the dispute to arbitration under Section C only after the expiration of that 180-day period.

(b)   Either Party may make any such report available to a tribunal constituted under Section C to decide the dispute referred to in this paragraph or a similar dispute, or to a tribunal constituted under Section B to decide a claim arising out of the same events or circumstances that gave rise to the dispute under Section C.

5.   Where a Party submits a dispute involving financial services to arbitration under Section C in conformance with paragraph 4, and on the request of either Party within 30 days of the date the dispute is submitted to arbitration, each Party shall, in the appointment of all arbitrators not yet appointed, take appropriate steps to ensure that the tribunal has expertise or experience in financial services law or practice. The expertise of particular candidates with respect to financial services shall be taken into account in the appointment of the presiding arbitrator.

6.   Notwithstanding Article 11(2) [Transparency – Publication], each Party shall, to the extent practicable,

(a)   publish in advance any regulations of general application relating to financial services that it proposes to adopt;

(b)   provide interested persons and the other Party a reasonable opportunity to comment on such proposed regulations.

7.   The terms "financial service" or "financial services" shall have the same meaning as in subparagraph 5(a) of the Annex on Financial Services of the GATS.

As a result of these provisions, the US Board of Governors of the Federal Reserve System and the US Securities Exchange Commission (as well as other US financial regulatory authorities) maintain their ability to limit or condition foreign investments in US financial institutions on compliance with US "safety and soundness" requirements. Additionally, non-discriminatory measures of general application taken by any

US public entity (including, most importantly, the US Federal Reserve Board and the US Department of the Treasury) in pursuit of monetary and related credit policies or exchange rate policies are exempt from the provisions of an IIA. However, such measures of general application may not be used to restrict the IIA's guarantees related to funds transfers or the limits on investment-related performance requirements.

The ability of a foreign investor to bring an investor–state arbitration claim against the US under an IIA is also subject to special procedural requirements if the US invokes the above financial services provisions as a defense. (See Article 20.3–20.5 of the 2004 US Model BIT.)

Taxation

US treaty practice is to limit the ability of a foreign investor to bring an investor–state arbitration claim on account of taxation measures. The recent US generation of IIAs protects investors only if: (1) the taxation measure constitutes expropriation; or (2) a tax advantage is conditioned on a prohibited investment-related performance measure. (See Article 21 of the 2004 US Model BIT.)

Essential security interests

Nothing in a US IIA prevents a treaty party from taking measures to protect its essential security interests or to fulfill its obligations with respect to international peace and security. Thus, Article 18 of the 2004 US Model BIT provides as follows:

> Article 18: Essential Security
> Nothing in this Treaty shall be construed;
> 1. to require a Party to furnish or allow access to any information the disclosure of which it determines to be contrary to its essential security interests; or
> 2. to preclude a Party from applying measures that it considers necessary for the fulfillment of its obligations with respect to the maintenance or restoration of international peace or security, or the protection of its own essential security interests.

Earlier generations of US BITs did not explicitly state whether this type of "essential security" exception is "self-judging" (that is, whether the host country's own determination that its essential security interests are at risk is binding or whether that determination instead may be subject to review in arbitration).

Several recent ICSID arbitration awards have concluded that the analogous provision in the US–Argentina BIT is not self-judging. Those arbitral panels have rejected the Argentina assertion that the economic and financial measures Argentina took in response to its economic crisis were excused on the basis that they were for the protection of Argentina's essential security interests. For example, in the recent *Enron* v. *Argentina*[19] award, an ICSID tribunal ruled that "[t]ruly exceptional and extraordinary clauses such as a self-judging provision normally must be expressly drafted to reflect that intent, as otherwise there can well be a presumption about it not having that meaning in view of its exceptional nature." The tribunal held that this drafting standard had not been met with respect to the US–Argentina BIT and therefore the "essential security interests" exception in that treaty was not self-judging. The tribunal then undertook to review for itself the validity of Argentina's assertion that its economic measures were in fact for "essential security interests," and ultimately rejected the argument. In contrast, the ICSID tribunal in the recent *LG&E* v. *Argentina*[20] case was more open to Argentina's position, holding that the treaty provision was not self-judging but that Argentina's conduct was partially excused by the somewhat analogous "state of necessity" exclusion under customary international law.

Importantly, all US IIAs since NAFTA in 1995 (including the 2004 US Model BIT and subsequent US FTAs) expressly specify that the "essential security interests" exception is available to a party for "measures that *it considers necessary* for . . . the protections of its own essential security interests." Based on that language it appears that the "essential security" exception in newer US treaties is self-judging. That interpretation was reinforced in the recent US bipartisan trade compromise permitting several FTAs to proceed toward ratification. In compliance with that compromise, the US and its treaty partners added the following express self-judging language to the US–Panama FTA, the US–Peru Trade Promotion Agreement, the US–Colombia Trade Promotion Agreement and the Republic of Korea–US FTA:

> For greater certainty, if a Party invokes [the essential security exception] in an arbitration proceeding initiated under [the investor–state arbitration provisions or the state–state arbitration provisions], the tribunal or panel hearing the matter shall find that the exception applies.

None of these IIAs defines the scope of the phrase "essential security interests." The US has carefully avoided publicly stating whether the term covers only national security interests or also covers economic crises. In, *inter alia*, the *CMS* v. *Argentina*;[21] *Enron* v. *Argentina* and *LG&E* v. *Argentina* ICSID awards, arbitral tribunals construing the "essential security interests" exception in the US–Argentina BIT have held that, depending on the particular facts and circumstances, the phrase may in fact cover economic crises.

6.1.4 APEC and OECD Non-Binding Investment Guidelines

International investment law is commonly seen as limiting the scope of permissible government behavior. Those "protections" may also be seen as setting out the parameters for government regulatory space. Therefore, it may be helpful to understand as well the non-binding principles to which the US has subscribed with respect to proper multinational corporate behavior. For example, the US has adhered to the OECD Guidelines for Multinational Enterprises and the APEC Non-Binding Investment Principles.

At present the 30 OECD countries, plus Argentina, Brazil, Chile, Egypt, Estonia, Israel, Latvia, Lithuania, Romania and Slovenia, adhere to the OECD Guidelines. China has not agreed to be bound by the OECD Guidelines. The OECD Guidelines apply wherever companies from adhering states operate, not just in the adhering countries. The non-binding OECD Declaration specifies that adhering countries (including the US) "should" grant treatment consistent with international law and "national treatment" to foreign-controlled enterprises, as follows:

> II. 1.   That adhering governments should, consistent with their needs to maintain public order, to protect their essential security interests and to fulfill commitments relating to international peace and security, accord to enterprises operating in their territories an owned or controlled directly or indirectly by nationals of another adhering government (hereinafter referred to as "Foreign-Controlled Enterprises") treatment under their

laws, regulations and administrative practices, consistent with international law and no less favourable than that accorded in like situations to domestic enterprises (hereinafter referred to as "National Treatment");

2. That adhering governments will consider applying "National Treatment" in respect of countries other than adhering governments;
3. That adhering governments will endeavor to ensure that their territorial subdivisions apply "National Treatment";
4. That this Declaration does not deal with the right of adhering governments to regulate the entry of foreign investment or the conditions of establishment of foreign enterprises.

Unlike US IIAs, the OECD Guidelines also contain chapters covering most aspects of company behavior, including employment and industrial relations, the environment and taxation. Most significantly, the OCED Guidelines are backed by an implementation procedure. Under that procedure, final responsibility for enforcement of the Guidelines lies with National Contact Points established by the adhering governments. If a company is believed to be in breach of the OECD Guidelines, then a trade union, an non-governmental organization (NGO) or another interested party can raise this as a case with either the National Contact Point in the country where the violation occurred (if it is an adhering country) or the National Contact Point in the country where the company is headquartered (if the problem arose in a non-adhering country). The National Contact Point should then try to resolve the issue, through a range of available options that include offering a forum for discussion for the parties concerned, allowing conciliation or mediation. Ultimately, if no agreement can be reached, the National Contact Point is required to issue an OECD public statement on the case. It could also make recommendations to the parties on how the Guidelines apply to the case. National Contact Points may, therefore, inform a corporation that its activities infringe the OECD Guidelines. Trade unions are also seeking to make the provision of export credits and investment guarantees to corporations conditional upon observance of the OECD Guidelines.

The Asia-Pacific Economic Cooperation (APEC) Non-Binding Investment Principles contain recommendations addressing many of the same issues as international investment law. As a member of APEC, China has accepted these principles, as has the US. Under the APEC Principles, signatory governments "aspire" to the following principles:

- Member economies will make all laws, regulations, administrative guidelines and policies pertaining to investment in their economies publicly available in a prompt, transparent and readily accessible manner.
- Member economies will extend to investors from any economy treatment in relation to the establishment, expansion, operation and protection of their investments, treatment no less favorable than that accorded in like situations to domestic investors.
- Member economies will not relax health, safety, and environmental regulations as an incentive to encourage foreign investment.
- Member economies will minimize the use of performance requirements that distort or limit expansion of trade and investment.
- Member economies will not expropriate foreign investments or take measures that have a similar effect, except for a public purpose and on a non-discriminatory basis, in accordance with the laws of each economy and principles of international law and against the prompt payment of adequate and effective compensation.
- Member economies will further liberalize towards the goal of the free and prompt transfer of funds related to foreign investment, such as profits, dividends, royalties, loan payments and liquidations, in freely convertible currency.

- Member economies accept that disputes arising in connection with a foreign investment will be settled promptly through consultations and negotiations between the parties to the dispute or, failing this, through procedures for arbitration in accordance with members' international commitments or through other arbitration procedures acceptable to both parties.
- Member economies will permit the temporary entry and sojourn of key foreign technical and managerial personnel for the purpose of engaging in activities connected with foreign investment, subject to relevant laws and regulations.
- Member economies will endeavour to avoid double taxation related to foreign investment.
- Acceptance of foreign investment is facilitated when foreign investors abide by the host economy's laws, regulations, administrative guidelines and policies, just as domestic investors should.
- Member economies accept that regulatory and institutional barriers to the outflow of investment will be minimized.

6.2   WTO INVESTMENT-RELATED OBLIGATIONS

> Chinese investments in US services businesses may be protected by the World Trade Organization (WTO) General Agreement on Trade in Services (GATS). In addition, under the WTO Agreement on Trade-Related Investment Measures (TRIMs Agreement), the US is restricted from imposing investment-related peformance measures on Chinese investments in the US. However, Chinese investors do not control their own claim under the GATS or the TRIMs Agreement, but instead must rely on their own government to pursue the claims against the US. Also, if the claim is successful, the ordinary WTO remedy will be withdrawal by China of trade benefits from US companies, not compensation for the injured Chinese investor.

In addition to investor protections under US IIAs, several agreements concluded under the auspices of the World Trade Organization (WTO) also afford Chinese investors certain protections for their investments in the US. The two most important agreements in this regard are the GATS and the TRIMs Agreement. Unlike IIAs, the obligations of host countries found in the GATS and the TRIMs Agreement are not independently enforceable by injured investors, nor are damage remedies available. Instead, breaches by a host country of its GATS or TRIMs commitments are enforceable by means of state–state arbitration under the WTO Dispute Settlement Understanding. The WTO dispute settlement system relies largely on principles of deterrence for its remedial tools, rather than compensation to the injured private party. If a WTO dispute panel determines that a host member country has breached one of its WTO obligations, and the host member does not remove the offending measure, then the claimant member state is entitled to withdraw trade benefits granted to the breaching state under the WTO system. The foreign investor does not control the claim in WTO dispute proceedings in a state–state process. Further, the injured investor will not be compensated for the injuries it has suffered from the breach, unless its own member country chooses to elect to withdraw trade benefits from the offending state so as to provide an advantage to the injured investor.

6.2.1 General Agreement on Trade in Services

The US and China are members of the GATS, which contains both general and specific commitments with respect to trade in services. About 60 percent of US gross domestic product (GDP) is comprised of services, including financial and insurance services, construction services, electricity generation, transmission and distribution, pipeline services, transportation services, engineering and design, health service and numerous other business activities. As a result, a significant proportion of Chinese investment in the US may well eventually involve the supply of services covered by the GATS. Indeed, the definition of "services" in Article 1.2(b) of the GATS is broad: "(b) 'services' includes any services in any sector except services supplied in the exercise of governmental authority." The exception in the quoted definition for services supplied "in the exercise of governmental authority" means only "services which are supplied neither on a commercial basis nor in competition with one or more service suppliers." (See GATS Art. 1.2(c).)

Importantly, the GATS defines "trade in services" in Article I.2 to include "the supply of a service . . . by a service supplier of one Member, through a commercial presence in the territory of any other Member." In turn, Article XXVIII of the GATS defines "commercial presence" to mean: "(d) any type of business or professional establishment, including through (i) the constitution, acquisition or maintenance of a juridical person, or (ii) the creation or maintenance of a branch or representative office, within the territory of a Member for the purpose of supplying a service."

By operation of these definitions, the GATS concepts of "trade in services" and the "supply of a service" include services supplied through a subsidiary (whether a newly established company or a company acquired from a prior owner), a branch office or a representative office – a "commercial presence." Within the GATS framework, supply of covered services through a "commercial presence" is known as "Mode 3." As is apparent, Mode 3 encompasses a variety of devices commonly utilized by foreign investors.

The GATS covers the supply of a service in the US by a Chinese service supplier through a "commercial presence" in the US. The supply of services by a Chinese enterprise through US subsidiaries, branch offices and representative offices is therefore included within GATS coverage.

Substantively, the GATS contains both "general" commitments and "specific" commitments. Specific commitments are undertakings by a member state that relate only to services sectors affirmatively listed in that member's schedule of specific commitments. General commitments, in contrast, are undertakings by all members of the GATS found in the text of the GATS. "General" commitments are applicable to all trade in services, for all sectors, and to all modes of supply (including Mode 3, "commercial presence"). A number of the "general" commitments under the GATS are of particular importance to Chinese investors utilizing a commercial presence in the US to supply services within the US; among them are commitments relating to: (1) most-favored-nation treatment; (2) domestic regulation; and (3) monopolies and exclusive service suppliers.

General commitment for most-favored-nation treatment

Article II of the GATS imposes on the US an MFN obligation with respect to Chinese services and service suppliers operating through a US "commercial presence."

> Under the GATS, Chinese services suppliers are entitled to MFN treatment in the US, subject to listed exceptions.

The GATS MFN article provides as follows:

Article II Most-Favored-Nation Treatment
1. With respect to any measure covered by this Agreement, each Member shall accord immediately and unconditionally to services and service suppliers of any other Member treatment no less favorable than that it accords to like services and service suppliers of any other country.
2. A Member may maintain a measure inconsistent with paragraph 1 provided that such a measure is listed in, and meets the conditions of, the Annex on Article II Exemptions.
3. The provisions of this Agreement shall not be so construed as to prevent any Member from conferring or according advantages to adjacent countries in order to facilitate exchanges limited to contiguous frontier zones of services that are both locally produced and consumed.

By virtue of this commitment, Chinese investors who establish a commercial presence in the US to supply services are entitled to MFN treatment, whether or not the protections of a US IIA cover the investment. Like the MFN obligation found in US IIAs, though, several interpretive issues exist, including what is meant by "like" services and service suppliers. Also, as Article II.2 of the GATS notes, a member may exempt specific measures affecting trade in services from this MFN commitment, by listing the excluded measures in that Member's Annex on Article II Exemptions. The US Annex on Article II Exemptions contains an array of exclusions from the Mode 3 commercial presence commitment for "market access" and "national treatment." While the list is too extensive to be included in this chapter, it may be found at http://tsdb.wto.org/wto/WTOHomepublic. htm. The list does not differ substantially from the similar list of MFN exclusions in US IIAs previously described in this chapter.

In addition, Article XIII of the GATS excludes certain government procurement from this MFN commitment: "laws, regulations, or requirements governing the procurement by governmental agencies of services purchased for governmental purposes and not with a view to commercial resale or with a view to use in the supply of services of commercial sale."

General commitment for domestic regulation

The GATS contains a "general" commitment in Article VI, binding on all members, with respect to domestic regulatory measures affecting trade in services. First, if a member has undertaken specific commitments with respect to a particular services sector, then GATS Article VI.1 requires that member to: "ensure that all measures of general application affecting trade in services [in that sector] are administered in a reasonable, objective and impartial manner."

> The GATS contains general commitments requiring the US to ensure that all of its measures of general application for specific covered services must essentially be administered in a reasonable, objective and impartial manner. In addition, the GATS requires the US to provide for independent, impartial and objective review of administrative decisions respecting trade in services. The GATS also restricts the ability of the US to employ qualification, technical or licensing requirements to create unnecessary barriers to trade in services through a commercial pre-serve.

This GATS commitment may overlap with the "fair and equitable treatment" commitment found in IIAs. To date, there are no WTO dispute panel determinations exploring the nature of this commitment. Chinese investors need to review those specific commitments to determine if their services offerings through a US commercial presence are covered. The US has undertaken an extensive array of specific GATS commitments with respect to trade in services.

Second, under Article VI.2 the GATS obligates its members to establish or maintain judicial, arbitral or administrative tribunals or procedures for prompt review of administrative decisions affecting trade in services. If the procedures are not independent of the agency making the administrative decision, the GATS obligates the member to ensure that the procedures in fact provide for an objective and impartial review. Thus, Chinese investors in the services sector are guaranteed under the GATS prompt, impartial and objective review of US administrative decisions affecting trade in such services. The system of administrative law judges and judicial review of US federal regulatory actions under the US Administrative Procedures Act is generally considered to satisfy these GATS obligations, but of course the possibility exists that individual reviews may be criticized for failure to conform to these GATS commitments.

Third, the GATS has established a Council for Trade in Services under GATS Article VI.4. That Council is entrusted with the responsibility for establishing disciplines to ensure that: "measures relating to qualification requirements and procedures, technical standards and licensing requirements do not constitute unnecessary barriers to trade in services." The Council has not yet established such disciplines. However, the drafters of the GATS anticipated the possibility of delays within the Council for Trade in Services. Therefore, Article VI.5 of the GATS provides that, pending entry into force of Council-developed disciplines, members are prohibited from applying licensing and qualification requirements and technical standards that:

nullify or impair . . . specific commitments [of that member] in a manner that (i) fails to comply with the following criteria and (ii) could not reasonably have been expected of that Member at the time the specific commitments in those sectors were made:
(a) based on objective and transparent criteria, such as competence and the ability to supply the service;
(b) not more burdensome than necessary to ensure the quality of the service;
(c) in the case of licensing procedures, not in themselves a restriction on the supply of the service.

As a consequence of Article VI.5, therefore, a Chinese investor providing services through a commercial presence in the US is entitled to protection against qualification requirements, technical standards and licensing procedures that constitute improper barriers to trade in the affected service.

I also refer readers to Article VI of the GATS for additional commitments relating to domestic regulation affecting trade in services.

General commitment relating to monopolies and exclusive services suppliers

> The GATS requires the US to ensure that monopoly services suppliers, which may include owners of crucial "interconnection" assets like certain electricity transmission lines, telecommunications switching nodes and petroleum pipelines, do not abuse their dominant economic position.

GATS Article VIII contains a number of "general" commitments that introduce competition (antitrust) law principles into a member's obligations with respect to monopoly services suppliers and exclusive services suppliers. These commitments are particularly important in many "public service" sectors in the US, such as the provision of electricity, gas and oil distribution, and telecommunication services. In such sectors, a single or limited number of companies may entirely control a crucial "interconnection" asset, such as the connections into transmission lines in US electricity networks or critical telecommunications switching nodes. Those monopoly or exclusive interconnection providers may use their control over that crucial asset to deny or limit access to interconnections, thereby abusing their dominant economic position in an anticompetitive manner. In a manner similar to (but more limited than) US domestic antitrust law and public services regulatory measures, GATS Article VIII establishes the following set of competition principles for such circumstances:

> Article VIII Monopolies and Exclusive Service Suppliers
> 1. Each Member shall ensure that any monopoly supplier of a service in its territory does not, in the supply of the monopoly service in the relevant market, act in a manner inconsistent with that Member's obligations under Article II and specific commitments.
> 2. Where a Member's monopoly supplier competes, either directly or through an affiliated company, in the supply of a service outside the scope of its monopoly rights and which is subject to that Member's specific commitments, the Member shall ensure that such a supplier does not abuse its monopoly position to act in its territory in a manner inconsistent with such commitments . . .
> 5. The provisions of this Article shall also apply to cases of exclusive service suppliers, where a Member, formally or in effect, (a) authorizes or establishes a small number of service suppliers and (b) substantially prevents competition among those suppliers in its territory.

Accompanying the GATS are an Annex on Telecommunications and a Basic Agreement on Telecommunications, to which both the US and China are parties. The Basic Agreement, the Annex and a related Reference Paper build upon the foregoing domestic regulation and competition commitments found in Articles VI and VIII of the GATS, and establish even more detailed commitments with respect to the telecommunications regulatory framework and interconnection to telecommunications networks and services. If a Chinese investor intends to employ a commercial preserve in the US to provide telecommunications services, it will be valuable to review the Basic Agreement, the Annex and the Reference Paper.[22]

General exceptions to general commitments

The GATS, like other WTO agreements, contains a broad array of general exceptions *inter alia* to protect public order; to protect human, animal or plant life or health; to secure compliance with laws relating to deceptive or fraudulent practices; to protect privacy and confidentiality; and for safety. These exceptions, however, are not available if the measure is "applied in a manner which would constitute a means of arbitrary or unjustifiable discrimination between countries where like conditions prevail, or a disguised restriction on trade in services."

The GATS contains a number of broad exceptions to its protections, including exceptions to protect public order, to protect human, animal or plant life or health, to secure compliance with anti-fraud and similar laws, to protect privacy and confidentiality, and for safety. These exceptions do not apply, though, to arbitrary or unjustifiably discriminatory measures or to disguised trade restrictions.

The following list of general exceptions is found in the GATS Article XIV:

Article XIV General Exceptions
Subject to the requirement that such measures are not applied in a manner which would constitute a means of arbitrary or unjustifiable discrimination between countries where like conditions prevail, or a disguised restriction on trade in services, nothing in this Agreement shall be construed to prevent the adoption or enforcement by any Member of measures:
(a) necessary to protect public morals or to maintain public order;
(b) necessary to protect human, animal or plant life or health;
(c) necessary to secure compliance with laws or regulations which are not inconsistent with the provisions of this Agreement including those relating to:
    (i) the prevention of deceptive and fraudulent practices or to deal with the effects of a default on services contracts;
    (ii) the protection of the privacy of individuals in relation to the processing and dissemination of personal data and the protection of confidentiality of individual records and accounts;
    (iii) safety;
(d) inconsistent with Article XVII [National Treatment], provided that the difference in treatment is aimed at ensuring the equitable or effective imposition or collection of direct taxes in respect of services or service suppliers of other Members;
(e) inconsistent with Article II [MFN], provided that the difference in treatment is the result of an agreement on the avoidance of double taxation or provisions on the avoidance of double taxation in any other international agreement or arrangement by which the Member is bound.

Security exceptions

Like US IIAs, the GATS contains in Article XIV bis an exception for "essential security interests." That exception is phrased as a "self-judging" standard ("any action which *it considers* necessary"). The GATS "essential security interest" exception is more specific than the comparable provisions in US IIAs, and is largely focused on national security interests rather than economic crises.

> Like US IIAs, the GATS contains an "essential security interests" exception.

Article XIV bis Security Exceptions
1.   Nothing in this Agreement shall be construed:
    (a)   to require any Member to furnish any information, the disclosure of which it considers contrary to its essential security interests; or
    (b)   to prevent any Member from taking any action which it considers necessary for the protection of its essential security interests:
        (i)   relating to the supply of services as carried out directly or indirectly for the purpose of provisioning a military establishment;
        (ii)   relating to fissionable and fusionable materials or the materials from which they are derived;
        (iii) taken in time of war or other emergency in international relations; or
    (c)   to prevent any Member from taking any action in pursuance of its obligations under the United Nations Charter for the maintenance of international peace and security.
2.   The Council for Trade in Services shall be informed to the fullest extent possible of measures taken under paragraphs 1(b) and (c) and of their termination.

There is no public interpretation of the final substantive phrase in Article XIV bis, clause i(b)(iii): "or other emergency in international relations." Accordingly, while the thrust of GATS Article XIV bis is national security, an argument that the provision encompasses economic crises currently remains available. It is not clear whether a WTO disputes panel would defer to a member's assertion that an economic crisis was an "emergency in international relations" on the basis that Article XIV bis is self-judging or would instead itself consider whether such an assertion fell within the scope of the "essential security interests" exception.

Balance-of-payments restrictions on payments and transfers
In the event of serious balance-of-payments and external financial difficulties, or the threat thereof, the GATS permits members to impose restrictions on payments or transfers for trade in services, so long as such restrictions: (1) do not discriminate among members; (2) are consistent with the International Monetary Fund's Articles of Agreement; (3) avoid unnecessary damage to commercial, economic and financial interests of other members, (4) do not exceed those restrictions necessary to deal with the balance-of-payments crisis; and (5) are temporary and phased out as the crisis situation improves.

> The GATS permits the US, in a situation of serious balance of payments and external financial difficulties, to impose temporary restrictions on payments and transfers for trade in services consistent with IMF Articles of Agreement. Under US IIAs, however, the US has bound itself to not exercise this GATS authority with respect to funds transfers relating to investments.

The pertinent provisions are found in GATS Articles XI and XII:

Article XI Payments and Transfers
1. Except under the circumstances envisaged in Article XII, a Member shall not apply restrictions on international transfers and payments for current transactions relating to its specific commitments.
2. Nothing in this Agreement shall affect the rights and obligations of the members of the International Monetary Fund under the Articles of Agreement of the Fund, including the use of exchange actions which are in conformity with the Articles of Agreement, provided that a Member shall not impose restrictions on any capital transactions inconsistently with its specific commitments regarding such transactions, except under Article XII or at the request of the Fund.

Article XII Restrictions to Safeguard the Balance of Payments
1. In the event of serious balance-of-payments and external financial difficulties or threat thereof, a Member may adopt or maintain restrictions on trade in services on which it has undertaken specific commitments, including on payments or transfers for transactions related to such commitments. It is recognized that particular pressures on the balance of payments of a Member in the process of economic development or economic transition may necessitate the use of restrictions to ensure, inter alia, the maintenance of a level of financial reserves adequate for the implementation of its program of economic development or economic transition.
2. The restrictions referred to in paragraph 1:
   (a) shall not discriminate among Members;
   (b) shall be consistent with the Articles of Agreement of the International Monetary Fund;
   (c) shall avoid unnecessary damage to the commercial, economic and financial interests of any other Member;
   (d) shall not exceed those necessary to deal with the circumstances described in paragraph 1;
   (e) shall be temporary and be phased out progressively as the situation specified in paragraph 1 improves.
3. In determining the incidence of such restrictions, Members may give priority to the supply of services which are more essential to their economic or development programs. However, such restrictions shall not be adopted or maintained for the purpose of protecting a particular service sector.

6.2.2 Agreement on Trade-Related Investment Measures

In recognition of the fact that investment measures can in certain cases cause trade-restrictive and distorting effects, the WTO also sponsored the TRIMs Agreement. Both the US and China are party to that agreement. The TRIMs Agreement applies only to investment measures related to trade in goods, not measures related to trade in services. The TRIMs Agreement provides that no member may apply any TRIM that is inconsistent with that member's "national treatment" and "elimination of quantitative restrictions" commitments in the General Agreement on Tariffs and Trade 1994 (GATT 1994).

Under the WTO TRIMs Agreement, the US has bound itself to not impose certain investment-related performance measures on trade in goods. The similar commitment in US IIAs covering "investments" is broader in coverage, both as to prohibited measures and as to services.

An annex to the TRIMs Agreement contains an illustrative list of TRIMs that are inconsistent with those commitments, as follows:

ANNEX: Illustrative List
1. TRIMs that are inconsistent with the obligation of national treatment provided for in paragraph 4 of Article III of GATT 1994 include those which are mandatory or enforceable under domestic law or under administrative rulings, or compliance with which is necessary to obtain an advantage, and which require:
    (a) the purchase or use by an enterprise of products of domestic origin or from any domestic source, whether specified in terms of particular products, in terms of volume or value of products, or in terms of a proportion of volume or value of its local production; or
    (b) that an enterprise's purchases or use of imported products be limited to an amount related to the volume or value of local products that it exports.

As the illustrative list makes clear, TRIMs covered by the agreement include conditioning investment on domestic content requirements and mandatory export requirements tied to import utilizations, as well as, in the case of quantitative restrictions, limiting access to foreign exchange to control imports. The US has taken no specific exceptions to its obligations under the TRIMs Agreement. However, Article 3 of the TRIMs Agreement provides that all exceptions under GATT 1994 apply to the TRIMS Agreement as well. Accordingly, a Chinese investor concerned about a possible US TRIM will need to review the extensive array of exceptions found in GATT 1994, including general exceptions, "essential security interest" exceptions and balance-of-payment exceptions similar to those found in the GATS and described above. If the protection of a US IIA is also available, that protection will be broader. IIAs cover a far more extensive range of investment-related performance measures. In addition, US IIAs cover services as well as goods. (See Article 8 of the 2004 US Model BIT.)

The obligations of a WTO member under the TRIMs Agreement may be enforced in state–state arbitration under the WTO Dispute Settlement Understanding, in the same manner as previously discussed with respect to the GATS. Again, withdrawal of trade benefits is the ordinary remedy, not damages to compensate the injured investor.

6.3   ENFORCEMENT OF FCN TREATIES IN THE US COURTS

Customary international law or treaty-based rights are not generally enforceable in US courts, unless there is a particular US statute granting jurisdiction to the courts or the treaty in question is considered by the US courts to be "self-executing."

> Older US "friendship, commerce and navigation" (FCN) treaties still exist. If a Chinese investor employs an intermediate business entity located in a US (FCN) treaty partner, the provisions of that FCN treaty may be relevant. An August 2008 US Court of Appeal decision rejected the possibility that an investor could enforce its rights under an FCN treaty in US courts.

US IIAs provide for special enforcement forums, investor–state arbitration and state–state arbitration. Similarly, the GATS and TRIMs Agreement provide for a special enforcement forum and disputes panels under the WTO Dispute Settlement Understanding. Therefore, it is highly unlikely that any of those agreements would be considered "self-executing." However, the older versions of US investment and commerce treaties, the so-called Friendship, Commerce and Navigation (FCN) treaties, usually make no mention of enforcement forums. The issue of whether rights of a foreign investor against the US under a still-extant FCN may be judicially enforced is therefore less clear. The US and China are not parties to an FCN treaty. Like the analysis above in Section 6.1 with respect to BITs, though, if a Chinese investor utilizes an intermediate company located in a state that is an FCN treaty partner with the US, then the provisions of that FCN treaty may become relevant.

In a recent US District Court decision involving Iran and McKesson Corp. stemming from the consequences of the 1978 Iranian Revolution, that court held the 1955 Treaty of Amity between the US and Iran (a still-existing older FCN) was in fact "self-executing." Accordingly, McKesson, an injured US investor, could bring an expropriation claim against Iran in the US courts. In August 2008, the US Court of Appeals for the District of Columbia Circuit overturned the District Court decision, rejecting the argument that McKesson had a private right of action under the FCN treaty. Even more so than US BITs, earlier US FCN treaties vary considerably from country to country. Consequently, if a Chinese investor sources a US investment through a third country that is a party to a still-effective FCN treaty with the US, that investor needs to review the terms of that FCN treaty to determine what investment protections, if any, are available under that treaty.

NOTES

*   This chapter was prepared in the context of the Deloitte–Vale Columbia Center on Sustainable International Investment project on "Is the US ready for FDI from China?" Copyright © 2009 by Columbia University and Deloitte Development LLC. All rights reserved.
1.   See "United States Launches Negotiations of an Investment Treaty With China," Fact Sheet, Bureau of Economic, Energy and Business Affairs, Washington, DC, June 20, 2008, http://www.state.gov/e/eeb/rls/fs/2008/106132.htm.
2.   Currently, the "new generation" China BITs are with Barbados, Belgium–Luxembourg, Benin, Bosnia and Herzegovina, Botswana, Brunei Darussalam, Congo, Costa Rica, Cyprus, Czech Republic, Djibouti, Finland, Germany, Guyana, Iran, Ivory Coast, Jordan, Kenya, Latvia, Myanmar, the Netherlands, Nigeria, the Democratic People's Republic of Korea, Sierra Leone, Spain, Swaziland, protocol to the BIT with Sweden, Trinidad and Tobago, Tunisia and Vanuatu. The investment chapter of the China–Pakistan Free Trade Agreement is similar to a new generation BIT.
3.   The full text of the 2004 US Model BIT is available at www.ustr.gov and www.state.gov.
4.   S.D. Myers Inc. v. Government of Canada (Award on Liability), 8 ICSID Rep. 3 (NAFTA/UNCITRAL 2000), pp. 52–55.
5.   Methanex Corp. v. U.S. (NAFTA/UNCITRAL 2005) at IV, Chapter B, Para. 19.
6.   Pope & Talbot Inc. v. Government of Canada (Award), 7 ICSID Rep. 43 (NAFTA/UNCITRAL 2002), at 107–125.
7.   *Id.*, at 119–120.
8.   [Minimum Standard of Treatment] shall be interpreted in accordance with Annex A [customary international law].
9.   UNCTAD, *Bilateral Investment Treaties 1995–2006: Trends in Investment Rulemaking* (Geneva: UNCTAD, 2007), p. 8.
10.   Counter-memorial of Respondent United States of America, in Glamis Gold, Inc. v. U.S., at 227–228 (footnotes omitted).

11. Article 6 [Expropriation] shall be interpreted in accordance with Annexes A [customary international law] and B [Expropriation].
12. See M. Kantor, "Fair and Equitable Treatment: Echoes of FDR's Court Packing Plan in the International Law Approach towards Regulatory Expropriation", 5 *The Law and Practice of International Courts and Tribunals* 231 (2006).
13. Phillips Petroleum Company Iran v. Iran, Award No. 425-39-2, June 29, 1989, Chamber Two, Iran – United States Claims Tribunal, at Paragraph 110.
14. See, for example, Annexes 10-E and 10-F of the US–Peru Trade Promotion Agreement, available at www. ustr.gov.
15. See www.state.gov/s/l/c3741.htm.
16. It is understood that the term "prudential reasons" includes the maintenance of the safety, soundness, integrity, or financial responsibility of individual financial institutions.
17. For greater certainty, measures of general application taken in pursuit of monetary and related credit policies or exchange rate policies do not include measures that expressly nullify or amend contractual provisions that specify the currency of denomination or the rate of exchange of currencies.
18. For purposes of this Article, "competent financial authorities" means, for the United States, the Department of the Treasury for banking and other financial services, and the Office of the United States Trade Representative, in coordination with the Department of Commerce and other agencies, for insurance; and for [Country], [ ].
19. Award, ICSID Case No. ARB/01/3 (May 22, 2007), Paragraph 335.
20. Award, ICSID Case No. ARB/02/1 (July 25, 2007).
21. Award, ICSID Case No. ARB/01/8 (May 12, 2005), and decision of the Ad Hoc Committee on the Application for Annulment of the Argentine Republic, ICSID Case No. ARB/01/8 Annulment Proceeding) (September 25, 2007).
22. See Mark Kantor, "Foreign direct investment in Chinese Telecoms: Changes in the Regulatory Scheme," 13 *Cambridge Review of International Affairs*, 136 (2000).

APPENDIX 6.1

Annex A   Items Excluded by the US from the National Treatment Protection in the US–Singapore FTA*

Sector: Atomic Energy
Measures: *Atomic Energy Act of 1954*, 42 USC. §§ 2011 *et seq.*
Description: Investment
A license issued by the United States Nuclear Regulatory Commission is required for any person in the United States to transfer or receive in interstate commerce, manufacture, produce, transfer, use, import, or export any nuclear "utilization or production facilities" for commercial or industrial purposes. Such a license may not be issued to any entity known or believed to be owned, controlled, or dominated by an alien, a foreign corporation, or a foreign government (42 USC. § 2133(d)). A license issued by the United States Nuclear Regulatory Commission is also required for nuclear "utilization and production facilities," for use in medical therapy, or for research and development activities. The issuance of such a license to any entity known or believed to be owned, controlled, or dominated by an alien, a foreign corporation, or a foreign government is also prohibited (42 USC. § 2134(d)).

Sector: Business Services
Measures: *Export Trading Company Act of 1982*, 15 USC. §§ 4011–4021
15 C.F.R. Part 325
Description: Cross-Border Services
Title III of the *Export Trading Company Act of 1982* authorizes the Secretary of Commerce to issue "certificates of review" with respect to export conduct. The Act provides for the issuance of a certificate of review where the Secretary determines, and the Attorney General concurs, that the export conduct specified in an application will not have the anticompetitive effects proscribed by the Act. A certificate of review limits the liability under federal and state antitrust laws in engaging in the export conduct certified. Only a "person" as defined by the Act can apply for a certificate of review. "Person" means "an individual who is a resident of the United States; a partnership that is created under and exists pursuant to the laws of any State or of the United States; a State or local government entity; a corporation, whether organized as a profit or nonprofit corporation, that is created under and exists pursuant to the laws of any State or of the United States; or any association or combination, by contract or other arrangement, between such persons." A foreign national or enterprise may receive the protection provided by a certificate of review by becoming a "member" of a qualified applicant. The regulations define "member" to mean "an entity (US or foreign) that is seeking protection under the certificate with the applicant. A member may be a partner in a partnership or a joint venture; a shareholder of a corporation; or a participant in an association, cooperative, or other form of profit or nonprofit organization or relationship, by contract or other arrangement."

Sector: Business Services
Measures: *Export Administration Act of 1979, as amended*, 50 USC. App. §§ 2401–2420
International Emergency Economic Powers Act, 50 USC. §§ 1701–1706
Export Administration Regulations, 15 C.F.R. Parts 730-774
Description: Cross-Border Services
With some limited exceptions, exports and re-exports of commodities, software, and technology subject to the Export Administration Regulations require a license from the Bureau of Industry and Security, US Department of Commerce (BIS). Certain activities of US persons, wherever located, also require a license from BIS. An application for a license must be made by a person in the United States. In addition, release of controlled technology to a foreign national in the United States is deemed to be an export to the home country of the foreign national and requires the same written authorization from BIS as an export from the territory of the United States.

Sector: Mining
Measures: *Mineral Lands Leasing Act of 1920*, 30 USC. Chapter 3A, 10 USC. § 7435
Description: Investment
Under the Mineral Lands Leasing Act of 1920, aliens and foreign corporations may not acquire rights-of-way for oil or gas pipelines, or pipelines carrying products refined from oil and gas, across on-shore federal lands or acquire leases or interests in certain minerals on on-shore federal lands, such as coal or oil. Non-US citizens may own a 100 percent interest in a domestic corporation that acquires a right-of-way for oil or gas pipelines across on-shore federal lands, or that acquires a lease to develop mineral resources on on-shore federal lands, unless the foreign investor's home country denies similar or like privileges for the mineral or access in question to US citizens or corporations, as compared with the privileges it accords to its own citizens or corporations or to the citizens or corporations of other countries (30 USC. §§ 181, 185(a)). Nationalization is not considered to be denial of similar or like privileges. Foreign citizens, or corporations controlled by them, are restricted from obtaining access to federal leases on Naval Petroleum Reserves if the laws, customs, or regulations of their country deny the privilege of leasing public lands to citizens or corporations of the United States (10 USC. § 7435).

Sector: All Sectors
Measures: 22 USC. §§ 2194 and 2198(c)
Description: Investment
The Overseas Private Investment Corporation insurance and loan guarantees are not available to certain aliens, foreign enterprises, or foreign-controlled domestic enterprises.

Sector: Air Transportation
Measures: 49 USC. Subtitle VII, *Aviation Programs*
14 C.F.R. Part 297 (foreign freight forwarders); 14 C.F.R. Part 380, Subpart E (registration of foreign (passenger) charter operators)
Description: Investment
Only air carriers that are "citizens of the United States" may operate aircraft in domestic air service (sabotage) and may provide international scheduled and non-scheduled air service as US air carriers. US citizens also have blanket authority to engage in indirect air transportation activities (air freight forwarding and passenger charter activities other than as actual operators of the aircraft). In order to conduct such activities, non-US citizens must obtain authority from the Department of Transportation. Applications for such authority may be rejected for reasons relating to the failure of effective reciprocity, or if the Department of Transportation finds that it is in the public interest to do so. Under 49 USC. § 40102(a)(15), a citizen of the United States means an individual who is a US citizen; a partnership in which each member is a US citizen; or a US corporation of which the president and at least two-thirds of the board of directors and other managing officers are US citizens, which is under the actual control of US citizens, and in which at least seventy-five percent of the voting interest in the corporation is owned or controlled by US citizens.

Sector: Air Transportation
Measures: 49 USC. Subtitle VII, *Aviation Programs*
49 USC. § 41703
14 C.F.R. Part 375
Description: Cross-Border Services
1. Authorization from the Department of Transportation is required for the provision of specialty air services in the territory of the United States.
   Investment
2. "Foreign civil aircraft" require authority from the Department of Transportation to conduct specialty air services in the territory of the United States. In determining whether to grant a particular application, the Department will consider, among other factors, the extent to which the country of the applicant's nationality accords US civil aircraft operators

effective reciprocity. "Foreign civil aircraft" are aircraft of foreign registry or aircraft of US registry that are owned, controlled, or operated by persons who are not citizens or permanent residents of the United States (14 C.F.R. § 375.1). Under 49 USC. § 40102(a)(15), a citizen of the United States means an individual who is a US citizen; a partnership in which each member is a US citizen; or a US corporation of which the president and at least two-thirds of the board of directors and other managing officers are US citizens, which is under the actual control of US citizens, and in which at least seventy-five percent of the voting interest in the corporation is owned or controlled by US citizens.

Sector: Transportation Services – Customs Brokers
Measures: 19 USC. § 1641(b)
Description: Cross-Border Services and Investment
A customs broker's license is required to conduct customs business on behalf of another person. Only US citizens may obtain such a license. A corporation, association, or partnership established under the law of any state may receive a customs broker's license if at least one officer of the corporation or association, or one member of the partnership, holds a valid customs broker's license.

Sector: All Sectors
Measures: *Securities Act of 1933*, 15 USC. §§ 77C(b), 77f, 77g, 77h, 77j, and 77s(a)
17 C.F.R. §§ 230.251 and 230.405
Securities Exchange Act of 1934, 15 USC. §§ 78l, 78m, 78o(d), and 78w(a)
17 C.F.R. § 240.12b-2
Description: Investment
Foreign firms, except for certain Canadian issuers, may not use the small business registration forms under the Securities Act of 1933 to register public offerings of securities or the small business registration forms under the Securities Exchange Act of 1934 to register a class of securities or file annual reports.

Sector: Communications – Radio communications
Measures: 47 USC. § 310
Foreign Participation Order 12 FCC Rcd 23891 (1997)
Description: Investment
The United States reserves the right to restrict ownership of radio licenses in accordance with the above statutory and regulatory provisions. Radio communications consists of all communications by radio, including broadcasting.

Sector: Professional Services – Patent Attorneys, Patent Agents, and Other Practice before the Patent and Trademark Office
Measures: 35 USC. Chapter 3 (practice before the US Patent and Trademark Office)
37 C.F.R. Part 10 (representation of others before the US Patent and Trademark Office)
Description: Cross-Border Services
As a condition to be registered to practice for others before the US Patent and Trademark Office (USPTO):
(a) a patent attorney must be a US citizen or an alien lawfully residing in the United States (37 C.F.R. § 10.6(a));
(b) a patent agent must be a US citizen, an alien lawfully residing in the United States, or a non-resident who is registered to practice in a country that permits patent agents registered to practice before the USPTO to practice in that country; the latter is permitted to practice for the limited purpose of presenting and prosecuting patent applications of applicants located in the country in which he or she resides (37 C.F.R. § 10.6(c)); and
(c) a practitioner in trademark and non-patent cases must be an attorney licensed in the United States, a "grandfathered" agent, an attorney licensed to practice in a country that

accords equivalent treatment to attorneys licensed in the United States, or an agent registered to practice in such a country; the latter two are permitted to practice for the limited purpose of representing parties located in the country in which he or she resides (37 C.F.R. § 10.14(a)-(c)).

Sector: All Sectors
Level of Government: Regional
Measures: All existing non-conforming measures of all states of the United States, the District of Columbia, and Puerto Rico
Description: Cross-Border Services and Investment

Note:

*   This text is quoted from Annex A to Investment Chapter of US–Singapore Free Trade Agreement, available at www.ustr.gov.

APPENDIX 6.2

Annex B   Items Excluded by the US from MFN Protection in the US–Singapore FTA*

Sector: Mining
Measures: *Mineral Lands Leasing Act of 1920*, 30 USC. Chapter 3A, 10 USC. § 7435
Description: Investment
Under the Mineral Lands Leasing Act of 1920, aliens and foreign corporations may not acquire rights-of-way for oil or gas pipelines, or pipelines carrying products refined from oil and gas, across on-shore federal lands or acquire leases or interests in certain minerals on on-shore federal lands, such as coal or oil. Non-US citizens may own a 100 percent interest in a domestic corporation that acquires a right-of-way for oil or gas pipelines across on-shore federal lands, or that acquires a lease to develop mineral resources on on-shore federal lands, unless the foreign investor's home country denies similar or like privileges for the mineral or access in question to US citizens or corporations, as compared with the privileges it accords to its own citizens or corporations or to the citizens or corporations of other countries (30 USC. §§ 181, 185(a)). Nationalization is not considered to be denial of similar or like privileges. Foreign citizens, or corporations controlled by them, are restricted from obtaining access to federal leases on Naval Petroleum Reserves if the laws, customs, or regulations of their country deny the privilege of leasing public lands to citizens or corporations of the United States (10 USC. § 7435).

Sector: All Sectors
Measures: 22 USC. §§ 2194 and 2198(c)
Description: Investment
The Overseas Private Investment Corporation insurance and loan guarantees are not available to certain aliens, foreign enterprises, or foreign-controlled domestic enterprises.

Sector: Air Transportation
Measures: 49 USC. Subtitle VII, *Aviation Programs*
14 C.F.R. Part 297 (foreign freight forwarders); 14 C.F.R. Part 380, Subpart E (registration of foreign (passenger) charter operators)
Description: Investment
Only air carriers that are "citizens of the United States" may operate aircraft in domestic air service (sabotage) and may provide international scheduled and non-scheduled air service as US air carriers. US citizens also have blanket authority to engage in indirect air transportation activities (air freight forwarding and passenger charter activities other than as actual operators of the aircraft). In order to conduct such activities, non-US citizens must obtain authority from the Department of Transportation. Applications for such authority may be rejected for reasons relating to the failure of effective reciprocity, or if the Department of Transportation finds that it is in the public interest to do so. Under 49 USC. § 40102(a)(15), a citizen of the United States means an individual who is a US citizen; a partnership in which each member is a US citizen; or a US corporation of which the president and at least two-thirds of the board of directors and other managing officers are US citizens, which is under the actual control of US citizens, and in which at least seventy-five percent of the voting interest in the corporation is owned or controlled by US citizens.

Sector: Air Transportation
Measures: 49 USC. Subtitle VII, *Aviation Programs*
49 USC. § 41703
14 C.F.R. Part 375
Description: Cross-Border Services
1. Authorization from the Department of Transportation is required for the provision of specialty air services in the territory of the United States.
   Investment

2. "Foreign civil aircraft" require authority from the Department of Transportation to conduct specialty air services in the territory of the United States. In determining whether to grant a particular application, the Department will consider, among other factors, the extent to which the country of the applicant's nationality accords US civil aircraft operators effective reciprocity. "Foreign civil aircraft" are aircraft of foreign registry or aircraft of US registry that are owned, controlled, or operated by persons who are not citizens or permanent residents of the United States (14 C.F.R. § 375.1). Under 49 USC. § 40102(a)(15), a citizen of the United States means an individual who is a US citizen; a partnership in which each member is a US citizen; or a US corporation of which the president and at least two-thirds of the board of directors and other managing officers are US citizens, which is under the actual control of US citizens, and in which at least seventy-five percent of the voting interest in the corporation is owned or controlled by US citizens.

Sector: All Sectors
Measures: *Securities Act of 1933*, 15 USC. §§ 77C(b), 77f, 77g, 77h, 77j, and 77s(a)
17 C.F.R. §§ 230.251 and 230.405
Securities Exchange Act of 1934, 15 USC. §§ 78l, 78m, 78o(d), and 78w(a)
17 C.F.R. § 240.12b-2
Description: Investment
Foreign firms, except for certain Canadian issuers, may not use the small business registration forms under the Securities Act of 1933 to register public offerings of securities or the small business registration forms under the Securities Exchange Act of 1934 to register a class of securities or file annual reports.

Sector: Professional Services – Patent Attorneys, Patent Agents, and Other Practice before the Patent and Trademark Office
Measures: 35 USC. Chapter 3 (practice before the US Patent and Trademark Office)
37 C.F.R. Part 10 (representation of others before the US Patent and Trademark Office)
Description: Cross-Border Services
As a condition to be registered to practice for others before the US Patent and Trademark Office (USPTO):
(a) a patent attorney must be a US citizen or an alien lawfully residing in the United States (37 C.F.R. § 10.6(a));
(b) a patent agent must be a US citizen, an alien lawfully residing in the United States, or a non-resident who is registered to practice in a country that permits patent agents registered to practice before the USPTO to practice in that country; the latter is permitted to practice for the limited purpose of presenting and prosecuting patent applications of applicants located in the country in which he or she resides (37 C.F.R. § 10.6(c)); and
(c) a practitioner in trademark and non-patent cases must be an attorney licensed in the United States, a "grandfathered" agent, an attorney licensed to practice in a country that accords equivalent treatment to attorneys licensed in the United States, or an agent registered to practice in such a country; the latter two are permitted to practice for the limited purpose of representing parties located in the country in which he or she resides (37 C.F.R. § 10.14(a)-(c)).

Sector: All Sectors
Level of Government: Regional
Measures: All existing non-conforming measures of all states of the United States, the District of Columbia, and Puerto Rico
Description: Cross-Border Services and Investment

Note:

*   This text is quoted from Annex B to Investment Chapter of US–Singapore Free Trade Agreement, available at www.ustr.gov.

APPPENDIX 6.3   AVAILABLE RESOURCES

The topic of international investment law protections (and limits) with respect to investments in the US by Chinese entities does not fit the model for a standard academic literature review. Investment law protections have generated voluminous writings over the past century. Moreover, the quantity of writings on substantive issues such as "fair and equitable treatment," "regulatory expropriation" and "most-favored-nation treatment" has simply exploded along with the dramatic growth of investment treaty arbitration since 2000. Even a summary review of that literature would take hundreds of pages.

With respect to limits on international investment laws protections (and, in particular, the issues of an investment treaty exclusion for "essential security" reasons and the related customary international law doctrine of "state of necessity"), the opposite is true. Almost nothing detailed has been written on those issues. Instead, one finds stray sentences or paragraphs here and there, buried inside commentary on the larger issue of investment law protections. That situation will undoubtedly change quickly for two reasons. First, the Annulment Committee in the *CMS* v. *Argentina* case released its decision in 2008 on challenges by Argentina to the award of the original ICSID tribunal in that dispute. In that decision, the Annulment Committee criticized the analysis of "essential security interests" and "state of necessity" issues in the decision of the original tribunal in *CMS* v. *Argentina*, but declined to overturn the original award because of the limited scope of annulment review under the ICSID Convention. That result leaves an open split in the Argentine awards over the proper approach to these limits to international investment law protections.

Second, the "self-judging" nature of the "essential security interests" exclusion was part of the May 2008 "bipartisan trade compromise" between Democratic Congressional leaders and the Republican administration, intended to enable several free trade agreements to move forward in the US Congress (the Peru, Panama, Colombia and Republic of Korea FTAs). Accordingly, the issue of the "essential security interests" exclusion is also receiving political attention in the US.

With these factors in mind, the following resources may be helpful.

General Information on International Investment Law Protections

Primary sources
Good online compendiums of international investment arbitration awards may be found at the following locations:

Investment Claims, at www.investmentclaims.com
NAFTA Claims, at www.naftaclaims.com
Investment Treaty Arbitration, at http://ita.law.uvic.ca/
The Peace Palace Library, bibliography for "New Aspects of International Investment Law," at http://www.ppl.nl/bibliographies/all/?bibliography=investment
International Centre for Settlement of Investment Disputes (ICSID), pending and concluded cases, available at http://www.worldbank.org/icsid/cases/cases.htm
Westlaw International Arbitration Awards database (by subscription only)

These sources are currently not easily searchable. The publishers of investmentclaims. com, in cooperation with Oxford University Press, are working on expanding the searchable nature of the investmentclaims.com website. The United Nations Conference on Trade and Development (UNCTAD) is also working on a publicly available searchable database of investment treaty awards.

Secondary sources
The Peace Palace Library contains a "Bibliography for New Aspects of International Investment Law" (available at http://www.ppl.nl/bibliographies/all/?bibliography= investment). According to the International Law Institute, this is perhaps the most comprehensive online search engine for searching for different materials on investor–state arbitration. The bibliography is hosted by The Hague Academy of International Law.

A recent "Select Bibliography" of books, official reports and articles on substantive international investment law is found at pp. 447–453 of C. McLachlan, L. Shore and M. Weiniger, *International Investment Arbitration: Substantive Principles* (Oxford: Oxford University Press 2007).

McLaughlan, Shore and Weiniger *supra* is the most recent treatise on substantive international investment law. The book covers, *inter alia*, detailed discussions of the development in international arbitration of principles of "fair and equitable treatment," "full protection and security," "national treatment," "most–favored-nation treatment," "expropriation," and "compensation."

International Law Institute (ILI), Alternative Dispute Resolution Center, "Research Guide for International Commercial and Investment Arbitration," available at http:// www.ili.org/adrc_research_guide.htm.

"Responsibilities of States for Internationally Wrongful Acts: Text of the Draft Articles with Commentaries thereto" (Crawford, Special Rapporteur), in *Report of the International Law Commission of its Fifty-Third Session (23 April–1 June and 2 July–10 August 2001), Official Records of the General Assembly Fifty-sixth Session*, Supplement No. 10, UN Doc A/56/10, 59-365.

British Institute of International and Comparative Law (BIICL), Papers from BIICL Investment Treaty Forum, published as *Investment Treaty Law* (2006) and *Investment Treaty Law: Current Issues* Vol. 2 (2007).

Karl, Joachim, Joerg Weber and James Zhan (forthcoming). "International investment rulemaking at the beginning of the 21st century: stocktaking and options for the way forward", in *The Evolving International Investment Regime: Expectations, Realities, Options* (Alvarez, Sauvant and Ahmed (eds), Oxford University Press, 2010).

OECD (2005). *International Investment Law: A Changing Landscape* (Paris: OECD Publishing).

Sauvant, Karl P. and Jorg Weber, eds (2004). *International Investment Agreements: Key Issues* (New York and Geneva: United Nations).

UNCTAD (2006). *Investor–state Disputes Arising from Investment Treaties: A Review.* (New York and Geneva: United Nations).

UNCTAD (2007). *Bilateral Investment Treaties 1995–2006: Trends in Investment Rulemaking.* (New York and Geneva: United Nations).

Information on Essential Security, State of Necessity and MFN

"Essential security" and "state of necessity"

Relevant investment treaty arbitration awards include (as of September 2008), the ICSID tribunal decisions in *CMS* v. *Argentina, Enron* v. *Argentina, LG&E* v. *Argentina, Sempras* v. *Argentina* and *Continental Casualty Co.* v. *Argentina*, the *Annulment Committee* decision in *CMS* v. *Argentina* and *BG Group PLC* v. *Argentina*. All of these decisions can be found at www.investmentclaims.com.

Burke-White and von Staden, "Investment Protection in Extraordinary Times: The Interpretation and Application of Non-Precluded Measures Provisions in Bilateral Investment Treaties" (April 25, 2007), University of Pennsylvania Law School Paper 152. Prof. Burke-White acted as an expert on behalf of the Republic of Argentina in a number of the investment treaty claims brought against Argentina before ICSID tribunals. In those cases, and in this paper, he (and co-author von Staden) argue that the treaty-based "essential security" and customary international law-based "state of necessity" exclusions, in the Argentine context: (1) are "self-judging;" (2) cover economic crises; and (3) are separate tests (with the threshold for proving the "essential security" exclusion being lower than the threshold for proving the "state of necessity" defense). The position espoused by Burke-White that the tests are "self-judging" was rejected in the *CMS, CMS Annulment Committee, Enron, LG&E* and *Sempras* tribunal decisions. The position espoused by Burke-White that the "essential security" and "state of necessity" tests are based on different standards was rejected by the *CMS, Enron* and *Sempras* tribunals. In the *LG&E* case and in the *CMS Annulment Committee* decision, Burke-White's positions were partially accepted. The *CMS Annulment Committee* agreed that the "essential security" test and the "state of necessity" test may be based on different standards, but held that the error in the ICSID tribunal's decision on this point was not a basis for annulling the *CMS* award. The *CMS Annulment Committee* also upheld the ruling of the *CMS* tribunal that, on the facts as found by the ICSID tribunal, Argentina had failed to satisfy the requirements for a "state of necessity" defense under customary international law. In *LG&E*, the ICSID tribunal accepted that, on essentially the same factual circumstances as existed in *CMS, Enron* and *Sempras*, a 17-month "state of necessity" existed and that the investor was not entitled to compensation for injuries suffered during that period, but was entitled to compensation for injuries suffered after that period. Argentina has sought Annulment Committee review of the tribunal decisions in *Enron, LG&E* and *Sempras*. Numerous other ICSID cases against Argentina will face the same issues, and further decisions are anticipated in the coming months and year.

US Office of the Special Trade Representative, Trade Facts, *Bipartisan Agreement On Trade Policy: Investment May 2007*, Port Security, available at http://www.ustr.gov/assets/Document_Library/Fact_Sheets/2007/asset_upload_file417_11285.pdf.

US Office of the Special Trade Representative, Trade Facts, *Bipartisan Trade Deal: Full Summary*, available at http://www.ustr.gov/assets/Document_Library/Fact_Sheets/2007/asset_upload_file127_11319.pdf.

"Most-favored-nation treatment"
Relevant investment treaty arbitration awards include (as of September 2008) *Maffezini* v. *Spain, Siemens* v. *Argentina, Gas Natural* v. *Argentina, Suez (Aguas de Barcelona)* v. *Argentina, Plama* v. *Bulgaria, Salini* v. *Jordan, Telenor* v. *Hungary, MTD* v. *Chile, MTD* v. *Chile Annulment Committee* and *BG Group PLC* v. *Argentina.*

Anglo Iranian Oil Co Case (Jurisdiction) (United Kingdom v. Iran), [1952] ICJ Rep 93.

Case Concerning the Rights of Nationals of the United States in Morocco (France v. United States of America) [1952] ICJ Rep 176.

Ambatielos Case (*Greece v. United Kingdom*), *International Court of Justice*, *[1953] ICJ Rep 10, Reports of International Arbitral Awards, Vol. XII, United Nations* (1956), pp. 82, 107.

Draft articles on most-favoured-nation clauses (International Law Commission (ILC) Draft), in *Yearbook of the International Law Commission* (1978), Vol. II, Part Two.

International Law Commission, 59th session, Geneva, 7 May–8 June and 9 July–10 August 2007, *Most-Favoured-Nation Clause, Report of the Working Group*, A/CN.4/L. 719, 20 July 2007.

Organisation for Economic Co-Operation and Development (OECD), *Most-Favoured-Nation Treatment in International Investment Law* (2004), available at http://www.oecd.org/dataoecd/21/37/33773085.pdf.

United Nations Conference on Trade and Development (UNCTAD), *Preserving Flexibility in IIAs: The Use of Reservations* (2006), available at http://www.unctad.org/Templates/webflyer.asp?docid=7145&intItemID=2340&lang=1.

McLaughlan, Shore and Weiniger *supra* at Paras 7.161–7.169, pp. 254–257.

7. Is the US ready for FDI from China? Lessons from Japan's experience in the 1980s

Curtis J. Milhaupt*

INTRODUCTION

Twenty years before China became a rising star in the global economy and a major potential source of outward foreign direct investment (FDI), another East Asian country – Japan – occupied this role. Japan's FDI flow into the United States skyrocketed from less than $1 billion annually in the 1980s to a peak of about $18 billion in 1990 alone. As a percentage of total stock, Japanese FDI in the US went from 6.2 percent in 1980 to 20.7 percent in 1990 (Kang 1997, p. 319, Table 5). This boom in Japanese FDI took place in an unsettled environment. Reactions in the United States were colored by trade friction, exchange rate controversy, cultural misperceptions, politically charged debates about the unique (and for many US observers, "unfair") underpinnings of Japanese capitalism, and the "threat" posed to US interests by Japan's economic ascendance. Any influx of Chinese FDI into the United States will take place against a backdrop that bears a striking resemblance to the situation two decades earlier.

This chapter examines the Japanese experience of US–directed FDI, principally in the 1980s, seeking to draw lessons for China. As detailed below, the chapter focuses principally on the 1980s because this decade marked the peak of Japanese FDI in the US and concomitant political and media debate about Japanese investment. Controversy over Japanese FDI died down significantly beginning in the early 1990s, as Japan's own economic problems caused a contraction in the overseas operations of Japanese firms.[1] Thus, some of the most salient lessons for Chinese executives are to be found in the hothouse environment of the 1980s. The chapter asks whether the parallels are sufficiently close that the Japanese experience can serve as a roadmap for understanding the patterns and likely pitfalls in Chinese FDI in the future. I then consider what lessons Chinese actors at the firm and governmental levels might learn from Japan's experience.

To state the conclusions very briefly at the outset, despite some important differences principally stemming from China's political orientation and geostrategic position vis-à-vis the United States, the background parallels between the two cases are striking. Moreover, an examination of Japan's experience in light of FDI theory indicates that the experience was not unique, despite major differences in US–Japanese organizational structures, regulatory policies and culture. Japanese firms did not rewrite the rules of FDI; to the contrary, they closely followed the trajectory and patterns suggested by standard FDI theories. This suggests a high degree of "fit" in the Japan analogy. If this is accurate, Chinese FDI is likely to be motivated by factors similar to, and produce a range of frictions closely resembling, those experienced by Japanese firms two decades before.

Today, Japan remains a major source of US–directed FDI, and Japanese affiliates are a significant source of employment for US workers. As detailed at the end of the chapter, the Japanese example provides some guidance on how Chinese firms might navigate the frictions they will inevitably face, and ultimately integrate into the local business communities in the United States.

The chapter is structured as follows: Section 7.1 briefly surveys several leading theories on the motivations for FDI, and shows that Japan's experience closely tracked the predictions of those theories. Section 7.2 provides a sketch of key phases in Japanese FDI into the United States, followed by an analysis of the underlying causes of controversy these investments engendered. Section 7.3 examines the response of Japanese firms and governmental actors to the frictions arising from US–directed FDI. Section 7.4 describes the current status of Japanese FDI into the United States. Section 7.5 draws lessons for China.

7.1   LITERATURE REVIEW AND ORIENTATION OF THE ANALYSIS

In the early stages of Japanese FDI, some commentators speculated that it would follow a unique pattern due to Japan's cultural distance from the US, as well as the perceived uniqueness of business structures and governmental linkages of Japanese firms. In particular, commentators pointed to the fact that Japanese firms tended to use affiliated trading companies (*sogo shosha*) as their agents in foreign markets, which was thought to lend a distinctive character to Japanese FDI (Vernon 1993, p. 70; Kojima 1978, pp. 85–87; Yoshida 1987, pp. 15–18). Moreover, some predicted that the mode of entry into the host country (greenfield investment versus acquisition) would be influenced by the lack of acquisition activity in Japan's home market.

By the early 1990s, however, it was evident that Japan's experience in the US was readily explainable by existing FDI theories (though its experience played a role in extending existing theories). As Vernon (1993, p. 70) noted, by this time "the patterns of foreign direct investment by Japanese firms were converging toward the norms recorded by their US and European rivals." Moreover, although Japanese firms may have displayed some early aversion to acquisitions as the mode of entry, any such aversion fell away rapidly in the mid-1980s.

While space constraints do not permit even a brief recitation of all potentially relevant theoretical literature, what ties these perspectives together is a view of FDI as a means by which multinational enterprises (MNEs) defend the market shares they gained through exporting by exploiting potential advantages in ownership, location or internalization.[2] FDI can be seen as the facilitating link in the natural transition from exporting, to assembling, to producing in the foreign market (see CRS 1989b). Viewed in this light, FDI has multiple motivations – some firm-specific, such as a desire to produce closer to the foreign market, achieve economies of scale, or reduce transaction costs. Other motivations are political, such as shifting production to avoid export restraints, or to fend off threatened protectionism in a foreign market. Still other motivations are based on the macroeconomic environment, such as movements in exchange rates, which can affect trade performance and competitiveness. The following paragraphs outline several leading theories on FDI behavior, and provide references to literature confirming Japan's conformance with the main predictions of these theories.

7.1.1   Micro-Analysis of FDI

Internalization theory: the MNE internalizes what would otherwise be an arm's-length market transaction in the host country. Inherent disadvantages of the firm operating in an alien commercial and legal setting are overcome by the opportunity to develop technological assets and extend organizational structures in the host country, building on strengths in the home country market.

From this perspective, exports and FDI are complementary. Exports reveal demand sufficient to warrant the higher fixed cost of FDI, which (partially) internalizes the production and/or distribution process in the export market.

Exploitation of internalization advantages is a component of the prevailing "eclectic theory" of FDI (see Dunning 1997), along with exploitation of ownership advantages (such as brands or economies of scale) and location advantages of managing the activity within an MNE's boundaries rather than through exports.

As will be shown in section 7.2 of this chapter, internalization, along with other elements of the eclectic theory, provide a solid explanation for the significant qualitative and quantitative changes in Japanese FDI that took place beginning in the late 1970s and early1980s. As Caves (1993, p. 279) noted: "[T]he microeconomic behavior underlying Japanese foreign investment does not differ qualitatively from what other countries' foreign investors have exhibited." He continued (p. 284): "Many company-level studies of the foreign investment process have observed a sequence in which a company first establishes itself as an exporter to a foreign market, then undertakes foreign investment to support and expand its position there. This sequence was strongly evident for Japanese foreign investment."

FDI behavior is motivated not only by responses to organizational and transaction cost factors operating at the firm or industry level; it is also heavily influenced by political economy variables. The most important of these are actual or threatened protectionist activity in host countries.

7.1.2   Macro-Analysis of FDI

Tariff-jumping FDI: firms engage in FDI to avoid existing tariffs and other trade protectionist measures in the host country.

As shown in the next part of the chapter, Japan's experience is a clear illustration of this phenomenon. Voluntary export restraints are cited as factors motivating Japanese investment in the US steel industry (CRS 1990, p. 11) and television-manufacturing activity (CRS 1982, p. 9). In response to voluntary export restraints on automobiles, "Japanese automakers fundamentally altered their US investment strategies," creating production facilities in the US and forming alliances with state and local governments, which were eager to influence plant location decisions with a variety of incentives (Encarnation 1992, pp. 131–133).

Quid pro quo FDI: investment occurs as an attempt to reduce the probability that threatened but as yet unimplemented protectionist measures will be imposed – "it is tariff-defusing" FDI (Bhagwati et al. 1992).

Japan's experience in the 1980s is quite literally a text book example of defensive FDI designed to defuse protectionist impulses in the host country. A survey of Japanese firms undertaking FDI between 1980 and 1986 by Japan's Ministry of International Trade and Industry (MITI) found that the overwhelming majority of firms cited "avoiding trade friction" as their main motivation (Bhagwati 1990; Bhagwati et al. 1992, p. 189). One commentator suggested that quid pro quo FDI was particularly salient to Japanese firms in the 1980s, because by that time their stake in major foreign markets such as the United States had become so huge and critical to their success: "the defensive motivations that commonly lie behind the creation and spread of multinational enterprises are likely to act even more powerfully on the Japanese than on their US-based and Europe-based competitors" (Vernon 1993, p. 69).

In addition to these political economy considerations, macroeconomic factors are of course also relevant to FDI behavior. Currency exchange rates, asset values in the home and host countries, and the balance of international trade can all influence the level and form of FDI.

7.1.3 Location Decisions

A second strand of FDI literature relevant to this chapter concerns industry location decisions: what factors influence foreign industry transplants to locate where they do? A threshold question relates to the countries in which MNEs choose to invest. For Japanese MNEs in the 1980s, as for Chinese MNEs today, the United States is a crucial and attractive overseas market due to its size, the quality of its physical infrastructure, the highly skilled nature of its labor force, and a host of related factors.

Some literature has also focused on industry location decisions within the United States. The Japanese location experience may be of limited direct relevance to Chinese firms, but as will be shown later in the chapter, the state-level dynamics of location decisions may be informative for prospective Chinese investors. Kong (1992) provided the most extensive discussion of these theories in relation to Japanese FDI. He proposed an organization–resource dependence model that predicts that transplanted industries will locate near required resources and services. Since similar industries have similar needs, a good location for one factory will be a good location for another with similar requirements. A "state model" predicts that location decisions are strongly affected by state government policies, with the state acting as an entrepreneur to lure transplants with a variety of tax and other incentives. Finally, a "class model" argues that strong unions are a negative factor in influencing industrial plant location decisions. Examining the Japanese automobile industry, Kong (1992) found that resource dependency provides the strongest explanation for location decisions. State government incentives were also very influential. Labor force unionization, however, did not appear to be a significant factor.

The bottom line from the theoretical literature as applied to Japan's experience is consistent and clear: organizational and transaction cost factors and political considerations figured prominently in the FDI decisions of Japanese firms in the 1980s. With a few exceptions discussed below, distinctive qualities of Japanese firms, government policies and culture – to the extent that they existed – did not lend a distinctive pattern or form to Japanese FDI. On the other hand, perceptions in the United States about these distinctive qualities were extremely important in coloring the US reaction to Japanese FDI as it developed in response to economic and political contexts.

This conclusion orients the analysis and increases the relevance of the Japan analogy for China. It suggests three analytical default positions that will animate the remainder of the chapter.[3] First, the basic motivations for and trajectory of Chinese FDI into the United States will resemble those of their Japanese counterparts, despite the distinctive setting from which such investments will emanate. Second, many of the frictions likely to be generated by Chinese FDI into the United States will have direct parallels with those generated by Japanese FDI in the 1980s. Third, as a result, the strategies and adaptations of Japanese firms operating in the US may offer useful lessons for China.

7.2   JAPANESE FDI IN THE 1980s: CHARACTERISTICS AND FRICTIONS

During the 1980s, Japan's total stock of assets held abroad increased 25-fold, and its share of total FDI flows into the United States rose from 19 percent in 1980 to 31 percent in 1987. Figure 7.1 traces the huge expansion in Japanese FDI inflows to the United States over the course of the 1980s.

This major expansion in Japanese investment over the decade generated a host of frictions. This section of the chapter examines the factors leading to the rapid increase in Japanese FDI, outlines the main characteristics of that investment and analyzes the key strands of criticism that Japanese FDI into the United States evoked.

7.2.1   Investment Trajectory and Characteristics

As noted above, in the first stages of development of Japan's multinational networks it was thought that Japanese MNEs would exhibit a quite different pattern of FDI than their US and European counterparts. Until the 1970s, Japanese investment in the US

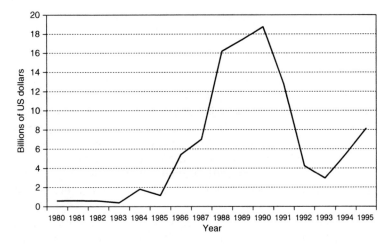

Source: US Bureau of Economic Analysis.

Figure 7.1   Japanese FDI flows in the United States, 1980–95

was an adjunct to international trade. Many Japanese producers were not large enough or enjoyed too few competitive advantages to engage in FDI; others relied on affiliated trading companies as their agents in foreign markets. Thus, the bulk of Japanese FDI at the time was undertaken by the trading companies and the banks that financed the trade. A handful of Japanese manufacturers made investments in the 1960s and early 1970s, but FDI related to trade activities predominated: in 1980, Japan's share of foreign investment in US wholesale trade was 37 percent, but in manufacturing it was less than 5 percent (Caves 1993, p. 281).

During the 1980s, the character of Japanese FDI in the United States changed significantly. Japanese investment in US manufacturing accelerated, and Japanese firms sought to replicate their operating systems in the United States. Heavy investments were made in the US distribution sector to support the marketing of autos and other goods that require extensive coordination of manufacturing and distribution. Many factors contributed to the shift, including increased Japanese R&D, the accumulation of intangible assets that support foreign investments, better learning about the transfer of intangible assets and skills to foreign markets, and increased sales promotion. Also important was the development of organizational skills and business practices of Japanese firms. The character of these organizational developments explains Japan's international comparative advantage in automobiles and other high-value-added durable goods, where systematic innovations in product quality are rapidly incorporated into the production process (Caves 1993, pp. 287–88).

This shift in Japanese FDI activity is in accord with the standard theory of investment based on transaction costs and exploitation of ownership and location advantages, in which distribution and other operational activities are brought in-house when they provide lower costs and greater benefits than arm's-length relationships. But some distinctive characteristics of Japanese investment in the United States did emerge. One was the high propensity of Japanese MNEs to control their production affiliates tightly from Japan, relying almost exclusively on Japanese input sources and Japanese nationals as top managers (Vernon 1993, pp. 71–72). The tendency of foreign affiliates to rely so heavily on sources in Japan was attributed to consensual decision-making processes, just-in-time production processes and other distinctive organizational features of Japanese firms (Vernon 1993, p. 72; Yoshida 1987, pp. 16–17).

By the mid-1980s, Japan-based firms were expanding their multinational networks at a rapid pace (Figure 7.1). Vernon (1993, p. 72) noted that some of the factors that had slowed the growth of these networks in the past now served to accelerate their proliferation. The desire, just noted, of Japanese firms to rely on Japanese input sources is one prominent example. This resulted in foreign affiliates of Japanese firms pulling large numbers of Japanese satellite suppliers with them into the foreign market. Again, this type of activity is highly consistent with internalization theory, which emphasizes the transaction cost-minimizing effects of expansion into foreign markets as a prime motive for FDI.

Turning to macroeconomic factors, the Plaza Accord in 1985 resulted in a major adjustment in the yen–dollar exchange rate. The depreciation of the dollar led to increased FDI from Japan, particularly in the form of acquisitions. Blonigen (1995), examining the period 1974–92, showed that a weaker dollar relative to the yen was strongly correlated with greater acquisition FDI by Japanese firms. As theory predicts, he found that the effect was strongest in industries in which the presence of intangible assets is more likely, such as manufacturing, particularly of high-tech products.[4]

A second macroeconomic factor boosting Japanese FDI in the latter half of the 1980s was Japan's speculative bubble economy. This was a period of massive asset inflation – particularly real estate and equities. Research by Blonigen (1995) showed that increases in the Japanese stock market index in the 1980s were highly correlated with increased Japanese acquisition activity. It is quite possible that the poor performance of some Japanese acquisitions in the United States at this time (for example, Sony's purchase of Columbia Pictures, overpaying for trophy assets such as Rockefeller Center and Pebble Beach Golf Course) was a spillover effect of speculative bubble activity in Japan.

A third macroeconomic factor leading to increased Japanese FDI was the bilateral trade imbalance. As noted above, FDI can be viewed as a complement to international trade – as Japanese exports grew, FDI continued to expand. At the same time, the continuing trade imbalance between the United States and Japan created a political environment highly conducive to FDI, as explained next.

Growing protectionist sentiment in the United States served as an important catalyst for Japanese FDI in the United States (CRS 1989b, pp. 89–447E, 7). Firms faced with protectionism established operations in the United States to protect their market share (Palugod 1990). It is well established in the literature that quantitative restrictions on Japanese exports were correlated with higher Japanese foreign investments (for example, Drake and Caves 1992). The starkest example of the correlation is the automobile industry. In 1981, Japanese firms began voluntarily restraining exports of autos to the United States to give the US auto industry a period of time to make the necessary adjustments to become more competitive with imports. The Japanese renewed their restraints in each subsequent year through 1984. The automobile voluntary restraint agreement (VRA) induced Japanese auto makers to locate operations in the United States. Three major Japanese auto producers, which accounted for almost 75 percent of US imports from Japan, began investing heavily in auto assembly facilities in the United States after imposition of the VRA (USITC 1985). A similar correlation between the imposition of export restraints and higher Japanese investment in the United States was exhibited in the color television industry and the semiconductor industry (Palugod 1990, pp. 101–102). Blonigen (1995) empirically confirmed that the threat of protectionism had a significant impact on Japanese FDI in the United States. Thus, it is plain that Japanese managers (and possibly government officials, if one credits MITI with a significant planning and coordination role in the economy at this time) took political factors into account in deciding whether to invest in the United States.

Mode of entry

As was true of other major investors in the 1980s, the cumulative expenditure of Japanese investors over the decade was heavily directed toward acquisitions. Table 7.1 shows annual investment by mode of entry.

As the table indicates, greenfield investments and acquisitions were roughly equivalent in the first half of the decade. The distinctive feature of Japanese acquisition activity is its huge increase in the latter half of the decade, as indicated by Figure 7.1. As just discussed, it is quite likely that the spike in acquisition activity in this period was motivated

Table 7.1   *Japanese FDI in the United States, by investment type, 1980–90 (millions of dollars)*

Year	Acquisitions	Greenfields
1980	521	75
1981	469	147
1982	137	450
1983	199	193
1984	1 352	454
1985	463	689
1986	1 250	4 166
1987	3 340	3 666
1988	12 232	3 956
1989	11 204	6 206

Source: Bureau of Economic Analysis.

by the twin macroeconomic factors of dollar depreciation and dramatic asset inflation in Japan.

It is helpful, however, to place Japanese acquisition activity in context. Although Japan was one of the top eight foreign acquirers in the late 1970s through mid-1980s, it ranked well below the UK, Canada, the Federal Republic of Germany and France in terms of numbers of acquisitions. For the period 1976–86, Japan accounted for only 4.5 percent of foreign purchases of US companies (CRS 1987, pp. 5–6). A significant portion of the Japanese acquisition activity, particularly in the latter part of the decade, consisted of real estate purchases. It is unlikely that Japanese acquisition activity became controversial at the end of the decade due solely to the sheer number or volume of transactions, but rather as a result of some high-profile acquisitions capping a decade of trade imbalances (see the discussion below). One possible exception was Japanese acquisitions in the US banking industry. As of 1989, 33 Japanese banks controlled about half of the total foreign banking assets in the United States – $329 billion. Their overall US banking asset market share as of that date was 10 percent, triple the market share of a decade earlier. Their market share in California was particularly high, with Japanese controlling the five largest banks in the state (CRS 1989a, pp. 89–407E, 3).

Location decisions

The location decisions of Japanese manufacturers in the 1980s followed predictable patterns. A study of start-up manufacturing plants in high-tech industries conducted in the early 1980s showed that, for the majority of companies, the quality of the labor force, proximity to markets and lack of labor unionization were the three most important factors in the location decision (cited in Yoshida 1987, pp. 65–67). California was the overwhelming choice for the firms surveyed (ibid.). Focusing on Japanese automobile transplants, Kong (1992) found that plant location decisions were driven by a combination of straightforward production factors (access to materials, skilled labor, distribution channels) and state-level government incentives. Japanese automobile factories were clustered in the lower Midwest (Ohio, Indiana, Illinois, Kentucky, Tennessee).

Surprisingly, this study found that, although Japanese automotive executives routinely expressed concerns about working with organized labor in the United States, labor unionization did not appear to be a highly salient factor in automobile plant location decisions. This finding, however, is in tension with the commonly accepted view that Japanese manufacturers sought to avoid locations with heavy populations of unionized labor.

7.2.2 Frictions and Controversies

Consonant with the (ultimately inaccurate) view that Japanese firms would exhibit unique foreign investment behavior, some predicted that Japanese FDI would be less controversial than FDI from some other nations. As Vernon (1993, p. 70) noted:

> [F]rom this early pattern [of Japanese FDI based on trade relations and led by the general trading companies], it appeared that the Japan-based multinational enterprise might root itself much more deeply in its foreign markets than did the US-based and Europe-based companies, with results that might prove more benign from the viewpoint of the host country.

Unfortunately for Japan, this prediction also turned out to be inaccurate. This part of the chapter outlines the principal sources of friction in the United States associated with Japanese FDI in the 1980s. The discussion is pursued in some detail because the parallels with contemporary China are striking, and thus this phase of Japanese FDI may be of particular interest to Chinese executives and policy-makers.

Reciprocity issues
The largest underlying cause of friction over Japanese FDI in the 1980s was the perception that, while the US was wide open to Japanese investment and imports, US firms faced substantial barriers to investment and trade in Japan. Reciprocity-based criticisms of Japanese FDI appeared frequently in Congressional hearings and public commentary throughout the decade.[5] Consider two reactions to high-profile Japanese acquisitions in 1989:

> The purchases of Columbia Pictures and Rockefeller Center occupied the headlines throughout the fall, and raised the question of whether the public reaction to these acquisitions was racist, since British and Dutch acquisitions – though not as dramatic – did not evoke the same reactions. While some of the reactions displayed an ugly racist tone, for the most part the reactions were based more on the perception that the Japanese were not playing fair with their trading practices; that in their failure to open their markets and remove their investment barriers, they were not in the same category as our major trading partners, who . . . are habituated to more open trade.[6]

An editorial in *Newsweek* made a similar point:

> Those who are uncomfortable with the Oct. 30 agreement to sell 51% of the company that owns Rockefeller Center . . . to Mitsubishi Estate Co. must realize that there is a connection: As long as Americans can't pay for Japanese products by exporting goods and services of their own, they will have to pay with real estate and other capital assets – even with a national treasure like Rockefeller Center . . . There will be no improvement in American access to Japanese markets until Washington makes up its mind to confront Japan with some formula that requires real reciprocity in trade for all US companies.[7]

Reciprocity was also central to the debate about Japanese investment in the US banking sector, which, as noted above, was one of the key targets of Japanese FDI in the 1980s. While the sheer magnitude of the investment was a concern to some observers, the most frequent complaint was that US banks were denied similar access to the Japanese financial sector (CRS 1989a, p. 7).

This precise line of criticism may not be available to critics of inbound Chinese FDI. The claim that China is "closed" to foreign investment and trade – a claim frequently made in relation to Japan in the 1980s – is fairly untenable.[8] China has been the largest destination for FDI among developing countries and among the top five destinations overall for over a decade running.[9] Moreover, for most of this decade, China has been the fastest-growing US export market, overtaking Japan as the third-largest export destination for the US in 2007.[10] While the reciprocity argument may not be open to China critics, the reciprocity critique of Japanese FDI took place against a complex economic and political backdrop. The underlying strands of that backdrop have many direct parallels with the US–China relationship today. Consider the following sources of friction in Japan–US trade and investment in the 1980s.

Spillover from the trade imbalance

The setting for inbound FDI from Japan was an unprecedented US trade imbalance with that country.[11] This imbalance colored US perceptions of Japan and served as the background against which the entire decade's debate over Japanese FDI played out. It seems safe to predict that perceptions of Chinese FDI will also be heavily colored by the overall state of the US–China trade relationship, in which, of course, the US currently runs a massive deficit ($262 billion in 2007, accounting for about 35 percent of the total US trade deficit). Large bilateral trade deficits get the attention of politicians and raise protectionist sentiment in Washington. Recent years have seen several signs of protectionism reminiscent of the climate in Washington in the 1980s.[12] The target has changed, but the Congressional rhetoric and action by the administration are similar to that of the 1980s. For example, in 2007, the Commerce Department imposed countervailing duties on Chinese coated paper, the first time it had taken such action against an imported product in 22 years, and the US Trade Representative (USTR) initiated three cases against China in the WTO.

As with criticism of the yen in the context of Japan's trade imbalance with the United States in the early 1980s,[13] many critics today claim that an undervalued yuan allows China to flood the US with cheap imports.[14] Protectionist and "anti-China" sentiment, concern over US jobs and a more generalized fear of growing Chinese economic might – all fuelled in some way by the trade imbalance – can be expected to color US views of Chinese FDI, just as they did in the 1980s with respect to Japan (CRS 2007). As Senator Max Baucus commented: "China's competitive challenge makes America nervous. From Wall Street to Main Street, Americans are nervous about China's effect on the American economy, American jobs, on the American way of life."[15]

Japan's economic threat to the US

Throughout the 1980s, some members of Congress and vocal critics in academia promoted the view that the Japanese posed a threat to US economic wellbeing. The argument, tied in part to the reciprocity complaint, was that the Japanese were not engaging in fair trade competition. The precise dimensions of the perceived unfairness varied with the critic, but several common themes were repeated. First, US–Japan trade and investment did not take place on a "level playing field" because Japanese firms received (generally undefined) "subsidies" from their government.[16] Second, Japanese firms were said to engage in anti-competitive practices in their home country and were exporting these practices through their investment activities in the United States. This view was articulated before Congress in 1989 by Japan critic Pat Choate:

> [W]e are seeing [that] foreign investment permits foreign corporations, particularly from Japan and, to a lesser degree, from Europe, to extend into the US market the operation of cartels that are prohibited under American law. These cartels are able to engage in anti-competitive practices. And what's more, under existing policies of the US government, they operate with a sort of diplomatic immunity.[17]

A deeper conspiracy behind Japanese FDI was seen by adherents of the "Japan, Inc." school that emerged in the late 1970s, fuelled by Chalmers Johnson's enormously influential book, *MITI and the Japanese Miracle*. In this view, Japan's economic success was a product of industrial policy formulated and executed through close cooperation between the economic bureaucrats at the Ministry of International Trade and Industry and the business sector, with the support of LDP politicians. In the most extreme version of the Japan, Inc. story, Japan's industrial policy consisted of the government "picking winners and losers," forming cartels and tolerating oligopolistic behavior in key sectors, ensuring a supply of low-cost bank finance to favored industries, and sheltering nascent industries from outside competition until they could dominate world markets. For adherents of this worldview, the Japanese "had developed a powerful, rapidly growing, purposively managed, and relentlessly self-interested economic juggernaut which was posing a fundamental challenge to US economic supremacy" (Yoshida 1987, p. 2). The Japan, Inc. school found adherents within Congress and certain sectors of the US administration, including the Commerce Department. The notion of Japan as a rising juggernaut that jeopardized US interests was widely shared by the public. In 1988, polls showed that more Americans feared the Japanese economy than the Soviet threat.[18]

Today, although the particulars differ considerably, similar complaints are raised about "unfair" Chinese trade practices (such as dumping and poor intellectual property protections) and "subsidies" from the Chinese government.[19] Today, as in the 1980s, some of the complaints will be lodged by US competitors most directly challenged by the entry of foreign players into the US market.[20] And, of course, public discourse in the United States is filled with references to the "threat" posed by China's economic rise. As a Congressional Research Service Report for Congress recently noted: "In many respects, the rise of China as a global economic power is subject to the same interpretation as the economic rise of Japan during the 1970s and 1980s and the impact that rise was thought to have on the US economy" (CRS 2007, p. 2).

Concerns about national security and political influence
Even though Japan was (and remains) a close military ally of the United States, Japanese acquisition activity in the 1980s was not immune to objections based on national security concerns. The most controversial transaction from a national security perspective was Fujitsu's attempted acquisition in 1986 of Fairchild Semiconductor (which ironically

was already controlled by Schlumberger, a French firm). Congressional objections to
the bid specifically and surrounding controversy over Japanese acquisitions of US high-
tech companies more generally eventually caused Fujitsu to withdraw its bid.[21] To give
a flavor of the public debate at the time, William Safire, in opposing the bid in his news-
paper column, noted that: "Japanese businessmen were accused of stealing secrets from
IBM and are suspected of technology diversions through Hong Kong."[22] Controversy
surrounding the Fujitsu–Fairchild transaction was a major impetus behind passage in
1988 of the Exon–Florio provision, which revised the Committee on Foreign Investment
in the United States (CFIUS) process for review of foreign acquisitions of US firms. It
authorized the President or his designee to investigate foreign acquisitions to determine
their effects on national security. Two decades later, another amendment to the CFIUS
process was motivated by a controversial Chinese bid for a US firm. In 2007, the Foreign
Investment and National Security Act[23] codified and clarified the CFIUS process in direct
response to CNOOC's politically charged and ultimately withdrawn bid for Unocal.

Post enactment of the Exon–Florio provision, other Japanese acquisitions proved
controversial as well. For example, an agreement by Fanuc Ltd, a Japanese machine
tool manufacturer, to acquire a minority equity stake in Moore Special Tool Company
of Connecticut, a maker of precision machine tools, triggered a CFIUS investigation
in October 1990, and was ultimately abandoned when a congressional challenge to the
transaction became apparent. The purchase by Nippon Sanso of Semi Gas Systems,
which produced gas systems for semiconductor production lines, was not blocked by
CFIUS, but it did generate a Senate subcommittee hearing in 1990 chaired by Al Gore
over its implications for US technological competitiveness.[24]

Because Japan was an important military ally, national security concerns over Japanese
acquisitions were often framed in terms of the potential for industrial espionage and
blended into angst about the sustainability of US economic and technological supremacy
in the face of Japan's perceived industrial policy.[25] Consider the statement of Senator
Frank Murkowski in regard to the Semi Gas acquisition, contrasting what he viewed as
the inability of CFIUS to gather detailed company-level information in reviewing the
deal with the workings of the Japanese government:

> Well, let me tell you what the French do and the Japanese do. They exchange this information
> . . . in order to achieve an objective and that objective is the advancement of technology in a
> competitive world . . . [In Japan,] every business, every industry there has a goal and a strategy
> to achieve the goal. Recognizing that resources are usually scarce, a successful Japanese strate-
> gic industry plan is adopted by MITI. It is coordinated, formulated . . . By targeting strategic
> markets, an infrastructure is built up which insures a solid basis for economic expansion . . .
> Thus in Japan, every technology becomes a stepping stone. Every product becomes the basis for
> another, and the resulting efficiencies of scale are enormous, as we have seen.[26]

A related concern was that heavy Japanese FDI could affect the US political process.
In Congressional testimony, Susan Tolchin, a frequent critic of Japanese FDI at the time,
asserted that over 100 political action committees run by foreign affiliates sought to "influence our public officials."[27] Congressman John Bryant asserted that "the sheer magnitude
of these [Japanese and other foreign] investments has increased foreign influence and leverage over US economic policymaking and political decisionmaking, and every Member
of Congress has already felt it."[28] He went on to complain: "the amount spent in 1988 by

Japanese interests to influence US policy is more than the combined budgets of the five most influential American business organizations in Washington . . ."[29]

In great contrast to Japan's status as a military ally of the United States (an "unsinkable aircraft carrier," as one striking metaphor, commonly attributed to Prime Minister Yasuhiro Nakasone, speaking in 1983, put it), China poses significant military and geostrategic challenges to the United States.[30] The Pentagon routinely expresses concern over China's rapid military build-up and the non-transparency of its military budget and goals.[31] The Taiwan issue constitutes a potential flashpoint for armed conflict in the region involving the United States and China. China already appears to be leveraging its economic rise into a more muscular foreign policy, particularly in the Asian region. It seems safe to predict that the long-range interests of the United States and China may diverge over a host of issues ranging from the economic to the military and political. Given this backdrop, and in view of the controversial nature of Japanese FDI in the 1980s, Chinese acquisitions involving technology, finance or natural resources are likely to evoke high levels of concern and scrutiny in Washington as well as widespread public controversy.

National security concerns are also likely to amplify controversy over China's "unfair" trade practices. For example, CRS (2007, p. 38) reported that some analysts believe national security considerations require the US to maintain an independent supply of steel. US steel producers have complained that overcapacity and overinvestment may cause China to dump cheap steel on world markets, jeopardizing US industry. This example is reminiscent of the argument, lodged by US manufacturers in several industries in the 1980s, that Japanese acquirers were deliberately targeting vulnerable US firms (Kang 1997, p. 318). But the fact that China is now the subject of criticism is likely to raise the stakes and heighten the linkage between "unfair" or "adversarial" economic competition and "national security threat."

Moreover, if a growing Japanese and Western European commercial presence in the 1980s provoked fears that the political process in Washington was being tainted, such concerns will surely be magnified by any significant lobbying efforts on behalf of Chinese business interests in the United States.

Employment practices

By the end of the 1980s, about 300,000 Americans worked for Japanese affiliates in the United States.[32] As noted previously, one distinctive feature of Japanese FDI was tight control over foreign affiliates, particularly with regard to the employment of high-level managers. Employment-related disputes were a constant source of trouble for Japanese firms in the United States in the 1980s and early 1990s. According to a *New York Times* article in 1990, Japanese firms commonly had at least one employment lawsuit pending against them, and losing a case cost at least $20 million in damages and legal expenses.[33] Japanese firms were most often hit with claims that they discriminated against non-Japanese and against women, including by engaging in sexual harassment, and were also accused of discriminating on the basis of race and age.[34] One such case, *Sumitomo Shoji* v. *Avagliano*,[35] was decided by the US Supreme Court and generated the important ruling that a wholly owned subsidiary of a Japanese firm operating in the United States is a US corporation and thus is subject to Title VII's anti-discrimination provisions. The US Equal Employment Opportunity Commission was also involved in several cases against

Japanese firms. Public perceptions of Japanese employment practices at the time were very negative. A national survey commissioned by Japanese firms in 1989 found that most Americans believed Japanese companies were more likely to discriminate against women, to be less open to advancement for Americans and to provide less job security than American firms. It also found that Americans were less willing to work for a Japanese firm than for a Canadian, British or German company.[36] It is impossible to know how much of this negative perception was attributable to wrongful conduct as opposed to misunderstandings about unfamiliar Japanese organizational practices, work habits and cultural norms. But Japanese employment practices undeniably generated a significant amount of ill will in the United States.

To date, we have insufficient experience with employment practices of Chinese foreign affiliates to draw comparisons with the Japanese situation. Indeed, a lack of literature on Chinese employment and managerial practices generally makes it difficult to assess whether this aspect of Chinese FDI potentially poses problems for Chinese affiliates in the United States. But given the continuing sensitivity of the US legal regime (and plaintiffs' attorneys) to employment discrimination in its various forms, Chinese foreign affiliates operating in the US would be well advised to take a cautionary note from the Japanese experience. Similarly, Chinese affiliates should scrupulously avoid any operational practices that could reinforce negative impressions about Chinese products or corporate conduct, such as unsafe labor practices, shirking on product quality standards or failure to respect intellectual property rights.

7.3   RESPONDING TO FRICTION

This part of the chapter examines the responses to friction over Japanese FDI in the United States. Of course, responses varied by actor and audience, and many strategies to defuse tension were pursued on a firm-level basis. It is difficult to gauge the full range and effectiveness of the efforts undertaken in this period, particularly at the firm level, as there seems to be limited institutional memory of this particular aspect of Japanese FDI in the United States in the 1980s. What follows is the most complete overview of the landscape I was able to assemble from the sources available. I have separated the discussion of responses into three parts: national level, state and local level, and firm level.

At the national level, the US and Japanese governments attempted to deal with the trade and investment imbalances through a series of negotiations in the late 1980s known as the Structural Impediments Initiative (SII). The SII talks were premised on the notion that many of the obstacles US firms investing in Japan faced were informal – tied to Japan's distinctive business structures and practices – rather than legal or regulatory restrictions. A General Accounting Office (GAO) report (1990, p. 18, Appendix III) stated:

> These informal barriers include a business environment in which Japanese companies are rarely sold; there are virtually no hostile takeovers; and cross-shareholding among allied companies leaves a low percentage of companies' common stock available for sale on the stock market. In addition, Japan's long-term supplier relationships, close ties between government and industry, and complex distribution system are considered imposing barriers, particularly to start-up investments.

The SII negotiations were launched in the fall of 1989 in an attempt to identify and solve "structural problems" that contributed to the trade and payments imbalance. While ostensibly the talks sought to identify problems in both countries, they focused most attention on impediments to trade and investment in Japan, such as the *keiretsu* system, shareholders' rights, the complex distribution system, and exclusionary trade practices; they even delved into Japanese saving and investment patterns. The talks resulted in a list of action steps to be taken by both governments. The US commitments focused on reducing the budget deficit and increasing the savings rate. The Japanese committed to a range of actions including increasing public spending, encouraging the formation of new businesses, deregulation and reviewing its antitrust policy. This is not the place to provide an in-depth assessment of these talks. Whatever the talks may have substantively achieved,[37] they did succeed in shining a spotlight on many idiosyncratic Japanese business practices that contributed to the country's extremely low levels of inbound FDI and strong preference for domestic products over imports. Currently, the US and China are engaged in similar talks to address frictions in the bilateral economic relationship. It seems safe to conclude that, while such negotiations may on balance be helpful in mitigating tensions, they are unlikely to alter the environment dramatically for inbound FDI in the United States.

It is important to recall that frictions over Japanese FDI at the time were cabined within the larger, generally healthy, US–Japan relationship. Japan had strong supporters within the US government to emphasize the mutual interests of the two countries as well as Japan's contributions to the bilateral relationship. These supporters helped counter negative rhetoric and dampen protectionist sentiment. I cite just two examples. First, at the peak of public perception that the Japanese were "buying up America," at the end of the decade, Elliot Richardson (who at that time was the chairperson of the Association for International Investment – see below) pointed out in congressional testimony that Japan was covering all of the costs of the US military presence in Japan and was working to increase access for US products. He contrasted the emotional nature of popular reaction to highly visible investments such as Rockefeller Center with the "steadier and clearer" perception of US and Japanese leaders concerning mutual interests and responsibilities.[38]

Second, Mike Mansfield, Ambassador to Japan throughout the period of trade and investment friction, coined the phrase, "the US–Japan relationship is the most important bilateral relationship in the world, bar none." This became the standard mantra for a succession of presidents and other high-level US government officials, ensuring that the rough spots in the economic relationship were viewed in the context of an otherwise close and crucial partnership. The US–Japan alliance also gave the US leverage in its approach to trade and investment problems with Japan – leverage that it may not have with respect to China.

Public relations efforts by private and public organizations acting on behalf of Japanese interests in the United States were also strengthened. The Association for International Investment (subsequently reorganized as the Organization for Foreign and International Investment, OFII) was established in the wake of Fujitsu's aborted acquisition of Fairchild. Elliot Richardson was its founding chairperson. The organization participated in the legislative process with respect to the Exon–Florio Amendment, helping to shape the legislation in a benign way from the perspective of foreign investors.[39] The

Keizai Koho Center, known in English as the Japanese Institute for Social and Economic Affairs, was established as an independent, non-profit organization in 1978. It is supported by Japanese firms, individuals and foreign affiliates. The Center engages in public relations efforts overseas, particularly with respect to the Japanese economy and business.[40] The Japanese government established the Japanese External Trade Organization (JETRO) in 1958 to promote mutual trade and investment between Japan and the rest of the world. In the 1980s, JETRO was active in gathering information about legal and political developments that might affect Japanese trade and investment opportunities abroad and published its findings in an annual white paper, which included detailed surveys of the investment climate in the United States and elsewhere. In this period of trade and investment friction, JETRO sought to position itself as a resource for US businesses seeking to pursue investment opportunities in Japan, a mission it still highlights today. Keidanren (the Japan Business Federation) maintains a Washington, DC office "to promote greater understanding in the United States of the importance of the bilateral trade and investment relationship to the US and Japanese economies, and to support policies that strengthen bilateral trade relations."[41]

Private-level diplomacy was another important strategy employed by Japanese firms in the 1980s (Yoshida 1987, pp. 139–142). Beginning in the 1960s, a number of organizations were established to foster communication between US and Japanese business people. Such groups include the Advisory Council on US–Japan Economic Relations and the Japan–US Economic Council. In 1983, the US–Japan Advisory Commission, composed of seven private citizens from each side, was formed at the request of President Reagan and Prime Minister Nakasone to review comprehensively the bilateral relationship. The Commission prepared a report stressing the prospects for long-term cooperation based on common interests, and endorsed direct investment as a means of increasing the flow of goods, capital, information, and skills, thereby strengthening the economic relationship (ibid.). In addition, numerous forums were established for exchange of ideas and information among business people and local, state, and federal government officials. The US–Japan Business Council is perhaps the most prominent example. It has several regional associations that provide opportunities for interaction among state government officials and business people.[42] These associations have annual meetings which alternate between the US and Japan. The governors of the states involved often attend these meetings, which are used to promote understanding of the benefits of FDI for the states, such as employment, increased tax revenue and technology transfer to local industries.

In contrast to the mostly critical tone of debate at the federal – and more specifically Congressional – level, state and local governments in the 1980s were generally very welcoming toward Japanese FDI (JETRO 1990, pp. 74–76). Although a number of bills were introduced in state legislatures to regulate or restrict foreign investment, only one state actually enacted such a bill into law. A Japanese government report attributes the contrast in climate to the fact that the beneficial effects of FDI in the form of job creation and tax receipts are felt most directly in regional economies (JETRO 1990).

In fact, states actively competed to attract Japanese FDI. The most common incentives were preferential tax treatment and low-cost financing, though some states offered free land, new roads, and schools for the children of Japanese managers. By 1990, more than 40 states had established offices in Tokyo to promote themselves as investment destinations (JETRO 1990, p. 77). Japanese MNEs skillfully played this competition to their benefit. For example, as noted above, although all the major Japanese auto-makers set up assembly operations in the same region of the United States, each was located in a different state, suggesting a bargaining strategy in which a later entrant leveraged the incentive package obtained by an earlier entrant. Kong (1992, p. 136) concluded that the Japanese auto manufacturers successfully "applied a strategy to maximize their political capital by spreading out the location in different states." He found that "all the winner states are in the high rank of number of tax and financial incentives available to industry" (ibid., p. 127). The upshot: "With so many available incentives, foreign investors clearly have the upper hand, using it to squeeze as much as they can out of the state" (ibid., p. 135).

This is not to suggest that the environment was completely welcoming to Japanese affiliates at the state and local level. As we have seen, the Japanese used greenfield investment in many industries to avoid or defuse protectionism in the United States. Greenfield investment is often thought to be the less politically problematic form of entry because it creates new jobs and tax revenues as opposed to the "mere" change of ownership entailed in an acquisition.[43] But greenfield investment can generate its own frictions. In the case of Japanese assembly and production affiliates in the United States, as noted, employment practices were a source of considerable tension. Also, local communities in the US sometimes argued that the entrance of foreign affiliates created excess capacity in an industry, resulting in the closure of US factories. Moreover, the public was sometimes critical of what it viewed as excessive incentives provided by state and local governments to woo foreign investors (JETRO 1990, p. 75).

At the firm level, concerns over community reaction sometimes shaped Japanese acquisitions of US assets. Public commitments to maintain existing headquarters, plants and facilities were sometimes made part of an acquisition agreement in order to allay local fears.[44] It was common for Japanese affiliates to retain public relations firms and undertake media campaigns to shape local sentiment toward their business activities in the community. Hitachi, embroiled in a number of US controversies in the 1980s, established an action program in 1985 that included efforts to expand production in the United States and to increase procurement from US sources. Similar steps were taken by other Japanese firms to defuse trade and investment tensions.

Another effort to engender goodwill at the local level entailed corporate social responsibility campaigns by Japanese affiliates. The affiliates made efforts to integrate into the local community by becoming involved in community affairs and making donations to local charities. A number of Japanese firms or corporate groups active in the United States at the time established foundations in support of education, endowed chairs at major universities,[45] and made other high-profile philanthropic gestures. For example, the Hitachi Foundation was established in 1985, with Elliot Richardson as its founding chairperson.[46] The Mitsui USA Foundation was established in 1987 to promote higher education and care for the disabled. The Toyota USA Foundation, also founded in the 1980s, promotes primary and high school education, particularly in math and science. These efforts reflected the unanimous advice given to Japanese affiliates by their supporters in the United States: if you want to be accepted, you must be good local citizens and demonstrate a commitment to the market and society as a whole.[47]

For all the controversy it engendered, studies have shown that Japanese investment in the United States in this period generally exhibited lower returns than comparable investments in the United States or Japanese investments elsewhere. Several reasons have been advanced to explain this result: an inability of Japanese firms to transplant the *keiretsu* network of suppliers and affiliates to the United States; misguided attempts to employ Japanese human resource policies and practices in their US affiliates; and the rushed or speculative nature of many investments in the 1980s as a response to anticipated trade restrictions in the United States and the growth of the bubble economy in Japan (for example, Bergsten et al. 2001, p. 123).

By the early 1990s, the friction and rhetoric over Japanese FDI in the United States had quieted considerably. The causes were likely several. Some or all of the strategies discussed above may have been successful in defusing tension. The eventual acclimation of the US public to Japanese products, brands and corporations may also have played a role. Japanese affiliates may have learned how to adapt better to their local environment – to overcome the "liability of foreignness" that Eden and Miller discuss in Chapter 5 of this volume. The overriding factor, however, was the bursting of the "bubble economy" in Japan. The Nikkei index peaked at the end of 1989 and eventually fell to one-third of the peak. Land prices declined steadily. A non-performing loan crisis occurred in the banking sector. Japan's serious economic problems caused a major retrenchment in overseas activities. As Figure 7.1 indicates, many Japanese firms shrank or withdrew altogether from US operations. During the post-bubble period, Japanese investment in the United States was on the same order of magnitude as that of Switzerland (Bergsten et al. 2001, p. 123). Japanese FDI in the United States ceased to be a major topic of public debate after about 1991.

7.4   THE CLIMATE FOR JAPANESE FDI IN THE 2000s

Today, the topic of Japanese FDI has completely disappeared from the US media and Congressional chambers. But Japanese investment in the United States is robust. By the end of 2007, the stock of Japanese investment in the United States was approximately $233 billion, second only to the UK and roughly 11 percent of the total stock. As of 2005, Japanese companies accounted for 614,000 jobs in the United States (about two-thirds of which were attributable to the automotive sector), and about 1 percent of private sector GDP (US–Japan Investment Initiative Report 2007, p. 11).

The bilateral investment relationship is continuously being re-examined and lubricated by a thick network of governmental and private sector actors. Several of the links in this network were described in Section 7.3 of this chapter, including the US–Japan Business Council and its regional associations. An important recent example is the United States–Japan Investment Initiative, launched in 2001 within the framework of the US–Japan Economic Partnership for Growth. The Initiative seeks to enhance the investment climate in both countries and to implement activities to facilitate FDI. Issues related to improving the investment climate in the United States raised by Japan include visa problems and the Exon–Florio and CFIUS review processes. Public outreach activities under the Initiative include investment seminars held in various cities of both countries.

Below the national level, states continue to woo Japanese foreign investment through their offices in Tokyo, while localities tout the opening of Japanese production facilities. A high-profile recent example is the 2006 opening of a $1.3 billion Toyota production facility in San Antonio, Texas.[48] Statements of the chairperson of the San Antonio

Chamber of Commerce indicate that the local hosts were anxious to accommodate the needs of Toyota and ensure that Toyota remained satisfied with its location decision.[49] As one of the world's premier companies, Toyota may be exceptional, but the case indicates that high-quality foreign affiliates enjoy a buyers' market in the United States with respect to their location decisions.

Thus, from a long-range perspective, despite considerable early frictions, the US not only remains open to Japanese foreign investment, but the climate at both the national and local levels could even be described as welcoming. The frictions of the 1980s have given way to a much calmer investment relationship characterized by emphasis on economic issues as opposed to political, cultural or national security concerns.

7.5   POSSIBLE LESSONS FOR CHINA

Is the US ready for FDI from China? Perhaps from the perspective of Japan's experience in the 1980s, the inquiry should be recast as a three-part question: First, have circumstances changed sufficiently to expect that a spike in Chinese FDI will create fewer frictions than was the case in the 1980s with Japanese FDI? Second, are Chinese firms prepared to help defuse the tensions that will inevitably arise out of a major influx of Chinese investment? Third, can we expect eventual normalization and maturation of investment relations between the United States and China?

As to the first question, nothing in the review of US reactions to the boom in Japanese FDI suggests that the experience will not be repeated in the case of another formidable East Asian nation, particularly one that does not share many of the strategic, political and military common interests with the US that muted and cabined the investment friction vis-à-vis Japan. Congress appears ready to play the "threat" card in respect of China at every opportunity, and large trade imbalances always create tempting targets for politicians. Moreover, it is easier for the media to report on trade wars, exchange rate controversies and political or human rights abuses in China than to undertake a nuanced assessment of the US–China economic relationship.

It might fairly be asked whether the attitudes of the US public and its political leadership have been tempered by the Japanese experience so that the next time around – with China – will be smoother. My own inclination is to conclude that any possible tempering effect will be offset by the fact that China is a potential adversary of the US on many levels, which will heighten suspicions of Chinese motives and exacerbate cultural misperceptions or racist undertones to the debate. Certainly it will not help that any forthcoming boom in Chinese FDI will follow massive media attention to Chinese product safety problems, a difficulty the Japanese did not face by the time investment flows into the US increased significantly. Another possibility is that Chinese FDI will be so qualitatively different from that of Japan in the 1980s that it will prove less politically and culturally sensitive. While some preliminary evidence might be interpreted as suggesting that Chinese FDI will prove to be different,[50] it is useful to bear in mind that patterns of Japanese FDI ultimately followed the theoretical models very closely, despite predictions that it would be distinctive and uniquely uncontroversial.

Thus, my rather pessimistic bottom-line conclusion to the first question, supported by FDI theory and the many background parallels between the Japanese and Chinese situations, is that history will repeat itself. Chinese firms will find many of the same motivations as the Japanese for a rapid expansion of US-directed FDI, and that surge – which will take place against a similar background of trade and exchange rate friction and charges of unfair business practices – will generate frictions at the national level very similar to those we experienced two decades earlier with Japan.

How might Chinese firms mitigate these forthcoming frictions? Here the Japanese experience offers a potentially more optimistic road map for China. Economic equivalence aside, greenfield investment is a less politically sensitive mode of entry than mergers and acquisitions. To the extent feasible, greenfield investments should be promoted and acquisitions – particularly unsolicited bids and deals involving aggressive tactics – should be avoided. Perhaps investments through sovereign wealth funds may also prove to be less politically sensitive than outright acquisitions of US corporations or assets. (China Investment Corporation's uncontroversial equity investments in US financial institutions following the subprime mortgage crisis is one example.) But it is too early to reach this conclusion firmly, particularly since sovereign wealth funds have begun to draw negative attention about their non-transparency and potential for politically motivated investments. Acquisitions should include measures to assuage public concern over transfer of sensitive technology or predatory investment practices. On this point, it is instructive to note that, in spite of such measures, Huawei's joint bid with Bain Capital for 3Com was withdrawn in early 2008 because it could not clear the CFIUS review process.

Regardless of mode of entry into the US, it will be important for Chinese affiliates to integrate quickly and deeply into local communities and to demonstrate their good corporate citizenship and respect for the US legal and market processes.[51] Scrupulous attention should be paid to avoiding even the appearance of employment discrimination or mistreatment of employees. Chinese affiliates should adopt best practices of corporate governance and appoint prominent and knowledgeable Americans as independent directors. Philanthropic activities should be undertaken where possible. Lobbying efforts should be low-key and pursued through collective organizations such as the OFII rather than on behalf of individual Chinese firms or interests. Efforts should be made to create good relations with state and local governments in the areas in which Chinese affiliates are located or consider locating.

Private-level diplomacy should be assiduously pursued through existing or new forums for discussion and debate between US and Chinese business people. Whenever feasible, policy-makers, academics and members of the media should be included in these forums to increase information flow and reduce cultural distance between the two countries. The US–China Business Council is certainly an important start in this regard, but at the time of writing this chapter the number and penetration of such organizations across the country is far lower than those of counterpart organizations for US–Japan business relations.

Whether Chinese affiliates and their political supporters in China are prepared to undertake these steps remains to be seen. Several questions deserve attention by those concerned about China's readiness for large-scale FDI in the United States. For example, will Chinese firms have sufficient political leeway to undertake the sort of integration into US communities and business associations that proved helpful to Japanese firms? Chinese firms are accustomed to receiving direction and guidance from political authorities, in Beijing or elsewhere.[52] Will Chinese executives have sufficient autonomy to respond flexibly to local conditions in the United States? Can Chinese firms effectively lobby policy-makers in Washington without triggering a backlash of criticism that agents of a communist regime are infiltrating the US political process? Will Chinese corporate governance practices in the United States be significantly better than those practices domestically, or will the problems (or at least perception) of poor disclosure, corruption and insider dealings follow Chinese firms to the US? Will the stigma of low or even dangerous quality that currently attaches to Chinese products exacerbate negative public reaction to Chinese FDI? Will Chinese firms (and their political managers) resist the temptation to acquire high-profile or sensitive assets in the United States that will enflame public opinion?

These questions are impossible to answer at this stage because they remain largely hypothetical. But Japan's experience suggests that Chinese executives and political leaders would do well to focus on these important questions as they contemplate investments in the United States.

From a long-term perspective, the Japanese experience in the United States should provide some grounds for optimism to Chinese investors. Despite the turbulence of the early boom years in Japanese FDI, today Japanese affiliates operate and thrive in the United States, while engendering virtually no political or media controversy. Thus, while the duration of the process may depend heavily on how well Chinese affiliates adapt to the US environment, Chinese investors can look forward to eventual normalization of the investment relationship.

NOTES

* This chapter was prepared in the context of the Deloitte–Vale Columbia Center on Sustainable International Investment project on "Is the US ready for FDI from China?" Helpful comments on an earlier draft were received from Hugh Patrick, Mark Ramseyer, Karl P. Sauvant, Mark West, and Charles Whitehead. Boyoon Choi provided excellent research assistance. Copyright © 2009 by Columbia University and Deloitte Development LLC. All rights reserved.
1. The quelling of controversy may also be attributed in part to learning effects by Japanese firms operating in the United States and "conditioning" of the US public to foreign investment from Japan. We will examine these possibilities below.
2. The "eclectic theory of FDI" associated with John H. Dunning represents a mix of three different theories in asserting that FDI is motivated by ownership advantages, location advantages and internalization advantages.
3. Subject, of course, to adjustment for the major differences in geopolitical relations vis-à-vis the United States and domestic political differences between China in the 2000s and Japan in the 1980s.
4. Because intangible assets acquired abroad can generate returns in the home country without a foreign currency transaction, currency depreciation in the country where the assets are acquired increases the return on those assets to the home country firm.
5. As Saxonhouse (1986, p. 245) recounted: "In 1982, when Senator Russell Long was discussing the so-called 'reciprocity legislation' in the United States, he said: 'No lesser mind than the Deity itself can keep up with all the subtleties and rules of Japanese import trade which are so effective in excluding American products.'"
6. Statement of Susan Tochin, Hearing before the Subcommittee on Economic Stabilization of the Committee on Banking, Finance and Urban Affairs, House of Rep, 101st Cong, 1st Sess., Nov. 15, 1989, p. 116.
7. *Newsweek*, November 13, 1989, p. 186.
8. Although China critics in Congress argue that China's WTO compliance is uneven, and former USTR Rob Portman argued that the US–China trade relationship lacks equity. See CRS (2007), pp. 34–35.
9. UNCTAD, World Investment Report 2007: Transnational Corporations, Extractive Industries and Development (New York and Geneva: United Nations, 2007), Annex table B.1., p. 251.

10. USTR, 2008 National Trade Estimate Report on Foreign Trade Barriers, p. 75. China, in turn, replaced the US as Japan's largest export destination.

11. See Saxonhouse (1986) for a thorough discussion of the trade imbalance and its policy implications.

12. See, for example, Heather Stewart, "US–China Trade War Looms," *Observer*, March 26, 2007, http://www.observer.guardian.couk/business/story/0,,1739428,00.html.

13. See, for example, Bergsten (1982).

14. One likely effect of a substantial adjustment in the yuan–dollar exchange rate is an increase in Chinese acquisitions of US firms. Although that effect of a revaluation of the yuan has received almost no attention, it is what the Japanese response to the Plaza Accord suggests, as shown above.

15. Statement of Senator Max Baucus, Senate Committee on Finance Hearing on US–China Relations, June 23, 2005, cited in CRS (2007), pp. 1–2.

16. See, for example, Statement of Susan Tolchin, Hearing before the Subcommittee on Economic Stabilization of the Committee on Banking, Finance and Urban Affairs, House of Rep, 101st Cong, 1st Sess., Nov. 15, 1989, p. 112.

17. Statement of Pat Choate, Hearing before the Subcommittee on Economic Stabilization of the Committee on Banking, Finance and Urban Affairs, House of Rep, 101st Cong, 1st Sess., Nov. 15, 1989, p. 15.

18. Cited in Green (2006), p. 108.

19. One of the key criticisms of the China Offshore Oil Corporation (CNOOC)'s attempt to acquire Unocal in 2005 was that its bid was "subsidized" by low-cost Chinese government financing because CNOOC is a state-owned enterprise.

20. In the 1980s, Congress frequently invited senior US executives from major industries such as automobiles and semiconductors to provide views on Japanese FDI. Not surprisingly, their views were almost uniformly negative, and their testimony was often laced with hyperbole about the threat Japan posed to US competitiveness and technological prowess.

21. From 1988 to 1992, Japan accounted for about two-thirds of all high-tech acquisitions in the US (Kang 1997, p. 320, Table 6). Alan Greenspan (prior to taking his position as Chairperson of the Fed) was critical of governmental interference in the Fujitsu–Fairchild acquisition. Greenspan commented that: "the incident frightened foreign investors and precipitated the decline in the dollar and the rise in interest rates . . . The end result: billions of dollars in additional interest costs for the US government and US consumers and businesses" (quoted in CRS 1987, pp. 16–17).

22. Cited in Kang (1997), p. 321.

23. Pub. L. No. 110-49, 121 Stat. 246. See David Fagan, Chapter 3 in this volume.

24. "The fact is that large parts of the US semiconductor equipment sector and the overall electronics industry are now being systematically acquired by foreign interests with potentially devastating effects for both US security and economic competitiveness, and the current administration shows little, if any, inclination to question these purchases at all." Statement of Senator Al Gore, Hearing before the Subcommittee on Science, Technology, and Space of the Committee on Commerce, Science and Transportation, US Senate, 101st Cong., 2d sess, Oct. 10, 1990, pp. 1–2.

25. Typical of works taking a critical view of Japan as a potential adversary and competitor is Prestowitz (1988).

26. Statement of Senator Frank H. Murkowski, Hearing before the Subcommittee on Foreign Commerce and Tourism of the Committee on Commerce, Science, and Transportation, US Senate, 101st Cong., 2d Sess., July 19, 1990, pp. 13–15.

27. Hearing before the Subcommittee on Economic Stabilization of the Committee on Banking, Finance and Urban Affairs, House of Rep, 101st Cong, 1st sess. Nov. 15, 1989, p. 110.

28. Statement of Hon. John Bryant, Hearings before the Subcommittee on Commerce, Consumer Protection, and Competitiveness of the Committee on Energy and Commerce, House of Rep., 101st Cong. 2d sess. June 13 and July 31, 1990.

29. Ibid., p. 72.

30. Japan was often criticized for not shouldering a heavier share of the costs of the military alliance. In effect, the claim was that the US had subsidized Japan's economic success by covering the costs of its defense. In this vein, Congressman Richard Gephardt once quipped that the United States and the Soviet Union fought the Cold War, and Japan won. China does not carry this type of baggage into its trade and investment relations with the United States. But this factor would scarcely offset the increased skepticism with which Chinese investments in the US are likely to be viewed on account of the potential military rivalry between the two countries.

31. See, for example, *New York Times*, November 5, 2007.

32. Jim Schachter and Nancy Yoshida, "US Workers Tested: Bosses from Japan bring Alien Habits," *Los Angeles Times*, July 19, 1988.

33. Deborah L. Jacobs, "Managing: Japanese–American Cultural Clash," *New York Times*, September 9, 1990.

34. See, for example, Leon Daniel Upi, "Americans Charge US-based Japanese Firms with Bias," United Press International, September 24, 1991 (reporting on testimony by American workers before Congressional panel).
35. 457 US 176 (1982).
36. William Armbruster, "Cultures Clash as Japanese Firms Set up Shop in the US," *Journal of Commerce*, March 1, 1989.
37. Perhaps a fair summation is that they resulted in a motley assortment of deregulatory measures and legal reforms in Japan of some – though probably modest – value, while signaling the seriousness with which the Japanese took the need to address the trade and investment imbalance to avoid damage to the bilateral relationship.
38. Statement of Elliot Richardson, Hearing before the Subcommittee on Economic Stabilization of the Committee on Banking, Finance, and Urban Affairs, House of Representatives, 101st Cong., 1st Sess. Nov. 15, 1989, pp. 6–12.
39. Interview with lawyer active in the establishment of the Association for International Investment and its reorganization as OFII.
40. http://www.kkc.or.jp/english/about_center/index.html. The Center says it "strives to close gaps in perception between Japan and other countries and between the business community and society at large."
41. http:www.kendanren-usa.org/about/keidanrenUSA/default.asp.
42. http://www.jusbc.gr.jp/eng/index/html.
43. This view is simplistic, as pointed out by Globerman and Shapiro in Chapter 2, this volume.
44. Author interview with legal counsel for a Japanese acquirer in the 1980s.
45. The author holds the Fuyo Professorship at Columbia Law School, which was established in 1980 by the Fuyo Group (one of the six major *keiretsu* corporate groups then in existence).
46. The Hitachi Foundation describes its mission as assisting economically isolated people in the United States.
47. Interview with advisor to the US affiliate of a major Japanese high-technology firm. See also Chapter 5 by Eden and Miller in this volume.
48. See http://www.sachamber.org/councils/ecodev/toyota/toyota_overview.php.
49. http://www.sachamber.org/councils/ecodev/toyota/SA_to_Toyota_Trip_Report_062603.PDF.
50. For example, it might be argued that non-controlling investments through a Chinese sovereign wealth fund will be less controversial than outright acquisitions by state-owned enterprises or even private Chinese firms. And it might plausibly be argued that Chinese firms are likely to avoid high-profile cultural irritants such as the purchase of Pebble Beach Golf Course by a Japanese investor in the 1980s, simply because such investments have little strategic value to the Chinese economy.
51. Toyota, one of the largest and most successful Japanese foreign investors in the United States, is widely viewed as a "great corporate citizen" by the communities in which it has invested. See, for example, the report of a study tour of Toyota's Indiana plant, available at http://www.sachamber.org/councils/ecodev/toyota/SA_to_Toyota_Trip_Report_062603.PDF.
52. For example, the General Chamber of Commerce of China in the United States is directed by the Chinese consulates in the US.

REFERENCES

Bergsten, C. Fred (1982). "What To Do about the US–Japan Economic Conflict," *Foreign Affairs*, 60 (2), pp. 1059–1075.

Bergsten, C. Fred, Takatoshi Ito and Marcus Nolan (2001). *No More Bashing: Building a New United States–Japan Economic Relationship* (Washington, DC: Institute for International Economics).

Bhagwati, Jagdish (1990). "The Theory of Political Economy, Economic Policy, and Foreign Investment," in M. Scott and D. Lal, eds, *Public Policy and Economic Development* (Oxford: Clarendon), pp. 27–54.

Bhagwati, Jagdish, Elias Dinopoulos and Kar-Yiu Wong (1992). "Quid Pro Quo Foreign Investment," *American Economic Review*, 82, pp. 186–190.

Blonigen, Bruce (1995). "Explaining Japanese Foreign Direct Investment in the United States," PhD dissertation, University of California, Davis.

Caves, Richard (1993). "Japanese Investment in the United States: Lessons for the Economic Analysis of Foreign Investment," *World Economy*, 16, pp. 279–300.

Congressional Research Service (CRS) (1982). "Foreign Investment in US Industry," Issue Brief No. IB78091 (Washington, DC: CRS).

Congressional Research Service (CRS) (1987). "Foreign Mergers and Acquisitions: Non-US Companies Acquiring US Companies," Report No. 87-711 E (Washington, DC: CRS).

Congressional Research Service (CRS) (1989a). "Foreign Investment in United States Banking," Report No. 89-407 E (Washington, DC: CRS).

Congressional Research Service (CRS) (1989b). "US Trade Restraints: Effects on Foreign Investment," Report No. 89-447 E (Washington, DC: CRS).

Congressional Research Service (CRS) (1990). "Foreign Direct Investment in the US Steel Industry," Report No. 90-297E (Washington, DC: CRS).

Congressional Research Service (CRS) (2007). "Is China a Threat to the US Economy?" Report No. RL33604 (Washington, DC: CRS).

Drake, T.A. and Robert Caves (1992). "Changing Determinants of Japanese Foreign Investment in the United States," *Journal of the Japanese and International Economies*, 6, pp. 228–246.

Dunning, John H. (1997). *Alliance Capitalism and Global Business* (London: Routledge).

Encarnation, Dennis (1992). *Rivals Beyond Trade: America versus Japan in Global Competition* (Ithaca, NY: Cornell University Press).

General Accounting Office (GAO) (1990). "Foreign Investment: Aspects of the US–Japan Relationship," Report No. GAO/NSIAD-90-203FS (Washington, DC: GAO)

Green, Michael J. (2006). "US–Japan Relations after Koizumi: Convergence or Cooling?" *Washington Quarterly*, 29 (4), pp. 101–110.

Japan External Trade Organization (JETRO) (1990). "White Paper on Foreign Direct Investments" (in Japanese) (Tokyo: JETRO).

Johnson, Chalmers (1982). *MITI and the Japanese Miracle: the Growth of Industrial Policy, 1925–1975* (Stanford, CA: Stanford University Press).

Kang, C.S. Eliot (1997). "US Politics and Greater Regulation of Inward Foreign Direct Investment," *International Organization*, 51, pp. 301–333.

Kojima, K. (1978). *Direct Foreign Investment: A Japanese Model of Multinational Business Operations* (New York: Praeger).

Kong, Fanying (1992). "The Political Economy of Industrial Location: The Case of Japanese Auto Transplants," PhD dissertation, Purdue University, IN.

Palugod, Nora Custodio (1990). "Japanese Multinationals in the United States: The Determinants of their Direct Investment," PhD Dissertation, University of Pittsburgh, PA.

Prestowitz, Clyde (1988). *Trading Places: How We Allowed Japan to Take the Lead* (New York: Basic Books).

Saxonhouse, Gary (1986). "Japan's Intractable Trade Surpluses", *World Economy*, 9, pp. 239–257.

United States International Trade Commission (USITC) (1985). "A Review of Recent Developments in the U.S. Automobile Industry Including an Assessment of the Japanese Voluntary Restraint Agreements," Preliminary Report to the Subcommittee on Trade, Committee on Ways and Means, of the U.S. House of Representative in Connection with Investigation No. 332-188.

United States–Japan Investment Initiative Report (2007). "US–Japan Economic Partnership for Growth," http://www.state.gov/p/eap/rls/rpt/2007/86082.htm.

Vernon, Raymond (1993). "Where are the Multinationals Headed?" in Kenneth Froot, ed., *Foreign Direct Investment* (Chicago, IL: University of Chicago Press), pp. 57–84.

Yoshida, Mamoru (1987). *Japanese Direct Manufacturing Investment in the United States* (New York: Praeger).

APPENDIX I

Exon–Florio Statute (50 USC App. § 2170):
Authority to Review certain Mergers, Acquisitions,
and Takeovers

50 USC App. § 2170

§ 2170. Authority to review certain mergers, acquisitions, and takeovers

---

(a) Definitions. For purposes of this section, the following definitions shall apply:
   (1) Committee; chairperson. The terms "Committee" and "chairperson" mean the Committee on Foreign Investment in the United States and the chairperson thereof, respectively.
   (2) Control. The term "control" has the meaning given to such term in regulations which the Committee shall prescribe.
   (3) Covered transaction. The term "covered transaction" means any merger, acquisition, or takeover that is proposed or pending after August 23, 1988, by or with any foreign person which could result in foreign control of any person engaged in interstate commerce in the United States.
   (4) Foreign government-controlled transaction. The term "foreign government-controlled transaction" means any covered transaction that could result in the control of any person engaged in interstate commerce in the United States by a foreign government or an entity controlled by or acting on behalf of a foreign government.
   (5) Clarification. The term "national security" shall be construed so as to include those issues relating to "homeland security", including its application to critical infrastructure.
   (6) Critical infrastructure. The term "critical infrastructure" means, subject to rules issued under this section, systems and assets, whether physical or virtual, so vital to the United States that the incapacity or destruction of such systems or assets would have a debilitating impact on national security.
   (7) Critical technologies. The term "critical technologies" means critical technology, critical components, or critical technology items essential to national defense, identified pursuant to this section, subject to regulations issued at the direction of the President, in accordance with subsection (h).
   (8) Lead agency. The term "lead agency" means the agency, or agencies, designated as the lead agency or agencies pursuant to subsection (k)(5) for the review of a transaction.

(b) National security reviews and investigations.
   (1) National security reviews.
      (A) In general. Upon receiving written notification under subparagraph (C) of any covered transaction, or pursuant to a unilateral notification initiated under subparagraph (D) with respect to any covered transaction, the President, acting through the Committee–
         (i) shall review the covered transaction to determine the effects of the transaction on the national security of the United States; and
         (ii) shall consider the factors specified in subsection (f) for such purpose, as appropriate.
      (B) Control by Foreign government. If the Committee determines that the covered transaction is a foreign government-controlled transaction, the Committee shall conduct an investigation of the transaction under paragraph (2).

(C) Written notice.
  (i)   In general. Any party or parties to any covered transaction may initiate
        a review of the transaction under this paragraph by submitting a written
        notice of the transaction to the Chairperson of the Committee.
  (ii) Withdrawal of notice. No covered transaction for which a notice was sub-
        mitted under clause (i) may be withdrawn from review, unless a written
        request for such withdrawal is submitted to the Committee by any party
        to the transaction and approved by the Committee.
  (iii) Continuing discussions. A request for withdrawal under clause (ii) shall not
        be construed to preclude any party to the covered transaction from con-
        tinuing informal discussions with the Committee or any member thereof
        regarding possible resubmission for review pursuant to this paragraph.
(D) Unilateral initiation of review. Subject to subparagraph (F), the President or the
     Committee may initiate a review under subparagraph (A) of–
  (i)   any covered transaction;
  (ii) any covered transaction that has previously been reviewed or investigated
        under this section, if any party to the transaction submitted false or
        misleading material information to the Committee in connection with
        the review or investigation or omitted material information, including
        material documents, from information submitted to the Committee; or
  (iii) any covered transaction that has previously been reviewed or investigated
        under this section, if–
        (I)   any party to the transaction or the entity resulting from consum-
              mation of the transaction intentionally materially breaches a miti-
              gation agreement or condition described in subsection (l)(1)(A);
        (II) such breach is certified to the Committee by the lead department or
              agency monitoring and enforcing such agreement or condition as
              an intentional material breach; and
        (III) the Committee determines that there are no other remedies or
              enforcement tools available to address such breach.
(E) Timing. Any review under this paragraph shall be completed before the end of
     the 30-day period beginning on the date of the acceptance of written notice
     under subparagraph (C) by the chairperson, or beginning on the date of the
     initiation of the review in accordance with subparagraph (D), as applicable.
(F) Limit on delegation of certain authority. The authority of the Committee to
     initiate a review under subparagraph (D) may not be delegated to any person,
     other than the Deputy Secretary or an appropriate Under Secretary of the
     department or agency represented on the Committee.

(2) National security investigations.
  (A) In general. In each case described in subparagraph (B), the Committee shall
       immediately conduct an investigation of the effects of a covered transaction on
       the national security of the United States, and take any necessary actions in con-
       nection with the transaction to protect the national security of the United States.
  (B) Applicability. Subparagraph (A) shall apply in each case in which–
    (i)   a review of a covered transaction under paragraph (1) results in a deter-
          mination that–
          (I)   the transaction threatens to impair the national security of the
                United States and that threat has not been mitigated during or
                prior to the review of a covered transaction under paragraph (1);
          (II) the transaction is a foreign government-controlled transaction; or
          (III) the transaction would result in control of any critical infrastruc-
                ture of or within the United States by or on behalf of any foreign
                person, if the Committee determines that the transaction could
                impair national security, and that such impairment to national
                security has not been mitigated by assurances provided or renewed

with the approval of the Committee, as described in subsection (l), during the review period under paragraph (1); or

    (ii)   the lead agency recommends, and the Committee concurs, that an investigation be undertaken.

(C)   Timing. Any investigation under subparagraph (A) shall be completed before the end of the 45-day period beginning on the date on which the investigation commenced.

(D)   Exception.

    (i)   In general. Notwithstanding subparagraph (B)(i), an investigation of a foreign government-controlled transaction described in subclause (II) of subparagraph (B)(i) or a transaction involving critical infrastructure described in subclause (III) of subparagraph (B)(i) shall not be required under this paragraph, if the Secretary of the Treasury and the head of the lead agency jointly determine, on the basis of the review of the transaction under paragraph (1), that the transaction will not impair the national security of the United States.

    (ii)   Nondelegation. The authority of the Secretary or the head of an agency referred to in clause (i) may not be delegated to any person, other than the Deputy Secretary of the Treasury or the deputy head (or the equivalent thereof) of the lead agency, respectively.

(E)   Guidance on certain transactions with national security implications. The Chairperson shall, not later than 180 days after the effective date of the Foreign Investment and National Security Act of 2007, publish in the Federal Register guidance on the types of transactions that the Committee has reviewed and that have presented national security considerations, including transactions that may constitute covered transactions that would result in control of critical infrastructure relating to United States national security by a foreign government or an entity controlled by or acting on behalf of a foreign government.

(3)   Certifications to Congress.

(A)   Certified notice at completion of review. Upon completion of a review under subsection (b) that concludes action under this section, the chairperson and the head of the lead agency shall transmit a certified notice to the members of Congress specified in subparagraph (C)(iii).

(B)   Certified report at completion of investigation. As soon as is practicable after completion of an investigation under subsection (b) that concludes action under this section, the chairperson and the head of the lead agency shall transmit to the members of Congress specified in subparagraph (C)(iii) a certified written report (consistent with the requirements of subsection (c)) on the results of the investigation, unless the matter under investigation has been sent to the President for decision.

(C)   Certification procedures.

    (i)   In general. Each certified notice and report required under subparagraphs (A) and (B), respectively, shall be submitted to the members of Congress specified in clause (iii), and shall include–

        (I)   a description of the actions taken by the Committee with respect to the transaction; and

        (II)   identification of the determinative factors considered under subsection (f).

    (ii)   Content of certification. Each certified notice and report required under subparagraphs (A) and (B), respectively, shall be signed by the chairperson and the head of the lead agency, and shall state that, in the determination of the Committee, there are no unresolved national security concerns with the transaction that is the subject of the notice or report.

    (iii)   Members of Congress. Each certified notice and report required under subparagraphs (A) and (B), respectively, shall be transmitted–

(I)   to the Majority Leader and the Minority Leader of the Senate;

(II)   to the chair and ranking member of the Committee on Banking, Housing, and Urban Affairs of the Senate and of any committee of the Senate having oversight over the lead agency;

(III)   to the Speaker and the Minority Leader of the House of Representatives;

(IV)   to the chair and ranking member of the Committee on Financial Services of the House of Representatives and of any committee of the House of Representatives having oversight over the lead agency; and

(V)   with respect to covered transactions involving critical infrastructure, to the members of the Senate from the State in which the principal place of business of the acquired United States person is located, and the member from the Congressional District in which such principal place of business is located.

(iv) Signatures; limit on delegation.

(I)   In general. Each certified notice and report required under subparagraphs (A) and (B), respectively, shall be signed by the chairperson and the head of the lead agency, which signature requirement may only be delegated in accordance with subclause (II).

(II)   Limitation on delegation of certifications. The chairperson and the head of the lead agency may delegate the signature requirement under subclause (I)–

(aa)   only to an appropriate employee of the Department of the Treasury (in the case of the Secretary of the Treasury) or to an appropriate employee of the lead agency (in the case of the lead agency) who was appointed by the President, by and with the advice and consent of the Senate, with respect to any notice provided under paragraph (1) following the completion of a review under this section; or

(bb)   only to a Deputy Secretary of the Treasury (in the case of the Secretary of the Treasury) or a person serving in the Deputy position or the equivalent thereof at the lead agency (in the case of the lead agency), with respect to any report provided under subparagraph (B) following an investigation under this section.

(4) Analysis by Director of National Intelligence.

(A) In general. The Director of National Intelligence shall expeditiously carry out a thorough analysis of any threat to the national security of the United States posed by any covered transaction. The Director of National Intelligence shall also seek and incorporate the views of all affected or appropriate intelligence agencies with respect to the transaction.

(B) Timing. The analysis required under subparagraph (A) shall be provided by the Director of National Intelligence to the Committee not later than 20 days after the date on which notice of the transaction is accepted by the Committee under paragraph (1)(C), but such analysis may be supplemented or amended, as the Director considers necessary or appropriate, or upon a request for additional information by the Committee. The Director may begin the analysis at any time prior to acceptance of the notice, in accordance with otherwise applicable law.

(C) Interaction with intelligence community. The Director of National Intelligence shall ensure that the intelligence community remains engaged in the collection, analysis, and dissemination to the Committee of any additional relevant information that may become available during the course of any investigation conducted under subsection (b) with respect to a transaction.

(D) Independent role of Director. The Director of National Intelligence shall be a non-voting, ex officio member of the Committee, and shall be provided with all notices received by the Committee under paragraph (1)(C) regarding covered transactions, but shall serve no policy role on the Committee, other than to provide analysis under subparagraphs (A) and (C) in connection with a covered transaction.

(5) Submission of additional information. No provision of this subsection shall be construed as prohibiting any party to a covered transaction from submitting additional information concerning the transaction, including any proposed restructuring of the transaction or any modifications to any agreements in connection with the transaction, while any review or investigation of the transaction is ongoing.

(6) Notice of results to parties. The Committee shall notify the parties to a covered transaction of the results of a review or investigation under this section, promptly upon completion of all action under this section.

(7) Regulations. Regulations prescribed under this section shall include standard procedures for–

   (A) submitting any notice of a covered transaction to the Committee;

   (B) submitting a request to withdraw a covered transaction from review;

   (C) resubmitting a notice of a covered transaction that was previously withdrawn from review; and

   (D) providing notice of the results of a review or investigation to the parties to the covered transaction, upon completion of all action under this section.

(c) Confidentiality of information. Any information or documentary material filed with the President or the President's designee pursuant to this section shall be exempt from disclosure under section 552 of title 5, United States Code, and no such information or documentary material may be made public, except as may be relevant to any administrative or judicial action or proceeding. Nothing in this subsection shall be construed to prevent disclosure to either House of Congress or to any duly authorized committee or subcommittee of the Congress.

(d) Action by the President.

   (1) In general. Subject to paragraph (4), the President may take such action for such time as the President considers appropriate to suspend or prohibit any covered transaction that threatens to impair the national security of the United States.

   (2) Announcement by the President. The President shall announce the decision on whether or not to take action pursuant to paragraph (1) not later than 15 days after the date on which an investigation described in subsection (b) is completed.

   (3) Enforcement. The President may direct the Attorney General of the United States to seek appropriate relief, including divestment relief, in the district courts of the United States, in order to implement and enforce this subsection.

   (4) Findings of the President. The President may exercise the authority conferred by paragraph (1), only if the President finds that–

      (A) there is credible evidence that leads the President to believe that the foreign interest exercising control might take action that threatens to impair the national security; and

      (B) provisions of law, other than this section and the International Emergency Economic Powers Act, do not, in the judgment of the President, provide adequate and appropriate authority for the President to protect the national security in the matter before the President.

   (5) Factors to be considered. For purposes of determining whether to take action under paragraph (1), the President shall consider, among other factors each of the factors described in subsection (f), as appropriate.

(e) Actions and findings nonreviewable. The actions of the President under paragraph (1) of subsection (d) and the findings of the President under paragraph (4) of subsection (d) shall not be subject to judicial review.

(f) Factors to be considered. For purposes of this section, the President or the President's designee may, taking into account the requirements of national security, consider–

(1) domestic production needed for projected national defense requirements,

(2) the capability and capacity of domestic industries to meet national defense requirements, including the availability of human resources, products, technology, materials, and other supplies and services,

(3) the control of domestic industries and commercial activity by foreign citizens as it affects the capability and capacity of the United States to meet the requirements of national security,

(4) the potential effects of the proposed or pending transaction on sales of military goods, equipment, or technology to any country–

(A) identified by the Secretary of State–

(i) under section 6(j) of the Export Administration Act of 1979 [50 USCS Appx. § 2405(j)], as a country that supports terrorism;

(ii) under section 6(l) of the Export Administration Act of 1979 [50 USCS Appx. § 2405(l)], as a country of concern regarding missile proliferation; or

(iii) under section 6(m) of the Export Administration Act of 1979 [50 USCS Appx. § 2405(m)], as a country of concern regarding the proliferation of chemical and biological weapons;

(B) identified by the Secretary of Defense as posing a potential regional military threat to the interests of the United States; or

(C) listed under section 309(c) of the Nuclear Non-Proliferation Act of 1978 [42 USCS § 2139a] on the "Nuclear Non-Proliferation-Special Country List" (15 C.F.R. Part 778, Supplement No. 4) or any successor list;

(5) the potential effects of the proposed or pending transaction on United States international technological leadership in areas affecting United States national security;

(6) the potential national security-related effects on United States critical infrastructure, including major energy assets;

(7) the potential national security-related effects on United States critical technologies;

(8) whether the covered transaction is a foreign government-controlled transaction, as determined under subsection (b)(1)(B);

(9) as appropriate, and particularly with respect to transactions requiring an investigation under subsection (b)(1)(B), a review of the current assessment of–

(A) the adherence of the subject country to nonproliferation control regimes, including treaties and multilateral supply guidelines, which shall draw on, but not be limited to, the annual report on "Adherence to and Compliance with Arms Control, Nonproliferation and Disarmament Agreements and Commitments" required by section 403 of the Arms Control and Disarmament Act [22 USCS § 2593a];

(B) the relationship of such country with the United States, specifically on its record on cooperating in counter-terrorism efforts, which shall draw on, but not be limited to, the report of the President to Congress under section 7120 of the Intelligence Reform and Terrorism Prevention Act of 2004 [unclassified]; and

(C) the potential for transshipment or diversion of technologies with military applications, including an analysis of national export control laws and regulations;

(10) the long-term projection of United States requirements for sources of energy and other critical resources and material; and

(11) such other factors as the President or the Committee may determine to be appropriate, generally or in connection with a specific review or investigation.

(g) Additional information to Congress; confidentiality.

(1) Briefing requirement on request. The Committee shall, upon request from any Member of Congress specified in subsection (b)(3)(C)(iii), promptly provide briefings on a covered transaction for which all action has concluded under this section, or on

compliance with a mitigation agreement or condition imposed with respect to such transaction, on a classified basis, if deemed necessary by the sensitivity of the information. Briefings under this paragraph may be provided to the congressional staff of such a Member of Congress having appropriate security clearance.

(2) Application of confidentiality provisions.

    (A) In general. The disclosure of information under this subsection shall be consistent with the requirements of subsection (c). Members of Congress and staff of either House of Congress or any committee of Congress, shall be subject to the same limitations on disclosure of information as are applicable under subsection (c).

    (B) Proprietary information. Proprietary information which can be associated with a particular party to a covered transaction shall be furnished in accordance with subparagraph (A) only to a committee of Congress, and only when the committee provides assurances of confidentiality, unless such party otherwise consents in writing to such disclosure.

(h) Regulations.

    (1) In general. The President shall direct, subject to notice and comment, the issuance of regulations to carry out this section.

    (2) Effective date. Regulations issued under this section shall become effective not later than 180 days after the effective date of the Foreign Investment and National Security Act of 2007.

    (3) Content. Regulations issued under this subsection shall–

        (A) provide for the imposition of civil penalties for any violation of this section, including any mitigation agreement entered into or conditions imposed pursuant to subsection (l);

        (B) to the extent possible–

            (i) minimize paperwork burdens; and

            (ii) coordinate reporting requirements under this section with reporting requirements under any other provision of Federal law; and

        (C) provide for an appropriate role for the Secretary of Labor with respect to mitigation agreements.

(i) Effect on other law. No provision of this section shall be construed as altering or affecting any other authority, process, regulation, investigation, enforcement measure, or review provided by or established under any other provision of Federal law, including the International Emergency Economic Powers Act [50 USCS §§ 1701 et seq.], or any other authority of the President or the Congress under the Constitution of the United States.

(j) Technology risk assessments. In any case in which an assessment of the risk of diversion of defense critical technology is performed by a designee of the President, a copy of such assessment shall be provided to any other designee of the President responsible for reviewing or investigating a merger, acquisition, or takeover under this section.

(k) Committee on Foreign Investment in the United States.

    (1) Establishment. The Committee on Foreign Investment in the United States, established pursuant to Executive Order No. 11858 [note to this section], shall be a multi agency committee to carry out this section and such other assignments as the President may designate.

    (2) Membership. The Committee shall be comprised of the following members or the designee of any such member:

        (A) The Secretary of the Treasury.

        (B) The Secretary of Homeland Security.

        (C) The Secretary of Commerce.

(D)   The Secretary of Defense.

(E)   The Secretary of State.

(F)   The Attorney General of the United States.

(G)   The Secretary of Energy.

(H)   The Secretary of Labor (nonvoting, ex officio).

(I)   The Director of National Intelligence (nonvoting, ex officio).

(J)   The heads of any other executive department, agency, or office, as the President determines appropriate, generally or on a case-by-case basis.

(3)   Chairperson. The Secretary of the Treasury shall serve as the chairperson of the Committee.

(4)   Assistant Secretary for the Department of the Treasury. There shall be established an additional position of Assistant Secretary of the Treasury, who shall be appointed by the President, by and with the advice and consent of the Senate. The Assistant Secretary appointed under this paragraph shall report directly to the Undersecretary of the Treasury for International Affairs. The duties of the Assistant Secretary shall include duties related to the Committee on Foreign Investment in the United States, as delegated by the Secretary of the Treasury under this section.

(5)   Designation of lead agency. The Secretary of the Treasury shall designate, as appropriate, a member or members of the Committee to be the lead agency or agencies on behalf of the Committee–

(A)   for each covered transaction, and for negotiating any mitigation agreements or other conditions necessary to protect national security; and

(B)   for all matters related to the monitoring of the completed transaction, to ensure compliance with such agreements or conditions and with this section.

(6)   Other members. The chairperson shall consult with the heads of such other Federal departments, agencies, and independent establishments in any review or investigation under subsection (a), as the chairperson determines to be appropriate, on the basis of the facts and circumstances of the covered transaction under review or investigation (or the designee of any such department or agency head).

(7)   Meetings. The Committee shall meet upon the direction of the President or upon the call of the chairperson, without regard to section 552b of title 5, United States Code (if otherwise applicable).

(l)   Mitigation, tracking, and postconsummation monitoring and enforcement.

(1)   Mitigation.

(A)   In general. The Committee or a lead agency may, on behalf of the Committee, negotiate, enter into or impose, and enforce any agreement or condition with any party to the covered transaction in order to mitigate any threat to the national security of the United States that arises as a result of the covered transaction.

(B)   Risk-based analysis required. Any agreement entered into or condition imposed under subparagraph (A) shall be based on a risk-based analysis, conducted by the Committee, of the threat to national security of the covered transaction.

(2)   Tracking authority for withdrawn notices.

(A)   In general. If any written notice of a covered transaction that was submitted to the Committee under this section is withdrawn before any review or investigation by the Committee under subsection (b) is completed, the Committee shall establish, as appropriate–

(i)   interim protections to address specific concerns with such transaction that have been raised in connection with any such review or investigation pending any resubmission of any written notice under this section with respect to such transaction and further action by the President under this section;

(ii)   specific time frames for resubmitting any such written notice; and

(iii) a process for tracking any actions that may be taken by any party to the transaction, in connection with the transaction, before the notice referred to in clause (ii) is resubmitted.

(B) Designation of agency. The lead agency, other than any entity of the intelligence community (as defined in the National Security Act of 1947), shall, on behalf of the Committee, ensure that the requirements of subparagraph (A) with respect to any covered transaction that is subject to such subparagraph are met.

(3) Negotiation, modification, monitoring, and enforcement.

(A) Designation of lead agency. The lead agency shall negotiate, modify, monitor, and enforce, on behalf of the Committee, any agreement entered into or condition imposed under paragraph (1) with respect to a covered transaction, based on the expertise with and knowledge of the issues related to such transaction on the part of the designated department or agency. Nothing in this paragraph shall prohibit other departments or agencies in assisting the lead agency in carrying out the purposes of this paragraph.

(B) Reporting by designated agency.

(i) Modification reports. The lead agency in connection with any agreement entered into or condition imposed with respect to a covered transaction shall–

(I) provide periodic reports to the Committee on any material modification to any such agreement or condition imposed with respect to the transaction; and

(II) ensure that any material modification to any such agreement or condition is reported to the Director of National Intelligence, the Attorney General of the United States, and any other Federal department or agency that may have a material interest in such modification.

(ii) Compliance. The Committee shall develop and agree upon methods for evaluating compliance with any agreement entered into or condition imposed with respect to a covered transaction that will allow the Committee to adequately assure compliance, without–

(I) unnecessarily diverting Committee resources from assessing any new covered transaction for which a written notice has been filed pursuant to subsection (b)(1)(C), and if necessary, reaching a mitigation agreement with or imposing a condition on a party to such covered transaction or any covered transaction for which a review has been reopened for any reason; or

(II) placing unnecessary burdens on a party to a covered transaction.

(m) Annual report to Congress.

(1) In general. The chairperson shall transmit a report to the chairman and ranking member of the committee of jurisdiction in the Senate and the House of Representatives, before July 31 of each year on all of the reviews and investigations of covered transactions completed under subsection (b) during the 12-month period covered by the report.

(2) Contents of report relating to covered transactions. The annual report under paragraph (1) shall contain the following information, with respect to each covered transaction, for the reporting period:

(A) A list of all notices filed and all reviews or investigations completed during the period, with basic information on each party to the transaction, the nature of the business activities or products of all pertinent persons, along with information about any withdrawal from the process, and any decision or action by the President under this section.

(B) Specific, cumulative, and, as appropriate, trend information on the numbers of filings, investigations, withdrawals, and decisions or actions by the President under this section.

(C) Cumulative and, as appropriate, trend information on the business sectors involved in the filings which have been made, and the countries from which the investments have originated.

(D) Information on whether companies that withdrew notices to the Committee in accordance with subsection (b)(1)(C)(ii) have later refiled such notices, or, alternatively, abandoned the transaction.

(E) The types of security arrangements and conditions the Committee has used to mitigate national security concerns about a transaction, including a discussion of the methods that the Committee and any lead agency are using to determine compliance with such arrangements or conditions.

(F) A detailed discussion of all perceived adverse effects of covered transactions on the national security or critical infrastructure of the United States that the Committee will take into account in its deliberations during the period before delivery of the next report, to the extent possible.

(3) Contents of report relating to critical technologies.

(A) In general. In order to assist Congress in its oversight responsibilities with respect to this section, the President and such agencies as the President shall designate shall include in the annual report submitted under paragraph (1)–

   (i) an evaluation of whether there is credible evidence of a coordinated strategy by 1 or more countries or companies to acquire United States companies involved in research, development, or production of critical technologies for which the United States is a leading producer; and

   (ii) an evaluation of whether there are industrial espionage activities directed or directly assisted by foreign governments against private United States companies aimed at obtaining commercial secrets related to critical technologies.

(B) Release of unclassified study. All appropriate portions of the annual report under paragraph (1) may be classified. An unclassified version of the report, as appropriate, consistent with safeguarding national security and privacy, shall be made available to the public.

(n) Certification of notices and assurances. Each notice, and any followup information, submitted under this section and regulations prescribed under this section to the President or the Committee by a party to a covered transaction, and any information submitted by any such party in connection with any action for which a report is required pursuant to paragraph (3)(B) of subsection (l), with respect to the implementation of any mitigation agreement or condition described in paragraph (1)(A) of subsection (l), or any material change in circumstances, shall be accompanied by a written statement by the chief executive officer or the designee of the person required to submit such notice or information certifying that, to the best of the knowledge and belief of that person–

(1) the notice or information submitted fully complies with the requirements of this section or such regulation, agreement, or condition; and

(2) the notice or information is accurate and complete in all material respects.

APPENDIX II

Regulations Pertaining to Mergers, Acquisitions, and Takeovers by Foreign Persons; Final Rule

Friday,
November 21, 2008

Part II

Department of the Treasury

Office of Investment Security

31 CFR Part 800
Regulations Pertaining to Mergers,
Acquisitions, and Takeovers by Foreign
Persons; Final Rule

DEPARTMENT OF THE TREASURY

Office of Investment Security

31 CFR Part 800

RIN 1505–AB88

Regulations Pertaining to Mergers, Acquisitions, and Takeovers by Foreign Persons

AGENCY: Department of the Treasury.
ACTION: Final rule.

SUMMARY: This Final Rule amends regulations in part 800 of 31 CFR that implement section 721 of the Defense Production Act of 1950 ("section 721"), as amended by the Foreign Investment and National Security Act of 2007, codified at 50 U.S.C. App. 2170. While the revised regulations retain many features of the prior regulations, a number of changes have been made to implement section 721, increase clarity, reflect developments in business practices over the past several years, and make additional improvements based on experiences with the prior regulations.

DATES: *Effective date:* This rule is effective December 22, 2008.

Applicability date: See § 800.103.

FOR FURTHER INFORMATION CONTACT: For questions about this Final Rule, contact: Nova Daly, Deputy Assistant Secretary, U.S. Department of the Treasury, 1500 Pennsylvania Avenue, NW., Washington, DC 20220, telephone: (202) 622–2752, e-mail: *Nova.Daly@do.treas.gov*; Welby Leaman, Senior Advisor, telephone: (202) 622–0099, e-mail: *Welby.Leaman@do.treas.gov*; Aimen Mir, Senior Policy Analyst, telephone: (202) 622–0184, e-mail: *Aimen.Mir@do.treas.gov*; or Mark Jaskowiak, Office Director, telephone: (202) 622–5052, e-mail: *Mark.Jaskowiak@do.treas.gov*.

SUPPLEMENTARY INFORMATION:

I. Background

The Foreign Investment and National Security Act of 2007 ("FINSA"), Public Law 110–49, 121 Stat. 246, which amends section 721 of the Defense Production Act of 1950 ("DPA") (50 U.S.C. App. 2170), requires the issuance of regulations implementing its provisions following public notice and comment.

FINSA was passed by Congress as H.R. 556, which adopted the language of S. 1610. Senate Report 110–80, accompanying S. 1610, provides a useful history of the various bills leading to the enactment of FINSA.

President Bush signed FINSA into law on July 26, 2007, and it became effective on October 24, 2007.

Section 721 authorizes the President to review mergers, acquisitions, and takeovers by or with any foreign person which could result in foreign control of any person engaged in interstate commerce in the United States, to determine the effects of such transactions on the national security of the United States. FINSA codifies aspects of the structure, role, process, and responsibilities of the Committee on Foreign Investment in the United States ("CFIUS" or "the Committee") and the role of executive branch departments, agencies, and offices in CFIUS's review of transactions for national security concerns. A brief summary of major aspects of the statute follows.

FINSA formally establishes CFIUS in statute. (Previously, the sole basis for the existence of CFIUS had been Executive Order 11858 of May 7, 1975, 40 FR 20263, 3 CFR, 1971–1975 Compilation, p. 990.) FINSA specifies the following as members of CFIUS: The Secretary of the Treasury (who serves as chairperson), the Attorney General, and the Secretaries of Homeland Security, Commerce, Defense, State, and Energy. FINSA also provides that CFIUS may include, generally or on a case-by-case basis as the President deems appropriate, the heads of any other executive department, agency, or office. The President designated the U.S. Trade Representative and the Director of the Office of Science and Technology Policy as additional members of CFIUS in Executive Order 11858, as amended most recently by Executive Order 13456, 73 FR 4677 (Jan. 23, 2008). In the same Executive Order, the President directed that "[t]he following officials (or their designees) shall observe and, as appropriate, participate in and report to the President on [CFIUS's] activities": (i) The Director of the Office of Management and Budget, (ii) the Chairman of the Council of Economic Advisors, (iii) the Assistant to the President for National Security Affairs, (iv) the Assistant to the President for Economic Policy, and (v) the Assistant to the President for Homeland Security and Counterterrorism. FINSA also establishes the Director of National Intelligence ("DNI") and the Secretary of Labor as *ex officio* members of CFIUS. FINSA specifies that the DNI is to provide independent analyses of any national security threats posed by transactions and is to have no other policy role. FINSA further provides that, for each transaction before CFIUS, the Department of the Treasury shall designate, as appropriate, one or more

lead agencies. The lead agency, on behalf of CFIUS, may negotiate, enter into or impose, monitor, and enforce mitigation agreements or conditions with parties to a transaction to address any threats to national security posed by the transaction. FINSA requires regulations to provide for an appropriate role for the Secretary of Labor with respect to mitigation agreements.

FINSA also formalizes the process by which CFIUS conducts national security reviews of any transaction that could result in foreign control of a person engaged in interstate commerce in the United States, which FINSA refers to as a "covered transaction." Specifically, FINSA provides for CFIUS review of covered transactions, which must be completed within 30 days, to determine the effect of the transaction on national security and to address any national security concerns. Subject to certain exceptions discussed below, FINSA requires an additional investigation, which must be completed within 45 days, in the following types of cases: (1) Where the transaction threatens to impair U.S. national security and that threat has not been mitigated prior to or during the 30-day review; (2) where the transaction is a foreign government-controlled transaction; (3) where the transaction results in foreign control over critical infrastructure that, in the determination of CFIUS, could impair national security, if that impairment has not been mitigated; or (4) where the lead agency recommends, and CFIUS concurs, that an investigation be undertaken. Executive Order 11858 also provides that CFIUS shall undertake an investigation if a member of CFIUS advises the chairperson that it believes that the transaction threatens to impair the national security and that the threat has not been mitigated.

To ensure accountability for CFIUS decisions, FINSA requires that a senior-level official of the Department of the Treasury and of the lead agency certify to Congress, for any covered transaction on which CFIUS has concluded action under section 721, that CFIUS has determined that there are no unresolved national security concerns. The certification must be made at a level no lower than an employee appointed by the President by and with the advice and consent of the Senate, for transactions on which CFIUS concludes action under section 721 after a review, and at the Deputy Secretary level or above for transactions on which CFIUS concludes action under section 721 after an investigation. If the President makes a decision on a transaction under section 721, then he must announce his decision publicly within 15 days of the completion of the investigation.

In addition, in order for CFIUS to conclude action under section 721 for a foreign government-controlled transaction without proceeding beyond a review to an investigation, the Department of the Treasury and the lead agency must determine, at the Deputy Secretary level or above, that the transaction "will not impair the national security." Similarly, in cases where the transaction would result in foreign control over critical infrastructure, the transaction could impair national security, but such impairment has been mitigated during the review period, CFIUS may conclude action under section 721 without proceeding beyond a review if the Department of the Treasury and the lead agency determine, at the Deputy Secretary level or above, that the transaction will not impair national security.

Where a covered transaction presents national security risks, FINSA provides statutory authority for CFIUS, or a lead agency acting on behalf of CFIUS, to enter into mitigation agreements with parties to the transaction or to impose conditions on the transaction to address such risks. This authority enables CFIUS to mitigate any national security risk posed by a transaction rather than recommending to the President that the transaction be prohibited because it could impair U.S. national security. FINSA also provides CFIUS with authority to impose civil penalties for violations of section 721, including violations of any mitigation agreement.

Finally, FINSA increases CFIUS's reporting to Congress concerning the work it has undertaken pursuant to section 721. In addition to the certifications described previously, which CFIUS must provide to Congress after concluding action on a transaction under section 721, CFIUS also must provide annual reports on its work, including a list of the transactions it has reviewed or investigated in the preceding 12 months, analysis related to foreign direct investment and critical technologies, and a report on foreign direct investment from certain countries.

II. Comments on the Proposed Rule

The Final Rule contained in this document is based on the Notice of Proposed Rulemaking published on April 23, 2008 ("Proposed Rule") (73 FR 21868), which proposed amendments to the regulations in part 800 of 31 CFR. The comment period for the Proposed Rule ended on June 9, 2008. The Department of the Treasury received a total of 25 written submissions and some oral comments that were principally provided at a public meeting held at the Department of the Treasury on May 2, 2008. The written and oral submissions comprised approximately 200 distinct comments. The comments represented a wide range of interests, including foreign governments, U.S. business groups, law firms, and a member of Congress. All comments received by the end of the comment period were posted for public viewing at *http://www.regulations.gov*.

Among the comments submitted were a number that welcomed the Proposed Rule as helping the Committee to safeguard U.S. national security in a manner consistent with the U.S. commitment to open investment. Although one commenter believed the Proposed Rule would result in the "great majority" of mergers and acquisitions being subject to reviews, the Committee does not expect the changes to the regulations to materially affect the number of transactions that it reviews. From 2005 through 2007, the Committee reviewed less than ten percent of foreign acquisitions in the United States.

We respond to the comments submitted in the detailed section-by-section analysis, below.

III. Discussion of Final Rule

Overview of Significant Issues

The Final Rule retains many of the basic features of the existing regulations, which were adopted in 1991 after the 1988 enactment of section 721 of the DPA. The system continues to be based on voluntary notices to CFIUS by parties to transactions, although FINSA provides CFIUS with the authority to review a transaction that has not been voluntarily notified. The principal new development with regard to the procedures for filing notices with CFIUS is that the Final Rule makes explicit CFIUS's current practice of encouraging parties to contact and engage with CFIUS before making a formal filing. By consulting with CFIUS in advance of filing and, where appropriate, providing CFIUS with a draft notice or some portion of the information that later may be included in the notice, parties can help ensure that their notice, once submitted, will contain the information CFIUS needs to do its work. Such pre-notice consultations can help ensure that reviews of covered transactions are concluded as efficiently as possible. Consistent with the requirement set forth in section 721(b)(2)(E), the Department of the Treasury, as Chairperson of CFIUS, will also be publishing in the **Federal Register** guidance on the types of transactions that CFIUS has reviewed and that have presented national security considerations. The guidance, among other things, will include a discussion of certain types of information the Committee, based on past experience, considers useful for parties filing a notice to provide.

The provisions of Subpart D pertaining to the contents of a voluntary notice have been expanded to reflect information that CFIUS now routinely seeks from notifying parties. By having the relevant information included in each notification, CFIUS will be better prepared to conduct an efficient and in-depth analysis as soon as a notice is accepted. As noted in the proposed regulations, personal identifier information, which is needed to examine the backgrounds of members of the boards of directors and senior company officials of entities in the ownership chain of the foreign acquirer, should be submitted in conjunction with each notification, and should be marked clearly and provided as a separate document to facilitate limited distribution of this information. In addition to the new information requirements, the Final Rule, consistent with FINSA, also requires each of the parties to a notified transaction to provide certifications regarding the accuracy and completeness of their notices, as to information about the party making the certification (including certain affiliated entities), the transaction, and all follow-up information. A notice will not be deemed complete if it lacks certifications that comply with these requirements, and CFIUS may reject a notice that has previously been accepted if the final certification required under § 800.701(d) has not been received. Furthermore, material misstatements or omissions made by a party in connection with a review or investigation may result in the rejection of the notice or the reopening of a completed review or investigation.

Consistent with the new authority provided by FINSA, the Final Rule provides for penalties for material misstatements or omissions made to CFIUS, for false certifications, or for breach of mitigation agreements or conditions entered into or imposed under section 721. The Final Rule also provides that a mitigation agreement may include provisions establishing liquidated damages for violations of the agreement. *See* § 800.801. Parties that receive a notice of the imposition of penalties will have the opportunity to submit to CFIUS a petition for reconsideration of the imposition of the penalties.

Additional changes to the regulations have been made, including revisions to or deletions of existing examples or provisions, to take into account FINSA, and to otherwise add clarity to the regulations. The following discussion addresses changes to several of the key concepts of the regulations.

Covered Transaction

FINSA introduced the term "covered transaction" to identify the types of transactions that are subject to review and investigation by CFIUS. The statutory definition of covered transaction maintains the scope of section 721 as pertaining to any merger, acquisition, or takeover by or with a foreign person that is proposed or pending after August 23, 1988, which could result in foreign control of any person engaged in interstate commerce in the United States (the latter type of person is defined in these regulations as a "U.S. business").

The Final Rule further clarifies the meaning of the term "covered transaction," *see* § 800.207, by specifying the scope of important elements of the term, including "transaction," "control," "U.S. business," and "foreign person." The definitions and clarification of these terms appear in Subpart B (Definitions) and in Subpart C (Coverage).

Transaction

The term "transaction" is defined in § 800.224, and implements the statutory requirement that a covered transaction be one that involves a "merger, acquisition, or takeover" that is proposed or pending after August 23, 1988, by encompassing both proposed and completed transactions. This definition continues to exclude start-up or "greenfield" investments and includes only a very limited type of long-term lease.

Control

FINSA does not define "control," but rather requires that CFIUS prescribe a definition by regulation. *See* FINSA, Public Law 110–49, section 2, adding section 721(a)(2). "Control" is and always has been a key threshold concept in section 721, as the authority provided under that section, from the authority to review or investigate a notified transaction to the authority of the President to take action to suspend or prohibit a transaction, is predicated on foreign *control* of a person engaged in interstate commerce in the United States. This focus on control suggests a fundamental congressional judgment

that national security risks are potentially highest in transactions that involve the acquisition by a foreign person of control of an entity operating in the United States. Indeed, Congress made clear in the 1988 Conference Report that accompanied the originally enacted version of section 721 that "[t]he Conferees in no way intend to impose barriers to foreign investment. * * * [section 721] is not intended to authorize investigations on investments that could not result in foreign control of persons engaged in interstate commerce * * *." *See* H.R. Conf. Rep. No. 100–576, at 926 (1988). Nothing in FINSA or its legislative history suggests any departure from this focus on control. Indeed, FINSA incorporates the concept of control in its definition of the new term "covered transaction," as discussed above.

The Final Rule maintains the long-standing approach of defining "control" in functional terms as the ability to exercise certain powers over important matters affecting an entity. Specifically, "control" is defined as the "power, direct or indirect, whether or not exercised, through the ownership of a majority or a dominant minority of the total outstanding voting interest in an entity, board representation, proxy voting, a special share, contractual arrangements, formal or informal arrangements to act in concert, or other means, to determine, direct, or decide important matters affecting an entity; in particular, but without limitation, to determine, direct, take, reach, or cause decisions regarding the [matters listed in § 800.204(a)], or any other similarly important matters affecting an entity." *See* § 800.204(a). Two points should be emphasized concerning this definition. First, it eschews bright lines. Consistent with the existing regulations, control is not defined in terms of a specified percentage of shares or number of board seats. Although share holding and board seats are relevant to a control analysis, neither factor on its own is necessarily determinative. Instead, all relevant factors are considered together in light of their potential impact on a foreign person's ability to determine, direct, or decide important matters affecting an entity. Second, echoing the congressional views expressed in the conference report accompanying the original legislation in 1988, the focus of the statute and therefore of these regulations is *control*. Even acknowledging the considerable flexibility necessarily inherent in a national security regulation, the statutory standard is not satisfied by anything less than control. Acquisition

of influence falling short of the definition of control over a U.S. business is not sufficient to bring a transaction under section 721. *See* § 800.302.

Demonstrating its significance to this regulatory framework, the concept of control appears in several different places throughout the regulations, both in those sections that define the nature of the acquirer and those that define the transaction itself. For example, control is a key concept in the definitions of "foreign person" and "foreign government-controlled transaction." A foreign person is any foreign national (*i.e.*, an individual who is not a U.S. national), foreign government, or foreign entity, or any "entity over which *control* is exercised or exercisable by a foreign national, foreign government, or foreign entity." *See* § 800.216 (emphasis added). A foreign government-controlled transaction is a covered transaction that "could result in the *control* of a U.S. business by a foreign government or a person *controlled by* or acting on behalf of a foreign government." *See* § 800.214 (emphases added). Similarly, "covered transaction" is defined in this Final Rule as "any transaction that is proposed or pending after August 23, 1988, by or with any foreign person, which could result in *control* of a U.S. business by a foreign person." *See* § 800.207 (emphasis added).

Conversely, transactions that could not result in foreign control of a U.S. business are not subject to section 721. Thus, a start-up or "greenfield" investment is not subject to section 721. *See* § 800.301(c), Example 3. Moreover, as noted below, a foreign person does not control an entity if it holds ten percent or less of the voting interest in the entity and it holds that interest "solely for the purpose of passive investment," as that term is defined in § 800.223. *See* § 800.302(b). However, the regulations do not provide, and never have provided, an exemption based solely on whether an investment is ten percent or less in a U.S. business. If a foreign person holds ten percent or less of the voting interest in a U.S. business but does not hold that interest solely for the purpose of passive investment, then the transaction still may be a covered transaction. For example, a transaction involving a foreign person's acquisition of nine percent of the voting shares of a U.S. business in which the foreign person has negotiated rights to determine, direct, decide, take, reach, or cause decisions regarding important matters affecting that business would be a covered transaction.

Section 800.204 lays out the basic definition of "control," provides an illustrative list of matters that are deemed to be important, states that CFIUS will consider certain relationships between persons in evaluating whether an entity is considered to be controlled by a foreign person, and identifies certain minority shareholder protections that are not considered in themselves to confer control over an entity. The regulations add a number of examples to provide greater clarity as to the application of this definition.

U.S. Business

Section 800.226 defines "U.S. business," a term contained in the regulatory definition of "covered transaction," to mean any entity engaged in interstate commerce in the United States, but only to the extent of its activities in interstate commerce in the United States. In determining whether a person is a U.S. business, CFIUS first will consider whether the subject of the transaction is an "entity" (which is defined to include any branch, partnership, group or sub-group, association, estate, trust, corporation or division of a corporation, or organization; assets, whether or not organized as a separate legal entity, operated by any one of the foregoing as a business undertaking in a particular location or for particular products or services; and any government). If the subject of the transaction is an entity, CFIUS will consider whether the entity is engaged in interstate commerce.

Foreign Person

The term "foreign person" is defined in § 800.216. The Final Rule introduces the new concept of a "foreign entity," further discussed below in the section-by-section analysis of § 800.212, and specifies that an entity that falls within the definition of a "foreign entity" will be deemed a foreign person.

Transactions That Are and Are Not Covered Transactions

Sections 800.301 and 800.302 illustrate the types of transactions that are and are not covered transactions, respectively. Section 800.301(a) further develops the reference in § 800.204 to "power, whether or not exercised," by making clear that, if a foreign person has the ability to exercise control over a U.S. business at the time a transaction is consummated, whether at will or after a particular period of time, then the person cannot avoid a determination that "control" exists for purposes of section 721 by voluntarily forgoing, or delaying, the exercise of control.

Section 800.302(b) provides a very limited qualification to the application of the general control principle. Pursuant to § 800.302(b), a foreign person does not control an entity if it satisfies a two-pronged test: (1) It holds ten percent or less of the voting interest in the entity; and (2) its interest is held solely for the purpose of passive investment. Section 800.223 lays out the test for whether an interest is held solely for the purpose of passive investment. Under that test, an interest would be held solely for the purpose of passive investment if the foreign person has no plan or intent to control the entity, neither possesses nor develops any purpose other than passive investment, nor takes any action that is inconsistent with an intent to hold the interest solely for the purpose of passive investment. This special rule applies to all types of investors equally, rather than assuming that certain types of institutions are passive investors.

Sections 800.301(c) and 800.302(c) further illustrate the extent to which particular types of transactions, such as greenfield investments; the acquisition of branch offices, assets from multiple sources, and defunct businesses; and the entry into commodity purchase contracts, service contracts, and technology license agreements, are or are not covered transactions. Section 800.301(d) addresses joint ventures, which may be covered transactions only if they involve the contribution of a U.S. business.

Sections 800.302(d) and (e) and § 800.303 establish special rules with regard to securities underwriting, insurance, and lending, to clarify certain circumstances in which a foreign person may obtain, in the ordinary course of its business, an interest in an entity that may not be considered control of that entity because of those circumstances.

Section-by-Section Analysis

Section 800.101—Scope

Section 800.101 of the Proposed Rule states that the regulations implement section 721, which authorizes the President and the Committee to take certain actions with respect to covered transactions that threaten to impair U.S. national security. Several commenters noted that the regulations do not define "national security" and other related terms. A commenter suggested that there is a perception that the scope of CFIUS's reviews is broader than national security. Another suggested that "national security" be specifically defined to encompass economic security. A commenter also suggested that the Committee identify certain

excepted industries or businesses, investments in which would not be subject to review.

The Committee will continue its practice of focusing narrowly on genuine national security concerns alone, not broader economic or other national interests. The longstanding policy of the U.S. Government, which was reaffirmed in the President's Statement on Open Economies on May 10, 2007, is to welcome foreign investment. Section 1 of Executive Order 11858, as amended, applies that policy to the Committee's work: "It is the policy of the United States to support unequivocally [international] investment, consistent with the protection of the national security." The Committee reviews transactions for national security concerns on a case-by-case basis. This approach allows the Committee to fully address the national security concerns that a particular transaction may raise, rather than identifying certain sectors in which foreign investment is prohibited, restricted, or discouraged. As directed by FINSA, the Department of the Treasury is also publishing guidance regarding the types of transactions that the Committee has reviewed and that have presented national security considerations.

Section 800.103—Applicability rule/ Section 800.210—Effective Date

Several commenters expressed concern that new provisions in the regulations will cause uncertainty for transactions completed prior to the effective date of FINSA or this Final Rule and that parties should be given sufficient time to adjust to any new standards.

As provided in section 721 as amended by FINSA and further elaborated in § 800.207 and § 800.601(b) of the Final Rule, the Committee has the authority to review any covered transaction. However, to allow parties time to adjust to this Final Rule, the amendments to part 800 made by this Final Rule will become effective thirty days after their publication in the **Federal Register**.

With respect to actions already taken by parties to transactions, the Committee does not intend for this Final Rule to disrupt certain expectations created by the provisions of the regulations, prior to their amendment by this Final Rule. *See* 31 CFR Part 800 (July 1, 2008) ("the prior regulations"), *available at http://www.access.gpo.gov/ nara/cfr/waisidx_08/31cfr800_08.html.* Therefore, consistent with § 800.103, the provisions of the prior regulations will continue to govern certain questions pertaining to past transactions and acts.

As provided in § 800.103(a), the provisions of this Final Rule apply as of the effective date of this Final Rule, with certain exceptions. These exceptions are spelled out in § 800.103(b), and consist of the various provisions that relate to whether a particular transaction is a covered transaction. Provisions that pertain to procedural matters are thus not listed in paragraph (b) but, rather, apply to all CFIUS reviews and investigations as of the effective date. Accordingly, for example, all notices filed with the Committee on or after the effective date of this Final Rule must contain the information specified in § 800.402 of this Final Rule, regardless of when the transaction occurred or will occur. Notices filed with the Committee prior to the effective date of this Final Rule are required to contain at least the information specified in § 800.402 of the prior regulations.

As provided in § 800.103(b), particular sections of subparts B and C of this Final Rule apply to any transaction for which the execution of the agreement, or other comparable action underlying the transaction, occurs on or after the effective date of this Final Rule. As noted above, these provisions concern the assessment of whether a transaction is a "covered transaction." Paragraphs (b)(1) through (b)(4) of § 800.103 specify the particular event that needs to occur on or after the effective date in order for the relevant provision of the Final Rule to apply to the transaction. For example, if a letter of intent establishing the material terms of a transaction is signed on or after the effective date of this Final Rule, then the provisions of the Final Rule will govern the analysis of whether the transaction is a "covered transaction." Conversely, if the letter of intent was signed before the effective date of this Final Rule, then the Committee will look at the provisions of the prior regulations in analyzing whether the transaction is a "covered transaction," even if the transaction was notified to the Committee after the effective date of this Final Rule.

Note that if parties sign a letter of intent prior to the effective date of this Final Rule, but the material terms differ in the final definitive agreement signed by the parties, then the Committee would look to the date on which that final definitive agreement was signed to determine the rules under which the assessment of whether the transaction is a "covered transaction" will be made.

When reviewing any transaction notified to the Committee on or after the effective date that falls within the scope of § 800.103(b) and that includes minority shareholder protections listed in § 800.204(c), the Committee will take into account § 800.204(c) of the Final Rule to the extent that doing so would support a conclusion that the transaction is not a covered transaction.

As provided in subpart H, the provisions concerning penalties will apply to any action after the effective date of this Final Rule that constitutes a violation under subpart H, regardless of when the related transaction occurred or when the mitigation agreement was signed. If, for example, after the effective date of this Final Rule, a party intentionally violates a mitigation agreement signed in 2000, the party may be subject to civil penalties under § 800.801(b) of the Final Rule. Damages provisions written into mitigation agreements entered into prior to the effective date of this Final Rule are independent of, and not affected by, this Final Rule.

Section 800.204—Control

The Proposed Rule made a number of changes to clarify the definition of "control," which is now at § 800.204. These include, among other revisions, clarification that control depends on powers over "important matters" affecting an entity, expansion of the illustrative list of "important matters," and the addition or revision of examples to demonstrate what constitutes control. The Overview of Significant Issues, above, like the preamble to the Proposed Rule, also explains that the acquisition of influence falling short of the definition of control over a U.S. business is not sufficient to bring a transaction under section 721. The Proposed Rule also introduced a new paragraph concerning minority shareholder protections, which is addressed below in the discussion of § 800.204(c) of the Final Rule.

Several commenters suggested that the Proposed Rule provided too expansive a definition of control, or, by not providing a more objective standard, risked inappropriate expansion of the definition. A commenter suggested that the definition of control would cause foreign investors to disclaim *pro rata* rights they obtain simply by right of their shareholdings and suggested that this would be detrimental to good governance. Several commenters asked for additional clarification regarding the difference between "control" and "influence falling short of the definition of control."

The Final Rule makes numerous modifications to the language of § 800.204(a) to provide greater clarification of what constitutes "control," including by clarifying circumstances where influence does not rise to the level of control. Examples in this section show that, although an investor might have influence within a business—for example, through a board seat, exercising *pro rata* voting rights attendant with share ownership, or otherwise—it does not have control unless it is able to determine, direct, take, reach, or cause decisions regarding the types of important matters listed in § 800.204(a).

Commenters suggested further clarification of several specific important matters listed in § 800.204(a). Several commenters suggested that the power to determine, direct, or decide a single important matter affecting an entity should not constitute control and that, at the least, the Committee should clarify that it will consider the totality of the circumstances in making its assessment. Another commenter asked whether there is an ownership threshold at which control will always be found.

The Final Rule makes no changes to the list of important matters at § 800.204(a) in response to the commenters' requests for specific clarifications. The Committee approaches its analysis of whether a transaction could result in foreign control on a case-by-case basis, considering the level of ownership interest, the rights that emanate from such ownership, other rights held, restrictions on the exercise of such rights, and all other relevant facts and circumstances. The examples in § 800.204 demonstrate this approach of considering together all relevant facts and circumstances in light of their potential impact on a person's ability to determine, direct, or decide important matters affecting an entity. As a result of this approach, the regulations provide no ownership threshold or other bright lines above which CFIUS would find control in all circumstances.

Several commenters suggested that the Proposed Rule did not adequately illustrate that ownership and control can be separated through certain transaction structures—for example, in private equity funds structured as limited partnerships. One commenter suggested that the Committee clarify that it will review transactions involving private equity funds. The Final Rule adds Examples 8 and 9 in § 800.204, which provide greater clarification of the relationship between ownership and control and make clear that the Committee will focus on "control," as defined, within any transaction structure rather than formalistically distinguishing among structures.

A commenter asked for clarification of the meaning of "indirect" power in § 800.204(a). The Final Rule, like the Proposed Rule, defines "control" in functional terms. Therefore, for example, a person that has the power to determine important matters of an entity does not avoid having control of that entity by voting the shares of a wholly-owned subsidiary that, in turn, votes the shares of the entity, or by acting through another intermediary or agent.

Section 800.204(b)—Arrangements to Act in Concert

The Proposed Rule provided that, in examining questions of control in situations where more than one foreign person has an ownership interest in an entity, consideration will be given, pursuant to what is now § 800.204(b), to whether the foreign persons are related or have formal or "informal" arrangements to act in concert. A commenter asked for clarification of what constitutes an "informal" arrangement and whether this would include a voting trust.

The Final Rule makes no change to the proposed language, which is now at § 800.204(b), in response to this comment. If a trustee has the legal authority to vote the shares of different parties, even if unrelated, then those shares would be considered as being voted in concert if the trustee can vote the shares according to its discretion or is required to vote all shares in the same way. Example 1 in § 800.204 illustrates an informal arrangement to act in concert, where no formal agreement is disclosed but it is clear from other evidence that the foreign persons have agreed to act as a group in the exercise of their powers over important matters affecting the U.S. business.

Section 800.204(c)—Minority Shareholder Protections

The Proposed Rule identified several minority shareholder protections at what is now § 800.204(c) and provided that the Committee will not deem those negative rights (*i.e.*, rights to prevent certain events from occurring) to confer control in themselves. Many commenters suggested negative rights that they believe should be added to the list of minority shareholder protections. This Final Rule expands the list of minority shareholder protections, now at § 800.204(c), to include two additional negative rights: The power to prevent an entity from voluntarily filing for bankruptcy or liquidation, and the power to prevent the change of existing legal rights or preferences of the

particular class of stock held by minority investors as provided in the relevant corporate documents governing such shares.

The list in § 800.204(c), however, expressly is not intended to be exhaustive of the rights that shall not in themselves be deemed to confer control over an entity. Section 800.204(c) includes a list of negative rights that the Committee recognizes as minority shareholder protections because they protect the investment-backed expectations of minority shareholders and do not affect strategic decisions on business policy or day-to-day management of an entity or other important matters affecting an entity.

The Committee recognizes, however, that other negative rights proposed by commenters for inclusion in § 800.204(c) are often provided to minority shareholders. Section 800.204(d) explicitly provides that the Committee will consider, on a case-by-case basis, whether minority shareholder protections other than those listed in § 800.204(c) do not confer control over an entity. Non-inclusion in § 800.204(c) of any particular right does not mean that the Committee has determined that such a right necessarily results in control and does not prejudge whether the Committee would determine under § 800.204(d) that such a right does not confer control in a particular transaction.

The Committee will consider favorably in the context of specific transactions notified to the Committee the parties' opinion that the following minority shareholder protections do not in themselves confer control: The power to prevent changes in the capital structure of the entity, including through mergers, consolidations, or reorganizations, that would dilute or otherwise impair existing shareholder rights; the power to prevent the acquisition or disposition of assets material to the business outside the ordinary course of business; the power to prevent fundamental changes in the business or operational strategy of the entity; the power to prevent incursion of substantial indebtedness outside the ordinary course of business; the power to prevent fundamental changes to the entity's regulatory, tax, or liability status; and the power to prevent any amendment of the Articles of Incorporation, constituent agreement, or other organizational documents of an entity. The Committee's favorable consideration of these rights does not preclude it from finding that the existence of one or a combination of these rights confers control under the

facts and circumstances of a particular transaction.

Section 800.204(e)—Incremental Acquisitions

A commenter asked that the regulations clarify whether CFIUS will review voluntary notices when a foreign person acquires an additional interest in a U.S. business after the Committee has concluded its review of a prior covered transaction involving the same parties and the President did not prohibit or suspend the transaction. The Proposed Rule did not address this point explicitly. The commenter suggested that clarifying this point would help to ensure that the Committee is not overburdened and can focus its resources appropriately on transactions that raise national security concerns.

This Final Rule adds § 800.204(e) and accompanying Example 7 to clarify the Committee's approach to incremental acquisitions. Pursuant to § 800.204(e), a transaction in which a foreign person acquires an additional interest in a U.S. business that was previously the subject of a covered transaction for which the Committee concluded all action under section 721 will not be considered a covered transaction.

If a prior investment by a foreign person in a U.S. business was not notified to CFIUS, or if CFIUS determined that the prior investment was not a covered transaction, then the subsequent investment may be a covered transaction, depending on whether the subsequent investment could result in the foreign person's control of the U.S. business.

With respect to any covered transaction, any mitigation agreement or conditions may include, subject to the requirements of section 721 and Executive Order 11858, measures to address any national security risk posed by the covered transaction, including any increased risk if the foreign acquirer were to have a greater ownership interest in the U.S. business.

Section 800.207—Covered Transaction

The Proposed Rule defined "covered transaction" consistent with the definition of that term in section 721. The Proposed Rule provided additional clarity about what transactions are covered by section 721 in numerous other provisions, including §§ 800.301 and 800.302 and the definitions of "control," "foreign person," and a "U.S. business." A commenter suggested that the Committee regularly release redacted descriptions of transactions that have been filed with the Committee, along with descriptions of the Committee's assessment of whether they were covered transactions.

The Final Rule does not adopt this suggestion. Public release of any assessment by the Committee of whether a transaction is a covered transaction would implicate significant potential national security and confidentiality concerns. The Final Rule, at §§ 800.207, 800.301 and 800.302, provides greater clarity regarding what transactions are covered by section 721. Parties to a transaction, at their own discretion, may make available to the public information about transactions that they have voluntarily notified to the Committee.

Section 800.208—Critical Infrastructure

The Proposed Rule defined "critical infrastructure" consistent with the definition of that term in section 721 and clarified that, in determining whether a covered transaction involves critical infrastructure, the Committee would consider the "particular" systems or assets involved, rather than defining certain classes of systems or assets as critical infrastructure. Several commenters expressed support for this approach. Others suggested that the scope of "critical infrastructure" be further illustrated by identifying infrastructure that would or would not be considered critical.

The Final Rule, at § 800.208, continues the case-by-case approach of section 721 and the Proposed Rule towards identifying critical infrastructure. Under this approach, the Committee determines whether (1) a particular transaction notified to it is a "covered transaction," (2) that particular covered transaction would result in foreign control of critical infrastructure of or within the United States, and (3) that particular covered transaction has potential national security effects. Accordingly, the definition of critical infrastructure turns on the national security effects of any incapacity or destruction of the particular system or asset over which a foreign person would have control as a result of a covered transaction. Consistent with this approach, the Committee will not deem classes of systems or assets to be, or not to be, critical infrastructure.

Section 800.211—Entity

The Proposed Rule made clear that an entity need not have a distinct legal personality in order to fall within the definition of "entity" under these regulations. A commenter asked for clarification of the circumstances in which assets with no distinct legal

personality would be considered an "entity."

The Final Rule amends the proposed text of § 800.211 to add a cross-reference to §§ 800.301(c) and 800.302(c), which provide additional clarity regarding when assets with no distinct legal personality can constitute an "entity" and, in turn, a "U.S. business." This additional clarification is provided, in particular, by Examples 6 and 7 in § 800.301(c) and Examples 1, 2, 4, and 5 in § 800.302(c).

Section 800.212—Foreign Entity

The Proposed Rule introduced a new term, "foreign entity," to refer to entities the Committee considers to be foreign persons based on either their place of organization and foreign exchange listing or the extent of their foreign ownership, even if no single foreign person controls the entity. Commenters expressed concern that the definition of "foreign entity" in the Proposed Rule would have captured entities that were incorporated outside of the United States if they were primarily traded on foreign exchanges, even if the entities were in fact majority-owned by U.S. nationals.

The Final Rule revises the proposed text of § 800.212 to cover entities organized under the laws of a foreign state if either its principal place of business is outside the United States or its equity securities are primarily traded on one or more foreign exchanges. The Final Rule excludes from the definition of "foreign entity," however, any entity that is able to demonstrate to the Committee that a majority of the equity interest in the entity is ultimately owned by U.S. nationals. Note that, under the definition of "foreign person" at § 800.216(b), any entity over which control is exercised or exercisable by a foreign person would still itself be deemed a foreign person, even if that entity does not constitute a "foreign entity." Accordingly, an entity controlled by a foreign person is itself a foreign person, even if it is majority owned by U.S. nationals.

Commenters also asked whether a foreign person's ownership of shares of an entity could result in that entity being considered a "foreign entity" if the right to vote that person's shares were transferred to U.S. nationals through a voting trust. Example 3 in § 800.301(a) of the Final Rule illustrates that an agreement to delay the exercise of voting rights for a limited period of time does not preclude a finding of control. Similarly, if a voting trust is revocable or time-limited, the Committee would consider the foreign

person that placed its shares in such a voting trust as still holding the shares.

Finally, a commenter asked whether the definition of "foreign entity" was intended to be a standard for determining foreign government control. The definition of "foreign entity" is not intended to be a standard for determining foreign government control. If an entity could be controlled by a foreign government, the question of whether it is a "foreign entity" would never arise, as "foreign entity" is a term that is intended to cover situations where there is significant foreign ownership but ownership is dispersed.

Section 800. 213—Foreign Government

The Proposed Rule defined the term "foreign government" to include non-elected heads of state with governmental responsibilities. A commenter said that the term "head of state" in § 800.213 was unclear.

The Final Rule amends § 800.213 to delete the clause referring to certain heads of state, since it imprecisely defined the circumstances under which the Committee may treat an investment by a government official as being an investment by a foreign government. Consistent with the reference in § 800.214 to a person "acting on behalf of a foreign government," the Final Rule permits the Committee to treat investments by foreign government officials as investments by foreign governments where the circumstances so warrant, such as in certain cases where an official invests to advance governmental objectives.

Section 800. 214—Foreign Government-Controlled Transaction

The Proposed Rule defined "foreign government-controlled transaction" to mean any covered transaction that could result in control of a U.S. business by a foreign government or a person controlled by or acting on behalf of a foreign government. Commenters suggested that, in considering whether a transaction is foreign government-controlled, the regulations should treat certain types of entities owned by foreign governments or that have a "government background" as not foreign government-controlled—for example, if they operate on a purely commercial and market-driven basis.

The Final Rule makes no changes to the proposed text of § 800.214. "Foreign government-controlled transaction" is defined by statute at section 721(a)(4) and may not be modified by regulation in a manner that is inconsistent with the statute. The statute makes clear that transactions are "foreign government-controlled transactions" if they could result in the control of any person engaged in interstate commerce in the United States by a foreign government or an entity controlled by or acting on behalf of a foreign government, regardless of whether the transaction has a purely commercial and market-driven basis. Accordingly, the regulations do not exclude transactions involving entities controlled by a foreign government, even if the entities operate on a commercial basis, nor entities that are controlled only indirectly by a foreign government through a person controlled by or acting on behalf of a foreign government. Consistent with section 721(b)(2)(E), however, the Department of the Treasury, as Chairperson of the Committee, is publishing guidance regarding the types of transactions that the Committee has reviewed and that have presented national security considerations. That guidance clarifies that whether a foreign government-controlled entity operates on a purely commercial and market-driven basis is among the important factors that the Committee takes into consideration when assessing whether foreign government control in a particular transaction poses concerns about possible impairment of U.S. national security.

Section 800.216—Foreign Person

The Proposed Rule expanded the definition of "foreign person" to include the term "foreign entity" and added a number of examples. A commenter suggested that the examples in § 800.216 and § 800.226, which respectively define "foreign person" and "U.S. business," be expanded to make clear that the two concepts are distinct. A commenter also expressed concern that an acquisition by an investment fund controlled by a foreign bank may be treated differently under the regulations than would an acquisition by an investment fund controlled by U.S. nationals.

The Final Rule makes no changes to the proposed text of § 800.216 and § 800.226. The terms "foreign person" and "U.S. business" are independent of one another and serve distinct purposes in the Final Rule. Accordingly, it is possible that a particular entity may be just a foreign person, just a U.S. business, both a foreign person and a U.S. business simultaneously, or neither a U.S. business nor a foreign person.

Section 721 and this Final Rule, which implements section 721, cover transactions after a certain date that could result in control of a U.S. business by a foreign person. Accordingly, whether a party that controls an investment fund is, or is not, a foreign person is central to the statutory and regulatory framework.

Section 800.220—Party or Parties to a Transaction

The Proposed Rule provided, at § 800.220(f), that any party in a role comparable to a party listed in paragraphs (a) through (e) of § 800.220 would also be deemed a "party to a transaction." A commenter suggested that § 800.220(f) provides the Committee with excessive discretion.

The Final Rule makes no change to the proposed text of § 800.220. Paragraph (f) of that section does not expand the scope of what constitutes a covered transaction. Rather, it identifies what persons, in circumstances other than those covered by paragraphs (a) through (e), are considered to be a "party to a transaction" and, therefore, may file a voluntary notice with the Committee consistent with the requirements of § 800.402.

Section 800.224—Transaction

The Proposed Rule replaced the term "acquisition" with the term "transaction," at § 800.224, in order to harmonize the terminology of the regulations with that of FINSA, and provided that a transaction is a "proposed or consummated merger, acquisition, or takeover." One commenter suggested that the Committee should not have the authority to review transactions after they have been completed. However, if a transaction is proposed after August 23, 1988 and could result in foreign control of a U.S. business, then it would be a "covered transaction," as defined in section 721, even if the transaction has been consummated by the time of review.

In addition to other clarifications of the definition, the Proposed Rule also clarified that certain joint ventures and long-term leases are "transactions." In particular, the Proposed Rule provided that long-term leases are transactions when, because of the terms of the lease and the extent of the lessee's authority over the U.S. business, the lessee operates the business as if it were the owner. A commenter asked whether a long-term lease in which a lessor retained only minimal oversight responsibilities and the ability to impose penalties in the event of a contractual breach would not constitute a "transaction" under § 800.224(f) and the example in § 800.224.

The Final Rule makes no change to § 800.224(f) or the example in § 800.224 in response to the comment. As a general matter, and as reflected in the example in § 800.224, the more significant the substantive responsibilities retained by the lessor over the leased property, the likelier that the lease would not be viewed as a transaction.

Section 800.301(d)—Joint Ventures

The Proposed Rule, in § 800.301(d), harmonized the application of the term "covered transaction" to joint ventures with its application to all other transactions. Thus, the Proposed Rule provided that the creation of a joint venture is a covered transaction if a U.S. business is contributed to the joint venture and a foreign person could gain control of that U.S. business through the creation of the joint venture. Example 1 in § 800.301(d) of the Proposed Rule stated that the creation of a 50/50 joint venture by a foreign person and a party that contributes a U.S. business is a covered transaction, with respect to the U.S. business. A commenter suggested that such a transaction should not be a covered transaction because the power that the foreign person has over the U.S. business is no greater than the other party's.

The Final Rule makes no change in response to the comment described above. To the extent that a joint venture involves the contribution of a U.S. business, a foreign 50/50 joint venture partner would obtain the same degree of power over the important matters affecting that joint venture—and therefore the U.S. business—as if the foreign person had made a direct investment in that U.S. business to obtain a 50 percent interest. The acquisition of a 50 percent interest in an existing U.S. business is not viewed differently with regard to foreign control based on whether it is structured as a direct investment or a joint venture. When all ownership interests in a U.S. business are held by two equal partners, each partner is able to veto all important matters affecting the U.S. business, so each partner controls the U.S. business.

Section 800.302(b) of the Regulations Issued in 1991—Corporate Reorganizations

The Proposed Rule omitted a provision that had been included in the 1991 regulations, at § 800.302(b). The omitted provision stated that an acquisition is not subject to review under section 721 if the parent of the entity making the acquisition is the same as the parent of the entity being acquired. A commenter suggested reintroducing the omitted provision or confirming that the principle continues to apply.

The Final Rule does not reintroduce the omitted provision. Section 721, as amended by FINSA, requires the Committee to review any transaction notified to it that could result in control of a U.S. business by a foreign person. A corporate reorganization that results in a new foreign person acquiring control of a U.S. business would be a covered transaction, even though the ultimate parent of the U.S. business may not have changed. Thus, the Committee must treat such a reorganization as a covered transaction. Such a reorganization, however, will present national security considerations only in exceptional cases, as is explained in greater detail in guidance that the Department of the Treasury, as Chairperson of the Committee, is publishing on the types of transactions that the Committee has reviewed and that have presented national security considerations.

Section 800.302(b)—Solely for the Purpose of Passive Investment

The Proposed Rule provided in § 800.302(c) that a transaction that results in a foreign person holding ten percent or less of the outstanding voting interests in a U.S. business is not a covered transaction if the transaction is "solely for the purpose of investment." In § 800.223, "solely for the purpose of investment" was defined to refer to ownership interests in which the person holding or acquiring such interests has no plan or intent to exercise control, and takes no actions that indicate otherwise. Some commenters suggested that the term "solely for the purpose of investment" was too vague and created additional uncertainty for portfolio investors. A commenter also suggested clarifying that investors holding less than ten percent of the interests of a business can wield significant influence.

The Final Rule addresses these comments by clarifying that the rule for holdings of ten percent or less of the outstanding voting interests in a U.S. business—which is now at § 800.302(b) of the Final Rule—applies only to interests that are held or acquired "solely for the purpose of passive investment." The addition of the word "passive" emphasizes that this rule does not pertain to a transaction if the foreign person plans or intends to gain control over the U.S. business. The example in § 800.223 of the Final Rule also makes clear that the Committee will consider whether the foreign person's negotiation of rights constitutes evidence that the foreign person possesses a purpose other than passive investment. Under the Final Rule, a transaction would not

be a "covered transaction" if the foreign person holds ten percent or less of the voting shares in a U.S. business and the investment is passive such as where, for example, the foreign investor has no affirmative rights other than the ability to vote its shares *pro rata* and no negative rights other than any minority shareholder protection listed in § 800.204(c) or as considered by the Committee on a case-by-case basis under § 800.204(d).

A commenter also suggested that the Proposed Rule be revised to identify a mechanism for tracking whether, after the Committee determines that this rule applies to a transaction, the foreign person develops plans or an intent to control the U.S. business or takes action inconsistent with passive intent. The Final Rule makes no change to the proposed language in response to this comment. The Committee will inform the parties if it determines a notified transaction is not a covered transaction because the investment is held or acquired solely for the purpose of passive investment. Should material facts change in the future relating to whether the foreign person has control of the U.S. business, the transaction may become a covered transaction subject to section 721.

A commenter also suggested that the rule regarding transactions solely for the purpose of passive investment should be expressed in terms of whether the foreign person has ten percent or less of the outstanding "ownership interest" in the U.S. business, rather than the "voting interest."

The Final Rule does not adopt this suggestion because it would not cover an investor whose voting power in a U.S. business is disproportionately large compared to its ownership interest. Such an investor could have the ability to exercise control, even though its ownership interest is under the ten percent threshold. For example, where a company has issued a class of non-voting stock, it is possible that a foreign person may have ten percent or less of the outstanding stock of a company, but still have greater than ten percent of the voting stock, possibly giving it powers that are disproportionate to its share of all outstanding stock.

Section 800.303—Lending Transactions

The Proposed Rule, at § 800.303, established a special rule that described the circumstances in which a foreign lender may obtain ownership of collateral but not be deemed to control that collateral. The Proposed Rule also intended to clarify that a lending transaction, even where accompanied by a security interest in property,

ordinarily does not convey control. Several commenters expressed concern that § 800.303 could be read to suggest that loans could be considered covered transactions based on the presence of standard negative covenants in the loan documents and requested that the Committee clarify that this is not the case.

This Final Rule revises § 800.303 to provide more clearly that loans themselves are not "transactions" (defined in § 800.224), except where the foreign person acquires economic or governance rights in the U.S. business characteristic of an equity investment, but not of a loan. Loan covenants that give the lender a negative right over certain decisions of the borrower, therefore, would not result in the loan itself being subject to these regulations, so long as the foreign person does not acquire economic or governance rights in the U.S. business characteristic of an equity investment but not of a loan. Consistent with that rule, and as provided in Example 3 in § 800.303 of the Final Rule, if the loan agreement were to extend to the lender the right to be on the board of the borrower and the right to receive dividends from the borrower, the loan would be considered a "transaction" and would be a covered transaction if these or other powers that the lender receives as a result of the loan would constitute "control," as defined in § 800.204. Note that the acquisition of control of a U.S. business by a foreign lender as a result of a borrower's default on a loan would still be considered a covered transaction, except in the circumstances described in § 800.303(c) or where the Committee determines that there is no control as a result of its assessment of the factors identified in § 800.303(a)(2).

Several commenters suggested that, in assessing whether a loan could give the lender control over the borrower, the Committee should take into account the fact that lending transactions and banks are subject to other regulatory regimes, both in the United States and abroad. Section 721, however, creates a separate statutory process from that created under banking and other laws, with different purposes and standards. The Committee's determinations regarding control are independent of such other laws.

The Proposed Rule, at § 800.303(a)(1), provides that the Committee will accept a notice when default becomes imminent or some "other condition" arises that would result in a "significant possibility" that the foreign lender may obtain control of the U.S. business. One commenter asked for further clarification of what "other conditions" are and what constitutes a "significant possibility." As a general matter, the Committee declines to accept notices of covered transactions where the occurrence of the transaction is speculative or remote. Accordingly, the Final Rule continues to provide that the Committee will accept notices of loans that do not, by themselves, constitute covered transactions, only when, because of imminent or actual default or other condition, there is a significant possibility that the foreign person may obtain control of the U.S. business. Such a "significant possibility" may exist, for example, where several persons other than the foreign lender also have security interests in the same collateral and it is very possible, but not certain, that the foreign lender will obtain control.

Several commenters expressed concern about the possible effect of § 800.303 on the validity of lenders' security interests. For example, a security interest, upon default, may result in "control" of the collateral by the lender, and section 721 authorizes the President to suspend or prohibit covered transactions in certain circumstances. To the extent that a security interest may be suspended or prohibited by the President under section 721 upon default, a commenter objected to the limitation on notifying the transaction until default becomes imminent or some other condition arises that would result in a significant possibility that the foreign lender may obtain control of the U.S. business in which it has a security interest. The commenters also requested that the Committee allow a reasonable period of time for a lender to transfer management decisions or day-to-day control over the U.S. business to U.S. nationals.

The Final Rule recognizes in § 800.303 that foreign persons that make loans in the ordinary course, such as commercial banks, do not do so in hopes of acquiring control over collateral in the event of default and retaining possession of the collateral indefinitely. Section 800.303(a)(2) allows the Committee to provide the foreign person with the time needed to dispose of collateral of which it has taken possession, so long as the foreign person has made arrangements to transfer management decisions or day-to-day control over the U.S. business to U.S. nationals during the interim period.

Section 800.304—Timing Rule for Convertible Voting Instruments

Several commenters expressed concern over the treatment of convertible voting instruments in § 800.302(b) of the Proposed Rule. One commenter suggested that the Proposed Rule might inadvertently eliminate the Committee's flexibility to determine on a case-by-case basis whether the acquisition of convertible voting instruments should be deemed to confer control even without the conversion of such instruments. Another commenter suggested that the Proposed Rule's treatment of convertible voting instruments inappropriately would cover transactions that result in foreign influence falling short of control, because it is only upon conversion that the holder receives rights relevant to control.

The Final Rule revises the provision, which now appears at § 800.304, to further clarify that the Committee will consider the circumstances of conversion in order to determine whether the Committee will include the rights that the holder will obtain upon conversion in its assessment of whether a notified transaction that includes such instruments could result in control. This rule allows the Committee to consider the rights that would result from the conversion of the instruments at an appropriate time. In some cases, such as where the results of conversion are reasonably ascertainable and the conversion is in the near future, the Committee will consider such rights when the acquisition of the convertible instruments is notified to the Committee. In other cases, such as where conversion is speculative or remote, the Committee may choose not to consider the rights that would result from conversion at the time of the notified transaction. In such cases, however, the Committee consistent with § 800.304(b), may, still consider whether the acquisition of the convertible voting instruments is a covered transaction because of any immediate rights that they convey to the holder with respect to the governance of the entity that issued the instruments. Furthermore, once the conversion of the instruments becomes imminent, it may be appropriate for the Committee to consider the rights that would result from conversion and whether the conversion is a covered transaction.

Section 800.401—Procedures for Notice

The Proposed Rule, at § 800.401, explicitly encouraged parties to a transaction to consult with the Committee prior to filing a notice. The preamble to the Proposed Rule made clear that pre-notice consultations give the Committee an opportunity to understand the transaction and to suggest information that the parties may wish to include in their notice to assist the Committee in addressing any national security considerations as efficiently as possible. Commenters asked for additional information regarding the purpose of such prefiling communications and when such communications would be appropriate.

The Final Rule leaves § 800.401(f) unchanged. Prefiling consultations may be particularly helpful where a party to the transaction has not previously prepared a notice for submission to the Committee or where a transaction is unusually complex. Included within the broad spectrum of prefiling consultations that may be helpful are: (1) Informing the Staff Chairperson orally or in writing of a transaction that may be filed and the date it may be filed; (2) requesting in writing that the Staff Chairperson modify a requirement in § 800.402, as further described below; (3) asking the Staff Chairperson procedural questions orally or in writing; (4) requesting a meeting with the Staff Chairperson, other Treasury official, or other Committee staff, to provide information on a transaction and to allow the Staff Chairperson and others to pose questions that may help the party identify information it may wish to include in a voluntary notice; and (5) providing a draft of the voluntary notice.

Several commenters suggested that the Committee provide a binding decision on whether a transaction is a covered transaction before a full voluntary notice is submitted to the Committee under § 800.401. One commenter expressed opposition to this proposal, suggesting that, prior to receipt of a full voluntary notice, the Committee might err on the side of caution in finding that transactions are covered transactions.

The Committee has not made any changes in the Final Rule in response to these comments. The Committee recognizes the potential utility of a preliminary determination on whether a transaction is a covered transaction. The proposal for a timely, yet binding, decision through a new and separate prefiling process, however, would create a substantial new burden on the CFIUS process, thus undermining the Committee's ability to meet its statutory deadlines. As a determination that might fall outside the statutorily defined review and investigation process, it also raises potential concerns regarding consistency with section 721 that would require further examination.

A commenter requested that the Department of the Treasury accept voluntary notices without requiring that they be broken into multiple electronic files. The Final Rule makes no changes to the proposed language of § 800.401, which makes no reference to this requirement. The Staff Chairperson does currently request, however, that large submissions be broken into smaller electronic files because information technology capabilities vary widely across the government departments and offices to which the Staff Chairperson forwards each notice. The Department of the Treasury is exploring options to improve the process for receipt and distribution of notices.

Section 800.402—Contents of Voluntary Notice

The Proposed Rule, at § 800.402, expanded the information that must be included in a voluntary notice submitted to the Committee to require certain additional information that the Committee routinely has requested of parties. Several commenters argued that the information requirements of § 800.402 are onerous and suggested that the significant time and expense that they predicted would be required to prepare a notice may discourage voluntary filings. Commenters stated that some of the information requirements may not be relevant in particular cases and suggested asking only for a narrower set of information in each case, supplemented by additional data based on the type of industry, transaction, or the parties. A commenter also suggested a short-form notice that would provide the parties something less than the safe harbor provided in § 800.601 upon the Committee's completion of its review.

The Final Rule makes several significant changes to the proposed language of § 800.402(c) to narrow the scope of some of the information required, as discussed further below. In those cases where the information sought under § 800.402(c) is not applicable to the notified transaction, the voluntary notice should state so. Except where the Staff Chairperson modifies a particular information requirement for a particular filer as described below or where a party states, and the Staff Chairperson agrees, that a request is not applicable, a voluntary notice will not comply with § 800.402 if any information required in § 800.402 is missing.

In extraordinary cases, parties may request that the Staff Chairperson modify an information requirement in these Final Rules for a particular transaction. All such requests must be submitted in writing to the Staff Chairperson before filing a notice. The Staff Chairperson will consider accommodating such a request only in the exceptional case where a

requirement would place an extraordinary burden on the parties and where modification would not impair the full and efficient consideration of the transaction. For example, the Staff Chairperson may consider a request by a small company to modify the requirement at § 800.701(b), to allow the company to submit a certified translation of only portions of its annual report. The Staff Chairperson, however, will not consider waiving the requirement at § 800.402(c)(6)(vi) for personal identifier information regarding certain key personnel. If the Staff Chairperson grants the request for modification, the justification that was provided in the written request must be included in the party's voluntary notice. Even after a request has been granted, the Committee may request the information after the notice has been submitted, in which case § 800.403(a)(3) will apply, and completion of the review or investigation, within the constraints of section 721, may take longer than if the information had been provided at the outset.

A commenter requested confirmation that submission of a voluntary notice is not an admission that a transaction is a covered transaction. The Committee will not treat a voluntary filing as an admission that the transaction is a covered transaction. Furthermore, the Final Rule makes a minor change to the proposed language of § 800.402(j), clarifying that parties filing a voluntary notice are required to state their "opinion" (rather than "full statement of [their] view," as provided in the Proposed Rule) as to whether the transaction is a covered transaction.

Commenters suggested changes to two proposed information requirements regarding the value of the transaction. The Final Rule modifies the proposed language of § 800.402(c)(1)(viii) to request a "good faith approximation of the net value of the interest acquired" rather than a statement of the full value of the transaction and a description of how it was derived. The Final Rule modifies the proposed language of § 800.402(c)(3)(i) to require identification of the methodology used to determine market share, rather than how the estimate was derived, although the Committee may request such an explanation on a case-by-case basis after a review is initiated.

The Proposed Rule, at § 800.402(c)(3)(iv), required filers to identify each contract that was in effect within the past three years with any U.S. Government agency. In response to comments suggesting that the Proposed Rule was unnecessarily broad, the Final Rule significantly narrows the proposed

language, requiring identification of any contract in effect within the past three years with any U.S. Government agency or component with national defense, homeland security, or other national security responsibilities, including law enforcement as it relates to defense, homeland security, or national security.

The Proposed Rule, at § 800.402(c)(3)(vi), required information regarding rebranding or incorporation of the U.S. business's products or services by another company or in another company's products. Several commenters suggested this requirement may prove highly burdensome in some cases. The Final Rule makes no change to the proposed language. In those exceptional cases where the requirement is extraordinarily burdensome, however, the filer may request that the Staff Chairperson modify this requirement, subject to the conditions stated above regarding such requests. Such a request may be considered, for example, where the U.S. business produces and sells a raw material to thousands of manufacturers.

The Proposed Rule, at § 800.402(c)(3)(vii), required identification of priority rated contracts or orders for the past three years. A commenter noted that the Proposed Rule requested information on the target company's plans to ensure that it or any new entity formed at the completion of the transaction would remain in compliance with the Defense Priorities and Allocations System (DPAS) regulations. The commenter suggested that the language be amended to request a statement of the plans of the acquiring party (rather than the U.S. business itself) to ensure compliance of the U.S. business or newly formed U.S. business with the DPAS regulations. The Final Rule makes the suggested changes. Another commenter suggested that the requirement that parties identify all priority rated contracts and orders for the past three years could require a voluminous production. The Final Rule makes no change in this regard. Parties that comply with the three-year record-keeping requirement of the DPAS regulations should not face a significant burden in complying with this subsection.

The Proposed Rule, at § 800.402(c)(3)(viii), required a description and copy of cyber security plans. A commenter suggested this may be irrelevant in some cases and could be misinterpreted to suggest that a cyber security plan is expected in conjunction with foreign acquisitions. The Final Rule makes no change to this proposed requirement. The subsection refers to plans that any company may have to protect its information technology systems, regardless of whether the company is in the information technology industry. The subsection requires submission of any such cyber security plan but does not state a view as to the appropriateness of a plan in any particular case.

A commenter interpreted § 800.402(c)(4)(i) of the Proposed Rule as requiring filers to identify and classify under the Export Administration Regulations ("EAR") almost every item that the U.S. business produces or trades in, since all items subject to the EAR bear at least the designation EAR99. As noted by other commenters, however, this subsection, which has not been modified by the Final Rule, allows filers to provide commodity classifications for items by general product categories, which does not require the identification or classification of every individual item produced or traded.

The Proposed Rule, at § 800.402(c)(4)(ii)(B), required filers to identify articles and services that have not been, but may be, designated or determined to be covered by the U.S. Munitions List pursuant to 22 CFR 120.3. Commenters suggested that the scope of this requirement was ambiguous. The Final Rule revises this provision to make clear that the requirement includes articles and services "under development" that may be designated or determined in the future to be defense articles or defense services pursuant to 22 CFR 120.3.

The Proposed Rule, at § 800.402(c)(5)(i), required filers to identify certain licenses, permits, and authorizations that have been granted by an agency of the U.S. Government. A commenter questioned whether this would extend to sewer permits, motor vehicle licenses, business licenses, and other similar state or local permits, licenses or authorizations. The Final Rule makes no change to the proposed subsection. The requirement applies only to licenses, permits, and authorizations that have been granted by an agency of the "United States Government," a term which refers only to federal—not state or local—government.

The Proposed Rule, at § 800.402(c)(6)(ii), required filers to identify the foreign person's plans with respect to the U.S. business's operations. A commenter suggested that this requirement has no relation to national security. The Final Rule makes no change in response to the comment because a foreign person's intentions with respect to the operations of the U.S. business may be central to the national security analysis, depending on the relevance of the business to U.S. national security interests.

The Proposed Rule, at § 800.402(c)(6)(iv)(D), required filers to state whether a foreign government has any affirmative or negative rights not already identified in the filing that could be relevant to the Committee's determination of whether the notified transaction is a foreign government-controlled transaction. A commenter suggested that the requirement be limited to "material" rights. The Final Rule makes no change to the proposed language because the requirement is already limited to rights "that could be relevant" to the determination of whether the transaction is a foreign government-controlled transaction.

The Proposed Rule, at § 800.402(c)(6)(vi) and (vii), required filers to provide certain biographical and personal identifier information for certain key personnel affiliated with the foreign acquirer and its parents. Commenters asked for clarification regarding how the two sections differ. Commenters also suggested that the information be required: Only for individuals affiliated with the immediate acquirer, the ultimate parent, and other entities that have control or have a role in the transaction; only if the information has not been provided in connection with another transaction in the preceding six months; or, with regard to shareholders, only at a threshold higher than five percent. Commenters also suggested that the scope of the requirement for information on government and military service be clarified and narrowed.

The Final Rule combines the two proposed subsections into § 800.402(c)(6)(vi) and identifies a single group of individuals for whom filers must provide a curriculum vitae or similar professional synopsis as part of the main notice, as well as certain other personal identifier information in a separate document to facilitate special handling. Such information must be provided for each member of the board of directors and each officer of the foreign person engaged in the transaction and its immediate, intermediate, and ultimate parents (see § 800.219 for the definition of "parent"), and for any individual having an ownership interest of five percent or more in the foreign person engaged in the transaction and in its ultimate parent. The Final Rule does not remove this requirement with respect to foreign acquirers that were involved in a transaction within the preceding six months because the storage and retrieval of such information would create substantial new burdens on the Committee. The Final Rule, at § 800.402(c)(6)(vi), also narrows the foreign military service information requirement. Filers are not required to provide details of foreign military service where the service was at a rank below the top two non-commissioned ranks of the foreign country. Filers must continue to provide the dates and nature of all other military and government service.

Section 800.403—Deferral, Rejection, or Disposition of Certain Voluntary Notices

The Proposed Rule provided in § 800.403(a)(3) that the Staff Chairperson of the Committee may reject a voluntary filing if a party fails to provide any follow-up information requested by CFIUS within two business days. Many commenters suggested that this requirement was too onerous and suggested expansion of the response time to three or five business days. One commenter also asked the Committee to clarify that holidays in both the United States and in the responding foreign party's home country would not be counted as business days.

The Final Rule revises § 800.403(a)(3) to extend the time allowed to a party to respond to a request for follow-up information to three business days, which appropriately balances the burden to parties to a transaction notified to CFIUS and the needs of the Committee to complete a review or investigation on a timely basis. The Final Rule also adds a definition of "business day" at § 800.201 to exclude legal public holidays in the United States. This definition does not exclude other countries' holidays, so as to encourage a uniformly efficient review process.

Section 800.503—Determination of Whether To Undertake an Investigation

The Proposed Rule reiterated in § 800.503(a) the standards provided by statute and Executive Order for initiating an investigation. Two commenters suggested that the standards were not clear or objective. They asked that the regulations identify the factors that agencies must consider in assessing whether there is a threat to national security and require disclosure of the rationale for the Committee's determination. Two commenters suggested that one of the standards in particular—at § 800.503(a)(1)—would make investigations inevitable in most cases, since it can be triggered by any one member of the Committee other than an *ex officio* member.

The Final Rule makes no changes to the proposed text of § 800.503. The standards for initiation of investigations are drawn directly from section 721(b)(2)(B) and section 6(b) of Executive Order 11858. Even after FINSA became effective on October 24, 2007, the vast majority of cases have been completed within the initial 30-day review period, demonstrating that the standards for initiation of investigations do not make investigations inevitable.

Section 721(f) identifies factors for the Committee to consider, as appropriate, in assessing effects of a covered transaction on national security. Guidance on the types of transactions that have raised national security considerations that the Department of the Treasury, as Chairperson of the Committee, will publish separately in the **Federal Register** consistent with with section 721(b)(2)(E) provides additional context for those factors. The Committee's assessment of the national security effects of covered transactions is based on, among other things, sensitive business information submitted by the parties and classified U.S. Government information. Thus, the rationale for the Committee's determination in any particular case cannot be made public. Safeguards in section 721 and Executive Order 11858, however, ensure that actions taken by the President or the Committee are taken only to address legitimate national security concerns. For example, any risk mitigation must be based on a written analysis of the national security risk posed by the covered transaction and of the risk mitigation measures believed to be reasonably necessary to address the risk. In addition, the President cannot exercise his authority to suspend or prohibit a covered transaction under section 721 unless he finds: (1) That there is credible evidence that leads the President to believe that the foreign interest exercising control might take action that threatens to impair the national security; and (2) that provisions of law, other than section 721 and the International Emergency Economic Powers Act, do not, in the judgment of the President, provide adequate and appropriate authority for the President to protect the national security.

A commenter also noted that the standard for initiating an investigation set forth in § 800.503(b)(2) of the Proposed Rule omits a phrase included in section 721(b)(2)(B)(i)(III). The commenter asked that the phrase "by assurances provided or renewed with the approval of the Committee" be added to the proposed text of § 800.503(b)(2), to remind parties that national security concerns may be mitigated by prior mitigation

agreements. The Final Rule does not make the requested addition. The point that the commenter wished to emphasize through the addition is correct. Entering into mitigation agreements, however, is not the only means of resolving any national security concerns. The Committee may also determine that any such concerns can be resolved through other applicable laws besides section 721 that adequately address national security risks raised by a covered transaction.

A commenter suggested that foreign government-controlled transactions should not be subject to an automatic investigation trigger. Section 721(b)(2)(B), however, requires that the Committee conduct an investigation of foreign government-controlled transactions. The Committee is allowed, pursuant to section 721(b)(2)(D) to conclude review of such a transaction without initiating an investigation if the Department of the Treasury and the lead agency determine at the Deputy Secretary level or higher that the transaction will not impair the national security of the United States.

A commenter also suggested that the review and investigation schedule be condensed to a shorter period than the statutory maximum 30-day review and 45-day investigation to minimize the impact on covered transactions reviewed by the Committee. Two commenters also asked that the regulations guarantee that the parties to a reviewed transaction will be informed several days before the end of the 30-day review period if risk mitigation will be required. The commenters noted that if the need for risk mitigation is not determined until near the end of the 30-day review, there may be insufficient time to reach resolution of concerns before the end of that period, resulting in an otherwise unnecessary 45-day investigation.

The Final Rule makes no changes to the proposed text of § 800.503 or other sections in response to these comments. The Committee seeks to conclude each case, as well as to engage parties regarding the need for risk mitigation, as soon as practicable. The maximum timeframes for reviews and investigations are established by section 721. They have proven in practice to be appropriate for numerous reasons: many officials from the various U.S. Government agencies that comprise the Committee, including senior officials, are involved in the Committee's determinations; the important national security responsibility entrusted to the Committee requires robust, often time-consuming analysis of each case; many of the transactions reviewed by the

Committee are complex; and the Committee's caseload is significant.

The Final Rule does implement changes to the CFIUS process that are intended to maximize efficiency and ensure timely consideration of transactions notified to the Committee. These changes include, among others, encouragement of prefiling consultations, expansion of the required contents of voluntary notices to include information that the Committee, in practice, has been requesting during the course of reviews, and requirements that the Staff Chairperson take certain administrative actions promptly or within defined periods of time.

Section 800.508—Role of the Secretary of Labor

The Proposed Rule, at § 800.508, provided a role for the Secretary of Labor with respect to mitigation agreements, as required by section 721(h)(3)(C). A commenter suggested that the role defined for the Secretary of Labor was too narrow and that the regulations should make clear that the Chairperson can seek the Secretary of Labor's input on other occasions, as appropriate. Another commenter suggested that the meaning of § 800.508 was ambiguous. A commenter also asked that the regulations make clear that mitigation agreements should not violate any U.S. laws, rather than only labor laws.

The Final Rule revises the proposed text of § 800.508 to expand the Secretary of Labor's role and to focus it on employment laws, rather than labor laws. The Final Rule also adds language to emphasize that the Secretary of Labor will have no other policy role. This reinforces the Committee's focus, consistent with section 721, on national security alone, rather than broader economic or other national interests, for example, the effect of foreign investment on domestic employment levels.

The Final Rule retains the provision addressing consistency of mitigation agreements with employment laws, rather than all U.S. laws, not because the Committee believes that mitigation agreements may be inconsistent with other applicable U.S. laws, but because § 800.508 addresses solely the advice that will be sought from the Secretary of Labor.

Section 800.601—Finality of Actions Under Section 721

The Proposed Rule revised § 800.601(a) to clarify the circumstances under which the authority under section 721(d) will not be exercised. Paragraph (1) of § 800.601(a) pertains to the situation in which the Committee finds that a transaction notified to it is not a covered transaction. Paragraphs (2) and (3) pertain to the situation in which a transaction notified to the Committee is found to be a covered transaction, and either the Committee has advised the parties in writing that it has concluded all action under section 721, or the President has announced his decision not to exercise his authority under section 721 with respect to the covered transaction. These provisions do not preclude exercise of authority under section 721(d) with respect to any other covered transaction.

The following example illustrates a situation in which § 800.601(a)(2) would apply and a situation in which it would not apply: Corporation A, a foreign person, owns a non-controlling interest in Corporation B, another foreign person. Corporation B notifies the Committee of a proposed purchase of a controlling interest in Corporation X, a U.S. business. The Committee determines that Corporation B's purchase is a covered transaction, and the parties are advised in writing that the Committee has concluded all action under section 721 with respect to that transaction. Section 800.601(a)(2) would apply to that transaction. Corporation A subsequently engages in another transaction to increase its interest in Corporation B to 51 percent and obtain control of Corporation B. Section 800.601(a)(2) would not apply to this later transaction. This later transaction would be a covered transaction because it results in Corporation A's control of Corporation X, a U.S. business.

The Proposed Rule excluded provisions in the 1991 regulations pertaining to the President's authority that are not necessary to include in regulation because they are already addressed in FINSA. The Proposed Rule also described circumstances under which the Committee may reopen a review of a covered transaction as to which the Committee previously had concluded all action under section 721. A commenter stated that the regulations should incorporate section 721(b)(1)(D)(iii), which permits reopening of a review as a result of certain intentional material breaches of mitigation agreements. Commenters also asked for clarification regarding the process the Committee would follow upon reopening a review.

The Final Rule amends the proposed text of § 800.601 to delete the description of circumstances under which the Committee may reopen a review of a covered transaction as to which the Committee previously had concluded all action. As provided under

Executive Order 11858, the Committee may reopen a review of a covered transaction for which the Committee has concluded action only in those extraordinary circumstances authorized under section 721, including section 721(b)(1)(D)(iii). In determining whether to reopen a review for material misstatement or omission, the Committee generally will not consider as material minor inaccuracies, omissions, or changes relating to financial or commercial factors not having a bearing on national security, as provided in the new § 800.509.

Where section 721 authorizes the Committee to reopen a review of a covered transaction as to which the Committee previously had concluded all action, the new review will be subject to the same procedural rules and requirements prescribed by section 721 and the regulations for notices of a covered transaction filed with the Committee by an agency under § 800.401(c).

Section 800.702—Confidentiality

The Proposed Rule, at § 800.702, clarified that confidentiality protections apply to information provided to CFIUS during the course of a withdrawal or with regard to a notice that is rejected under § 800.403. The preamble to the Proposed Rule noted that, under § 800.401(f), information provided during the course of pre-notice consultations is also protected by the confidentiality provisions of section 721(c) and § 800.702. In addition, § 800.702(c) made clear that public statements of the Chairperson or his designee may reflect information that the parties to the transaction have already themselves publicly disclosed.

Several commenters suggested that the confidentiality provisions of § 800.702 were inadequate because they may not extend to information provided during the course of pre-notice consultations if no notice is ultimately filed with the Committee and because they do not provide clear civil remedies to parties for violations of confidentiality. Two commenters also expressed concern over the potential involvement of Congress during the course of the Committee's review of a covered transaction.

The Final Rule amends the proposed text of § 800.702 to explicitly extend the confidentiality provisions under the section to information or documentary material provided during the course of pre-notice consultations pursuant to § 800.401(f), regardless of whether a notice is ultimately filed with the Committee. Further, the Final Rule makes clear that the confidentiality

provisions will continue to apply even when the transaction is no longer before the Committee.

The Final Rule makes no changes in response to the comments regarding civil remedies for violations of confidentiality. The confidentiality requirements under section 721(c) and § 800.702 bind the entire Executive Branch. Further, section 721(g)(2)(A) applies section 721(c) to briefings provided to the U.S. Congress under section 721(g)(1), and section 721(g)(2)(B) provides additional confidentiality assurances regarding proprietary information provided to Congress. Nothing in the regulations prevents parties from seeking any remedies available under existing law to prevent or redress violation of these confidentiality provisions. The Committee may also refer violations of these provisions to the Department of Justice for investigation and prosecution under 50 U.S.C. App. 2155(d), which provides for fines and imprisonment. It is also important to note that FINSA provides for reporting to Congress on each covered transaction only after all deliberative action is complete.

Section 800.801—Penalties

The Proposed Rule, at § 800.801, provided for the imposition of civil penalties for any violation of section 721, including a violation of any mitigation agreement entered into or conditions imposed pursuant to section 721(l). The preamble to the Proposed Rule made clear that civil monetary penalties could be imposed with regard to transactions entered into on or after the effective date of FINSA, October 24, 2007. In addition, § 800.801(c) authorized CFIUS to include in any mitigation agreement described in section 721(l) a liquidated damages provision tied to the harm to the national security that could result from a breach.

A commenter expressed concern that the civil penalties provided for in § 800.801 of the Proposed Rule were so high as to potentially discourage parties from filing voluntary notices with the Committee. Another commenter, noting that penalties for certain breaches of mitigation agreements may be up to the value of the transaction, suggested that the Committee set an upper bound to such penalties for particularly large transactions. A commenter also asked whether penalties for violations of mitigation agreements under section 721 will be separate from penalties assessed by the Department of Defense under agreements to mitigate foreign ownership, control, and influence under the National Industrial Security Program Operating Manual (NISPOM).

The Final Rule amends the proposed text of § 800.801 to specify that civil penalties may be imposed under the section only if the action that could give rise to civil penalties occurs on or after the effective date of the Final Rule. The Final Rule also adds a requirement that the determination to impose civil penalties under § 800.801 must be made by the members of the Committee named in FINSA and Executive Order 11858, except to the extent delegated by such official.

The Final Rule makes no other changes to the proposed text of § 800.801 in response to public comments received. CFIUS retains the discretion to impose less than the maximum penalty identified in § 800.801, depending on the nature of the violation. The Final Rule also affords parties the opportunity to submit a petition for reconsideration of any decision to impose a penalty. Furthermore, the maximum penalty amounts provided for in § 800.801 are consistent with the statutory penalty scheme under the International Emergency Economic Powers Act, a statute that provides the authority for a number of regulations related to national security.

Mitigation agreements or conditions entered into or agreed to pursuant to section 721(l) are separate from agreements reached under the NISPOM pursuant to separate legal authority of the Department of Defense. In general, the remedy and penalty provisions of the former type of mitigation agreements or conditions have no bearing on the applicability or enforceability of remedy and penalty provisions in the latter type of agreement.

Executive Order 12866

These regulations are not subject to the requirements of Executive Order 12866 because they relate to a foreign affairs function of the United States.

Paperwork Reduction Act

The collection of information contained in this rule has been approved by the Office of Management and Budget in accordance with the Paperwork Reduction Act of 1995 (44 U.S.C. 3507(d)) and assigned control number 1505–0121.

Under the Paperwork Reduction Act, an agency may not conduct or sponsor, and a person is not required to respond to, a collection of information unless it displays a valid control number assigned by the Office of Management and Budget.

Regulatory Flexibility Act

The Regulatory Flexibility Act ("RFA") (5 U.S.C. 601 *et seq.*) generally requires an agency to prepare a regulatory flexibility analysis unless the agency certifies that the rule will not have a significant economic impact on a substantial number of small entities. The RFA applies when an agency is required to publish a general notice of proposed rulemaking under section 553(b) of the Administrative Procedure Act (5 U.S.C. 553(b)), or any other law. As set forth below, because regulations issued pursuant to the Defense Production Act of 1950 (50 U.S.C. App. 2170) are not subject to the Administrative Procedure Act, or other law requiring the publication of a general notice of proposed rulemaking, the RFA does not apply.

This regulation implements section 721 of the DPA. Section 709 of the DPA (50 U.S.C. App. 2159, as amended by section 136 of the Defense Production Act Amendments of 1992 (Pub. L. 102–558)) provides that the regulations issued under it are not subject to the rulemaking requirements of the Administrative Procedure Act. Section 709 of the DPA instead provides that any regulation issued under the DPA be published in the **Federal Register** and opportunity for public comment be provided for not less than 30 days. (Similarly, FINSA requires the President to direct the issuance of implementing regulations subject to notice and comment.) Section 709 of the DPA also provides that all comments received during the public comment period be considered and the publication of the final regulation contain written responses to such comments. Legislative history demonstrates that Congress intended that regulations under the DPA be exempt from the notice and comment provisions of the Administrative Procedure Act and instead provided that the agency include a statement that interested parties were consulted in the formulation of the regulation. *See* H.R. Conf. Rep. No. 102–1028, at 42 (1992) and H.R. Rep. No. 102–208 pt. 1, at 28 (1991). The limited public participation procedures described in the DPA do not require a general notice of proposed rulemaking as set forth in the RFA. Further, the mechanisms for publication and public participation are sufficiently different to distinguish the DPA procedures from a rule that requires a general notice of proposed rulemaking. In providing the President with the authority to suspend or prohibit the acquisition, merger, or takeover of a domestic firm by a foreign firm if such action would threaten to impair the national security, Congress could not have contemplated that regulations implementing such authority would be subject to RFA analysis. For these reasons, the RFA does not apply to these regulations.

Notwithstanding the inapplicability of the RFA, we certify that this rule would not have a significant economic impact on a substantial number of small entities. These regulations provide for a voluntary system of notification, and historically fewer than 10 percent of all foreign acquisitions of U.S. businesses are notified to CFIUS. Typically, some of the notices filed with CFIUS concern U.S. companies that would qualify as small entities. It is estimated that an average filing requires about 100 hours of preparation time. It is estimated that between 100 and 200 notices will be filed with CFIUS annually over the next few years. Few cases end with mitigation agreements. There were 16 mitigation agreements in 2006, 14 in 2007, and fewer than 5 to date in 2008. As such, a substantial number of entities are not impacted by these rules regardless of their size. We also note that these regulations, to a substantial degree, merely provide a detailed explanation of the current burdens of complying with CFIUS procedures and do not impose significant new burdens on entities subject to CFIUS.

List of Subjects in 31 CFR Part 800

Foreign investments in the United States, Investigations, National defense, Reporting and recordkeeping requirements.

■ Accordingly, under the authority at 50 U.S.C. App. 2170(h), for the reasons stated in the preamble, the Department of the Treasury amends 31 CFR chapter VIII as follows:

CHAPTER VIII—OFFICE OF INVESTMENT SECURITY, DEPARTMENT OF THE TREASURY

■ 1. The heading for chapter VIII is revised to read as set forth above.

■ 2. Part 800 is revised to read as follows:

PART 800—REGULATIONS PERTAINING TO MERGERS, ACQUISITIONS, AND TAKEOVERS BY FOREIGN PERSONS

Subpart A—General

Sec.
800.101 Scope.
800.102 Effect on other law.
800.103 Applicability rule; prospective application of certain provisions.
800.104 Transactions or devices for avoidance.

Authority: 50 U.S.C. App. 2170; E.O. 11858, as amended, 73 FR 4677.

Subpart A—General

§ 800.101   Scope.

The regulations in this part implement section 721 of title VII of the Defense Production Act of 1950 (50 U.S.C. App. 2170), as amended, hereinafter referred to as "section 721." The definitions in this part are applicable to section 721 and these regulations. The principal purpose of section 721 is to authorize the President to suspend or prohibit any covered transaction when, in the President's judgment, there is credible evidence to believe that the foreign person exercising control over a U.S. business might take action that threatens to impair the national security, and when provisions of law other than section 721 and the International Emergency Economic Powers Act (50 U.S.C. 1701–1706), do not, in the judgment of the President, provide adequate and appropriate authority for the President to protect the national security in the matter before the President. It is also a purpose of section 721 to authorize the Committee to mitigate any threat to the national security of the United States that arises as a result of a covered transaction.

§ 800.102   Effect on other law.

Nothing in this part shall be construed as altering or affecting any other authority, process, regulation, investigation, enforcement measure, or review provided by or established under any other provision of federal law, including the International Emergency Economic Powers Act, or any other authority of the President or the Congress under the Constitution of the United States.

§ 800.103   Applicability rule; prospective application of certain provisions.

(a) Except as provided in paragraph (b) of this section and otherwise in this part, the regulations in this part apply from the effective date (as defined in Section 800.210).

(b) Sections 800.204 (Control), 800.205 (Conversion), 800.206 (Convertible voting instrument), 800.211 (Entity), 800.212 (Foreign entity), 800.216 (Foreign person), 800.220 (Party or parties to a transaction), 800.223 (Solely for the purpose of passive investment), 800.224 (Transaction), 800.226 (U.S. business), and 800.228 (Voting interest), and the regulations in subpart C (Coverage) do not apply to any transaction for which the following has occurred before the effective date, in which case corresponding provisions of

the regulations in this part that were in effect the day before the effective date will apply:

(1) The parties to the transaction have executed a written agreement or other document establishing the material terms of the transaction;

(2) A party has made a public offer to shareholders to buy shares of a U.S. business;

(3) A shareholder has solicited proxies in connection with an election of the board of directors of a U.S. business or has requested the conversion of convertible voting securities; or

(4) The parties have, in the Committee's view, otherwise made a commitment to engage in a transaction.

Note to § 800.103: See subpart H of this part for specific applicability rules pertaining to that subpart.

§ 800.104   Transactions or devices for avoidance.

Any transaction or other device entered into or employed for the purpose of avoiding section 721 shall be disregarded, and section 721 and the regulations in this part shall be applied to the substance of the transaction.

Example. Corporation A is organized under the laws of a foreign state and is wholly owned and controlled by a foreign national. With a view towards avoiding possible application of section 721, Corporation A transfers money to a U.S. citizen, who, pursuant to informal arrangements with Corporation A and on its behalf, purchases all the shares in Corporation X, a U.S. business. That transaction is subject to section 721.

Subpart B—Definitions

§ 800.201   Business day.

The term *business day* means Monday through Friday, except the legal public holidays specified in 5 U.S.C. 6103 or any other day declared to be a holiday by federal statute or executive order.

§ 800.202   Certification.

(a) The term *certification* means a written statement signed by the chief executive officer or other duly authorized designee of a party to a transaction filing a notice or information, certifying that the notice or information filed:

(1) Fully complies with the requirements of section 721, the regulations in this part, and any agreement or condition entered into with the Committee or any member of the Committee, and

(2) Is accurate and complete in all material respects, as it relates to:

(i) The transaction, and

(ii) The party providing the certification, including its parents, subsidiaries, and any other related entities described in the notice or information.

(b) For purposes of this section, a *duly authorized designee* is:

(1) In the case of a partnership, any general partner thereof;

(2) In the case of a corporation, any officer or director thereof;

(3) In the case of any entity lacking officers, directors, or partners, any individual within the organization exercising executive functions similar to those of an officer or director of a corporation or a general partner of a partnership; and

(4) In the case of an individual, such individual or his or her legal representative.

(c) In each case described in paragraphs (b)(1) through (b)(4) of this section, such designee must possess actual authority to make the certification on behalf of the party to the transaction filing a notice or information.

Note to § 800.202: A sample certification may be found at the Committee's section of the Department of the Treasury Web site at *http://www.treas.gov/offices/international-affairs/cfius/index.shtml.*

§ 800.203 Committee; Chairperson of the Committee; Staff Chairperson.

The term *Committee* means the Committee on Foreign Investment in the United States. The *Chairperson of the Committee* is the Secretary of the Treasury. The *Staff Chairperson* of the Committee is the Department of the Treasury official so designated by the Secretary of the Treasury or by the Secretary's designee.

§ 800.204 Control.

(a) The term *control* means the power, direct or indirect, whether or not exercised, through the ownership of a majority or a dominant minority of the total outstanding voting interest in an entity, board representation, proxy voting, a special share, contractual arrangements, formal or informal arrangements to act in concert, or other means, to determine, direct, or decide important matters affecting an entity; in particular, but without limitation, to determine, direct, take, reach, or cause decisions regarding the following matters, or any other similarly important matters affecting an entity:

(1) The sale, lease, mortgage, pledge, or other transfer of any of the tangible or intangible principal assets of the entity, whether or not in the ordinary course of business;

(2) The reorganization, merger, or dissolution of the entity;

(3) The closing, relocation, or substantial alteration of the production, operational, or research and development facilities of the entity;

(4) Major expenditures or investments, issuances of equity or debt, or dividend payments by the entity, or approval of the operating budget of the entity;

(5) The selection of new business lines or ventures that the entity will pursue;

(6) The entry into, termination, or non-fulfillment by the entity of significant contracts;

(7) The policies or procedures of the entity governing the treatment of non-public technical, financial, or other proprietary information of the entity;

(8) The appointment or dismissal of officers or senior managers;

(9) The appointment or dismissal of employees with access to sensitive technology or classified U.S. Government information; or

(10) The amendment of the Articles of Incorporation, constituent agreement, or other organizational documents of the entity with respect to the matters described in paragraphs (a)(1) through (9) of this section.

(b) In examining questions of control in situations where more than one foreign person has an ownership interest in an entity, consideration will be given to factors such as whether the foreign persons are related or have formal or informal arrangements to act in concert, whether they are agencies or instrumentalities of the national or subnational governments of a single foreign state, and whether a given foreign person and another person that has an ownership interest in the entity are both controlled by any of the national or subnational governments of a single foreign state.

(c) The following minority shareholder protections shall not in themselves be deemed to confer control over an entity:

(1) The power to prevent the sale or pledge of all or substantially all of the assets of an entity or a voluntary filing for bankruptcy or liquidation;

(2) The power to prevent an entity from entering into contracts with majority investors or their affiliates;

(3) The power to prevent an entity from guaranteeing the obligations of majority investors or their affiliates;

(4) The power to purchase an additional interest in an entity to prevent the dilution of an investor's *pro rata* interest in that entity in the event that the entity issues additional

instruments conveying interests in the entity;

(5) The power to prevent the change of existing legal rights or preferences of the particular class of stock held by minority investors, as provided in the relevant corporate documents governing such shares; and

(6) The power to prevent the amendment of the Articles of Incorporation, constituent agreement, or other organizational documents of an entity with respect to the matters described in paragraphs (c)(1) through (5) of this section.

(d) The Committee will consider, on a case-by-case basis, whether minority shareholder protections other than those listed in paragraph (c) of this section do not confer control over an entity.

(e) Any transaction in which a foreign person acquires an additional interest in a U.S. business that was previously the subject of a covered transaction for which the Committee concluded all action under section 721 shall not be deemed to be a transaction that could result in foreign control over that U.S. business (*i.e.*, it is not a covered transaction). However, if a foreign person that did not acquire control of the U.S. business in the prior transaction is a party to the later transaction, the later transaction may be a covered transaction.

Example 1. Corporation A is a U.S. business. A U.S. investor owns 50 percent of the voting interest in Corporation A, and the remaining voting interest is owned in equal shares by five unrelated foreign investors. The foreign investors jointly financed their investment in Corporation A and vote as a single block on matters affecting Corporation A. The foreign investors have an informal arrangement to act in concert with regard to Corporation A, and, as a result, the foreign investors control Corporation A.

Example 2. Same facts as in Example 1 with regard to the composition of Corporation A's shareholders. The foreign investors in Corporation A have no contractual or other commitments to act in concert, and have no informal arrangements to do so. Assuming no other relevant facts, the foreign investors do not control Corporation A.

Example 3. Corporation A, a foreign person, is a private equity fund that routinely acquires substantial interests in companies and manages them for a period of time. Corporation B is a U.S. business. In addition to its acquisition of seven percent of Corporation B's voting shares, Corporation A acquires the right to terminate significant contracts of Corporation B. Corporation A controls Corporation B.

Example 4. Corporation A, a foreign person, acquires a nine percent interest in the shares of Corporation B, a U.S. business. As part of the transaction, Corporation A also acquires certain veto rights that determine important matters affecting Corporation B.

including the right to veto the dismissal of senior executives of Corporation B. Corporation A controls Corporation B.

Example 5. Corporation A, a foreign person, acquires a thirteen percent interest in the shares of Corporation B, a U.S. business, and the right to appoint one member of Corporation B's seven-member Board of Directors. Corporation A receives minority shareholder protections listed in § 800.204(c), but receives no other positive or negative rights with respect to Corporation B. Assuming no other relevant facts, Corporation A does not control Corporation B.

Example 6. Corporation A, a foreign person, acquires a twenty percent interest in the shares of Corporation B, a U.S. business. Corporation A has negotiated an irrevocable passivity agreement that completely precludes it from controlling Corporation B. Corporation A does, however, receive the right to prevent Corporation B from entering into contracts with majority investors or their affiliates and to prevent Corporation B from guaranteeing the obligations of majority investors or their affiliates. Assuming no other relevant facts, Corporation A does not control Corporation B.

Example 7. Corporation A, a foreign person, acquires a 40 percent interest and important rights in Corporation B, a U.S. business. The documentation pertaining to the transaction gives no indication that Corporation A's interest in Corporation B may increase at a later date. Following its review of the transaction, the Committee informs the parties that the notified transaction is a covered transaction, and concludes action under section 721. Three years later, Corporation A acquires the remainder of the voting interest in Corporation B. Assuming no other relevant facts, because the Committee concluded all action with respect to Corporation A's earlier investment in the same U.S. business, and because no other foreign person is a party to this subsequent transaction, this subsequent transaction is not a covered transaction.

Example 8. Limited Partnership A comprises two limited partners, each of which holds 49 percent of the interest in the partnership, and a general partner, which holds two percent of the interest. The general partner has sole authority to determine, direct, and decide important matters affecting the partnership and a fund operated by the partnership. The general partner alone controls Limited Partnership A and the fund.

Example 9. Same facts as in Example 8, except that each of the limited partners has the authority to veto major investments proposed by the general partner and to choose the fund's representatives on the boards of the fund's portfolio companies. The general partner and the limited partners each have control over Limited Partnership A and the fund.

Note to § 800.204: See § 800.302(b) regarding the Committee's treatment of transactions in which a foreign person holds or acquires ten percent or less of the outstanding voting interest in a U.S. business solely for the purpose of passive investment.

§ 800.205   Conversion.

The term *conversion* means the exercise of a right inherent in the ownership or holding of particular financial instruments to exchange any such instruments for voting instruments.

§ 800.206   Convertible voting instrument.

The term *convertible voting instrument* means a financial instrument that currently does not entitle its owner or holder to voting rights but is convertible into a voting instrument.

§ 800.207   Covered transaction.

The term *covered transaction* means any transaction that is proposed or pending after August 23, 1988, by or with any foreign person, which could result in control of a U.S. business by a foreign person.

§ 800.208   Critical infrastructure.

The term *critical infrastructure* means, in the context of a particular covered transaction, a system or asset, whether physical or virtual, so vital to the United States that the incapacity or destruction of the particular system or asset of the entity over which control is acquired pursuant to that covered transaction would have a debilitating impact on national security.

§ 800.209   Critical technologies.

The term *critical technologies* means:
(a) Defense articles or defense services covered by the United States Munitions List (USML), which is set forth in the International Traffic in Arms Regulations (ITAR) (22 CFR parts 120–130);
(b) Those items specified on the Commerce Control List (CCL) set forth in Supplement No. 1 to part 774 of the Export Administration Regulations (EAR) (15 CFR parts 730–774) that are controlled pursuant to multilateral regimes (*i.e.*, for reasons of national security, chemical and biological weapons proliferation, nuclear nonproliferation, or missile technology), as well as those that are controlled for reasons of regional stability or surreptitious listening;
(c) Specially designed and prepared nuclear equipment, parts and components, materials, software, and technology specified in the Assistance to Foreign Atomic Energy Activities regulations (10 CFR part 810), and nuclear facilities, equipment, and material specified in the Export and Import of Nuclear Equipment and Material regulations (10 CFR part 110); and
(d) Select agents and toxins specified in the Select Agents and Toxins

regulations (7 CFR part 331, 9 CFR part 121, and 42 CFR part 73).

§ 800.210   Effective date.

The term *effective date* means December 22, 2008.

§ 800.211   Entity.

The term *entity* means any branch, partnership, group or sub-group, association, estate, trust, corporation or division of a corporation, or organization (whether or not organized under the laws of any State or foreign state); assets (whether or not organized as a separate legal entity) operated by any one of the foregoing as a business undertaking in a particular location or for particular products or services; and any government (including a foreign national or subnational government, the United States Government, a subnational government within the United States, and any of their respective departments, agencies, or instrumentalities). (See examples following §§ 800.301(c) and 800.302(c).)

§ 800.212   Foreign entity.

(a) The term *foreign entity* means any branch, partnership, group or sub-group, association, estate, trust, corporation or division of a corporation, or organization organized under the laws of a foreign state if either its principal place of business is outside the United States or its equity securities are primarily traded on one or more foreign exchanges.
(b) Notwithstanding paragraph (a) of this section, any branch, partnership, group or sub-group, association, estate, trust, corporation or division of a corporation, or organization that demonstrates that a majority of the equity interest in such entity is ultimately owned by U.S. nationals is not a foreign entity.

§ 800.213   Foreign government.

The term *foreign government* means any government or body exercising governmental functions, other than the United States Government or a subnational government of the United States. The term includes, but is not limited to, national and subnational governments, including their respective departments, agencies, and instrumentalities.

§ 800.214   Foreign government-controlled transaction.

The term *foreign government-controlled transaction* means any covered transaction that could result in control of a U.S. business by a foreign government or a person controlled by or acting on behalf of a foreign government.

§ 800.215   Foreign national.

The term *foreign national* means any individual other than a U.S. national.

§ 800.216   Foreign person.

The term *foreign person* means:

(a) Any foreign national, foreign government, or foreign entity; or

(b) Any entity over which control is exercised or exercisable by a foreign national, foreign government, or foreign entity.

Example 1. Corporation A is organized under the laws of a foreign state and is only engaged in business outside the United States. All of its shares are held by Corporation X, which controls Corporation A. Corporation X is organized in the United States and is wholly owned and controlled by U.S. nationals. Assuming no other relevant facts, Corporation A, although organized and only operating outside the United States, is not a foreign person.

Example 2. Same facts as in the first sentence of Example 1. The government of the foreign state under whose laws Corporation A is organized exercises control over Corporation A through government interveners. Corporation A is a foreign person.

Example 3. Corporation A is organized in the United States, is engaged in interstate commerce in the United States, and is controlled by Corporation X. Corporation X is organized under the laws of a foreign state, its principal place of business is located outside the United States, and 50 percent of its shares are held by foreign nationals and 50 percent of its shares are held by U.S. nationals. Both Corporation A and Corporation X are foreign persons. Corporation A is also a U.S. business.

Example 4. Corporation A is organized under the laws of a foreign state and is owned and controlled by a foreign national. A branch of Corporation A engages in interstate commerce in the United States. Corporation A (including its branch) is a foreign person. The branch is also a U.S. business.

Example 5. Corporation A is a corporation organized under the laws of a foreign state and its principal place of business is located outside the United States. Forty-five percent of the voting interest in Corporation A is owned in equal shares by numerous unrelated foreign investors, none of whom has control. The foreign investors have no formal or informal arrangement to act in concert with regard to Corporation A with any other holder of voting interest in Corporation A. Corporation A demonstrates that the remainder of the voting interest in Corporation A is held by U.S. nationals. Assuming no other relevant facts, Corporation A is not a foreign person.

Example 6. Same facts as Example 5, except that one of the foreign investors controls Corporation A. Assuming no other relevant facts, Corporation A is not a foreign entity pursuant to § 800.212(b), but it is a foreign person because it is controlled by a foreign person.

§ 800.217   Hold.

The terms *hold(s)* and *holding* mean legal or beneficial ownership, whether direct or indirect, whether through fiduciaries, agents, or other means.

§ 800.218   Lead agency.

The term *lead agency* means an agency designated by the Chairperson of the Committee to have primary responsibility, on behalf of the Committee, for the specific activity for which the Chairperson designates it as a lead agency, including all or a portion of a review, an investigation, or the negotiation or monitoring of a mitigation agreement or condition.

§ 800.219   Parent.

(a) The term *parent* means a person who or which directly or indirectly:

(1) Holds or will hold at least 50 percent of the outstanding voting interest in an entity; or

(2) Holds or will hold the right to at least 50 percent of the profits of an entity, or has or will have the right in the event of the dissolution to at least 50 percent of the assets of that entity.

(b) Any entity that meets the conditions of paragraphs (a)(1) or (2) of this section with respect to another entity (*i.e.*, the intermediate parent) is also a parent of any other entity of which the intermediate parent is a parent.

Example 1. Corporation P holds 50 percent of the voting interest in Corporations R and S. Corporation R holds 40 percent of the voting interest in Corporation X; Corporation S holds 50 percent of the voting interest in Corporation Y, which in turn holds 50 percent of the voting interest in Corporation Z. Corporation P is a parent of Corporations R, S, Y, and Z, but not of Corporation X. Corporation S is a parent of Corporation Y and Z, and Corporation Y is a parent of Corporation Z.

Example 2. Corporation A holds warrants which when exercised will entitle it to vote 50 percent of the outstanding shares of Corporation B. Corporation A is a parent of Corporation B.

§ 800.220   Party or parties to a transaction.

The terms *party to a transaction* and *parties to a transaction* mean:

(a) In the case of an acquisition of an ownership interest in an entity, the person acquiring the ownership interest, and the person from which such ownership interest is acquired, without regard to any person providing brokerage or underwriting services for the transaction;

(b) In the case of a merger, the surviving entity, and the entity or entities that are merged into that entity as a result of the transaction;

(c) In the case of a consolidation, the entities being consolidated, and the new consolidated entity;

(d) In the case of a proxy solicitation, the person soliciting proxies, and the person who issued the voting interest;

(e) In the case of the acquisition or conversion of convertible voting instruments, the issuer and the person holding the convertible voting instruments; and

(f) In the case of any other type of transaction, any person who is in a role comparable to that of a person described in paragraphs (a) through (e) of this section.

§ 800.221   Person.

The term *person* means any individual or entity.

§ 800.222   Section 721.

The term *section 721* means section 721 of title VII of the Defense Production Act of 1950, 50 U.S.C. App. 2170.

§ 800.223   Solely for the purpose of passive investment.

Ownership interests are held or acquired *solely for the purpose of passive investment* if the person holding or acquiring such interests does not plan or intend to exercise control, does not possess or develop any purpose other than passive investment, and does not take any action inconsistent with holding or acquiring such interests solely for the purpose of passive investment. (See § 800.302(b).)

Example. Corporation A, a foreign person, acquires a voting interest in Corporation B, a U.S. business. In addition to the voting interest, Corporation A negotiates the right to appoint a member of Corporation B's Board of Directors. The acquisition by Corporation A of a voting interest in Corporation B is not solely for the purpose of passive investment.

§ 800.224   Transaction.

The term *transaction* means a proposed or completed merger, acquisition, or takeover. It includes:

(a) The acquisition of an ownership interest in an entity.

(b) The acquisition or conversion of convertible voting instruments of an entity.

(c) The acquisition of proxies from holders of a voting interest in an entity.

(d) A merger or consolidation.

(e) The formation of a joint venture.

(f) A long-term lease under which a lessee makes substantially all business decisions concerning the operation of a leased entity, as if it were the owner.

Note to § 800.224(b): See § 800.304 regarding factors the Committee will consider in determining whether to include the rights to be acquired by a foreign person upon the conversion of convertible voting instruments as part of the Committee's assessment of whether a transaction that involves such instruments is a covered transaction.

Example. Corporation A, a foreign person, signs a concession agreement to operate the toll road business of Corporation B, a U.S. business, for 99 years. Corporation B, however, is required under the agreement to perform safety and security functions with respect to the business and to monitor compliance by Corporation A with the operating requirements of the agreement on an ongoing basis. Corporation B may terminate the agreement or impose other penalties for breach of these operating requirements. Assuming no other relevant facts, this is not a transaction.

§ 800.225   United States.

The term *United States* or *U.S.* means the United States of America, the States of the United States, the District of Columbia, and any commonwealth, territory, dependency, or possession of the United States, or any subdivision of the foregoing, and includes the Outer Continental Shelf, as defined in 43 U.S.C. 1331(a). For purposes of these regulations and their examples, an entity organized under the laws of the United States of America, one of the States, the District of Columbia, or a commonwealth, territory, dependency, or possession of the United States is an entity organized "in the United States."

§ 800.226   U.S. business.

The term *U.S. business* means any entity, irrespective of the nationality of the persons that control it, engaged in interstate commerce in the United States, but only to the extent of its activities in interstate commerce.

Example 1. Corporation A is organized under the laws of a foreign state and is wholly owned and controlled by a foreign national. It engages in interstate commerce in the United States through a branch or subsidiary. Its branch or subsidiary is a U.S. business. Corporation A and its branch or subsidiary is each also a foreign person should any of them engage in a transaction involving a U.S. business.

Example 2. Same facts as in the first sentence of Example 1. Corporation A, however, does not have a branch office, subsidiary, or fixed place of business in the United States. It exports and licenses technology to an unrelated company in the United States. Assuming no other relevant facts, Corporation A is not a U.S. business.

Example 3. Corporation A, a company organized under the laws of a foreign state, is wholly owned and controlled by Corporation X. Corporation X is organized in the United States and is wholly owned and controlled by U.S. nationals. Corporation A does not have a branch office, subsidiary, or fixed place of business in the United States. It exports goods to Corporation X and to unrelated companies in the United States.

Assuming no other relevant facts, Corporation A is not a U.S. business.

§ 800.227   U.S. national.

The term *U.S. national* means a citizen of the United States or an individual who, although not a citizen of the United States, owes permanent allegiance to the United States.

§ 800.228   Voting interest.

The term *voting interest* means any interest in an entity that entitles the owner or holder of that interest to vote for the election of directors of the entity (or, with respect to unincorporated entities, individuals exercising similar functions) or to vote on other matters affecting the entity.

Subpart C—Coverage

§ 800.301   Transactions that are covered transactions.

Transactions that are covered transactions include, without limitation:

(a) A transaction which, irrespective of the actual arrangements for control provided for in the terms of the transaction, results or could result in control of a U.S. business by a foreign person.

Example 1. Corporation A, a foreign person, proposes to purchase all of the shares of Corporation X, which is a U.S. business. As the sole owner, Corporation A will have the right to elect directors and appoint other primary officers of Corporation X, and those directors will have the right to make decisions about the closing and relocation of particular production facilities and the termination of significant contracts. The directors also will have the right to propose to Corporation A, the sole shareholder, the dissolution of Corporation X and the sale of its principal assets. The proposed transaction is a covered transaction.

Example 2. Same facts as in Example 1, except that Corporation A plans to retain the existing directors of Corporation X, all of whom are U.S. nationals. Although Corporation A may choose not to exercise its power to elect new directors for Corporation X, Corporation A nevertheless will have that exercisable power. The proposed transaction is a covered transaction.

Example 3. Corporation A, a foreign person, proposes to purchase 50 percent of the shares in Corporation X, a U.S. business, from Corporation B, also a U.S. business. Corporation B would retain the other 50 percent of the shares in Corporation X, and Corporation A and Corporation B would contractually agree that Corporation A would not exercise its voting and other rights for ten years. The proposed transaction is a covered transaction.

(b) A transaction in which a foreign person conveys its control of a U.S. business to another foreign person.

Example. Corporation X is a U.S. business, but is wholly owned and controlled by

Corporation Y, a foreign person. Corporation Z, also a foreign person, but not related to Corporation Y, seeks to acquire Corporation X from Corporation Y. The proposed transaction is a covered transaction because it could result in control of Corporation X, a U.S. business, by another foreign person, Corporation Z.

(c) A transaction that results or could result in control by a foreign person of any part of an entity or of assets, if such part of an entity or assets constitutes a U.S. business. (See § 800.302(c).)

Example 1. Corporation X, a foreign person, has a branch office located in the United States. Corporation A, a foreign person, proposes to buy that branch office. The proposed transaction is a covered transaction.

Example 2. Corporation A, a foreign person, buys a branch office located entirely outside the United States of Corporation Y, which is incorporated in the United States. Assuming no other relevant facts, the branch office of Corporation Y is not a U.S. business, and the transaction is not a covered transaction.

Example 3. Corporation A, a foreign person, makes a start-up, or "greenfield," investment in the United States. That investment involves such activities as separately arranging for the financing of and the construction of a plant to make a new product, buying supplies and inputs, hiring personnel, and purchasing the necessary technology. The investment may involve the acquisition of shares in a newly incorporated subsidiary. Assuming no other relevant facts, Corporation A will not have acquired a U.S. business, and its greenfield investment is not a covered transaction.

Example 4. Corporation A, a foreign person, purchases substantially all of the assets of Corporation B. Corporation B, which is incorporated in the United States, was in the business of producing industrial equipment, but stopped producing and selling such equipment one week before Corporation A purchased substantially all of its assets. At the time of the transaction, Corporation B continued to have employees on its payroll, maintained know-how in producing the industrial equipment it previously produced, and maintained relationships with its prior customers, all of which were transferred to Corporation A. The acquisition of substantially all of the assets of Corporation B by Corporation A is a covered transaction.

Example 5. Corporation A, a foreign person, owns businesses both outside the United States and in the United States. Corporation B, a foreign person, acquires Corporation A. The acquisition of Corporation A by Corporation B is a covered transaction with respect to Corporation A's businesses in the United States.

Example 6. Corporation X, a foreign person, seeks to acquire from Corporation A, a U.S. business, an empty warehouse facility located in the United States. The acquisition would be limited to the physical facility, and would not include customer lists, intellectual property, or other proprietary information, or other intangible assets or the transfer of personnel. Assuming no other relevant facts, the facility is not an entity and therefore not a U.S. business, and the proposed acquisition of the facility is not a covered transaction.

Example 7. Same facts as Example 6, except that, in addition to the proposed acquisition of Corporation A's warehouse facility, Corporation X would acquire the personnel, customer list, equipment, and inventory management software used to operate the facility. Under these facts, Corporation X is acquiring a U.S. business, and the proposed acquisition is a covered transaction.

(d) A joint venture in which the parties enter into a contractual or other similar arrangement, including an agreement on the establishment of a new entity, but only if one or more of the parties contributes a U.S. business and a foreign person could control that U.S. business by means of the joint venture.

Example 1. Corporation A, a foreign person, and Corporation X, a U.S. business, form a separate corporation, JV Corporation, to which Corporation A contributes only cash and Corporation X contributes a U.S. business. Each owns 50 percent of the shares of JV Corporation and, under the Articles of Incorporation of JV Corporation, both Corporation A and Corporation X have veto power over all of the matters affecting JV Corporation identified under § 800.204(a)(1) through (10), giving them both control over JV Corporation. The formation of JV Corporation is a covered transaction.

Example 2. Corporation A, a foreign person, and Corporation X, a U.S. business, form a separate corporation, JV Corporation, to which Corporation A contributes funding and managerial and technical personnel, while Corporation X contributes certain land and equipment that do not in this example constitute a U.S. business. Corporations A and B each have a 50 percent interest in the joint venture. Assuming no other relevant facts, the formation of JV Corporation is not a covered transaction.

§ 800.302 Transactions that are not covered transactions.

Transactions that are not covered transactions include, without limitation:

(a) A stock split or pro rata stock dividend that does not involve a change in control.

Example. Corporation A, a foreign person, holds 10,000 shares of Corporation B, a U.S. business, constituting ten percent of the stock of Corporation B. Corporation B pays a 2-for-1 stock dividend. As a result of this stock split, Corporation A holds 20,000 shares of Corporation B, still constituting ten percent of the stock of Corporation B. Assuming no other relevant facts, the acquisition of additional shares is not a covered transaction.

(b) A transaction that results in a foreign person holding ten percent or less of the outstanding voting interest in a U.S. business (regardless of the dollar value of the interest so acquired), but only if the transaction is solely for the purpose of passive investment. (See § 800.223.)

Example 1. In an open market purchase solely for the purpose of passive investment, Corporation A, a foreign person, acquires seven percent of the voting securities of Corporation X, which is a U.S. business. Assuming no other relevant facts, the acquisition of the securities is not a covered transaction.

Example 2. Corporation A, a foreign person, acquires nine percent of the voting shares of Corporation X, a U.S. business. Corporation A also negotiates contractual rights that give it the power to control important matters of Corporation X. The acquisition by Corporation A of the voting shares of Corporation X is not solely for the purpose of passive investment and is a covered transaction.

Example 3. Corporation A, a foreign person, acquires five percent of the voting shares in Corporation B, a U.S. business. In addition to the securities, Corporation A obtains the right to appoint one out of eleven seats on Corporation B's Board of Directors. The acquisition by Corporation A of Corporation B's securities is not solely for the purpose of passive investment. Whether the transaction is a covered transaction would depend on whether Corporation A obtains control of Corporation B as a result of the transaction.

(c) An acquisition of any part of an entity or of assets, if such part of an entity or assets do not constitute a U.S. business. (See § 800.301(c).)

Example 1. Corporation A, a foreign person, acquires, from separate U.S. nationals: (a) products held in inventory, (b) land, and (c) machinery for export. Assuming no other relevant facts, Corporation A has not acquired a U.S. business, and this acquisition is not a covered transaction.

Example 2. Corporation X, a U.S. business, produces armored personnel carriers in the United States. Corporation A, a foreign person, seeks to acquire the annual production of those carriers from Corporation X. under a long-term contract. Assuming no other relevant facts, this transaction is not a covered transaction.

Example 3. Same facts as Example 2, except that Corporation X, a U.S. business, has developed important technology in connection with the production of armored personnel carriers. Corporation A seeks to negotiate an agreement under which it would be licensed to manufacture using that technology. Assuming no other relevant facts, neither the proposed acquisition of technology pursuant to that license agreement, nor the actual acquisition, is a covered transaction.

Example 4. Same facts as Example 2, except that Corporation A enters into a contractual arrangement to acquire the entire armored personnel carrier business operations of Corporation X, including production facilities, customer lists, technology, and staff. This transaction is a covered transaction.

Example 5. Same facts as Example 2, except that Corporation X suspended all activities of its armored personnel carrier business a year ago and currently is in bankruptcy proceedings. Existing equipment provided by Corporation X is being serviced by another company, which purchased the service contracts from Corporation X. The business's production facilities are idle but still in working condition, some of its key former employees have agreed to return if the business is resuscitated, and its technology and customer and vendor lists are still current. Corporation X's personnel carrier business constitutes a U.S. business, and its purchase by Corporation A is a covered transaction.

(d) An acquisition of securities by a person acting as a securities underwriter, in the ordinary course of business and in the process of underwriting.

(e) An acquisition pursuant to a condition in a contract of insurance relating to fidelity, surety, or casualty obligations if the contract was made by an insurer in the ordinary course of business.

§ 800.303 Lending transactions.

(a) The extension of a loan or a similar financing arrangement by a foreign person to a U.S. business, regardless of whether accompanied by the creation in the foreign person of a secured interest in securities or other assets of the U.S. business, shall not, by itself, constitute a covered transaction.

(1) The Committee will accept notices concerning a loan or a similar financing arrangement that does not, by itself, constitute a covered transaction only at the time that, because of imminent or actual default or other condition, there is a significant possibility that the foreign person may obtain control of a U.S. business as a result of the default or other condition.

(2) Where the Committee accepts a notice concerning a loan or a similar financing arrangement pursuant to paragraph (a)(1) of this section, and a party to the transaction is a foreign person that makes loans in the ordinary course of business, the Committee will take into account whether the foreign person has made any arrangements to transfer management decisions and day-to-day control over the U.S. business to U.S. nationals for purposes of determining whether such loan or financing arrangement constitutes a covered transaction.

(b) Notwithstanding paragraph (a) of this section, a loan or a similar financing arrangement through which a foreign person acquires an interest in profits of a U.S. business, the right to appoint members of the board of directors of the U.S. business, or other comparable financial or governance rights characteristic of an equity investment but not of a typical loan may constitute a covered transaction.

(c) An acquisition of voting interest or assets of a U.S. business by a foreign person upon default or other condition involving a loan or a similar financing arrangement does not constitute a covered transaction, provided that the loan was made by a syndicate of banks in a loan participation where the foreign lender (or lenders) in the syndicate:

(1) Needs the majority consent of the U.S. participants in the syndicate to take action, and cannot on its own initiate any action vis-à-vis the debtor; or

(2) Does not have a lead role in the syndicate, and is subject to a provision in the loan or financing documents limiting its ability to control the debtor such that control for purposes of § 800.204 could not be acquired.

Example 1. Corporation A, which is a U.S. business, borrows funds from Corporation B, a bank organized under the laws of a foreign state and controlled by foreign persons. As a condition of the loan, Corporation A agrees not to sell or pledge its principal assets to any person. Assuming no other relevant facts, this lending arrangement does not alone constitute a covered transaction.

Example 2. Same facts as in Example 1, except that Corporation A defaults on its loan from Corporation B and seeks bankruptcy protection. Corporation A has no funds with which to satisfy Corporation B's claim, which is greater than the value of Corporation A's principal assets. Corporation B's secured claim constitutes the only secured claim against Corporation A's principal assets, creating a high probability that Corporation B will receive title to Corporation A's principal assets, which constitute a U.S. business. Assuming no other relevant facts, the Committee would accept a notice of the impending bankruptcy court adjudication transferring control of Corporation A's principal assets to Corporation B, which would constitute a covered transaction.

Example 3. Corporation A, a foreign bank, makes a loan to Corporation B, a U.S. business. The loan documentation extends to Corporation A rights in Corporation B that are characteristic of an equity investment but not of a typical loan, including dominant minority representation on the board of directors of Corporation B and the right to be paid dividends by Corporation B. This loan is a covered transaction.

§ 800.304 Timing rule for convertible voting instruments.

(a) For purposes of determining whether to include the rights that a holder of convertible voting instruments will acquire upon conversion of those instruments in the Committee's assessment of whether a notified transaction is a covered transaction, the Committee will consider factors that include:

(1) The imminence of conversion;

(2) Whether conversion depends on factors within the control of the acquiring party; and

(3) Whether the amount of voting interest and the rights that would be acquired upon conversion can be reasonably determined at the time of acquisition.

(b) When the Committee, applying paragraph (a) of this section, determines that the rights that the holder will acquire upon conversion will not be included in the Committee's assessment of whether a notified transaction is a covered transaction, the Committee will disregard the convertible voting instruments for purposes of that transaction except to the extent that they convey immediate rights to the holder with respect to the governance of the entity that issued the instruments.

Example 1. Corporation A, a foreign person, notifies the Committee that it intends to buy common stock and debentures of Corporation X, a U.S. business. By their terms, the debentures are convertible into common stock only upon the occurrence of an event the timing of which is not in the control of Corporation A, and the number of common shares that would be acquired upon conversion cannot now be determined. Assuming no other relevant facts, the Committee will disregard the debentures in the course of its covered transaction analysis at the time that Corporation A acquires the debentures. In the event that it determines that the acquisition of the common stock is not a covered transaction, the Committee will so inform the parties. Once the conversion of the instruments becomes imminent, it may be appropriate for the Committee to consider the rights that would result from the conversion and whether the conversion is a covered transaction. The conversion of those debentures into common stock could be a covered transaction, depending on what percentage of Corporation X's voting securities Corporation A would receive and what powers those securities would confer on Corporation A.

Example 2. Same facts as Example 1, except that the debentures at issue are convertible at the sole discretion of Corporation A after six months, and if converted, would represent a 50 percent interest in Corporation X. The Committee may consider the rights that would result from the conversion as part of its assessment.

Subpart D—Notice

§ 800.401 Procedures for notice.

(a) A party or parties to a proposed or completed transaction may file a voluntary notice of the transaction with the Committee. Voluntary notice to the Committee is filed by sending:

(1) One paper copy of the notice to the Staff Chairperson, Office of Investment Security, Department of the Treasury, 1500 Pennsylvania Avenue, NW.,

Washington, DC 20220, that includes, in English only, the information set out in § 800.402, including the certification required under paragraph (l) of that section; and

(2) One electronic copy of the same information required in paragraph (a)(1) of this section. See the Committee's section of the Department of the Treasury Web site, at *http:// www.treas.gov/offices/international-affairs/cfius/* for electronic submission instructions.

(b) If the Committee determines that a transaction for which no voluntary notice has been filed under paragraph (a) of this section may be a covered transaction and may raise national security considerations, the Staff Chairperson, acting on the recommendation of the Committee, may request the parties to the transaction to provide to the Committee the information necessary to determine whether the transaction is a covered transaction, and if the Committee determines that the transaction is a covered transaction, to file a notice under paragraph (a) of such covered transaction.

(c) Any member of the Committee, or his designee at or above the Under Secretary or equivalent level, may file an agency notice to the Committee through the Staff Chairperson regarding a transaction for which no voluntary notice has been filed under paragraph (a) of this section if that member has reason to believe that the transaction is a covered transaction and may raise national security considerations. Notices filed under this paragraph are deemed accepted upon their receipt by the Staff Chairperson. No agency notice under this paragraph shall be made with respect to a transaction more than three years after the date of the completion of the transaction, unless the Chairperson of the Committee, in consultation with other members of the Committee, files such an agency notice.

(d) No communications other than those described in paragraphs (a) and (c) of this section shall constitute the filing or submitting of a notice for purposes of section 721.

(e) Upon receipt of the certification required by § 800.402(l) and an electronic copy of a notice filed under paragraph (a) of this section, the Staff Chairperson shall promptly inspect such notice for completeness.

(f) Parties to a transaction are encouraged to consult with the Committee in advance of filing a notice and, in appropriate cases, to file with the Committee a draft notice or other appropriate documents to aid the Committee's understanding of the transaction and to provide an opportunity for the Committee to request additional information to be included in the notice. Any such pre-notice consultation should take place, or any draft notice should be provided, at least five business days before the filing of a voluntary notice. All information and documentary material made available to the Committee pursuant to this paragraph shall be considered to have been filed with the President or the President's designee for purposes of section 721(c) and § 800.702.

(g) Information and other documentary material provided by the parties to the Committee after the filing of a voluntary notice under § 800.401 shall be part of the notice, and shall be subject to the certification requirements of § 800.402(l).

§ 800.402   Contents of voluntary notice.

(a) If the parties to a transaction file a voluntary notice, they shall provide in detail the information set out in this section, which must be accurate and complete with respect to all parties and to the transaction. (See also paragraph (l) of this section and § 800.701(d) regarding certification requirements.)

(b) In the case of a hostile takeover, if fewer than all the parties to a transaction file a voluntary notice, each notifying party shall provide the information set out in this section with respect to itself and, to the extent known or reasonably available to it, with respect to each non-notifying party.

(c) A voluntary notice filed pursuant to § 800.401(a) shall describe or provide, as applicable:

(1) The transaction in question, including:

(i) A summary setting forth the essentials of the transaction, including a statement of the purpose of the transaction, and its scope, both within and outside of the United States;

(ii) The nature of the transaction, for example, whether the acquisition is by merger, consolidation, the purchase of voting interest, or otherwise;

(iii) The name, United States address (if any), Web site address (if any), nationality (for individuals) or place of incorporation or other legal organization (for entities), and address of the principal place of business of each foreign person that is a party to the transaction;

(iv) The name, address, website address (if any), principal place of business, and place of incorporation or other legal organization of the U.S. business that is the subject of the transaction;

(v) The name, address, and nationality (for individuals) or place of incorporation or other legal organization (for entities) of:

(A) The immediate parent, the ultimate parent, and each intermediate parent, if any, of the foreign person that is a party to the transaction;

(B) Where the ultimate parent is a private company, the ultimate owner(s) of such parent; and

(C) Where the ultimate parent is a public company, any shareholder with an interest of greater than five percent in such parent;

(vi) The name, address, website address (if any), and nationality (for individuals) or place of incorporation or other legal organization (for entities) of the person that will ultimately control the U.S. business being acquired;

(vii) The expected date for completion of the transaction, or the date it was completed; (viii) A good faith approximation of the net value of the interest acquired in the U.S. business in U.S. dollars, as of the date of the notice; and

(ix) The name of any and all financial institutions involved in the transaction, including as advisors, underwriters, or a source of financing for the transaction;

(2) With respect to a transaction structured as an acquisition of assets of a U.S. business, a detailed description of the assets of the U.S. business being acquired, including the approximate value of those assets in U.S. dollars;

(3) With respect to the U.S. business that is the subject of the transaction and any entity of which that U.S. business is a parent (unless that entity is excluded from the scope of the transaction):

(i) Their respective business activities, as, for example, set forth in annual reports, and the product or service categories of each, including an estimate of U.S. market share for such product or service categories and the methodology used to determine market share, and a list of direct competitors for those primary product or service categories;

(ii) The street address (and mailing address, if different) within the United States and website address (if any) of each facility that is manufacturing classified or unclassified products or producing services described in paragraph (c)(3)(v) of this section, their respective Commercial and Government Entity Code (CAGE Code) assigned by the Department of Defense, their Dun and Bradstreet identification (DUNS) number, and their North American Industry Classification System (NAICS) Code, if any;

(iii) Each contract (identified by agency and number) that is currently in

effect or was in effect within the past five years with any agency of the United States Government involving any information, technology, or data that is classified under Executive Order 12958, as amended, its estimated final completion date, and the name, office, and telephone number of the contracting official;

(iv) Any other contract (identified by agency and number) that is currently in effect or was in effect within the past three years with any United States Government agency or component with national defense, homeland security, or other national security responsibilities, including law enforcement responsibility as it relates to defense, homeland security, or national security, its estimated final completion date, and the name, office, and telephone number of the contracting official;

(v) Any products or services (including research and development):

(A) That it supplies, directly or indirectly, to any agency of the United States Government, including as a prime contractor or first tier subcontractor, a supplier to any such prime contractor or subcontractor, or, if known by the parties filing the notice, a subcontractor at any tier; and

(B) If known by the parties filing the notice, for which it is a single qualified source (i.e., other acceptable suppliers are readily available to be so qualified) or a sole source (i.e., no other supplier has needed technology, equipment, and manufacturing process capabilities) for any such agencies and whether there are other suppliers in the market that are available to be so qualified;

(vi) Any products or services (including research and development) that:

(A) It supplies to third parties and it knows are rebranded by the purchaser or incorporated into the products of another entity, and the names or brands under which such rebranded products or services are sold; and

(B) In the case of services, it provides on behalf of, or under the name of, another entity, and the name of any such entities;

(vii) For the prior three years—

(A) The number of priority rated contracts or orders under the Defense Priorities and Allocations System (DPAS) regulations (15 CFR part 700) that the U.S. business that is the subject of the transaction has received and the level of priority of such contracts or orders ("DX" or "DO"); and

(B) The number of such priority rated contracts or orders that the U.S. business has placed with other entities and the level of priority of such contracts or orders, and the acquiring party's plan to ensure that any new entity formed at the completion of the notified transaction (or the U.S. business, if no new entity is formed) complies with the DPAS regulations; and

(viii) A description and copy of the cyber security plan, if any, that will be used to protect against cyber attacks on the operation, design, and development of the U.S. business's services, networks, systems, data storage, and facilities;

(4) Whether the U.S. business that is being acquired produces or trades in:

(i) Items that are subject to the EAR and, if so, a description (which may group similar items into general product categories) of the items and a list of the relevant commodity classifications set forth on the CCL (i.e., Export Control Classification Numbers (ECCNs) or EAR99 designation);

(ii) Defense articles and defense services, and related technical data covered by the USML in the ITAR, and, if so, the category of the USML; articles and services for which commodity jurisdiction requests (22 CFR 120.4) are pending; and articles and services (including those under development) that may be designated or determined in the future to be defense articles or defense services pursuant to 22 CFR 120.3;

(iii) Products and technology that are subject to export authorization administered by the Department of Energy (10 CFR part 810), or export licensing requirements administered by the Nuclear Regulatory Commission (10 CFR part 110); or

(iv) Select Agents and Toxins (7 CFR part 331, 9 CFR part 121, and 42 CFR part 73);

(5) Whether the U.S. business that is the subject of the transaction:

(i) Possesses any licenses, permits, or other authorizations other than those under the regulatory authorities listed in paragraph (c)(4) of this section that have been granted by an agency of the United States Government (if applicable, identification of the relevant licenses shall be provided); or

(ii) Has technology that has military applications (if so, an identification of such technology and a description of such military applications shall be included); and

(6) With respect to the foreign person engaged in the transaction and its parents:

(i) The business or businesses of the foreign person and its ultimate parent, as such businesses are described, for example, in annual reports, and the CAGE codes, NAICS codes, and DUNS numbers, if any, for such businesses;

(ii) The plans of the foreign person for the U.S. business with respect to:

(A) Reducing, eliminating, or selling research and development facilities;

(B) Changing product quality;

(C) Shutting down or moving outside of the United States facilities that are within the United States;

(D) Consolidating or selling product lines or technology;

(E) Modifying or terminating contracts referred to in paragraphs (c)(3)(iii) and (iv) of this section; or

(F) Eliminating domestic supply by selling products solely to non-domestic markets;

(iii) Whether the foreign person is controlled by or acting on behalf of a foreign government, including as an agent or representative, or in some similar capacity, and if so, the identity of the foreign government;

(iv) Whether a foreign government or a person controlled by or acting on behalf of a foreign government:

(A) Has or controls ownership interests, including convertible voting instruments, of the acquiring foreign person or any parent of the acquiring foreign person, and if so, the nature and amount of any such instruments, and with regard to convertible voting instruments, the terms and timing of their conversion;

(B) Has the right or power to appoint any of the principal officers or the members of the board of directors of the foreign person that is a party to the transaction or any parent of that foreign person;

(C) Holds any contingent interest (for example, such as might arise from a lending transaction) in the foreign acquiring party and, if so, the rights that are covered by this contingent interest, and the manner in which they would be enforced; or

(D) Has any other affirmative or negative rights or powers that could be relevant to the Committee's determination of whether the notified transaction is a foreign government-controlled transaction, and if there are any such rights or powers, their source (for example, a "golden share," shareholders agreement, contract, statute, or regulation) and the mechanics of their operation;

(v) Any formal or informal arrangements among foreign persons that hold an ownership interest in the foreign person that is a party to the transaction or between such foreign person and other foreign persons to act in concert on particular matters affecting the U.S. business that is the subject of the transaction, and provide a copy of any documents that establish those rights or describe those arrangements;

(vi) For each member of the board of directors or similar body (including external directors) and officers (including president, senior vice president, executive vice president, and other persons who perform duties normally associated with such titles) of the acquiring foreign person engaged in the transaction and its immediate, intermediate, and ultimate parents, and for any individual having an ownership interest of five percent or more in the acquiring foreign person engaged in the transaction and in the foreign person's ultimate parent, the following information:

(A) A curriculum vitae or similar professional synopsis, provided as part of the main notice, and

(B) The following "personal identifier information," which, for privacy reasons, and to ensure limited distribution, shall be set forth in a separate document, not in the main notice:

(1) Full name (last, first, middle name);

(2) All other names and aliases used;

(3) Business address;

(4) Country and city of residence;

(5) Date of birth;

(6) Place of birth;

(7) U.S. Social Security number (where applicable);

(8) National identity number, including nationality, date and place of issuance, and expiration date (where applicable);

(9) U.S. or foreign passport number (if more than one, all must be fully disclosed), nationality, date and place of issuance, and expiration date and, if a U.S. visa holder, the visa type and number, date and place of issuance, and expiration date; and

(10) Dates and nature of foreign government and foreign military service (where applicable), other than military service at a rank below the top two non-commissioned ranks of the relevant foreign country; and

(vii) The following "business identifier information" for the immediate, intermediate, and ultimate parents of the foreign person engaged in the transaction, including their main offices and branches:

(A) Business name, including all names under which the business is known to be or has been doing business;

(B) Business address;

(C) Business phone number, fax number, and e-mail address; and

(D) Employer identification number or other domestic tax or corporate identification number.

(d) The voluntary notice shall list any filings with, or reports to, agencies of the United States Government that have been or will be made with respect to the transaction prior to its closing, indicating the agencies concerned, the nature of the filing or report, the date on which it was filed or the estimated date by which it will be filed, and a relevant contact point and/or telephone number within the agency, if known.

Example. Corporation A, a foreign person, intends to acquire Corporation X, which is wholly owned and controlled by a U.S. national and which has a Facility Security Clearance under the Department of Defense Industrial Security Program. See Department of Defense, "Industrial Security Regulation," DOD 5220.22–R, and "Industrial Security Manual for Safeguarding Classified Information," DOD 5220.22–M. Corporation X accordingly files a revised Form DD SF–328, and enters into discussions with the Defense Security Service about effectively insulating its facilities from the foreign person. Corporation X may also have made filings with the Securities and Exchange Commission, the Department of Commerce, the Department of State, or other federal departments and agencies. Paragraph (d) of this section requires that certain specific information about these filings be reported to the Committee in a voluntary notice.

(e) In the case of the establishment of a joint venture in which one or more of the parties is contributing a U.S. business, information for the voluntary notice shall be prepared on the assumption that the foreign person that is party to the joint venture has made an acquisition of the existing U.S. business that the other party to the joint venture is contributing or transferring to the joint venture. The voluntary notice shall describe the name and address of the joint venture and the entities that established, or are establishing, the joint venture.

(f) In the case of the acquisition of some but not all of the assets of an entity, § 800.402(c) requires submission of the specified information only with respect to the assets of the entity that have been or are proposed to be acquired.

(g) Persons filing a voluntary notice shall, with respect to the foreign person that is a party to the transaction, its immediate parent, the U.S. business that is the subject of the transaction, and each entity of which the foreign person is a parent, append to the voluntary notice the most recent annual report of each such entity, in English. Separate reports are not required for any entity whose financial results are included within the consolidated financial results stated in the annual report of any parent of any such entity, unless the transaction involves the acquisition of a U.S. business whose parent is not being acquired, in which case the notice shall

include the most recent audited financial statement of the U.S. business that is the subject of the transaction. If a U.S. business does not prepare an annual report and its financial results are not included within the consolidated financial results stated in the annual report of a parent, the filing shall include, if available, the entity's most recent audited financial statement (or, if an audited financial statement is not available, the unaudited financial statement).

(h) Persons filing a voluntary notice shall, during the time that the matter is pending before the Committee or the President, promptly advise the Staff Chairperson of any material changes in plans, facts and circumstances addressed in the notice, and information provided or required to be provided to the Committee under § 800.402, and shall file amendments to the notice to reflect such material changes. Such amendments shall become part of the notice filed by such persons under § 800.401, and the certification required under § 800.402(l) shall apply to such amendments. (See also § 800.701(d).)

(i) Persons filing a voluntary notice shall include a copy of the most recent asset or stock purchase agreement or other document establishing the agreed terms of the transaction.

(j) Persons filing a voluntary notice shall include:

(1) An organizational chart illustrating all of the entities or individuals above the foreign person that is a party to the transaction up to the person or persons having ultimate control of that person, including the percentage of shares held by each; and

(2) The opinion of the person regarding whether:

(i) It is a foreign person;

(ii) It is controlled by a foreign government; and

(iii) The transaction has resulted or could result in control of a U.S. business by a foreign person, and the reasons for its view, focusing in particular on any powers (for example, by virtue of a shareholders agreement, contract, statute, or regulation) that the foreign person will have with regard to the U.S. business, and how those powers can or will be exercised.

(k) Persons filing a voluntary notice shall include information as to whether:

(1) Any party to the transaction is, or has been, a party to a mitigation agreement entered into or condition imposed under section 721, and if so, shall specify the date and purpose of such agreement or condition and the United States Government signatories; and

(2) Any party to the transaction has been a party to a transaction previously notified to the Committee.

(l) Each party filing a voluntary notice shall provide a certification of the notice consistent with § 800.202. A sample certification may be found on the Committee's section of the Department of the Treasury Web site, available at *http://www.treas.gov/offices/ international-affairs/cfius/index.shtml.*

(m) Persons filing a voluntary notice shall include with the notice a list identifying each document provided as part of the notice, including all documents provided as attachments or exhibits to the narrative response.

§ 800.403   Deferral, rejection, or disposition of certain voluntary notices.

(a) The Committee, acting through the Staff Chairperson, may:

(1) Reject any voluntary notice that does not comply with § 800.402 and so inform the parties promptly in writing;

(2) Reject any voluntary notice at any time, and so inform the parties promptly in writing, if, after the notice has been submitted and before action by the Committee or the President has been concluded:

(i) There is a material change in the transaction as to which notification has been made; or

(ii) Information comes to light that contradicts material information provided in the notice by the parties;

(3) Reject any voluntary notice at any time after the notice has been accepted, and so inform the parties promptly in writing, if the party or parties that have submitted the voluntary notice do not provide follow-up information requested by the Staff Chairperson within three business days of the request, or within a longer time frame if the parties so request in writing and the Staff Chairperson grants that request in writing; or

(4) Reject any voluntary notice before the conclusion of a review or investigation, and so inform the parties promptly in writing, if one of the parties submitting the voluntary notice has not submitted the final certification required by § 800.701(d).

(b) Notwithstanding the authority of the Staff Chairperson under paragraph (a) of this section to reject an incomplete notice, the Staff Chairperson may defer acceptance of the notice, and the beginning of the thirty-day review period, to obtain any information required under this section that has not been submitted by the notifying party or parties or other parties to the transaction. Where necessary to obtain such information, the Staff Chairperson may inform any non-notifying party or parties that notice has been filed with respect to a proposed transaction involving the party, and request that certain information required under this section, as specified by the Staff Chairperson, be provided to the Committee within seven days after receipt of the Staff Chairperson's request.

(c) The Staff Chairperson shall notify the parties when the Committee has found that the transaction that is the subject of a voluntary notice is not a covered transaction.

Example 1. The Staff Chairperson receives a joint notice from Corporation A, a foreign person, and Corporation X, a company that is owned and controlled by U.S. nationals, with respect to Corporation A's intent to purchase all of the shares of Corporation X. The joint notice does not contain any information described under § 800.402(c)(3)(iii) and (iv) concerning classified materials and products or services supplied to the U.S. military services. The Staff Chairperson may reject the notice or defer the start of the thirty-day review period until the parties have supplied the omitted information.

Example 2. Same facts as in the first sentence of Example 1, except that the joint notice indicates that Corporation A does not intend to purchase Corporation X's Division Y, which is engaged in classified work for a U.S. Government agency. Corporations A and X notify the Committee on the 25th day of the 30-day notice period that Division Y will also be acquired by Corporation A. This fact constitutes a material change with respect to the transaction as originally notified, and the Staff Chairperson may reject the notice.

Example 3. The Staff Chairperson receives a joint notice by Corporation A, a foreign person, and Corporation X, a U.S. business, indicating that Corporation A intends to purchase five percent of the voting securities of Corporation X. Under the particular facts and circumstances presented, the Committee concludes that Corporation A's purchase of this interest in Corporation X could not result in foreign control of Corporation X. The Staff Chairperson shall advise the parties in writing that the transaction as presented is not subject to section 721.

Example 4. The Staff Chairperson receives a voluntary notice involving the acquisition by Company A, a foreign person, of the entire interest in Company X, a U.S. business. The notice mentions the involvement of a second foreign person in the transaction, Company B, but states that Company B is merely a passive investor in the transaction. During the course of the review, the parties provide information that clarifies that Company B has the right to appoint two members of Company X's board of directors. This information contradicts the material assertion in the notice that Company B is a passive investor. The Committee may reject this notice without concluding review under section 721.

Subpart E—Committee Procedures: Review and Investigation

§ 800.501 General.

(a) The Committee's review or investigation (if necessary) shall examine, as appropriate, whether:

(1) The transaction is by or with any foreign person and could result in foreign control of a U.S. business;

(2) There is credible evidence to support a belief that any foreign person exercising control of that U.S. business might take action that threatens to impair the national security of the United States; and

(3) Provisions of law, other than section 721 and the International Emergency Economic Powers Act, provide adequate and appropriate authority to protect the national security of the United States.

(b) During the thirty-day review period or during an investigation, the Staff Chairperson may invite the parties to a notified transaction to attend a meeting with the Committee staff to discuss and clarify issues pertaining to the transaction. During an investigation, a party to the transaction under investigation may request a meeting with the Committee staff; such a request ordinarily will be granted.

(c) The Staff Chairperson shall be the point of contact for receiving material filed with the Committee, including notices.

(d) Where more than one lead agency is designated, communications on material matters between a party to the transaction and a lead agency shall include all lead agencies designated with regard to those matters.

§ 800.502 Beginning of thirty-day review period.

(a) The Staff Chairperson of the Committee shall accept a voluntary notice the next business day after the Staff Chairperson has:

(1) Determined that the notice complies with § 800.402; and

(2) Disseminated the notice to all members of the Committee.

(b) A thirty-day period for review of a transaction shall commence on the date on which the voluntary notice has been accepted, agency notice has been received by the Staff Chairperson of the Committee, or the Chairperson of the Committee has requested a review pursuant to § 800.401(b). Such review shall end no later than the thirtieth day after it has commenced, or if the thirtieth day is not a business day, no later than the next business day after the thirtieth day.

(c) The Staff Chairperson shall promptly and in writing advise all parties to a transaction that have filed a voluntary notice of:

(1) The acceptance of the notice;

(2) The date on which the review begins; and

(3) The designation of any lead agency or agencies.

(d) Within two business days after receipt of an agency notice by the Staff Chairperson, the Staff Chairperson shall send written advice of such notice to the parties to a covered transaction. Such written advice shall identify the date on which the review began.

(e) The Staff Chairperson shall promptly circulate to all Committee members any draft pre-filing notice, any agency notice, any complete notice, and any subsequent information filed by the parties.

§ 800.503 Determination of whether to undertake an investigation.

(a) After a review of a notified transaction under § 800.502, the Committee shall undertake an investigation of any transaction that it has determined to be a covered transaction if:

(1) A member of the Committee (other than a member designated as *ex officio* under section 721(k)) advises the Staff Chairperson that the member believes that the transaction threatens to impair the national security of the United States and that the threat has not been mitigated; or

(2) The lead agency recommends, and the Committee concurs, that an investigation be undertaken.

(b) The Committee shall also undertake, after a review of a covered transaction under § 800.502, an investigation to determine the effects on national security of any covered transaction that:

(1) Is a foreign government-controlled transaction; or

(2) Would result in control by a foreign person of critical infrastructure of or within the United States, if the Committee determines that the transaction could impair the national security and such impairment has not been mitigated.

(c) The Committee shall undertake an investigation as described in paragraph (b) of this section unless the Chairperson of the Committee (or the Deputy Secretary of the Treasury) and the head of any lead agency (or his or her delegee at the deputy level or equivalent) designated by the Chairperson determine on the basis of the review that the covered transaction will not impair the national security of the United States.

§ 800.504 Determination not to undertake an investigation.

If the Committee determines, during the review period described in § 800.502, not to undertake an investigation of a notified covered transaction, action under section 721 shall be concluded. An official at the Department of the Treasury shall promptly send written advice to the parties to a covered transaction of a determination of the Committee not to undertake an investigation and to conclude action under section 721.

§ 800.505 Commencement of investigation.

(a) If it is determined that an investigation should be undertaken, such investigation shall commence no later than the end of the thirty-day review period described in § 800.502.

(b) An official of the Department of the Treasury shall promptly send written advice to the parties to a covered transaction of the commencement of an investigation.

§ 800.506 Completion or termination of investigation and report to the President.

(a) The Committee shall complete an investigation no later than the 45th day after the date the investigation commences, or, if the 45th day is not a business day, no later than the next business day after the 45th day.

(b) Upon completion or termination of any investigation, the Committee shall send a report to the President requesting the President's decision if:

(1) The Committee recommends that the President suspend or prohibit the transaction;

(2) The members of the Committee (other than a member designated as ex officio under section 721(k)) are unable to reach a decision on whether to recommend that the President suspend or prohibit the transaction; or

(3) The Committee requests that the President make a determination with regard to the transaction.

(c) In circumstances when the Committee sends a report to the President requesting the President's decision with respect to a covered transaction, such report shall include information relevant to sections 721(d)(4)(A) and (B), and shall present the Committee's recommendation. If the Committee is unable to reach a decision to present a single recommendation to the President, the Chairperson of the Committee shall submit a report of the Committee to the President setting forth the differing views and presenting the issues for decision.

(d) Upon completion or termination of an investigation, if the Committee determines to conclude all deliberative action under section 721 with regard to a notified covered transaction without sending a report to the President, action under section 721 shall be concluded. An official at the Department of the Treasury shall promptly advise the parties to such a transaction in writing of a determination to conclude action.

§ 800.507 Withdrawal of notice.

(a) A party (or parties) to a transaction that has filed notice under § 800.401(a) may request in writing, at any time prior to conclusion of all action under section 721, that such notice be withdrawn. Such request shall be directed to the Staff Chairperson and shall state the reasons why the request is being made. Such requests will ordinarily be granted, unless otherwise determined by the Committee. An official of the Department of the Treasury will promptly advise the parties to the transaction in writing of the Committee's decision.

(b) Any request to withdraw an agency notice by the agency that filed it shall be in writing and shall be effective only upon approval by the Committee. An official of the Department of the Treasury shall advise the parties to the transaction in writing of the Committee's decision to approve the withdrawal request within two business days of the Committee's decision.

(c) In any case where a request to withdraw a notice is granted under paragraph (a) of this section:

(1) The Staff Chairperson, in consultation with the Committee, shall establish, as appropriate:

(i) A process for tracking actions that may be taken by any party to the covered transaction before notice is refiled under § 800.401; and

(ii) Interim protections to address specific national security concerns with the transaction identified during the review or investigation of the transaction.

(2) The Staff Chairperson shall specify a time frame, as appropriate, for the parties to resubmit a notice and shall advise the parties of that time frame in writing.

(d) A notice of a transaction that is submitted pursuant to paragraph (c)(2) of this section shall be deemed a new notice for purposes of the regulations in this part, including § 800.601.

§ 800.508 Role of the Secretary of Labor.

In response to a request from the Chairperson of the Committee, the Secretary of Labor shall identify for the Committee any risk mitigation provisions proposed to or by the Committee that would violate U.S.

employment laws or require a party to violate U.S. employment laws. The Secretary of Labor shall serve no policy role on the Committee.

§ 800.509 Materiality.

The Committee generally will not consider as material minor inaccuracies, omissions, or changes relating to financial or commercial factors not having a bearing on national security.

Subpart F—Finality of Action

§ 800.601 Finality of actions under section 721.

(a) All authority available to the President or the Committee under section 721(d), including divestment authority, shall remain available at the discretion of the President with respect to covered transactions proposed or pending on or after August 23, 1988. Such authority shall not be exercised if:

(1) The Committee, through its Staff Chairperson, has advised a party (or the parties) in writing that a particular transaction with respect to which voluntary notice has been filed is not a covered transaction;

(2) The parties to the transaction have been advised in writing pursuant to § 800.504 or § 800.506(d) that the Committee has concluded all action under section 721 with respect to the covered transaction; or

(3) The President has previously announced, pursuant to section 721(d), his decision not to exercise his authority under section 721 with respect to the covered transaction.

(b) Divestment or other relief under section 721 shall not be available with respect to transactions that were completed prior to August 23, 1988.

Subpart G—Provision and Handling of Information

§ 800.701 Obligation of parties to provide information.

(a) Parties to a transaction that is notified under subpart D shall provide information to the Staff Chairperson that will enable the Committee to conduct a full review and/or investigation of the proposed transaction, and shall promptly advise the Staff Chairperson of any material changes in plans or information pursuant to § 800.402(h). If deemed necessary by the Committee, information may be obtained from parties to a transaction or other persons through subpoena or otherwise, pursuant to 50 U.S.C. App. 2155(a).

(b) Documentary materials or information required or requested to be filed with the Committee under this part shall be submitted in English. Supplementary materials, such as annual reports, written in a foreign language, shall be submitted in certified English translation.

(c) Any information filed with the Committee by a party to a covered transaction in connection with any action for which a report is required pursuant to section 721(l)(3)(B) with respect to the implementation of a mitigation agreement or condition described in section 721(l)(1)(A) shall be accompanied by a certification that complies with the requirements of section 721(n) and § 800.202. A sample certification may be found at the Committee's section of the Department of the Treasury Web site at *http:// www.treas.gov/offices/international-affairs/cfius/index.shtml.*

(d) At the conclusion of a review or investigation, each party that has filed additional information subsequent to the original notice shall file a final certification. (See § 800.202.) A sample certification may be found at the Committee's section of the Department of the Treasury Web site at *http:// www.treas.gov/offices/international-affairs/cfius/index.shtml.*

§ 800.702 Confidentiality.

(a) Any information or documentary material filed with the Committee pursuant to this part, including information or documentary material filed pursuant to § 800.401(f), shall be exempt from disclosure under 5 U.S.C. 552 and no such information or documentary material may be made public, except as may be relevant to any administrative or judicial action or proceeding. Nothing in this part shall be construed to prevent disclosure to either House of Congress or to any duly authorized committee or subcommittee of the Congress, in accordance with subsections (b)(3) and (g)(2)(A) of section 721.

(b) This section shall continue to apply with respect to information and documentary material filed with the Committee in any case where:

(1) Action has concluded under section 721 concerning a notified transaction;

(2) A request to withdraw notice is granted under § 800.507, or where

notice has been rejected under § 800.403;

(3) The Committee determines that a notified transaction is not a covered transaction; or

(4) Such information or documentary material was filed pursuant to § 800.401(f) and the parties do not subsequently file a notice pursuant to § 800.401(a).

(c) Nothing in paragraph (a) of this section shall be interpreted to prohibit the public disclosure by a party of documentary material or information that it has filed with the Committee. Any such documentary material or information so disclosed may subsequently be reflected in the public statements of the Chairperson, who is authorized to communicate with the public and the Congress on behalf of the Committee, or of the Chairperson's designee.

(d) The provisions of 50 U.S.C. App. 2155(d) relating to fines and imprisonment shall apply with respect to the disclosure of information or documentary material filed with the Committee under these regulations.

Subpart H—Penalties

§ 800.801 Penalties.

(a) Any person who, after the effective date, intentionally or through gross negligence, submits a material misstatement or omission in a notice or makes a false certification under §§ 800.402(l) or 800.701(c) may be liable to the United States for a civil penalty not to exceed $250,000 per violation. The amount of the penalty assessed for a violation shall be based on the nature of the violation.

(b) Any person who, after the effective date, intentionally or through gross negligence, violates a material provision of a mitigation agreement entered into with, or a material condition imposed by, the United States under section 721(l) may be liable to the United States for a civil penalty not to exceed $250,000 per violation or the value of the transaction, whichever is greater. Any penalty assessed under this paragraph shall be based on the nature of the violation and shall be separate and apart from any damages sought pursuant to a mitigation agreement

under section 721(l), or any action taken under section 721(b)(1)(D).

(c) A mitigation agreement entered into or amended under section 721(l) after the effective date may include a provision providing for liquidated or actual damages for breaches of the agreement by parties to the transaction. The Committee shall set the amount of any liquidated damages as a reasonable assessment of the harm to the national security that could result from a breach of the agreement. Any mitigation agreement containing a liquidated damages provision shall include a provision specifying that the Committee will consider the severity of the breach in deciding whether to seek a lesser amount than that stipulated in the contract.

(d) A determination to impose penalties under paragraph (a) or (b) of this section must be made by the named members of the Committee, except to the extent delegated by such official. Notice of the penalty, including a written explanation of the penalized conduct and the amount of the penalty, shall be sent to the penalized party by U.S. mail.

(e) Upon receiving notice of the imposition of a penalty under paragraph (a) or (b) of this section, the penalized party may, within 15 days of receipt of the notice of the penalty, submit a petition for reconsideration to the Staff Chairperson, including a defense, justification, or explanation for the penalized conduct. The Committee will review the petition and issue a final decision within 15 days of receipt of the petition.

(f) The penalties authorized in paragraphs (a) and (b) of this section may be recovered in a civil action brought by the United States in federal district court.

(g) The penalties available under this section are without prejudice to other penalties, civil or criminal, available under law.

Dated: November 14, 2008.

Clay Lowery,
Assistant Secretary (International Affairs).
[FR Doc. E8–27525 Filed 11–17–08; 11:15 am]

BILLING CODE 4810–25–P

APPENDIX III

Executive Order further amending Executive Order 11858 Concerning Foreign Investment in the United States, January 23, 2008

Executive Order

Further Amendment of Executive Order 11858 Concerning Foreign Investment in the United States

By the authority vested in me as President by the Constitution and the laws of the United States of America, including section 721 of the Defense Production Act of 1950, as amended (50 U.S.C. App. 2170), and section 301 of title 3, United States Code, it is hereby ordered as follows:

Section 1. Amendment to Executive Order 11858. Executive Order 11858 of May 7, 1975, as amended, is further amended to read as follows:

"FOREIGN INVESTMENT IN THE UNITED STATES
By the authority vested in me as President by the Constitution and the laws of the United States of America, including section 721 of the Defense Production Act of 1950, as amended (50 U.S.C. App. 2170), and section 301 of title 3, United States Code, it is hereby ordered as follows:

Section 1. Policy.   International investment in the United States promotes economic growth, productivity, competitiveness, and job creation. It is the policy of the United States to support unequivocally such investment, consistent with the protection of the national security.

Sec. 2. Definitions.
- (a)   The "Act" as used in this order means section 721 of the Defense Production Act of 1950, as amended.
- (b)   Terms used in this order that are defined in subsection 721(a) of the Act shall have the same meaning in this order as they have in such subsection.
- (c)   "Risk mitigation measure" as used in this order means any provision of a risk mitigation agreement or a condition to which section 7 of this order refers.

Sec. 3. Establishment.
- (a)   There is hereby established the Committee on Foreign Investment in the United States (the "Committee") as provided in the Act.
- (b)   In addition to the members specified in the Act, the following heads of departments, agencies, or offices shall be members of the Committee:
  - (i)   The United States Trade Representative;
  - (ii)   The Director of the Office of Science and Technology Policy; and
  - (iii) The heads of any other executive department, agency, or office, as the President or the Secretary of the Treasury determines appropriate, on a case-by-case basis.
- (c)   The following officials (or their designees) shall observe and, as appropriate, participate in and report to the President on the Committee's activities:
  - (i)   The Director of the Office of Management and Budget;
  - (ii)   The Chairman of the Council of Economic Advisers;
  - (iii) The Assistant to the President for National Security Affairs;

(iv) The Assistant to the President for Economic Policy; and

(v) The Assistant to the President for Homeland Security and Counterterrorism.

Sec. 4. Duties of the Secretary of the Treasury.

(a) The functions of the President under subsections (b)(1)(A) (relating to review and consideration after notification), (b)(1)(D) (relating to unilateral initiation of review and consideration), and (m)(3)(A) (relating to inclusion in annual report and designation) of the Act are assigned to the Secretary of the Treasury.

(b) The Secretary of the Treasury shall perform the function of issuance of regulations under section 721(h) of the Act. The Secretary shall consult the Committee with respect to such regulations prior to any notice and comment and prior to their issuance.

(c) Except as otherwise provided in the Act or this order, the chairperson shall have the authority, exclusive of the heads of departments or agencies, after consultation with the Committee:

(i) to act, or authorize others to act, on behalf of the Committee; and

(ii) to communicate on behalf of the Committee with the Congress and the public.

(d) The chairperson shall coordinate the preparation of and transmit the annual report to the Congress provided for in the Act and may assign to any member of the Committee, as the chairperson determines appropriate and consistent with the Act, responsibility for conducting studies and providing analyses necessary for the preparation of the report.

(e) After consultation with the Committee, the chairperson may request that the Director of National Intelligence begin preparing the analysis required by the Act at any time, including prior to acceptance of the notice of a transaction, in accordance with otherwise applicable law. The Director of National Intelligence shall provide the Director's analysis as soon as possible and consistent with section 721(b)(4) of the Act.

Sec. 5. Lead Agency.

(a) The lead agency or agencies ("lead agency") shall have primary responsibility, on behalf of the Committee, for the specific activity for which the Secretary of the Treasury designates it a lead agency.

(b) In acting on behalf of the Committee, the lead agency shall keep the Committee fully informed of its activities. In addition, the lead agency shall notify the chairperson of any material action that the lead agency proposes to take on behalf of the Committee, sufficiently in advance to allow adequate time for the chairperson to consult the Committee and provide the Committee's direction to the lead agency not to take, or to amend, such action.

Sec. 6. Reviews and Investigations.

(a) Any member of the Committee may conduct its own inquiry with respect to the potential national security risk posed by a transaction, but communication with the parties to a transaction shall occur through or in the presence of the lead agency, or the chairperson if no lead agency has been designated.

(b) The Committee shall undertake an investigation of a transaction in any case, in addition to the circumstances described in the Act, in which following a review a member of the Committee advises the chairperson that the member believes that the transaction threatens to impair the national security of the United States and that the threat has not been mitigated.

(c) The Committee shall send a report to the President requesting the President's decision with respect to a review or investigation of a transaction in the following circumstances:

(i) the Committee recommends that the President suspend or prohibit the transaction;

(ii) the Committee is unable to reach a decision on whether to recommend that the President suspend or prohibit the transaction; or

(iii) the Committee requests that the President make a determination with regard to the transaction.

(d) Upon completion of a review or investigation of a transaction, the lead agency shall prepare for the approval of the chairperson the appropriate certified notice or report to the Congress called for under the Act. The chairperson shall transmit such notice or report to the Congress, as appropriate.

Sec. 7. Risk Mitigation.

(a) The Committee, or any lead agency acting on behalf of the Committee, may seek to mitigate any national security risk posed by a transaction that is not adequately addressed by other provisions of law by entering into a mitigation agreement with the parties to a transaction or by imposing conditions on such parties.

(b) Prior to the Committee or a department or agency proposing risk mitigation measures to the parties to a transaction, the department or agency seeking to propose any such measure shall prepare and provide to the Committee a written statement that: (1) identifies the national security risk posed by the transaction based on factors including the threat (taking into account the Director of National Intelligence's threat analysis), vulnerabilities, and potential consequences; and (2) sets forth the risk mitigation measures the department or agency believes are reasonably necessary to address the risk. If the Committee agrees that mitigation is appropriate and approves the risk mitigation measures, the lead agency shall seek to negotiate such measures with the parties to the transaction.

(c) A risk mitigation measure shall not, except in extraordinary circumstances, require that a party to a transaction recognize, state its intent to comply with, or consent to the exercise of any authorities under existing provisions of law.

(d) The lead agency designated for the purpose of monitoring a risk mitigation measure shall seek to ensure that adequate resources are available for such monitoring. When designating a lead agency for those purposes, the Secretary of the Treasury shall consider the agency's views on the adequacy of its resources for such purposes.

(e) (i) Nothing in this order shall be construed to limit the ability of a department or agency, in the exercise of authorities other than those provided under the Act, to:

(A) conduct inquiries with respect to a transaction;

(B) communicate with the parties to a transaction; or

(C) negotiate, enter into, impose, or enforce contractual provisions with the parties to a transaction.

(ii) A department or agency shall not condition actions or the exercise of authorities to which paragraph (i) of this subsection refers upon the exercise, or forbearance in the exercise, of its authority under the Act or this order, and no authority under the Act shall be available for the enforcement of such actions or authorities.

(f) The Committee may initiate a review of a transaction that has previously been reviewed by the Committee only in the extraordinary circumstances provided in the Act.

Sec. 8. Additional Assignments to the Committee. In addition to the functions assigned to the Committee by the Act, the Committee shall review the implementation of the Act and this order and report thereon from time to time to the President, together with such recommendations for policy, administrative, or legislative proposals as the Committee determines appropriate.

Sec. 9. Duties of the Secretary of Commerce. The Secretary of Commerce shall:

(a) obtain, consolidate, and analyze information on foreign investment in the United States;

(b) monitor and, where necessary, improve procedures for the collection and dissemination of information on foreign investment in the United States;

(c) prepare for the public, the President or heads of departments or agencies, as appropriate, reports, analyses of trends, and analyses of significant developments in appropriate categories of foreign investment in the United States; and

(d) compile and evaluate data on significant transactions involving foreign investment in the United States.

Sec. 10. General Provisions.

(a) The heads of departments and agencies shall provide, as appropriate and to the extent permitted by law, such information and assistance as the Committee may request to implement the Act and this order.

(b) Nothing in this order shall be construed to impair or otherwise affect:
   (i)   authority granted by law to a department or agency or the head thereof;
   (ii)   functions of the Director of the Office of Management and Budget relating to budget, administrative, or legislative proposals; or
   (iii) existing mitigation agreements.

(c) This order shall be implemented consistent with applicable law and subject to the availability of appropriations.

(d) Officers of the United States with authority or duties under the Act or this order shall ensure that, in carrying out the Act and this order, the actions of departments, agencies, and the Committee are consistent with the President's constitutional authority to:
   (i)   conduct the foreign affairs of the United States;
   (ii)   withhold information the disclosure of which could impair the foreign relations, the national security, the deliberative processes of the Executive, or the performance of the Executive's constitutional duties;
   (iii) recommend for congressional consideration such measures as the President may judge necessary and expedient; and
   (iv) supervise the unitary executive branch.

Sec. 11. Revocation. Section 801 of Executive Order 12919 of June 3, 1994, is revoked."

Sec. 2. General Provision. This order is not intended to, and does not, create any right or benefit, substantive or procedural, enforceable at law or in equity, by any party against the United States, its departments, agencies or entities, its officers, employees, or agents, or any other person.

THE WHITE HOUSE

Index

3Com–Bain Capital/Huawei transaction 35, 46, 63, 67–8, 69, 72, 75, 76, 77, 88, 99, 204

absorptive capacity 28, 29, 30, 38
accountability 37, 55, 69, 143
accounting practices 36, 50, 129–30, 132
acquisition attempt failures 15–16, 26, 137–8, 195–6
  see also CNOOC–Unocal transaction; Maytag–Haier transaction; Huawei/Bain Capital–3Com transaction
acquisitions
  characteristics 24, 25
  versus greenfield investments 5, 8–9, 16, 25–6, 27, 28, 29, 30, 31–3, 40, 186, 191–2, 201, 204
  and institutional distance/liability of foreignness 125, 127, 134
  Japan 15, 137, 186, 191–2, 193
Administration Procedure Act 1946 (US) 144, 167
American Depository Receipts (ADRs) 128, 129–30
Anderson, E. 132
"anti-boycott" laws 131
anti-bribery 50, 73–4, 127–9, 134
anti-China attitudes 18, 89, 90–91, 92, 125, 132–3, 134, 194
  see also Congressional China Caucus (CCC); political opposition to Chinese investment in the US
anti-competitiveness 195, 197, 199
anti-corruption 50, 73–4, 76, 127–9, 134
  see also "most-favored-nation" (MFN) treatment; "national treatment"
anti-trust laws 10, 51, 52, 99, 168, 175
APEC Non-Binding Investment Principles 162, 163–4
arbitration 14, 15, 143, 150, 157–8, 159–60, 161–2, 167, 172, 173, 181, 183
Argentina 161–2, 181, 183, 184
Arms Export Control Act 1976 (AECA) (US) 130–31
Asia Pacific Foundation of Canada 22, 39
assets 1, 4, 25, 26–7, 28, 36, 37, 40, 187

"assurances," in CFIUS national security reviews under Exon–Florio/FINSA 62
attitudes to Chinese FDI
  by individuals and groups 18, 89–92, 115–21, 132–3, 134, 194, 195, 203
  and political institutions 92–100, 195, 197, 203
attitudes to Japanese FDI 15–16, 193–7, 198, 199
automobile industry 4, 16, 187, 190, 191, 192–3, 201, 202

Bain Capital/Huawei–3Com transaction 35, 46, 63, 67–8, 69, 72, 75, 76, 77, 88, 99, 204
balance-of-payments 10, 170–71, 172, 188
Bank Holding Company (BHC) Act 1956 (US) 53, 54
Bank Secrecy Act 1970 (BSA) (US) 130
banking sector 53–4, 128, 130, 159–61, 192, 193
Barton, Joe 68
Bhagwati, Jagdish 187, 188
bilateral investment treaties (BITs) 14–15, 142, 143, 144–5, 154
  see also US–Argentina BIT; US Model Bilateral Investment Treaty (BIT); US–Singapore FTA
Blackstone Group 40, 69, 134
Blonigen, Bruce 32, 190–91
boards of directors, in US Model Bilateral Investment Treaty (BIT) 156
brands 5, 16, 17, 25, 37, 187
bribery 50, 73–4, 133
Brouthers, Keith 24, 27
"bubble economy" (Japan) 192, 202
Bush, George W. 9, 45, 67, 98, 142–3
business associations 17, 89–90, 110, 143, 199–200, 202, 204
business practices/structures, Japan 186, 190, 199, 202
Business Roundtable 89, 90, 110

Canada 6, 7, 18, 22, 39, 136, 143, 145, 148–9, 150, 192
capital investment 30, 31
cartels 195